Legal Aspects of
SPORTS
SECOND EDITION

John J. Miller, PhD

Professor
Troy University
Troy, AL

Kristi L. Schoepfer, JD

Associate Professor
Winthrop University
Rock Hill, SC

JONES & BARTLETT
LEARNING

World Headquarters
Jones & Bartlett Learning
5 Wall Street
Burlington, MA 01803
978-443-5000
info@jblearning.com
www.jblearning.com

Jones & Bartlett Learning books and products are available through most bookstores and online booksellers. To contact Jones & Bartlett Learning directly, call 800-832-0034, fax 978-443-8000, or visit our website, www.jblearning.com.

Substantial discounts on bulk quantities of Jones & Bartlett Learning publications are available to corporations, professional associations, and other qualified organizations. For details and specific discount information, contact the special sales department at Jones & Bartlett Learning via the above contact information or send an email to specialsales@jblearning.com.

07870-1

Production Credits
VP, Executive Publisher: David D. Cella
Publisher: Cathy L. Esperti
Acquisitions Editor: Sean Fabery
Editorial Assistant: Hannah Dziezanowski
Senior Vendor Manager: Sara Kelly
Director of Marketing: Andrea DeFronzo
VP, Manufacturing and Inventory Control: Therese Connell
Composition and Project Management: Cenveo® Publisher
    Services

Cover Design: Kristin E. Parker
Rights & Media Specialist: Jamey O'Quinn
Media Development Editor: Troy Liston
Cover Image: © Darrin Klimek/Getty Images
Printing and Binding: Edwards Brothers Malloy
Cover Printing: Edwards Brothers Malloy

Library of Congress Cataloging-in-Publication Data
Names: Miller, John J. (John James), 1956- author. | Schoepfer, Kristi L., author.
Title: Legal aspects of sports / John J. Miller and Kristi L. Schoepfer.
Description: Edition 2. | Burlington, MA : Jones & Bartlett Learning, 2017. | Includes bibliographical references and index.
Identifiers: LCCN 2016043261 | ISBN 9781284072471 (pbk. : alk. paper)
Subjects: LCSH: Sports—Law and legislation—United States. | LCGFT: Textbooks.
Classification: LCC KF3989 .T48 2017 | DDC 344.73/099—dc23
LC record available at https://lccn.loc.gov/2016043261

6048

Printed in the United States of America
21 20 19 18 17   10 9 8 7 6 5 4 3 2

DEDICATION

To Laura and my girls, Kelsey and Jackie: you help me be a better person. To Mom and Dad, thanks for naming me after a writer. I guess it helps!

John J. Miller

To Michael for your endless support, to Dad for giving me my love of sports, and to Mom for making me believe anything is possible.

Kristi L. Schoepfer

Brief Contents

CONTENTS

3   Intentional Torts   39

4   Tort Defenses   59

9   Antitrust Law   151

10   Labor Relations in Sports   173

..

FOREWORD

Forty-five years ago, I wrote *From the Gym to the Jury*, one of the first four books written in the field of sport law. Of my next 28 books, 18 used sport law and legal issues in sport to define the content. My books were written for professors, undergraduate and graduate students, as well as practitioners. My focus came about as an alarming number of lawsuits were being filed in the field of sport.

John Miller and Kristi Schoepfer have written a unique text that allows for an in-depth study of the legal aspects of sport. Sport law texts are proliferating and are become virtually outdated before they are published. To combat this, Miller and Schoepfer suggest using the Internet to "stay current about the legal issues affecting sports," and—most important—they plan on providing updated cases on an annual basis using Jones & Bartlett Learning's online resources. Thus, while the core text information might stay the same, new cases will be added to keep the content current. This is a refreshing approach to a topic that continues to need attention.

The authors use their experience and background to convey to the reader not only the legal implications of sport issues, but to offer a portrait of modern society as sports litigation reveals it.

Herb Appenzeller, EdD
Jefferson-Pilot Professor of Sport Management, Emeritus
Guilford College
Greensboro, NC

PREFACE

We live in a very litigious society. Every day the news is filled with individuals suing or threatening to sue another person or organization for a perceived wrong. This is particularly true in the field of sport management. Failing to understand the legal consequences of certain actions can have a meaningful and negative connotation to a sport organization. The understanding of legal concepts as applied to sport can influence employee attitudes and organizational effectiveness. Accordingly, understanding the effects of the legal aspects of sport and strategies that may be used to manage them is of paramount importance. As such, this book is written to inform future sport managers about the issues that they are most likely to encounter in their careers.

CONCEPTUAL APPROACH

Like some points of the Mississippi River, the study of the legal aspects of sport can be a mile wide and a foot deep. Although this text provides the breadth of subject matter, it differs from the Mississippi River by providing the reader an opportunity for an in-depth study of legal aspect of sport. The question as to what constitutes sports law has been asked by students, academics, lawyers, and laypersons for years. For example, a number of textbooks that use sport-specific examples and apply them to specific legal components have been written for law students. This text, however, was written with a focus to educate future sport practitioners and administrators about the legal aspects as they apply to the sports field. In its present form, it is intended as a teaching resource that can be used in sport management undergraduate or graduate courses.

This text is designed to be supplemented by online resources. The field of sports law or legal aspects of sport is developing at an incredibly rapid pace, and there is a constant concern that a text may be out of date as soon as it is published. In light of current trends, Jones & Bartlett Learning has made applicable cases available online; the intention is to update these cases on an annual basis as needed. Thus, the book changes even if the chapter information stays the same.

ORGANIZATION OF TEXT

Coverage of the legal aspects of sport can be overwhelming. This book condenses this information into particular areas that will be of concern to future sport managers and coaches into 13 chapters. Chapter 1 discusses the influence that sport has had on society. Examples of previous discrimination, ethics, and commercialization issues are presented from a historical viewpoint to create a foundation for the legal aspects sport managers face in today's society. Chapter 2 focuses on unintentional torts, specifically negligence, as applied to several sport settings. The importance of this chapter is reflected in the significant number of negligence lawsuits filed against sport organizations and personnel every year. Chapter 3 introduces intentional torts in sport, which signifies the increase of individuals involved in sport who are intentionally trying to injure another person. Chapter 4, on tort defenses, identifies tactics that sport managers may utilize to protect themselves and their organizations in the event of litigation. Chapter 5 on risk management explains how sport managers can employ everyday strategies to assist in making the activity as safe as possible without diminishing the inherent risk of the activity.

Chapter 6 considers gender, sexual orientation, transgender, religious, racial, age, and disability-related discrimination, as well as sexual harassment issues that are present in sports. Legal areas such as Title IX, Title VII, the Americans with Disabilities Act, and the Age Discrimination in Employment Act as applied to sport are discussed in this chapter. Chapter 7 is devoted to issues of drug testing at a variety of sports levels including professional, intercollegiate, and interscholastic sports. Chapter 8 focuses on the relevant aspects of contract issues in sport, whereas chapter 9 addresses anti-trust issues in sport and Chapter 10 examines labor relations, primarily between professional sport team owners and players associations among the four major leagues in North America. Chapter 11 examines the legal concerns in sport regarding agents. Chapter 12 addresses constitutional issues, including freedom of speech and freedom of privacy, that are faced by intercollegiate and interscholastic sport administrators, coaches, and athletes. Finally, Chapter 13 considers legal aspects that are relevant at the international sport level, such as ambush marketing and doping policies.

FEATURES AND BENEFITS

Each chapter includes the following features:

- *Learning Objectives* present the chapter's desired outcome to the reader.
- A list of *Related Cases* indicates the cases that are available online.
- *Discussion Questions* prompt readers to more closely engage with the material presented in each chapter.
- A list of *Key Terms* helps the reader quickly identify critical new terms, with definitions included in the end-of-text Glossary.

INSTRUCTOR RESOURCES

Qualified instructors can receive access to the full suite of Instructor Resources, including the following:

- Slides in PowerPoint format
- Test Bank
- Instructor's Manual

John J. Miller, PhD
Professor
Troy University

Kristi L. Schoepfer, JD
Associate Professor
Winthrop University

ABOUT THE AUTHORS

John J. Miller, PhD, earned his undergraduate degree in Physical Education from the University of Wisconsin-Oshkosh, Master of Arts degree in Sport Psychology from the University of Minnesota, and Doctorate in Sport Administration from the University of New Mexico. Miller coached intercollegiate men's and women's swimming for 16 years, in which time 26 swimmers achieved National Association of Intercollegiate Athletics (NAIA) All-America status. Additionally, one of the female swimmers Miller coached won four national individual NAIA swimming championships. Twelve of his teams also achieved Academic All-America status. He was elected president of the NAIS Swimming and Diving Coaches Association, selected conference coach of the year four times, and NAIA National Swimming and Diving Champion Meet director twice.

After concluding his coaching career, Miller was hired at Texas Tech University as an assistant professor where he eventually rose to full professor status. He is currently a full professor of Sport Management at Troy University, Alabama. Miller has more than 30 years of teaching experience, having taught Coaching of Sport, Legal Aspects of Sport, Research Methods in Sport Management, Sport Event Management, Sport Management Internship, Sport Facilities Planning and Management, and Financial Aspects of Sport. Miller has served the Sport Recreation and Law Association as member at large, president, and conference host as well as the editor of the *Journal of Legal Aspects of Sport*. He has more than 60 peer-review publications and more than 100 national presentations, most of which deal with legal issues in sport. He is a research fellow in Sport and Recreation Law Association, Research Consortium, and the North American Society of Health, Physical Education, Recreation, Sport and Dance Professionals. He has been awarded the Betty van der Smissen Leadership Award, Herb Appenzeller Honor Award, and President's Award by the Sport and Recreation Law Association, as well as the Sport Management Outstanding Achievement Award by the National Association for Sport and Physical Education.

Kristi L. Schoepfer, JD, earned her Bachelor of Science in Education from the University of Dayton in 1998 and a Juris Doctorate, with certification in Sports Law, from Marquette University Law School in 2001. She is currently an associate professor of Sports Law and Sports Management at Winthrop University, South Carolina. Prior to joining the faculty at Winthrop, Schoepfer was an assistant professor of Sports Law for five years at the University of Wisconsin-Parkside. In total, Schoepfer has 16 years of experience teaching Sports Law courses. At present, she teaches courses on Risk Management in Sport, Sport Law, as well as Research and Writing in Sport Management, Sport Ethics and Governance, and Introduction to Sport Management.

In addition to her teaching at Winthrop University, Schoepfer is a member of the Board of Advisors for the National Sport Law Institute, a former board member of the Sport and Recreation Lawyers Association, and a national presenter on sport law issues. For her accomplishments in teaching, research, and service, Schoepfer was awarded the 2009 Marquette University Law School Charles W. Mentkowski Sport Law Alumna of the Year Award and the 2016 Sport and Recreation Law Association Herb Appenzeller Honor Award.

CONTRIBUTORS

John T. Wendt, JD
Professor
University of St. Thomas
Minneapolis, MN
Chapter 13, International Sports

REVIEWERS

The following reviewers provided feedback about Patrick K. Thornton's *Sports Law*, which served as the foundation for this text.

Matthew Garrett, PhD
Professor
Loras College
Dubuque, IA

Tonya Gimbert, PhD
Adjunct Instructor
Indiana State University
Terre Haute, IN

Martin Josie, MS
Instructor
Coppin State University
Baltimore, MD

Marcia J. Mackey, PhD
Associate Professor
Central Michigan University
Mt. Pleasant, MI

Stephen T. Mumford, MBA
Assistant Professor
Gwynedd Mercy University
Gwynedd Valley, PA

Tim Sceggel, MS
Director of Athletics
Instructor
Covenant College
Lookout Mountain, GA

William P. Schuber, JD
Assistant Professor
Fairleigh Dickinson University
Teaneck, NJ

SPORTS IN SOCIETY

LEARNING OBJECTIVES

By the end of the chapter, the reader will be able to:

1. Appreciate the influence of sports and the role of sports in society
2. Understand the impact of the *commercialization* of sport
3. Comprehend and provide examples of the integration of sport ethics and sports law
4. Analyze the increase of violence in sports at all levels
5. Depict the influence of race in sports
6. Understand how the use of mascots in sports may relate to racial discrimination

RELATED CASES

Case 1.1   Harjo v. Pro-Football, Inc., 1999 TTAB LEXIS 181, 50 U.S.P.Q.2d (BNA) 1705 (Trademark Trial & App. Bd. Apr. 2, 1999)

Case 1.2   McKichan v. St. Louis Hockey Club, L...., 967 S.W.2d 209, 1998 Mo. App. LEXIS 489 (Mo. Ct. App. 1998)

Case 1.3   Popov v. Hayashi 2002 WL 31833731 (Cal. Superior 2002)

Case 1.4   Bellecourt v. Cleveland 104 Ohio St.3d (Ohio 2004)

Case 1.5   Cox v. National Football League 889 F. Supp. 118 (S.D. N.Y. 1995)

Case 1.6   Hale V. Antoniou 2004 WL 1925551 (Me. 2004)

THE INFLUENCE OF SPORTS

Sports have had a stronghold on Americans for over a century. Boys, girls, men, and women have enjoyed participating in and watching a variety of professional and amateur sports for many years. Sports in many ways are a metaphor for life. Young people can learn teamwork, sportsmanship, and perseverance and develop many other admirable qualities when participating in sports. Boys and girls alike dream of hitting a home run in the bottom of the ninth inning and winning the championship while playing for their favorite ball club. Over the years, the sports industry has become one of the largest in the United States eclipsing real estate, health care, banking, and transportation (Coakley, 2007). Arguably the most visible components of the industry are sporting events. According to Higgs and McKinley (2009), sport in the United States parallels what is occurring in the rest of American society. These authors continue that if aliens viewed a sports event for the first time they might very well associate the sport with the business world because of the business signage that appeared in the stadium or on the television. The perception may very well reflect the reality that sport itself is a microcosm of American culture (Higgs & McKinley, 2009).

Maybe that displays a little too much commitment, but many fans take their sports very seriously. Eric James Torpy, for example, was always a big fan of Celtics great Larry Bird. After his lawyer reached a plea agreement for a 30-year prison term, Torpy decided he wanted to spend 33 years in prison instead of 30 to match Larry Bird's jersey number 33. Torpy was accused of robbery and shooting with intent to kill. According to Oklahoma County District Judge Ray Elliott, "He said if he was going to go down, he was going to go down in Larry Bird's jersey. We accommodated his request and he was just as happy as he could be" (Offbeat, 2005, para. 3). Scott Wiese was a dedicated fan of the Chicago Bears—so dedicated that

he signed a pledge at a Chicago bar in front of other fans two days before the 2007 Super Bowl promising to change his name to Peyton Manning if the Bears lost. The score was Colts 29, Bears 17. Wiese started the process of the name change the next week. His lawyer commented, "I never doubted him. He's a man of his word" (Reid, 2007, para. 7).

COMMERCIALIZATION OF SPORTS

Certainly, sports have become more commercialized in the last 20 years. Players and coaches make more money. ESPN's biography program, *Sports-Century*, listed the greatest 100 athletes of the 20th century in January 1999 (MacCambridge, 1999). The most represented sport was baseball, with 23 athletes in the top 100. Interestingly, Jim Thorpe was listed in the baseball, football, and track and field categories. The top 50 are shown in Table 1-1. Do you agree with *Sports Century*'s list? Where was Tiger Woods? Fifteen years later Woods was recognized as the second greatest athlete of the first decade of the twenty-first century. Notably, the same athlete, Michael Jordan was listed as the most outstanding athlete in the twentieth century as well as the first decade of the twenty-first century.

Intercollegiate athletics, within the universities, also continues to grow and operate as a big business enterprise (Duderstadt, 2007; Flowers, 2007; Splitt, 2009). Orszag and Orszag (2005) reported that the share of operating athletic and overall higher education spending has increased over time. Further, they revealed that total athletic spending increased by roughly 20% in nominal terms between 2001 and 2003 while total institutional spending rose by less than 5% during the same period. Wieberg, Upton, Perez, and Berkowitz (2009) discovered that the average public school subsidy for athletics was $8.8 million which equated to almost 80% more than revenue generated. Four years later, in 2013, there were

TABLE 1-1 Bowl Schedule and Payouts: 2013–2014

Bowl Game	Per Team Pay-Out
BCS National Championship Game	$18,000,000
Fiesta Bowl	$17,000,000
Sugar Bowl	$17,000,000
Orange Bowl	$17,000,000
Rose Bowl	$17,000,000
Capital One Bowl	$4,550,000
Chick-fil-A Bowl	$3,970,000 (ACC $2,930,000 (SEC)
Cotton Bowl	$3,375,000
Gator Bowl	$3,500,000
Buffalo Wild Wings Bowl	$3,350,000
Alamo Bowl	$3,175,000
Outback Bowl	$2,500,000
Russell Athletic Bowl	$2,275,000
Holiday Bowl	$2,075,000
Sun Bowl	$2,000,000
Music City Bowl	$1,837,000
Pinstripe Bowl	$1,800,000
Belk Bowl	$1,700,000
Texas Bowl	$1,700,000
Liberty Bowl	$1,437,500
Independence Bowl	$1,150,000
Las Vegas Bowl	$1,100,000
Heart of Dallas Bowl	$1,100,000
Military Bowl	$1,000,000
Kraft Fight Hunger Bowl	$925,000
BBVA Compass Bowl	$1,000,000 (SEC) $900,000 (ACC)
GoDaddy.com Bowl	$750,000
Little Caesars Pizza Bowl	$750,000
Hawaii Bowl	$650,000
Armed Forces Bowl	$600,000
Beef 'O' Brady's	$537,500
Poinsettia	$500,000

(continues)

TABLE 1-1 **Bowl Schedule and Payouts: 2013–2014 (*continued*)**

Bowl Game	Per Team Pay-Out
New Orleans	$500,000
New Mexico	$456,250
Famous Idaho Potato Bowl	$325,000

Source: Collins (2014).
According to CollegeFootballPoll.com (2016):
"Amounts shown do not necessarily reflect what each school receives. The conferences have different methods by which bowl money is divided among its membership. Some bowl agreements call for higher payouts to one conference than the other, depending on such factors as which is the 'host' conference. Many of the above payouts are reflective of past actual payouts, while others are published estimates of anticipated payouts for the current year (para. 2).

13 intercollegiate athletic departments that exceeded $100 million dollars in total revenue (Berkowitz, Upton, & Brady, 2013). However, only 10% (23 of 228) of the *National Collegiate Athletic Association (NCAA)* Division I public institutions generated sufficient amounts of money from media rights contracts, ticket sales, donations and other sources (not including subsidies from institutional or government support or student fees) to cover their expenses in 2012 (Berkowitz et al., 2013). LSU, Nebraska, Ohio State, Oklahoma, Penn State, Purdue, and Texas were the only schools to report no subsidy money in 2012 (Berkowitz et al., 2013). Moreover, while the other 16 schools received some type of subsidy, 10 (63%) received more subsidy money in 2012 than they did in 2011 (Berkowitz et al., 2013). Rutgers, for instance, spent $28 million more than the revenue it generated. This deficit was satisfied by receiving $18.5 million from the school and $9.5 million in student fees (Berkowitz et al., 2013).

Successful football and basketball head coaches in Division I-A intercollegiate athletics often sign multi-year, seven figure contracts that usually contain incentive bonuses. The salaries of intercollegiate coaches, particularly in football and men's basketball, have increased dramatically over the past ten years. For example, in 2004, a head football coach's base salary was $388,600 (Slywester & Witosky, 2004). In 2009, *USA Today* revealed that at least 25 college head football coaches were making $2 million or more during the 2009 season which represented an increase of slightly more than double since 2007 (Wieberg et al., 2009). Further, Wieberg et al. (2009) reported that the average pay for a head football coach at a *Football Bowl Subdivision (FBS)* institution was $1.36 million which represents nearly $1 million per head coach in five years. Wieberg et al. (2009) also indicated that coaching salaries made up the single greatest percent of athletics' operating budgets in the top-tier FBS schools. Additionally, coaching compensation accounted for more than half of capital projects (Wieberg et al., 2009).

More recently, the average compensation package for major-college coaches has been estimated $1.81 million, a rise of about $170,000, or 10%, since the previous season, and more than 90% since 2006 (Brady, Schnaars, & Berkowitz, 2013). The salaries of head football coaches such as Nick Saban at the University of Alabama and head men's basketball coaches such as Mike Krzyzewski have reached astronomical numbers. In 2014, Saban's contract was increased from $5.4 million dollars annually to nearly $7 million while Krzyzewski's annual salary was more than $9 million.

SPORTS ETHICS

Most would argue that cheating in sports is unethical and unsportsmanlike. How should sports treat cheating? Should participants be fined, suspended, or both? What are the appropriate penalties for a player who bends the rules a little? Does it matter whether a player intentionally cheats or just unknowingly breaks the rules of the game? Do some sports tolerate cheating more than other sports? Situations exist in which the pursuit of sport excellence becomes so obsessive that a competitor loses sight of what might be fair. To be sure, this is not a new concept as nearly seventy years ago the pursuit of breaking records as well as the desire to please a demanding public was becoming more important to athletes of the day than their own health (Boje, 1939). Because of this desire to achieve excellence or success, athletes have looked for avenues to gain an advantage or edge for many years.

Hughes and Coakley (1991) identified the following four norms as constituting the sport ethic:

1. Athletes are dedicated to "the game" above all else and demonstrate dedication through unwavering commitment, making sacrifices to play, and meeting the expectations of fellow athletes.
2. Athletes strive for distinction by relentlessly seeking to improve and achieve perfection; winning becomes important as a marker of achievement and one's willingness to push limits.
3. Athletes accept risks and play through pain to prove to teammates and coaches that they will not succumb to pressure or fear in any situation in which the game and teammates depend on their participation.
4. Athletes accept no obstacles in the pursuit of possibilities in their sport, even when the odds are against them.

The identity implications of conforming to sport ethic norms is often the foundation of sport cultures to the point that athletes accept them without question or qualification as they seek to have their identity claims acknowledged, accepted, and continuously reaffirmed over time (Coakley, 2007). As a result, pervasive patterns of dangerous normative over-conformity, such as taking performance enhancing drugs or reducing weight, in which athletes put the health and well-being of their bodies on the line (Coakley, 2007).

Sports and sports law involve ethical decision making. Sports lawyers and managers are faced with *ethical dilemmas* in everyday practice. *Sports ethics* is a burgeoning field, and much has been written recently in this area. For many who compete in sports, pursuing success or excellence is an ideal to be admired. On a regular basis the media depicts a present (Tiger Woods) or former (Michael Jordan) athlete as being a "winner" because they are great competitors. Winning, which is the ultimate form of success, is the most visible and therefore may be considered the most important goal in sports. As the old saying goes winning isn't a sometime thing, it is the only thing. While this quote was directed to professional athletes it has permeated through other levels of sport competition including interscholastic sports.

How many people would do what professional golfer Brian Davis did in 2010? He disqualified himself after he ticked a loose reed during his backswing on the first playoff hole. By calling a two-stroke penalty on himself, Jim Furyk emerged with the victory at the 2010 Verizon Heritage (Associated Press, 2010). Davis's error, a violation of rule 13.4 against moving a loose impediment during a takeaway, was indiscernible but for slow motion replays.

However, Davis immediately asked for PGA Tour tournament director to help determine what happened. The tournament director conferred with officials who reviewed TV replays. These officials verified that the violation cost him a chance at his first PGA Tour victory (Associated Press, 2010). Furyk earned $1,026,000 million for the victory while Davis earned $615,000 for his fourth second-place finish on the PGA Tour. How much integrity does it take to have someone confirm something that only slow motion replay could detect and leave more than $400,000 on the table?

In a 1991 football game between the University of Colorado and the University of Missouri, Colorado was given five downs and scored a touchdown on the fifth, winning the game 33–31. Colorado won the National Championship in 1991 with an 11–1–1 record. No concessions were made after the game. Should there have been? What action should have been taken by the university? The coach? Alumni? What repercussions would have resulted from a Colorado concession? Colorado coach Bill McCartney later founded Promise keepers, a Christian men's group, in 1990. He later admitted he was "truly remorseful" about the fifth-down play and the result (Associated Press, 1990). He retired as the Colorado coach in 1994.

Performance-Enhancing Drugs

Professional sports has seen its' share of cheating by those who took performance enhancing drugs. In 1963 Alvin Roy, the first strength coach employed by a professional football team, allegedly provided some San Diego Chargers with Dianabol (Gilbert, 1969). The prevalence of *anabolic steroids* apparently increased in the 1970s and 1980s as several notable players such as National Football League (NFL) Hall of Fame member, Howie Long, once estimated that at least 50% of NFL linemen in the late 1980s used steroids (Zimmerman, 1986). This estimation was substantiated by the NFL drug advisor who reported that the use of steroids was unbridled during the 1970s and 1980s (Miller, 1996). Ultimately, the death of Lyle Alzado due to complications brought on by steroid use throughout his career spotlighted the dangers of such abuse (Watson, 2009).

Professional baseball, while most recently in the news due to alleged use of steroids by notable players, has also had a history of players taking *performance-enhancing drugs (PEDs)*. For example, in 1998 a front office executive stated that use of anabolic steroids was rampant and thereby changing the nature of the game (Yesalis, Courson, & Wright, 2000). Kevin Towers, longtime general manager of the San Diego Padres, perceived that steroids were more common in major league clubhouses than alcohol, tobacco, or any other substance (Yesalis et al., 2000).

The *steroids era* refers to a period of time in Major League Baseball (MLB) when the increase of scoring was attributed to a perception that a large number of players used performance-enhancing drugs (ESPN-MLB, 2012). For example, In 1998, Mark McGwire of the St. Louis Cardinals and Sammy Sosa of the Chicago Cubs waged a two person contest for the National League home run title. Both McGwire (70 home runs) and Sosa (66 home runs) were more than the previous record holder, Roger Maris set 37 years earlier. However, a mere three years later Barry Bonds slugged 73 home runs, thereby surpassing McGwire's record. Although both Bonds and Sosa have not admitted using PEDs, McGwire admitted to performance-enhancing drug use (ESPN-MLB, 2012). Ken Caminiti admitted to taking steroids during his 1999 MVP season with the San Diego Padres. Should MLB rescind the MVP award because of his admission?

Falsifying Information

Ron McKelvey had a great college football career—about eight years long, to be exact. By using fake Social Security numbers, he was able to play football at several schools, including the University of Texas. Once his fraud was revealed, he was immediately dismissed from the university. Tim Johnson was the manager of the Toronto Blue Jays in 1998 and led them to a third-place finish. He was fired because he lied about serving in Vietnam as a Marine. George O'Leary resigned as head coach at the University of Notre Dame after discrepancies were found in his academic background. How should these acts be viewed? What action should be taken?

SPORTS VIOLENCE

Unfortunately, *violence* has become a major issue in both amateur and professional sports, and violence by both fans and players has increased in the last few years. Professional leagues and owners have attempted to take steps to ensure that violence does not threaten fan safety. Owners do not want fans afraid to attend games for fear of violent acts.

There are too many incidents to name here, but a few are instructive. One of the more famous events that took place in the National Basketball Association (NBA) game was a fight between the Detroit Pistons and the Indiana Pacers. This brawl eventually spilled over into the stands, and fans and players began to fight each another. The NBA levied heavy fines and suspensions to all players involved. Latrell Sprewell was suspended by the NBA and fined for his alleged choking of his coach, P.J. Carlesimo. The event garnered national attention.

In an infamous incident in baseball in 1966, San Francisco Giants pitcher Juan Marichal hit Dodgers catcher John Roseboro in the head with a bat. Marichal was subsequently suspended. Roseboro sued Marichal but eventually dropped the lawsuit. Marichal was fined $1750 and suspended for a week. Years later Marichal expressed remorse for the incident. In one of the darker days of boxing, Mike Tyson bit off part of the ear of boxer Evander Holyfield during a boxing match.

Tennis great Monica Seles was stabbed by a Steffi Graf fan, Gunter Parche, in Hamburg, Germany, while playing in a match in 1993. Before that she had won 30 single titles in just five years. Player and fan violence took a turn for the worse on May 16, 2000, when Dodgers catcher Chad Krueter was punched in the back of the head by a fan who took the cap off his head (Greenstein, 2000). Krueter and several teammates rushed into the crowd, and a major brawl broke out between fans and players. Several Dodgers players and coaches were suspended as a result. An injured spectator was arrested for disorderly conduct (Greenstein, 2000). Several lawsuits were filed against the players, the Dodgers, and the Cubs as a result.

Hockey has always had a reputation for fighting. In fact, hockey is one of the few sports that employs the services of a penalty box, which suspends a player's participation privileges for a short period of time for breaking the rules of the game. Most other sports will merely toss a player out of the game for misconduct. How much violence should professional hockey tolerate?

Two hockey incidents garnered significant attention because of the excessive violence involved. In 2000, Donald Brashear was assaulted on the ice during a game by noted enforcer Marty McSorley. McSorley was convicted of assault with a deadly weapon. He received an 18-month conditional discharge sentence and no jail time. Brashear suffered injuries as the result of the attack. In 2004, Steve Moore was struck across the head with a stick in a vicious attack by Todd Bertuzzi of the Vancouver Canucks. Bertuzzi was suspended by the league and lost over $500,000 in pay as a result of the suspension. Moore sued Bertuzzi in a civil lawsuit seeking millions of dollars in damages. National Hockey League (NHL) commissioner Gary Bettman stated, "This is not a part of our game, it has no place in our game, and it will not be tolerated in our game." Bertuzzi was suspended and was eventually reinstated 17 months later. He pled guilty to criminal charges, received a year probated sentence, and was forced to do 80 hours of community service.

One of the more violent acts in the history of sports was committed by Kermit Washington of the Los Angeles Lakers against NBA All-Star and head coach Rudy Tomjanovich of the Houston Rockets. Washington violently attacked Tomjanovich, punching him in the face and destroying his face beyond recognition. Tomjanovich later sued the Lakers and won a large verdict, primarily due to his attorney's skilled representation. Attorney Nick Nichols handled the case for Tomjanovich and was able to persuade a jury to return a large verdict in his client's favor. The case was later settled before a hearing on the appeal.

Football is by its nature a violent sport. In 2006, Albert Haynesworth stepped on the head of Dallas Cowboys center Andre Gurode with his cleats while Gurode was helmetless. He later apologized to Gurode but was suspended by the NFL. More recently, in 2014, the Minnesota Vikings removed star running back, Adrian Peterson, from the active roster after he was charged with a felony child-abuse charge. In that same year, Ray Rice, formerly of the Baltimore Ravens, was indefinitely suspended by the National Football League yet the NFL Players Association filed an appeal to lift the suspension. How much on-field violence should be tolerated by a professional football league? How should off-the-field violence be treated? What role should a players union have in ensuring a player receives fair discipline from the team, league, or commissioner for acts of violence?

Violence in youth sports has also increased. What can be done to curb the violence in youth sports? Is there too much parental supervision in sports for children? Are there too many organized sports for youth? What about instituting a parent-free zone at the youth sports events where only kids and referees are allowed to participate? Should there be sportsmanship rules for parents and coaches when they participate in youth sports? On July 5, 2000, in Boston, Massachusetts, a fight took place in a youth hockey game between a player's father and his coach. The coach died the day after the fight. The parent was convicted of involuntary manslaughter and sentenced to six to ten years in prison (Butterfield, 2002).

RACE AND SPORTS

It is unquestionable that sports have a substantial influence on the American landscape. They have influenced our culture, politics, and moral outlook over the past 200 years. Sports are replete with examples of how athletes have influenced our culture. *Jesse Owens* put to rest the myth of Aryan supremacy in the 1936 Olympics before a cast of Nazi soldiers and Adolf Hitler himself by winning four Olympic gold medals. However, upon his return to the United States, Owens remarked, "When I came back home, I couldn't live where I wanted. I wasn't invited to shake hands with Hitler, but I wasn't invited to the White House to shake hands with the president, either" (Simmons & Robotham, 2016, p. 40). The upset victory of Texas Western (now the University of Texas–El Paso), with the first all-African American lineup in college basketball, over the perennial college basketball power Kentucky was a major landmark for *race* and sports. Jackie Robinson, an All-American football player at UCLA, was the first to break baseball's color barrier in 1947 and endured racial hatred while doing so.

Sports and race have been the subject of much discussion for many years. In baseball the color barrier was broken in 1947 by Jackie Robinson of the Brooklyn Dodgers. The Dodgers general manager, Branch Rickey, specifically chose Robinson because of his character as well as athletic skill because he knew Robinson would face harassment and discrimination when he came to the major leagues. Black players played in the Negro Leagues for many years before the color barrier was broken in baseball. Today MLB has players from many different countries and different races.

Early Lloyd was the first black player in the NBA in 1952, playing with the Boston Celtics. Bill Russell won 11 championships as a player with the Boston Celtics in 13 seasons and was also named player manager of the Celtics in 1966. Russell experienced racism early in his life and was outspoken on civil rights issues. Above all else, Bill

Russell was a winner, and isn't that the essence of sports—to win?

A number of African-American female athletes have emerged as trailblazers in their particular sports over the years, from track and field and tennis to figure skating and basketball. The labor and toil of pioneers such as Alice Coachman, Althea Gibson, Wilma Rudolph and Lynette Woodard helped clear the paths for generations of female sports greats that followed like Jackie Joyner-Kersee, Sheryl Swoopes and Venus and Serena Williams (History Channel, n.d.). Hurdles continued to be conquered as Gibson was the first African-American woman to be voted as the Female Athlete of the Year in both 1957 and 1958. In 1964, Gibson began another pioneering effort when she became the first black woman to join the Ladies Professional Golf Association (History Channel, n.d.).

Consider the following statements made by athletes and executives in sports. Are the statements racist? Are they inappropriate? Are they to be considered free speech? How should they be viewed? When an athlete, coach, or sports executive makes a comment that could be considered racist or disparaging, what discipline measures should be taken?

In 2004 Larry Bird said that he thought the NBA lacked enough white superstars. "You know, when I played, you had me and Kevin [McHale] and some others throughout the league. I think it's good for a fan base because, as we all know, the majority of the fans are white America. And if you just had a couple of white guys in there, you might get them a little excited" (Martzke, 2004). What do you think of Bird's remarks? Would it have been different if Bird were an active player? The NBA took no action against Bird for his remarks. Did "Larry the Legend" get a break because of his stature and contributions to the league?

Golfer Fuzzy Zoeller said of Tiger Woods after he won the Masters Golf Tournament, "That little boy is driving well and he's putting well. He's doing everything it takes to win. So, you know what you guys do when he gets in here? You pat him on the back and say congratulations and enjoy it and tell him not to serve fried chicken next year. Got it? … [O]r collard greens or whatever the hell they serve" (Porter, 2013, para. 7). Zoeller lost several endorsement contracts as a result of his remarks. Do you consider his remarks racist? Should the PGA have taken steps to discipline Zoeller? Is this a different situation because golf is an individual sport? How do you compare these remarks to those of Bird? Should any of these remarks be considered free speech?

Consider some of the outrageous statements made by Marge Schott, former owner of the Cincinnati Reds, such as saying that "Hitler was good in the beginning, but he went too far" (Berkow, 1992). Why she was discussing Adolf Hitler at all is still a mystery, but she must have felt compelled to comment on the most hated person in the history of the world for some reason. She was also said to have used racial remarks in describing players. She was suspended from baseball on February 3, 1993, for one year and fined $25,000 for language the executive council stated was "racially and ethically offensive." Should she have been treated differently because she was the owner of a team instead of a player? What disciplinary power does a commissioner of a league have over an owner for conduct detrimental to the league?

On ESPN's *Sunday NFL Countdown*, Rush Limbaugh commented on Philadelphia Eagles quarterback Donovan McNabb, stating:

Sorry to say this, I don't think he's been that good from the get-go. I think what we've had here is a little social concern in the NFL. The media has been very desirous that a black quarterback do well. There is a little hope invested in McNabb, and he got a lot of credit for the performance of his team that he didn't deserve. The defense carried this team. (Limbaugh's comments touch off controversy, 2003, para. 4)

Do you believe Limbaugh should have been fired for his comments? Do you consider them racist?

Well-respected professor Kenneth Shropshire (2000) discussed sports and their role in society as a whole:

> In the past, I've written that sports is a microcosm of society. I have concluded recently that this is an overstatement. Among other differences, the absence of inter-gender relationships reduces the value of sports as the ideal model. Further, the basketball model is Black and White, quite different from the real America. Baseball, with its increasing Latino component, is potentially a better model, but it is not as entrenched in urban culture as is basketball. Taking a hard look at the racial realities in basketball, a business perceived to be a bastion of equal opportunity for African Americans, provides a view of where we are in broader American society. For greater progress in the legislatures, our courts, and other sectors of society, more of those who have not directly felt or seen racism and other forms of discrimination need to believe it still exists. (p. 13)

Considering Shropshire's statement's do you believe that racism exists in sports? How have sports promoted progress against racism in society recently?

Use of Mascots in Sports

A number of universities have changed their logos as a result of the appropriateness of using a minority population when depicting a *mascot*. For example, Marquette University changed its name from the Warriors (using a Native American profile) to the Golden Eagles; St. John's University in New York changed their nickname from the Redmen to the Red Storm; and Stanford University changed their nickname from the Indians to the Cardinal. Some universities have appealed the NCAA's ruling and received waivers for the use of their mascots. Catawba College (Catawba Indians), Central Michigan University (Chippewas), Florida State University (Seminoles), Mississippi College (Choctaws), and the University of Utah (Utes) won their appeals against the NCAA after each showed it had the approval of local tribes to use the nicknames.

The NCAA has taken a position in this matter, banning the use of Native American mascots by sports teams during postseason play. In 2005, he NCAA distributed a self evaluation to 31 colleges to analyze the use of potentially offensive imagery of Native Americans with their mascot choice (Brutlag Hosick, 2005). As a result of the self evaluation, nineteen intercollegiate teams were cited as having potentially "hostile or abusive" names, mascots, or images, that would be banned from displaying them during post-season play, and prohibited from hosting tournaments (Brand, 2005).

Professional sports have team names such as Braves, Indians, Chiefs, Warriors, and Blackhawks. Should sports teams use Native American tribes as names for teams and as mascots? What arguments can you make that Native American mascots are insulting and demeaning to Native Americans? The U.S. Commission on Civil Rights (2001) weighed in on the mascot issue:

> The U.S. Commission on Civil Rights calls for an end to the use of Native American images and team names by non-Native schools. The Commission deeply respects the rights of all Americans to freedom of expression under the First Amendment and in no way would attempt to prescribe how people can express themselves. However, the Commission believes that the use of Native American images and nicknames in school is insensitive and should be avoided. In addition, some Native American and civil rights advocates maintain that these mascots may violate antidiscrimination laws. (para. 1)

Recently, the *United States Patent and Trademark Office (USPTO)* indicated that the

Washington Redskins nickname is "disparaging of Native Americans" and that the team's federal trademarks for the name must be cancelled (White, 2014). The decision means that the team can continue to use the Redskins name, but it would lose a significant portion of its ability to protect the financial interests connected to its use (Associated Press, 2014). If others printed the name on sweatshirts, apparel, or other team material, it becomes more difficult to go after groups who use it without permission. The decision by the *Trademark Trial and Appeal Board* is similar to one it issued in 1999. That ruling was overturned in 2003 in large part on a technicality after the courts decided that the plaintiffs were too old and should have filed their complaint soon after the Redskins registered their nickname in 1967 (Associated Press, 2014).

Team owners strongly dispute any racism behind the mascot and won't change it, saying the Redskins name honors the team's history, legacy, and tradition (Jackson, 2013). Yet, Ray Halbritter, CEO of Oneida Nation Enterprises, stated:

> Lets be clear. The name, the R word, is defined in the dictionary as an offensive term. It's a racial epithet. Its a racial slur. I think there is a broader discussion to be had about using mascots generally and the damage it does to people and their self-identity. But certainly there's no gray area on this issue. (as quoted in Martinez, 2013, para. 20)

Should there be a distinction between college and professional teams regarding the use of mascot imagery?

PROFESSIONAL SPORTS

Professional sports leagues dominate the landscape in the United States, where there are what most consider four major sports: baseball, football, basketball, and hockey. Millions of fans attend professional sports events in the United States every year. The Super Bowl is one of the most watched television events every year, and commercial advertisers pay millions of dollars to advertise to people watching the game. The World Series is a staple of American life in October. Professional sports players have seen huge increases in salary in the recent past, and players unions have led the charge in securing higher salaries and better benefits for players. Athletes have always been celebrities in the United States, but with the ever-increasing popularity of sports and the increase in television exposure, many professional athletes have become household names.

Leagues, unions, players, and commissioners are the major players in the governance of professional sports. There are many legal and business issues in professional sports, which are addressed in later chapters. For example, since the mid-1960s professional sports have seen a rapid increase in the number of teams in each of the four major sports leagues. Franchise movement has been a major issue in recent years. Teams have moved from one city to another at a steady pace. Numerous new stadiums have been built. Many teams have been lured away to a new city because of a promise to build a new stadium or arena. Professional sports can garner major television revenue as well. Networks continue to pay large amounts of money to telecast a variety of professional sports in the United States. The PGA Tour displays the talents of the top golfers in the world, including Tiger Woods. In addition to the four major sports, U.S. sports leagues exist for lacrosse, soccer, bowling, tennis, stock car racing (NASCAR), and a few other sports. Minor league baseball is also extremely popular in America.

AMATEUR SPORTS

Amateur sports exist at many levels in the United States. Millions of people participate in individual and team sports. Adults and children play a variety of sports in recreational, YMCA, or adult sports leagues. Millions of others participate just for the enjoyment of playing individual or team sports. This section functions as a short introduction to the issues involved in amateur sports. Chapters 10 and 11 deal specifically with the NCAA and eligibility in amateur sports. The concept of amateurism is discussed fully in those chapters.

High school and college sports are very popular, with millions of fans attending games at both levels, and both are highly regulated in the United States. Each has bodies that address a variety of legal issues relating to eligibility, drug testing, and amateur status. Millions of students play college sports, ranging from the junior college level to big-time college athletics. An NCAA final or Bowl Championship Series (BCS) game will be watched by millions, with large payouts to the winning schools. The following quote from *United States ex rel. Sollazzo v. Esperdy* (1961) discusses the positives and negatives of amateur sports:

> Indeed, corruption of an amateur athlete is peculiarly distasteful. The athlete generally performs before the child in him wholly turns to man and thus is still unformed in character. Since at least as long ago as the founding of the republic, we have thought that participation in amateur sports is a valuable training for our youth, for their responsibilities in the armed services, in their civilian occupations and generally as citizens. Indeed few quotations are better known and more approved than the remark attributed to the Duke of Wellington that the Battle of Waterloo was won on the playing fields of Eton. We have believed that participation in athletics is not only healthful exercise but that it also inculcates and nourishes such desirable qualities as steadfastness, spirit, loyalty and team play. Violation of 382(1) can only tend to subvert the basic principles of amateur sport. Virtue there is in striving with one's whole spirit,

but only evil can come from lack of effort that is bought. (pp. 3–4)

College sports in America are extremely popular and can also be very lucrative. Student-athletes participate at a variety of collegiate levels in a myriad of difficult sports ranging from football to rodeo. Bowl games for college football teams can provide a large payday to the university, especially if the game is designated as a BCS game. Additionally, each of the Power 5 conferences (ACC, Big 10, Big 12, PAC-12, SEC) receive approximately $50 million, whether or not it qualifies a team for the playoffs (CollegeFootballPoll.com, 2016). Furthermore, an anticipated $6 million bonus will be paid for each team a conference sends to the semifinals, $4 million for participating in one of the primary bowl games (Rose Bowl, Fiesta Bowl, Sugar Bowl, Orange Bowl). However, for teams that reach the championship game only expenses, estimated at $2 million, will be allotted (CollegFootballPoll, 2016). Table 1-1 provides an example of how lucrative it can be to have one's school appear in a bowl game. How do bowl payouts for universities affect the salary and bonuses of coaches? How do they affect the university as a whole? How do they affect a university's football schedule or the conference in which the university plays?

CONCLUSION

As one reads through this chapter it becomes clear that the integration of sport and society is significantly intertwined. From issues such as race in the cases of Jackie Robinson and Althea Gibson to the commercialization of intercollegiate sports to the ethical manner in which parents, coaches, and athletes perform to the violence depicted on and off the field by athletes, society is reflected as microcosm within the sports arena. Additionally, these influences often lead to increased litigation.

One only has to read the paper or peruse the Internet to see how someone affiliated to sports is suing another due to discrimination, contract issues, negligence, assault, assault and battery, drug testing, due process, sexual harassment, or premises liability. All of these areas as well as several others will be discussed in this book. In the age of litigation, it is important for those in the management of sport at all levels to have an understanding of these issues. However, it is painfully apparent that, without at least a rudimentary introduction, a comprehension of legal aspects of sport cannot be fully appreciated without an understanding of the relationship to society.

NOTES AND DISCUSSION QUESTIONS

The Influence of Sports

1. How have sports changed society? How have sports changed over the past 50 years? How have sports changed America over the last 100 years? How have sports influenced politics? Religion?
2. Americans participate in a variety of sports and attend both professional and amateur sports activities at increasing rates. NASCAR and professional wrestling are both popular among Americans and are also "big business."
3. There are very few professional athletes in the United States when compared with the population. The chances of a person becoming a professional athlete are very slim. There has been much debate about whether athletes should be role models for children. Are they? Should they be?

Sports Ethics

1. Define sports ethics. What other ethical considerations do sports present? How should ethical decisions be applied in professional sports? Amateur sports?

Sports Violence

1. What can be done to stem the tide of violence in sports? How should violence against spectators be dealt with on the professional level? Should fans be banned from further events? How would a league or team enforce such a ruling?
2. What rules and procedures should be in place to prevent violent acts from occurring in amateur sports? What can be done to curtail the "win at all costs" attitude in youth sports? How can a balance be achieved between being competitive and allowing the kids to have fun?

(continues)

NOTES AND DISCUSSION QUESTIONS (CONTINUED)

Race and Sports

1. Should professional teams take action against the use of Native American mascots such as that taken by the NCAA? How would the league or commissioner enforce such a ban?
2. For an interesting case exploring the relationship between sports law, religion, free speech, and race, see *Williams v. Eaton* (1971). Fourteen football players sued after they were suspended from the team for a protest. They wore black arm bands in protest of the university's and conference's use of student monies and facilities to play host to Brigham Young University, alleging racist policies on the part of the Mormon Church.

Professional Sports

1. The ball hit by Mark McGwire to break Roger Maris's long-standing single-season home run record of 61 sold for $3.2 million (Schoenfield, 2007) . How does the reputation of the player who hit the ball affect its selling price? Eddie Murray's 500th home run ball was auctioned for $500,000 (Schoenfield, 2007). Why do baseball fans value such items to such a large extent?

Amateur Sports

1. The recruiting practices of high school basketball are examined in the movie *Hoop Dreams*. The film can be viewed as a documentary and a comment on winning at all costs at the high school level. After viewing the film, consider what affects recruiting practices have on student-athletes. What ethical considerations are present for coaches in such situations? William Gates, one of the high school basketball players who was depicted in the movie aptly stated: "People always say to me, 'When you get to the NBA, don't forget about me.' Well, I should've said back, 'If I don't make it to the NBA, don't forget about me" (*Hoop Dreams*, 1994).

KEY TERMS

Anabolic steroids
Commercialization
Ethical dilemma
Falsifying information
Football Bowl Subdivision (FBS)
Jesse Owens
Mascot
National Collegiate Athletic Association (NCAA)

Performance-enhancing drugs (PEDs)
Race
Sports ethics
Steroids era
Trademark Trial and Appeal Board
United States Patent and Trademark Office (USPTO)
Violence

REFERENCES

2016-2017 College Football Bowl Game Schedule. (2016). Retrieved from http://www.collegefootballpoll.com /bowl_games_bowl_schedule.html.

Associated Press. (1990). McCartney "remorseful" about fifth down play. SI.com. Retrieved from http:// sportsillustrated.cnn.com/football/collegenews /1998/06/20/mccartney_fifthdown/.

Associated Press. (2010). Davis concedes playoff to champ Furyk. Retrieved from http://sports.espn.go.com/golf /news/story?id=5110442.

Associated Press. (2014). Washington Redskins trademark cancelled as patent office rules name is "disparaging of Native Americans." *National Post.* Retrieved from http://sports.nationalpost.com/2014/06/18 /washington-redskins-trademark-cancelled-as -patent-office-rules-name-is-disparaging-of-native -americans/.

Berkow, I. (1992). Marge Schott: Baseball's Big Red headache. *New York Times.* Retrieved from http://www.nytimes .com/1992/11/29/sports/baseball-marge-schott -baseball-s-big-red-headache.html?pagewanted=all.

Berkowitz, S., Upton, J., & Brady, E. (2013). Most NCAA Division I athletic departments take subsidies. *USA Today.* Retrieved from http://www.usatoday.com /story/sports/college/2013/05/07/ncaa-finances -subsidies/2142443/.

Boje, O. (1939). Doping. *Bulletin of the Health Organization of the League of Nations*, 8, 439–469.

Butterfield, F. (2002). Father in killing at hockey rink is given sentence of 6 to 10 years. *New York Times.* Retrieved from http://www.nytimes.com/2002/01/26/us/father -in-killing-at-hockey-rink-is-given-sentence-of-6-to -10-years.html.

Brady, E., Schnaars, C., & Berkowitz, S. (2013). *The average compensation package for major-college football coaches is now $1.81 million per year. USA Today.* Retrieved from http://www.usatoday.com/story/sports/ncaaf /2013/11/06/college-football-coaches-salary-colorado -pay-mike-macintyre/3449695/.

Brand, M. (October 24, 2005). NCAA correctly positioned as a catalyst for social change. *NCAA News Archives.* Retrieved from http://fs.ncaa.org/Docs /NCAANewsArchive/2005/Editorial/ncaa+correctly +positioned+as+a+catalyst+for+social+change+-+10 -24-05+ncaa+news.html.

Brutlag Hosick, M. (March 14, 2005). Mascot matter fits into proper-environment discussion. *NCAA News.* Retrieved from http://fs.ncaa.org/Docs /NCAANewsArchive/2005/Association-wide /mascot+matter+fits+into+proper-environment +discussion+-+3-14-05+ncaa+news.html.

Coakley, J. (2007). *Sport in society: Issues and controversies.* 9th ed. Boston: McGraw-Hill.

Collins, M. (2014). 2013-2014 college football bowl game matchuups, payouts. Retrieved from http:// yellowjackedup.com/2013/12/08/2013-14-college -football-bowl-game-matchups/.

Duderstadt, J.J. (2007). *The view from the helm: Leading the American University during an era of change.* Ann Arbor: University of Michigan Press.

ESPN-MLB. (2012). The steroid era. Retrieved from http:// espn.go.com/mlb/topics/_/page/the-steroids-era.

Flowers, R.D. (2007). "Win one for the Gipper": Organizational foundations of intercollegiate athletics. *Journal for the Study of Sports and Athletes in Education*, 1(2), 121–140.

Gilbert, B. (June 23, 1969). Drugs in sport: Part 1. Problems in a turned-on world. *Sports Illustrated*, 64–72.

Greenstein, T. (2000). The not-so-friendly confines. *Chicago Tribune.* Retrieved from http://articles.chicagotribune .com/2000-05-17/sports/0005170270_1_dodgers -bullpen-cubs-chad-kreuter.

Higgs, C., & McKinley, B. (2009). Why sports matter. In A. Gillentine and B. Crowe (Eds.), *Foundations of Sport Management*, 2nd ed., pp. 15–28. Morgantown, WV: Fitness Information Technology.

History Channel. (n.d.). Black women in sports. Retrieved from http://www.history.com/topics/black-history /black-women-in-sports.

Hoop Dreams. (1994). Quotes. Retrieved from http://www .imdb.com/title/tt0110057/quotes.

Hughes, R. & Coakley, J. (1991). Positive deviance among athletes: The implications of over-conformity to the sport ethic. *Sociology of Sport Journal*, 8(4), 307–325.

Jackson, D. (2013). Redskins attorney responds to Obama. Retrieved from http://www.usatoday.com/story /theoval/2013/10/06/obama-washington-redskins -football-lanny-j-davis/2931859/.

Limbaugh's comments touch off controversy. (2003). ESPN .com. Retrieved from http://www.espn.com/nfl/news /story?id=1627887.

MacCambridge, M., Ed. (1999). *ESPN Sports Century.* New York: Hyperion Books.

Martinez, M. (2013). A slur or term of "honor"? Controversy heightens about Washington Redskins. CNN.com. Retrieved from http://www.cnn.com/2013/10/12/us/redskins-controversy/.

Martzke, R. (2004). Bird: NBA need more white stars. *USA Today.* Retrieved from http://usatoday30.usatoday.com/sports/basketball/nba/2004-06-08-bird-interview_x.htm.

Miller, A. (May 3, 1996). Reports of steroid use down, but abuse, not over, some say. *Atlanta Journal/Atlanta Constitution,* G4.

Offbeat. (2005). Man requests prison term to match Larry Bird's jersey. *USA Today.* Retrieved from http://usatoday30.usatoday.com/news/offbeat/2005-10-21-jail-bird_x.htm.

Orszag, J.M., & Orszag, P.R. (2005). *The empirical effects of collegiate athletics: An update.* Washington, D.C.: Compass.

Porter, K. (2013). A history of racist remarks aimed at Tiger Woods. CBS Sports. Retrieved from http://www.cbssports.com/golf/news/a-history-of-racist-remarks-aimed-at-tiger-woods/.

Reid, T. (2007). Diehard Bears fan lives up to bet, files to change name to Peyton Manning. *Herald & Review.* Retrieved from http://herald-review.com/news/local/diehard-bears-fan-lives-up-to-bet-files-to-change/article_6ad679e0-35fb-5488-b534-3e528fdc245a.html.

Schoenfield, D. (2007). Eddie Murray's 500th home run ball went for how much? ESPN.com. Retrieved from http://www.espn.com/espn/page2/story?page=070807/homeruns.

Shropshire, K.L. (2000). Beyond Sprewell: The new American dream. *Journal of Gender, Race, & Justice,* 4, 1–13.

Simmons, E., & Robotham, R. (2016). *Overcome: My life in pursuit of a dream.* Minneapolis: Mill City Press.

Slywester, M., & Witosky, T. (2004, Feb. 18). Athletic spending grows as academic funds dry up. *USA Today,* A01.

Splitt, F. G. (2009). The Knight Commission on intercollegiate athletics: Why it needs fixing. Retrieved from file http://thedrakegroup.org/Splitt_Knight_Commission.pdf.

United States ex rel. Sollazzo v. Esperdy, 285 F.2d 341, 1961 U.S. App. LEXIS 5567 (2d Cir. N.Y. 1961).

U.S. Commission on Civil Rights. (2001). Statement of U.S. Commission on Civil Rights on the use of Native American images and nicknames as sports symbols. Retrieved from http://www.usccr.gov/press/archives/2001/041601st.htm.

Watson, L. (2009). Steroids: Is it time to legalize and regulate their use? Retrieved from http://bleacherreport.com/articles/135947-steroids-is-it-past-time-to-legalize-and-regulate-their-use-in-sports.

Wieberg, S., Upton, J., Perez, A.J., & Berkowitz, S. (2009). College football coaches see salaries rise in down economy. *USA Today.* Retrieved from http://www.usatoday.com/sports/college/football/2009-11-09-coaches-salary-analysis_N.htm.

White, J. (2014). "We're in this until the name changes": Debate over Washington Redskins more intense than ever. Associated Press. Retrieved from http://sports.nationalpost.com/2014/08/10/were-in-this-until-the-name-changes-debate-over-washington-redskins-more-intense-than-ever/.

Williams v. Eaton, 333 F. Supp. 107 (D. Wyo. 1971).

Yesalis, C.E., Courson, S.P., & Wright, J.E. (2000). History of anabolic steroid use in sport and exercise. In C.E. Yesalis (Ed.), *Anabolic steroids in sport and exercise,* 2nd ed., pp. 51–71. Champaign, IL: Human Kinetics.

Zimmerman, P. (1986, Nov. 10). The agony must end. *Sports Illustrated,* 17–21.

UNINTENTIONAL TORTS

LEARNING OBJECTIVES

By the end of the chapter, the reader will be able to:

1. Appreciate the need for tort law in sports
2. Understand the concept and types of negligence and its application to sports
3. Understand the elements of negligence as they apply to sports
4. Comprehend and provide examples of the liabilities of coaches
5. Comprehend and provide examples of the liabilities of athletic administrators
6. Understand and provide examples of the liabilities of sports officials and referees
7. Comprehend and provide examples of the liabilities of sport team physicians
8. Analyze the liabilities of sport participants

RELATED CASES

Case 2.1   Pelham v. Board of Regents of the University System of Georgia, 743 SE2d 469

Case 2.2   Coomer v. Kan. City Royals Baseball Corp, 2013 Mo. App. LEXIS 46 (Mo. Ct. App. Jan. 15, 2013)

Case 2.3   Hawley v. Binghampton Mets Baseball Club Inc., 691 N.Y.S.2d 626 (N.Y. 1999)

Litigation in Sport and Society

As society has grown to be more litigious, there has been an acceptance of blaming others. Those involved in sports and recreational activities sue even though they either know or have reason to know the risks that are simply inherent in all sports and recreational activities. Centner (2006) stated, "American sports participants experiencing a mishap are more likely to blame the sport provider for not implementing greater safety precautions" (p. 40). A person might "conclude that something is terribly wrong with a society in which the most commonly-accepted aspects of play—a traditional source of a community's conviviality and cohesion—spurs litigation" (*Crawn v. Campo*, 1994, p. 24).

Tort law provides for remedies to plaintiffs who are injured and seeking redress. Under tort law, an injured party can bring a civil lawsuit to seek compensation for a wrong done to the party or the party's property. A *tort* can be either intentional or unintentional in nature and may be defined as "conduct that amounts to a legal wrong and causes harm for which courts will impose civil liability" (Dobbs, 2000, p. 1). If the tort is intentional it means that the individual intended to act or not act in preventing harm to another person. Conversely, if the tort is deemed to be unintentional, the person did not intend to cause harm. Negligence is an unintentional tort. This chapter does not attempt to discuss every unintentional tort in the law but only those pertinent to the discussion of the legal aspects of sport.

Negligence

Negligence is an unintentional tort in which the alleged wrongdoer does not intend the consequences of his or her actions to another a person, property, or reputation. Negligence considers whether there were acts of omission or commission that resulted in the harm of another person. The commission of an act is one in which that a prudent person would not have done. If a person could have prevented an action from occurring but choose not to, it would be considered and act of omission. Conversely, the omission of an act is one that a prudent person would have fulfilled, resulting in damages. If a person purposely created a situation in which another person was injured albeit not intentionlly, it could be construed as an act of omission. There are several types of negligence and each must be addressed in a different manner.

The most common types of negligence are:

1. *Comparative Negligence*—This type of negligence occurs when the plaintiffs are marginally responsible for the injuries to themselves. As such, the plaintiff may be required to pay a percentage of the damages in a comparative negligence case.
2. *Contributory Negligence*—In contributory negligence cases, if the plaintiff caused his own injury in any manner, the plaintiff cannot collect damages at all. This type of negligence is being abandoned in many areas. In the example for comparative negligence above, if contributory negligence applied, the individuals would not receive any damages because they partially contributed to their own injury in some way.
3. *Mixed Contributory & Comparative Negligence*—This form of negligence is a combination of contributory and comparative. Mixed negligence occurs when the plaintiff is determined to be more than 50% responsible of the injury. If this is determined by the court, the plaintiff may receive either a percentage of damages or none at all.

Accidents happen. However, a plaintiff will not have a cause of action based on negligence arising from an accident unless the plaintiff can establish fand prove the following four elements:

1. A duty of care was owed to the plaintiff.
2. The defendant breached that duty.
3. The breach of the duty was a proximate cause or legal cause of the plaintiff's injuries.
4. The plaintiff suffered damages.

If the plaintiff fails to prove all four elements, then the negligence case fails (*Sanders v. Kuna Joint School District*, 1994).

DUTY

A *duty* is a special relationship between two or more parties that may be created by statute, contract, or common law (Dobbs, 2000). In deciding whether a duty of care has been breached, a jury will determine how a reasonable person would have acted under the same or similar circumstances. Under negligence law, if an individual is found to owe a duty of care to others, then that individual must conduct himself or herself in a manner so as to avoid additional injury. Whether a duty exists is usually a question of law that depends on the relationship between the parties and the risks involved (*Thomas v. Wheat*, 2006). There is no tort liability unless the defendant is found to owe a duty to the plaintiff (*Henderson v. Volpe-Vito, Inc.*, 2006).

As has been noted quite often, the imposition of a duty is nothing more than a threshold requirement that if satisfied, merely opens the courthouse doors (*McCain v. Florida Power*, 1992). Once this duty is satisfied, an injured party must still prove the remaining elements of a negligence claim, including the much more specific proximate cause requirement (Drake, 2004). Drake (2004) further indicated that the imposition of a legal duty is more than a threshold requirement for getting into court; it is a formal judicial recognition of a legal

obligation to conform to a particular standard of conduct toward another. That obligation may have social or economic consequences far beyond its violation resulting in access to the court.

BREACH OF DUTY

A *breach of duty* occurs if a judge or jury determines that a reasonable person in the position of the defendant acted negligently. Whether a person's conduct constitutes a breach of duty is determined on a case-by-case basis. The question is not necessarily how a particular person would act but rather how society would judge that an ordinarily prudent person (i.e., a "reasonable person") would act under the same or similar circumstances. Owen (2007) stated;

> A person who acts carelessly-unreasonably, without *due care-breaches* the duty of care, and such conduct is characterized as "negligent." And so, within the *tort* of negligence (which we might label Negligence with a capital "N"), the second *element* is negligent action or inaction, often referred to simply as "negligence." (p. 1677)

To determine the existence of a breach of duty, negligence law often evaluates the defendant's conduct to an "objective" standard to measure by how a reasonable, prudent person would have acted in the circumstances with respect to imposing risks on others (Holmes, 1881/1963). Such a standard may include, but not limited to, the American Red Cross life saving procedures or professional teaching and coaching standards. In order to prevail under a negligence theory, a plaintiff must establish that the defendant owed a duty and that duty was breached. According to the court in *Hemady v. Long Beach Unified School District* (2006):

> In the area of sports activities, the court decides the existence and scope of a defendant's duty of care as a question of law. The

applicable duty of care depends on the nature of the sport at issue and the parties' general relationship to the sport. (p. 468)

In some cases, the negligence may be considered to border being an intentional tort. Terms such as gross negligence, willful or wanton misconduct, and reckless conduct ignore foreseeable risks that may be used in tort law to differentiate between conduct that is merely negligent and conduct that is perceived to be reckless (Dobbs, 2000). *Gross negligence* has been defined as willfully and intentionally disregarding the consequences for others by acting or failing to act when there is a duty to do so (*Koffman v. Garnett*, 2003). In these cases the negligence was so careless it showed a complete lack of concern for the safety of others. As a result, gross negligence is a much more serious form of negligence that goes beyond simple careless action.

Willful or wanton misconduct is more egregious than gross negligence and is depicted as intentionally doing or omitting to do something with the knowledge that such action or inaction will result in harm of another individual or with a disregard of the consequences (Dobbs, 2000). According to the court in *New Light Co., Inc v. Wells Fargo* (1994) willful and wanton negligence "exists where a defendant had actual knowledge that because of its actions, a danger existed to the plaintiff and the defendant intentionally failed to prevent a harm that is reasonably likely to result" (p. 13). Reckless conduct requires an injured plaintiff to prove that the defendant's conduct was either reckless or intentionally injurious. It requires a conscious choice of a course of action, either with knowledge of the serious danger to others involved or with knowledge of facts that would disclose this danger to any reasonable person. In determining whether defendant acted recklessly, the trier of fact will have to consider both the nature of the game and the totality of circumstances surrounding the shot. Sixteen states require reckless conduct to hold a defendant liable for injuries to

a plaintiff in a sporting contest. These states are California, Colorado, Connecticut, Hawaii, Iowa, Kentucky, Massachusetts, Michigan, Missouri, Nebraska, New Hampshire, New Jersey, North Carolina, Ohio, Rhode Island and West Virginia (Cole, 2007). Additionally, six states (Florida, Minnesota, Nevada, Oregon, Virginia, and Wisconsin) apply ordinary negligence. While Vermont and Wyoming completely bar any cause of action attempting to hold a participant in an athletic contest liable (Cole, 2007).

Hackbart v. Cincinnati Bengals

The seminal case of reckless conduct in sport may be applied to *Hackbart v. Cincinnati Bengals, Inc.* (1977, 1979). During a professional football game Denver Broncos defensive back Dale Hackbart was intentionally hit in the back of the head by the Bengals Charles "Booby" Clark. At the district court level, the court disallowed Hackbart's claim stating that "professional football is a species of warfare and that so much physical force is tolerated and the magnitude of the force exerted is so great that it renders injuries not actionable in court; that even intentional batteries are beyond the scope of the judicial process" (p. 2).

The court determined that while Clark's intentional blow may be perceived result as a criminal assault and battery charge outside the game of football, the football field is different as it represents a battlefield in which the same restraints of the law did not apply (*Hackbart v. Cincinnati Bengals*, 1977). Further the court ruled that applying professional football players to the law, it would be "wholly incongruous to talk about a professional football player's duty of care for the safety of opposing players when he has been trained and motivated to be heedless of injury to himself" (p. 11).

On appeal, the circuit court stated that Clark's conduct went beyond mere negligence (*Hackbart v. Cincinnati Bengals, Inc.*, 1979). Therefore, the court permitted Hackbart to recover monetary damages for his injuries. Further, the court reported that roughness of the sport did not justify the allowance of tortious acts to occur, particularly if the action is forbidden by the rules of the game. The court indicated that reckless conduct is different than negligent conduct in that recklessness involves making a "choice or adoption of a course of action either with knowledge of the danger or with knowledge of facts which would disclose this danger to a reasonable man," while negligence consists of "mere inadvertence [or] lack of skillfulness or failure to take precautions…" (*Hackbart v. Cincinnati Bengals, Inc.*, 1979, p. 21).

PROXIMATE CAUSE

Essential to any successful tort case is that the plaintiff prove that the defendant's wrongful activity caused the harm or injury to the plaintiff. Proximate cause can also be described as legal cause. Owen (2007) stated that "proximate cause assumes the existence of actual causation and inquires into whether the relationship between the wrong and harm was sufficiently close—whether the causal link was proximate rather than remote" (p. 1674). As with duty, proximate cause is a jury question as to "Whether a principal's or teacher's failure to supervise a student was the proximate cause of injuries suffered by a student is the issue most consistently litigated in negligent school supervision cases" (*Broward County School Board v. Ruiz*, 1986, p. 478).

Proximate cause occurs when the breach by the defendant actually and proximately cause the plaintiff's injury. It should be noted that defendant may still be liable even if his or her breach is not sole cause of injury, but makes significant contribution to the incurred damage (Hekmat, 2002). To determine whether the causation element has been met, two questions are posed: Is there causation in fact? Were the defendant's actions a proximate cause of the injury? If an injury would not have occurred without the defendant's conduct, then the causation in fact requirement is met.

Causation in fact is also referred to as the "but for" test. But for the wrongful acts of the defendant, the injury would not have occurred. However, causation in fact is easily met in virtually every scenario. A plaintiff could argue, for example, that if the defendant had not been born then the wrongful conduct would not have occurred. Its application is virtually limitless. Because of this, courts have established proximate cause or legal cause as the benchmark for meeting the third element of a negligence case.

Proximate cause or legal cause is present when the nexus between the wrongful conduct of the defendant and the plaintiff's injuries is strong enough to require imposing liability on the tortfeasor. Both causation in fact and proximate cause must be present for the plaintiff to succeed in a negligence action. If a defendant's conduct meets the test of causation in fact but a court determines that the defendant's wrongful conduct is not the proximate cause or legal cause of the injury, then the plaintiff's negligence case will fail. A plaintiff is not required to eliminate all of the other potential causes in proving proximate cause. They only need to prove a sufficient evidentiary basis from which causation can be reasonably inferred and furthermore, the causation is only required to be a "substantial factor" in causing the injury.

DAMAGES

For a plaintiff to prove a negligence case, the party must also have suffered *damages*. If an alleged wrongdoer breached a duty of care and causation was present, the plaintiff must still have suffered a significant injury, either physically or emotionally, to have a viable negligence claim. The most common remedy for a tort victim is money damages. However, plaintiffs can also seek injunctive relief under tort law if money damages are deemed inadequate.

Damages can be categorized as nominal, compensatory, or punitive. *Nominal damages* are obviously a very small award. These damages are awarded when the law recognizes a technical invasion of the plaintiff's rights, but no economic harm has been done to the plaintiff. In *United States Football League v. National Football League* (1988), a jury awarded nominal damages of $1 to the USFL in an antitrust lawsuit against the NFL. The amount awarded was then trebled to $3 as required under antitrust law.

Compensatory damages are available to make the plaintiff "whole." In a personal injury lawsuit, the plaintiff can seek damages for wage loss, pain and suffering, disfigurement, and medical expenses. The purpose behind *punitive damages* is to punish the wrongdoer and to prevent the wrongdoer and others from engaging in similar conduct in the future; however, punitive damages are not available to a plaintiff in every state.

LIABILITIES OF COACHES

Athletic coaches often attain results by employing methods that could legally be thought of as "wanton" or "grossly" negligent in any other context (Hurst & Knight, 2003). Others believe that it requires 110% player effort to be a great football player so they push past their physical limitations in exchange for a chance at huge salaries, national attention, and superhero position (Kreidler, 2001). Steve Mariucci, former coach of the San Francisco 49er's stated that: "Part of that conditioning is pushing through it. Athletes don't stop because they're a little sweaty, you know? Some of 'em [sic] are so darned tough that they ignore the symptoms—try to push through it" (qtd. in Kriedler, 2001). Coaches often have to push their athletes to allow them to reach new levels of competence and to achieve the best results for the team. According to *Kahn v. East Side* (2003), coaches should be permitted to push their players to levels that may beyond their abilities and that the improper application of potential legal liability

would deter the coaches from doing their jobs. In other words, a coach should not be held liable for merely encouraging the student attempt to reach a new level of competency since this would leave an undesirable "chilling" effect on teaching and learning new skills.

Sports provide situations where athletes may get injured. Schools or organizations are not required to insure the safety on their student-athletes, nor are they held strictly liable for their injuries (Dobbs, 2000). However, if a student-athlete perceives that they have been wronged the must prove that the school or coach committed an act of negligence in order to recover for their injuries (Dobberstein, 2007). Because coaches generally have the most direct control over those involved in their respective sport, they are normally the principal defendants in lawsuits brought by participants (Karns, 1986). Most cases regarding the legal liability of coaches involve injuries to participants of a particular sport. In this regard, the basis for this type of liability is generally predicated upon the theory of negligence.

With regard to negligence, as applied to coaches, "while a coach generally will not be held liable in negligence for conduct involving risks inherent to a sport, liability may ensue when a coach's conduct amounts to something more than simple negligence" (Davis, 2008, p. 573). Although coaches do not owe a duty to their athletes to totally eliminate risks that arise from a sport, they do owe a duty of care not to increase risks that are inherent in a sport (*Kahn v. East Side Union High School District*, 2003; *Knight v. Jewett*, 1992). Specifically related to the duty owed by coaches, a concurring opinion in *Kahn* stated that:

> a coach, while far from being the insurer of students' safety, is also very differently situated in knowledge, training, experience, and responsibilities from the casual football player whose duty we considered in *Knight*. It might be said that a participant's extreme

departure from the degree of care shown by an ordinarily prudent person is an inherent risk of certain vigorous competitive sports, for in the heat of a game or the excitement of a race a contestant may lose sight of virtually everything except his or her goal. But a coach or instructor stands somewhat apart from the fray; the coach's role includes observing and directing the competition, and he or she is expected to keep a cooler head than the competitors themselves. When the instructor or coach is a school teacher, moreover, the safety of the minor students will usually be a primary consideration. (p. 1020)

Since coaches are often hired because of their experience and knowledge of the sport, some courts have imposed a heightened duty of care on authority figures, especially when those individuals are responsible for teaching an inherently dangerous activity (*Kahn v. East Side Union High School District*, 2003; *Knight v. Jewett*, 1992). To ensure that the athlete is adequately prepared to perform an action, the coach has a duty to properly teach the elements of progression as well as consider the complexity of the action, athlete readiness, and safety (Doleschal, 2006). Because of their lack of knowledge of the symptoms, young athletes need to be monitored since it has been asserted that because of the "nature of their jobs, sports coaches bear the special heightened duty of minimizing the risk of injury to all participants, especially those under their control" (Hekmat, 2002, p. 619). An empirical study reported that breach of duty was the focus of the majority (65%) of the decisions and accounted for the highest success rate for plaintiffs (50%) (Chitwood Smith, 2005). According to the court in *Knight v. Jewett* (1992):

A sports instructor may be found to have breached a duty of care to a student or athlete only if the instructor intentionally injures the student or engages in conduct that is reckless in the sense that it is "totally outside the range of the ordinary activity" involved in teaching or coaching the sport. (p. 318)

Pre-existing injuries aggravated by the alleged breach of duty, may be included in the claim (Hekmat, 2002). As such, a plaintiff can establish that the defendant breached his or her duty of care by providing evidence that the defendant's conduct failed to conform to a reasonable standard of care. Since a coach and an athlete have an established relationship custom and experience often offer a robust guide to the rights and responsibilities that flow between the parties (Owen, 2007). However, applying an objective, reasonable-person standard of behavior to complex situations requires considered thought. For example, should an athlete suffer a cardiac arrest in practice and certified medical personnel are not immediately available, the coach may or may not initiate cardiopulmonary resuscitation until medical personnel arrive. If the coach does so (an act of commission) but cracks some ribs, the athlete survives. However, should the coach not initiate CPR (act of omission), the athlete may die. In either case the proximate cause of an injury or "but for" test must be considered. The determination of whether a defendant has breached that duty is a question of fact for the jury (*Kleinknecht v. Gettysburg College*, 1993).

DUTY TO SUPERVISE

Coaches have a duty to supervise their athletes any time that they are serving in an official capacity representing the school (*Beckett v. Clinton Prairie School Corp.*, 1987; *Benitz v. New York City Board of Education*, 1989). As such, coaches must be physically present to supervise their athletes in the locker rooms and practice areas, before, during, and after games, in transportation situations on buses and in bus-loading areas, during overnight stays necessitated by attendance at tournaments out of town (Doleschal, 2006). This duty requires coaches to make certain that appropriate sport facilities are locked and that student-athletes are cannot gain access unless an authorized staff member is physically present in the immediate area to supervise. In *Prejean v. East Baton Rouge Parish School Board* (1999), an elementary school basketball player suffered a severe injury when a fellow player fell on him after being accidentally bumped by a coach during a drill. As the plaintiff, one other player, and the coach all ran for a loose ball during the drill, the coach bumped into the other player, who fell on the plaintiff's leg, fracturing it. The trial court found that by participating in the scrimmage and by attempting to recover the loose ball in the way he had, the coach had breached his duty. However, an appellate court later ruled that the coach had not breached his duty to supervise his players in a reasonable manner.

In *Moose v. Massachusetts Institute of Technology* (1997), the plaintiff was a pole vaulter on his college track and field team. While practicing pole vault, under the supervision of two track coaches, the plaintiff suffered a fractured skull. As a result, Moose sued the coaches as well as the university, alleging that the coaches negligently supervised him during his pole vault practice. The court found for the Moose by finding that the coaches knew about previous incidents in which other vaulters were sprung off of the landing pit because it was too short. The coaches also failed to place additional padding around the pit on the day of the accident, although this safety feature was available and it had been a previous practice. Moreover, the supervising coach had Moose perform with a training pole, which was too light to support his weight. After at least one vault, the coach suggested that that Moose should either change to a heavier pole, elevate his grip on the pole of decrease his approach run. However, the coach did warn Moose to make such modifications prior to the vault in which he was injured.

DUTY TO PROVIDE EMERGENCY CARE

When developing and implementing the care for an emergency situation, coaches should make certatin that the appropriate first aid equipment and auxiliary equipment, such as spine boards and automatic electronic defibrillators, and emergency contact phone number are available and up-to-date. Additionally, there should be at least one person on duty at all times who possesses emergency training such as CPR or is trained to use the emergency equipment.

In *Mogabgab v. Orleans Parish School Board* (1970), a high school football player who suffered from heat stroke and heat exhaustion at a high school football practice and subsequently died. The mother and father of Mogabgab, as the plaintiffs, alleged that their son's death was a result of the negligence of the coaches and others. The Louisiana Court of Appeals found the coaches liable. Specifically the coaches failed to exercise their duty to provide all necessary and reasonable safeguards to prevent injuries. Furthermore, the coaches did not follow the recommendations of the American Medical Association for the prevention of heat stroke and heat exhaustion during football. The key in *Mogabgab* was the lack of a reasonable standard of care in which the coaches delayed getting medical treatment for their son.

LIABILITIES OF ATHLETIC ADMINISTRATORS

Since athletics has so many areas in which a lawsuit may be filed, it is essential that athletic administrators understand the steps that should be taken to decrease potential risks. Similar to coaches, athletic administrators have a duty to use a reasonable standard of care which does not increase the risks to a participant (Dobbs, 2000). As noted previously, coaches are most often named as the primary defendant in a lawsuit. However, an athletic administrator may be named in a lawsuit due to the *respondeat superior doctrine*. According to McCaskey and Biedzynski (1996) courts have imposed liability on third parties for the actions of coaches, under the theories of respondeat superior and vicarious liability. If a coach is negligent, the university that employs the coach may be held liable under the doctrine of respondeat superior. The respondeat superior doctrine,

> literally means "let the master answer," holds a principal (a "master") liable for the acts of an agent (a "servant") provided that the agent was acting negligently and at the time was also acting within the scope of his employment. If an employer knew or should have known that the employee or volunteer was "unstable" or had a history of behaving inappropriately the organization may be held liable if it failed to take action that would have prevented the behavior. (Martinez, 2003, p. 154)

Respondeat superior is a type of vicarious liability, which allows a third party to be held liable for a defendant's negligence in some cases, even if the third party wasn't there when the injury occurred and did not cause the injury or make it worse. The liability on third parties for the actions of coaches, under the theories of respondeat superior and vicarious liability have been imposed by the courts. For example, if a coach is alleged to be negligent in actions within the scope of their employment, the university that employs the coach may be held liable under the doctrine of respondeat superior. According to Fleming (1953),

> In vicarious liability, *A* is held liable to *C* for damages which *B's* negligence has caused *C*, even though *A* has been free from negligence or other fault. In such a case *A* is made vicariously liable for *B's* fault, such liability is being imposed because of some relationship between *A* and *B*. (p. 161)

Thus, the supervisor, such as an athletic director, of a coach is also responsible for the coach's alleged negligent actions. Examples of respondeat superior in which the employing school district, school administrators, athletic directors as well as coaches were named as defendents in a lawsuit include *Mogabgab v. Orleans Parish School Board* (1970); *Roventini v. Pasadena School District* (1997); and *Stowers v. Clinton Central School Corporation* (2006). In each case, the school district, school principal, athletic administrator, and coaches were named in the lawsuit. In another example, although the parents alleged negligence on the part of a high school football coach and his assistants, it was the Jefferson County Public Schools in Louisville, Kentucky settled a case in which the school's insurers paid $1.75 million to the parents of a high school football player who died of heat stroke at a high school football practice in 2008 (Beahm, 2010). However, as part of the civil settlement, the defendants did not admit to any liability in the settlement.

In *Kavanagh v. Trustees of Boston University* (2003), a basketball player for Manhattan College was punched during an intercollegiate game against Boston University. As Kavanagh intervened to break up a scuffle between Boston University and Manhattan College players, he was punched in the nose by a Boston University player. The Boston University player was summarily ejected from the game. Kavanagh was treated for a broken nose but returned to play later in the game. Kavanagh sued the trustees of Boston University and Boston University's basketball coach contending that both parties were negligent and the University was vicariously liable for the conduct of a student athlete. The court found in favor of the defendants.

In *McKichan v. St. Louis Hockey Club* (1998), a professional hockey goaltender sued the opposing player and the owner of an opposing team for injuries the goaltender received when the opposing player charged into him. The defendant player filed a counterclaim against the goaltender for injuries the former had suffered. The players dismissed their claims against one another prior to trial and the case proceeded to trial solely against the owner on a theory of vicarious liability, asserting that the owner was responsible for the acts of his players. A jury returned an award of $175,000, but on appeal the trial court judgment was reversed.

It is important to note that respondeat superior does not apply in every case. To hold a supervisor liable for an employee's negligence, the injured plaintiff must prove *all* of the following:

1. The injury occurred while the defendant was actually working for the employer;
2. The injury was caused by something the defendant would ordinarily do while working for the employer; and
3. The employer benefited in some way from whatever the defendant was doing that caused the injury, even if the benefit was very small or indirect.

Duty for Emergency Care

Athletic administrators must be certain that emergency care actions are in place and communicated with all appropriate parties. According to the court in *Kleinknecht* (1993) the school owed a duty to the student-athlete to provide sufficiently proactive emergency medical measures. In *Pinson v. Tennessee* (1995), a football player was injured during two different practices several weeks apart. After the first incident, the university's athletic trainer did not notify the hospital doctors of the observed neurological conditions of the student-athlete. Additionally, the trainer never informed the team physician of the student's frequent headaches prior to the second episode. The injuries incurred by the student-athlete resulted in significant and permanent neurological damage. The court ruled in favor of the student because a "special relationship" existed

between the student and university predicated on the student having participated in scheduled athletic practices under the university's supervision. The *Pinson* court found that a "special relationship" existed between the athlete and the university which created the duty of the university to offer prompt medical care. Thus, it is imperative that the appropriate instructions regarding the course of action to take in case of injury or emergency be communicated to athletes and repeated often with athletes and members of the coaching staff for reinforcement (Doleschal, 2006).

Duty to Supervise

Supervision responsibilities also pertain to athletics administrators who are expected to be able to supervise coaching staff members competently. In addition, athletics administrators are expected to supervise contests to ensure that spectators do not create an unsafe or disruptive environment (*Leahy v. School Board of Hernando County*, 1984). A further extension of this duty is the need to supervise the condition, safe usage, maintenance and upkeep of equipment and facilities. Finally, athletics administrators will be expected to ensure coaches are capable of providing proper instruction, supervision, safe conditions and activities.

A recent and relatively notorious sport-related case regarding the lack of supervision by athletic administrators concerned Penn State University and Jerry Sandusky, a former defensive coordinator for the university's football team. In 1977, Sandusky founded Second Mile, a charity dedicated to assisting children with dysfunctional families. According the court, Second Mile always had significant social and financial association to Penn State University (*Doe v. Pa. State University*, 2013). As the founder of the charity, Penn State University permitted Sandusky to bring children from Second Mile to the university's premises. Importantly, the school also allowed Sandusky and these children to use the Penn State facilities without any supervision (*Doe v. Pa. State University*, 2013). While the court upheld Penn State's motion dismiss Doe's claim of vicarious liability, legendary football coach Joe Paterno, Penn State University president Graham Spanier, Penn State senior vice president for finance Gary Schultz, and Penn State athletic director Tim Curley were either placed on administrative leave, retired or fired due to a lack of supervision regarding Sandusky's actions.

DUTY TO PROVIDE SAFE TRANSPORTATION

In 2007 five members of the Bluffton University baseball team were killed when their bus crashed (Grant, 2013). On February 26, 2013, a charter bus carrying the University of Maine women's basketball team veered across northbound lanes and went down an embankment (Associated Press, 2013). One of the player suffered a broken hand, the head coach incurred minor facial cuts, and the driver was seriously injured. Later in 2013, the driver and the pregnant head coach of the Seton Hill University women's lacrosse team were killed when the bus allegedly went off the road and crashed into a tree (*USA Today*, 2013). By all indications, none of the buses involved in these accidents was equipped with seatbelts.

Recently, vehicular accidents involving student-athletes provided insights into the issue of team safety travel. On August 22, 2015, a bus carrying a Wisconsin high school volleyball team struck a car, killing the drive of the car, a mother and her three year old daughter, as well as injuring 16 others (CBS Minnesota, 2015). All of the student-athletes, coaches, and bus driver emerged from the crash without significant injuries. Also, in California three vans filled with a cross country team of community college athletes were rear-ended by an inattentive driver of a gravel truck (Duranty, 2015). The collision triggered a domino effect which resulted in minor injuries to nine people of the 30 men and woment as well as damage to two vans (Duranty, 2015).

According to the former head of the National Highway Traffic Safety Administration, David Strickland stated:

> While travel on motorcoaches is overall a safe form of transportation, when accidents do occur, there is the potential for a great number of deaths and serious injuries due to the number of occupants and high speeds at which vehicles are traveling. Adding seat belts to motorcoaches increases safety for all passengers and drivers, especially in the event of a rollover crash. (Grant, para. 12)

Due to these types of incidents, the Motorcoach Enhanced Safety Act was passed in 2012. Among the items covered in the Motorcoach Enhanced Safety Act of 2012 requires that all such vehicles (i.e., busses and vans) have:

1. Improved seating designs, to substantially decrease the risk of passengers being thrown from their seats and hitting other passengers, interior surfaces, and components;
2. Safety seat belts installed at each designated seating position;
3. Superior glazing must installed in each motorcoach portal to avoid the partial or complete ejection of the travelers;
4. Improved roof standards to withstand rollovers;
5. Fire suppression systems that automatically subdues all fires;
6. Improved emergency evacuation designs including exit windows, doors, roof hatch, and wheelchair lift doors to expedite access and use by passengers of motorcoaches under all emergency circumstances, including crashes and fires;
7. Enhanced occupant impact protection standards for motorcoach interiors to reduce substantially serious injuries for all passengers of motorcoaches.

Athletic administrators have a duty to provide safe transportation of the participants to and from events at which the sport takes place, including practices (Doleschal, 2006). However, safe transportation of student-athletes is an often neglected issue facing athletics administrators. In cases where the event is well-organized and managed, should a vehicular accident involving one or more of the participating teams occur a certain pall will be associated to the event. In a Louisiana case, a van accident in which a student driver who did not possess a chauffeur's license was unable to control the van after one of its tires blew (*Clement v. Griffin*, 1994). The van rolled three times, ejecting several of the baseball team's 13 members. The students filed suit against the driver, the college, the state, and boards connected to the college. An appellate court found the college had duties to properly maintain vehicles (the tire was found to be under-inflated), select qualified drivers, properly train its drivers, and that it had failed to properly operate the vehicle. The plaintiffs were awarded amounts ranging from $25,000 to $1.6 million (*Clement v. Griffin*, 1994).

As cited in LaVetter (2005), a 2005 study of National Junior College Athletic Association and National Association of Intercollegiate Athletics athletic directors revealed that:

1. Only 11% allow nine or fewer passengers in 15-passenger vans. It is important to note that the National Highway Traffic Safety Administration reported 15-passenger vans with 10 or more occupants had a rollover rate in single-vehicle crashes that is nearly three times the rate of those that were lightly loaded with fewer than five occupants.
2. Fifty percent of two- and four-year colleges continued to use student drivers.
3. Thirty-eight percent of athletics administrators said they did not place any van travel restrictions during inclement weather.

To fulfill their duty to provide safe transportation, athletic administrators should develop, implement, and enforce clear policies on vehicle maintenance as well as decrease the use of 15-passenger vans. According to the National Highway Transportation Safety Administration (NHTSA) likelihood of being in an accident in which there are more than 10 passengers in a 15-passenger van is three times as great when more than nine passengers travel. Further, 15-passenger vans potential for a rollover increases significantly at speeds over 50 miles an hour and on curved roads. Finally, many younger drivers, even in college, may not be qualified or experienced to drive 15-passenger vans. The National Interscholastic Athletic Administration Association (NIAAA) has indicated that the least recommended transportation activity is to allow student-athletes to transport themselves and others to practices or contests or out-of-town driving (Blackburn, Forsyth, Olson, & Whitehead, 2014).

While it may not be financially feasible for schools to use buses to transport teams to every game, it is important that athletic administrators develop and implement a well-defined policy as to who can drive team vans. For example, at the college level, some schools allow students over 21 to drive the vans to and from games. However, because of their inexperience driving large vans, or the possibility of fatigue after playing in an athletic contest, if at all possible the only people allowed to transport teams should be coaches or other school personnel (LaVetter, 2005).

Some states require a Type II bus driver certification, which permits a designated school official to transport athletes in a vehicle that has a capacity of 10–16 people (LaVetter, 2005). However, the National Association of Independent Schools has recommended that schools contract buses for all team travel—even those located a short distance away (Wilson, 2002). Contract components that should be considered when negotiating with a transportation company include unlimited mileage, vehicle usage limitations, gas prices and vehicular maintenance. Although the athletic administrator should possess knowledge of state laws as well as federal mandates when renting or using vehicles other than regulated buses, the most cost-efficient method is to employ a rental company to maintain the vehicles and comply with federal and state safety regulations. This has a legal as well as a safety benefit since the use commercial buses allows school is able to transfer liability for providing safe transportation from the school to the bus company.

To avoid litigation being brought under the respondeat superior doctrine, athletic administrators should be in regular communication with all coaches, parents/guardians of athletes, and participants regarding the rules and regulations under which the athletic program will be conducted. Athletic administrators should provide all safety rules in writing and distribute them to all coaches, parents/guardians of athletes and athletes prior to first day of practice and reiterated on a regular basis throughout the sport season. Finally, all rules must be strictly enforced on a regular basis.

LIABILITIES OF SPORT OFFICIALS AND REFEREES

Sports officials in the United States can found from the grass-roots recreational community leagues to the bright lights of professional sports. With the exception of the professional sports officials, many officials receive little pay and do it for the love of the sport. There has been a longstanding reluctance to hold sports officials negligent (*Pape v. State*, 1982). However, sports officials and referees have been sued for "failure to inspect playing fields, failure to cancel an athletic contest because of bad weather, failure to control use of equipment, failure to enforce rules, failure to control the conduct of players, and failure to render first aid" (Wolin & Lange, 2013, p. 84). Referees do

have to enforce the rules of the game, but there is no independent tort for referee malpractice (*Bain v. Gillispie*, 1984). No court has recognized a viable cause of action for misapplication of a game rule or error in judgment (*Georgia High School Association v. Waddell*, 1981).

In 2008, University of Houston wide receiver Patrick Edwards broke his leg during an intercollegiate football game when he ran into a metal cart used by the Marshall University (MU) band. It should be noted that metal cart was located very near the end zone when Edwards hit after attempting to catch a long pass. The injury not only cost Edwards $30,000 in medical expenses. As a remedy, Edwards sued Marshall University, Conference USA, and the game referee, citing the National Collegiate Athletic Association NCAA football rules requiring that "all markers and obstructions within the playing enclosure shall be placed or constructed in such a manner as to avoid any possible hazard to players" (MU's tab $250,300 …, 2012, para. 3). The case settled for $250,300 (MU's tab $250,300 …, 2012).

During an NFL game, a player suffered a significant injury to his eye as a result of being struck by a weighted penalty flag that was thrown by a referee. The reason for the damage was that the official weighted his penalty flag with BB pellets rather than the customary popcorn kernels (Slotnick, 2011). As a result of the injury, Brown filed a $200 million lawsuit against the NFL, that his career was prematurely shortened (Slotnick, 2011). He eventually came to a settlement in 2002 which awarded him at least $15 million (Slotnick, 2011).

There has been legislation introduced at the state level that grants immunity to officials or limits their liability in some fashion. For example, the Mississippi State Legislature, for example, has enacted.

Miss. Code Ann. § 95-9-3 statute with regard to the immunity of officials:

1. Sports officials who officiate athletic contests at any level of competition in this

state shall not be liable to any person or entity in any civil action for injuries or damages claimed to have arisen by virtue of actions or inactions related in any manner to officiating duties within the confines of the athletic facility at which the athletic contest is played.

2. For purposes of this section, sports officials are defined as those individuals who serve as referees, umpires, linesmen and those who serve in similar capacities but may be known by other titles and are duly registered or members of a local, state, regional or national organization which is engaged in part in providing education and training to sports officials.

3. Nothing in this section shall be deemed to grant the protection set forth to sports officials who cause injury or damage to a person or entity by actions or inactions which are intentional, willful, wanton, reckless, malicious or grossly negligent.

SOURCE: Courtesy of Westlaw; reprinted with permission.

LIABILITIES OF TEAM PHYSICIANS

Athletes at all levels are should be at their best physical condition to perform at their very best for their teams. Being at the top physical condition is especially important to a professional athlete as his or her body is an asset to the team and the athlete. The team has an interest in ensuring that a player can perform at a top level to fulfill his or her contractual obligations to the team. The standard player contract in all major sports requires the player to maintain good physical condition. All professional and collegiate athletes are given extensive physical examinations to ensure they are ready to engage in athletic competition. Professional sports teams retain the services of

a physician who will provide medical care and advice to their players. The team physician's main function is to provide medical care for team members. In the course of that duty, the physician will typically provide both medical advice and treatment. This creates a patient/physician relationship between the team physician and the player. Many team physicians actually pay for the privilege of being the team physician.

Colleges and high schools also hire physicians and medical care personnel to perform physical examinations and to provide emergency medical care to participants in athletic events. Two prominent cases, *Kleinknecht v. Gettysburg College* (1993) and *Pinson v. Tennessee* (1995), dealt with duties owed by colleges and universities to their student-athletes. According to the court in *Kleinknecht* (1993) the college owed a duty to the student-athlete to provide sufficiently proactive emergency medical measures. The court in *Kleinknecht* stressed that the plaintiff student-athlete was different from the normal student population because he had been recruited to play in a school-sponsored athletic activity when the incident occurred, in other words there was "a distinction between a student injured while participating as an intercollegiate athlete in a sport for which he was recruited and a student injured at a college while pursuing his private interests" (*Kleinknecht*, p. 1367).

In *Pinson v. Tennessee* (1995), a football player was injured during two different practices several weeks apart. After the first incident, the university's athletic trainer did not notify the hospital doctors of the observed neurological conditions of the student-athlete. Additionally, the trainer never informed the team physician of the student's frequent headaches prior to the second episode. The injuries incurred by the student-athlete resulted in significant and permanent neurological damage. The court ruled in favor of the student because a "special relationship" existed between the student and university predicated on the student having participated in scheduled athletic practices under the university's supervision. Thus, the *Pinson* court found that a "special relationship" existed between the athlete and the university which created the duty of the university to offer prompt medical care, and that the university owed a duty to make certain that proper medical treatment was available in case athletes were injured in regularly scheduled practices and contests (*Pinson v. Tennessee*, 1995).

Regarding the question of breach of a duty, the *Kleinknecht* (1993) court found that the defendant college breached its duty of care by failing to have any medical personnel at a school-sponsored practice and competition. Finally, although medical team personnel were present at a football practice in *Pinson* (1995), the athletic trainer failed to notify the physician about the neurological symptoms the player had exhibited. Both *Kleinknecht* and *Pinson* show that a university may be held liable if an athlete is injudiciously put into competition following injury.

Within the context of the exercise reasonable care, medical personnel have duties for the health and safety of athletes for which they are entrusted. For example, a team physician has a duty to athletes to determine when they can return to play after an injury (Osborne, 2001). If the physician believes that an athlete may be exposed to greater harm by returning to play, the physician has the duty to deny the athlete that opportunity (Di Luca, 2008). Specifically dealing with injuries, legally recognized duties may include the duty to properly assess the athlete's condition, to provide or obtain proper medical treatment, to inform the athlete of the risks of athletic participation given the particular medical condition, and to provide clearance to participate (Osborne, 2001).

Team doctors can be pressured by many sources, including owners, coaches, or even players themselves, to find that a player is in condition to play, when in fact circumstances exist that might prove otherwise. Plaintiffs have sued a variety of medical providers, such as team physicians, athletic trainers, and universities, for failing to render proper medical care or advice. Courts have tended to adhere to a consistent standard of care, particularly when medical treatment is required (Di Luca, 2008). Of particular interest is that a medical malpractice claim is much easier to prove when there is not a standard to be judged against (Hecht, 2002). If a medical provider such as a doctor, hospital, or nurse fails to render proper care or treatment, the plaintiff may have a *medical malpractice* claim. A medical expert must testify on behalf of the plaintiff to establish the appropriate standard of care for the medical provider and state whether the standard of care has been breached. *Medical malpractice* is conduct that deviates from a reasonable standard of care.

A plaintiff in a medical malpractice action is required to establish the following elements: (1) a duty owed by the health care provider to act according to the applicable standard(s) of care; (2) a breach of that duty; (3) an injury; and (4) a causal connection between the breach of the standard and the injury. With respect to the causation element, the plaintiff must show evidence that to a reasonable degree of medical probability, the injury claimed was proximately caused by the negligence of the defendant (*Brumfield v. Ruyle*, 2007).

LIABILITIES OF PARTICIPANTS

Participants are those who are either directly or indirectly involved in the sports activity (Schubert, Smith, & Trentadue, 1986). As such, referees, assistants, and even ancillary personnel such as timekeepers and team physicians involved in a sports activity are all considered participants (Schubert et al., 1986). However, the primary participants in most sports are the athletes. While athletic administrators, coaches, and officials have duties to create and maintain a reasonably safe environment for the athletes to compete, the athletes themselves have responsibilities to prevent unnecessary exposure of harm to each other. Recent examples of athletes not living up their duties include a soccer player intentionally biting the shoulder of an opponent or a professional football player stomping on an opposing player's leg.

In one of the earliest cases regarding participant liability for another athlete is the case of *Nabozny v. Barnhill* (1975) which involved a soccer match between two amateur teams. The plaintiff was the goalkeeper, and the defendant was a forward on the opposing team. During the match, the defendant kicked the plaintiff in the head, causing injury, when the plaintiff was down on one knee holding the ball to his chest. Organizational rules stated that players were prohibited from making contact with the goalkeeper when he was in the penalty area and had possession of the ball. The court found in favor of the plaintiff.

Tomjanovich v. California Sports, Inc. (1979), is one the most famous tort sports case involving participant liability. Kermit Washington punched Rudy Tomjanovich during an NBA game, causing severe injuries to Tomjanovich, who sustained a skull fracture, concussion, and facial injuries that diminished his career as a professional player. Tomjanovich was actually trying to break up a fight at the time of the incident. He sued the Los Angeles Lakers, arguing they encouraged players to start fights with other teams and asserting they were liable for the acts of Washington. Noted Houston sports attorney Nick Nichols was able to persuade a California jury that Tomjanovich was entitled to damages in excess of $1 million (United Press International, 1981).

Bill Romanowski of the National Football League Oakland Raiders was sued by Marcus Williams for injuries Williams suffered when Romanowski hit him in the face during a practice drill in 2003. The punch ended Williams's career, causing some brain damage when his eye socket was crushed by Romanowski. The Raiders asserted they were not responsible for the conduct of Romanowski and fined him $60,000. Romanowski had been fined over $100,000 by the league in his career for head butting, headkicking, and spearing, all illegal activities in the NFL. The case went to trial in March 2005, and a jury awarded Williams $340,000. Williams was not satisfied with the verdict and was seeking a new trial when he and Romanowski agreed to settle the case for $415,000. Professional football is a violent game that would not usually lend itself to lawsuits between participants; however, because of the violent nature of the act committed by Romanowski, the matter was considered outside the scope of risk assumed even by a professional football player.

One of the most notorious incidents of participant versus participant violence in sports led to a civil lawsuit against Todd Bertuzzi of the Vancouver Canucks (Associated Press, 2006). Steve Moore, former Colorado Avalanche forward and Moore's parents, filed a civil lawsuit against Bertuzzi, his teammate Brad May, Canucks head coach Mark Crawford, and Canucks general manager Brian Burke. The lawsuit arose out of an incident that occurred on February 16, 2004, in a National Hockey League game between Colorado and Vancouver. The lawsuit alleged that Bertuzzi carried out an assault on the plaintiff at the request of the administration of the Vancouver hockey club. Todd Bertuzzi pled guilty to the charge of assault in a British Columbia court and was suspended from the league for the assault on Moore. Bertuzzi also received a $500,000 fine for his violent outburst against Moore, one of the largest fines ever issued in professional sports history.

CONCLUSION

The possibility of a participant suffering an injury exists in all sports. A negligence case arising from a sports injury can be based on failing to employ a competent coach, failing to provide adequate training or supervision, failing to provide safe equipment or facilities, requiring individuals to play, or even allowing mismatched players to compete against one another (Doleschal, 2006). It is relatively startling how often participants in sports and recreational activities choose to sue participants, coaches, spectators, officials, volunteers or the organization that conducts the activity. Coaches and athletic administration have legal duties in providing a reasonably safe environment for all participants. While some cases may have succeeded in which the facts pointed toward a coaches' total disregard for a player's well-being, overall the courts have been often been timid in applying liability to the coach or school, on the general principle that "the law should not place unreasonable burdens on the free and vigorous participation in sports" (*Foronda v. Hawaii International Boxing Club*, 2001, p. 838). Without this knowledge it is very likely that they may be faced with a lawsuit that could have been averted.

DISCUSSION QUESTIONS

Negligence

1. In *Lindaman v. Vestal Cent. School District* (2004), the court denied the defendant's motion for summary judgment, finding a question of fact existed as to whether the defendant was negligent. In your opinion, is this type of game appropriate for children of this age group? If not, what age is appropriate?

2. For an interesting case involving the concept of duty under negligence law, see *Kleinknecht v. Gettysburg College* (1993), which addressed the issue of the duty owed to an intercollegiate athlete if he or she is injured while participating in sports on campus. What duty of care does a university owe an intramural participant in providing for his or her safety?

Participant Versus Participant Liability

1. Consider the heated exchange that took place between Roger Clemens and Mike Piazza in the 2000 World Series. Piazza has had much success against Clemens in his career. During an at bat, Piazza's shattered bat flew in the direction of Clemens, who quickly scooped up the bat and discarded it in general direction of Piazza. If the bat had hit and injured Piazza, would Piazza have had grounds for a civil lawsuit against Clemens for damages? On what basis could a jury find Clemens liable?

2. Can a violation of a safety rule form the basis of a lawsuit? Consider an NFL player who commits a flagrant foul and receives an unsportsmanlike conduct penalty for hitting a player while he is out of bounds. If the latter player is injured as a result, would the violation of a rule of the game—in this case, unsportsmanlike conduct—form the basis of a civil lawsuit? What if a baseball player "corked" his bat and then during an at bat lined a foul ball off the third-base coach's head, injuring him? (Corking a bat is a violation of league rules and allegedly assists the player in hitting the ball harder and farther.) Could the thirdbase coach prevail in a lawsuit against the player on the basis that the player had violated a rule of the game?

(continues)

DISCUSSION QUESTIONS (CONTINUED)

Liabilities of Team Physicians

1. Does a team physician have a duty to the team or to the player? Could a player sue a team doctor for failure to diagnose an injury? Consider the case of Jeff Novak, a former Southwest Texas State standout who sued the Jacksonville Jaguars team physician, Stephen Lucke. Novak was awarded $4.35 million by a Jacksonville jury in July 1999. The verdict was overturned less than a week later by Judge Frederick Tygart, who indicated that he saw no evidence of negligence by Dr. Lucke. Novak best described the position of the team physician: "I think it's probably the toughest environment a doctor can have in the whole world. You've got coaches that want them on the field. You've got physicians who are tied up in wanting that team to win as well, and wanting to make the coach happy so he can be there again next year as the team doctor of the Jacksonville Jaguars." Novak had filed a medical malpractice lawsuit against the Jaguars's team physicians for medically clearing him to practice with a hematoma on his right leg. Coach Tom Coughlin testified in his deposition in the lawsuit that he "can and will exert as much pressure on the player and the doctors to get the player on the field" (Roberts, 2004, para. 8). The case eventually settled for $2.2 million.

Liability of Coaches and Athletic Administrators

1. In the appeal of *Kahn v. East Side Union High School District* (2003), the defendant was a 14 year old novice swimmer on the junior varsity swim team. While participating at a swim meet, the defendant broke her neck as a result of executing a racing dive into the shallow part of the pool. Several triable issues existed with respect to the whether the coachs' behavior was negligent. These issues included: 1) lack of training in the shallow water dive, especially as sequenced teaching methods were recommended in an available manual; 2) the coach's awareness of the plaintiff's severe fear of race diving; 3) the coach's promise that the plaintiff would not be required to dive; 4) his last minute breach of that promise after the swim meet began; 5) the coach's threat to remove the plaintiff from the team if she did not do a racing dive. Explain the elements of negligence as they apply to this case. How would the doctrine of respondeat superior be applied the athletic administrator in this case?
2. In which of the following scenarios could a coach be held liable for injuries to a student-athlete? In your answer, explain how each of the elements of negligence would apply.
    a. Making a student run extra laps for being late to practice, as result of which the student suffers injuries.
    b. Requiring players to perform one-on-one tackling drills with a weight difference of 70 pounds between the two players.
    c. Requiring a player to continue playing notwithstanding that the player has suffered an injury.

DISCUSSION QUESTIONS (CONTINUED)

Liability of Officials or Referees

1. Under what circumstances can a referee be held liable for negligence? What about a referee who accidentally gives a football team an extra down that allows the opposite team to score a touchdown and win the championship? What about a referee who miscalculates the time left in the game and allows one team extra time to kick a winning field goal?

KEY TERMS

Breach of duty

Comparative negligence

Compensatory damages

Contributory Negligence

Damages

Duty

Gross negligence

Medical malpractice

Mixed contributory & comparative negligence

Negligence

Nominal damages

Proximate cause

Punitive Damages

Respondeat superior doctrine

Tort

Willful or wanton misconduct

REFERENCES

Associated Press. (February 15, 2006). Moore seeking $15M in lost wages, more in damages. *ESPN NHL.* Retrieved from http://sports.espn.go.com/nhl/news /story?id=2331878

Associated Press. (February 27, 2013). Maine bus crashes north of Boston. Retrieved from http://espn.go.com /womens-college-basketball/story/_/id/8993677 /maine-black-bears-women-basketball-team-bus -crashes-north-boston-driver-hurt

Bain v. Gillispie, 357 N.W.2d 47 (Iowa Ct. App. 1984).

Bates, T.A., & Bates, S.T. (2005). Landlord's liability for failure to protect tenant from criminal acts of third person. *American Law Reports* (5th ed., vol. 749, 206–208).

Beahm, J. (2010). Max Gilpin school football death suit settles. *FindLaw.* Retrieved from http://blogs.findlaw .com/injured/2010/09/max-gilpin-school-football -death-suit-settles.html.

Beckett v. Clinton Prairie School Corp., 504 N.E.2d 552, 552 (Ind. 1987).

Benitz v. New York City Bd. of Education, 541 N.E.2d 29, 29 (N.Y. 1989).

Blackburn, M., Forsyth, E., Olson, J., & Whitehead, B. (2014). Get creative to manage athletic transportation budgets. Retrieved from http://www.humankinetics .com/excerpts/excerpts/get-creative-to-manage -athletic-transportation-budgets.

Broward County School Board v. Ruiz, 493 So. 2d 474 (1986).

Brumfield v. Ruyle, 2007 WL 1018475 (Tex. Ct. App.-Ft. Worth 2007).

CBS Minnesota. (August 23, 2015). Wis. Officials: Mother, child dead after crash with school bus. Retrieved from http://minnesota.cbslocal.com/2015/08/23 /wis-officials-mother-child-dead-after-crash-with -school-bus/

Centner, T.J. (2006). Equestrian immunity and sport responsibility statutes: Altering obligations and placing them on participants. *Villanova Sports and Entertainment Law Journal,* 13, 37–64.

Chitwood Smith, T.M. (2005). *A comprehensive analysis of judicial response to negligence cases in the elementary school* (unpublished doctoral dissertation). University of Louisville, Kentucky.

Clement v. Griffin, La. 94-0777, 637 So. 2d 478, 1994 La. LEXIS 1342 (La. May 20, 1994).

Cole, M.G. (2007). No blood no foul: The standard of care in Texas owed by participants to one another in athletic contests. *Baylor Law Review*, 59, 438–483.

Coomer v. Kan. City Royals Baseball Corporation, 2013 Mo. App. LEXIS 46 (Mo. Ct. App. Jan. 15, 2013).

Crawn v. Campo, 643 A.2d 600, 136 N.J. 494 (1994).

Davis, T. (2008). Tort liability of coaches for injuries to professional athletes: Overcoming policy and doctrinal barriers. *University of Missouri-Kansas City Law Review*, 76, 571–596.

Di Luca, T.R. (2008). Medical malpractice and the modern day athlete: A whole different ballgame … or is it? *Westchester Bar Journal*, 35, 17–26.

Dobberstein, M.J. (2007). Give me the ball, coach: A scouting report on the liability of high schools and coaches for injuries to high school pitcher's arms. *Sport Lawyer's Journal*, 14, 49–70.

Dobbs, D.B. (2000). *The law of torts*. St. Paul, Minn.: West Group.

Doe v. Pa. State Univ., 982 F. Supp. 2d 437, 2013 U.S. Dist. LEXIS 158752 (E.D. Pa. 2013).

Doleschal, J.K. (2006). Managing risk in interscholastic athletic programs: 14 legal duties of care. *Marquette Sports Law Review*, 17(1), 295–339.

Drake, W.N. (2004). Foreseeable zone of risk: Confusing foreseeability with duty in Florida negligence law. *The Florida Bar Journal*, 78, 10–17.

Duranty, A. (Aug. 21, 2015). Saddleback College athletes hurt after gravel truck rear-ends van, causing domino effect. *Orange County Register*. Retrieved from http://www.ocregister.com/articles/students-678769-vans-gravel.html

Fleming, J.F. (1953). Vicarious liability. *Tulane Law Review*, 28(2), 161–215.

Foronda v. Haw. Int'l Boxing Club, 96 Haw. 51, 25 P.3d 826, 2001 Haw. App. LEXIS 117 (Haw. Ct. App. 2001).

Georgia High School Ass'n v. Waddell, 285 S.E.2d 7 (Ga. 1981).

Grant, A. (2013). Deadly crash of bus carrying Bluffton University baseball team behind new rule on seat belts. *Plain Dealer*. Retrieved from http://www.cleveland.com/metro/index.ssf/2013/11/deadly_crash_of_bus_carrying_b.html

Hackbart v. Cincinnati Bengals, Inc. 435 F. Supp. 352, 1977 U.S. Dist. LEXIS 14408 (D. Colo. 1977).

Hackbart v. Cincinnati Bengals, Inc. 601 F.2d 516, 1979 U.S. App. LEXIS 14111, 4 Fed. R. Evid. Serv. (CBC) 1042 (10th Cir. Colo. 1979).

Hemady v. Long Beach Unified School District, 2006 Cal. App. LEXIS 1691 (Cal. App. 2d Dist. Oct. 30, 2006).

Hekmat, R.R. (2002). Malpractice during practice: Should NCAA coaches be liable for negligence? *Loyola of Los Angeles Entertainment Law Review*, 22, 613–642.

Hecht, A.N. (2002). Legal and ethical aspects of sports-related concussions: The Merrill Hoge story. *Seton Hall Journal of Sport Law*, 12, 17–64.

Henderson v. Volpe-Vito, Inc., 2006 WL 1751832 (Mich. Ct. App. 2006).

Holmes, O.W. (1881/1963). *The common law*. Howe, M.D. (Ed.)., Cambridge, Mass: Belknap Press of Harvard University Press.

Hurst, T.R., & Knight, J.N. (2003). Coaches' liability for athletes' injuries and deaths. *Seton Hall Journal of Sport Law*, 13(27), 40–51.

Kahn v. East Side Union High School District, 75 P. 3d 30 (Cal. 2003).

Karns, J.E. (1986). Negligence and secondary school sports injuries in North Dakota: Who bears the legal responsibility? *North Dakota Law Review*, 62, 455–486.

Kavanagh v. Trustees of Boston University, 440 Mass. 195, 795 N.E.2d 1170, 2003 Mass. LEXIS 643 (2003).

Kleinknecht v. Gettysburg College, 989 F.2d 1360 (1993).

Knight v. Jewett, 834 P.2d 696, 710 (Cal. 1992).

Koffman v. Garnett, 574 S.E.2d 258, 260 (Va. 2003).

Kreidler, M. (2001). *Tragedy won't stop athletes' push to the limit*. ESPN.com. Retrieved from http://msn.espn.go.com/nfl/columns/kreidler mark/1234262.html

LaVetter, D. (2005). Safety must drive decisions in van use. *NCAA News Archives*. Retrieved from http://fs.ncaa.org/Docs/NCAANewsArchive/2005/Editorial/safety+must+drive+decisions+in+van+use+-+12-5-05+ncaa+news.html

Leahy v. Sch. Bd. of Hernando County, 450 So. 2d 883, 885 (Fla. Dist. Ct. App. 1984).

Lindaman v. Vestal Cent. Sch. Dist., 12 A.D.3d 916, 785 N.Y.S.2d 549, 2004 N.Y. App. Div. LEXIS 13799 (N.Y. App. Div. 3d Dep't 2004).

Martinez, J.M. (2003). Liability and volunteer organization: A survey of the law. *Nonprofit Management and Leadership*, 14(2), 151–169.

McCain v. Florida Power, 593 So. 2d 500, 503 n.2 (Fla. 1992).

McCaskey, A.S., & Biedzynski, K.W. (1996). A guide to the legal liability of coaches for a sports participant's injuries. *Seton Hall Journal of Sport Law*, 6, 7–125.

McKichan v. St. Louis Hockey Club, L.P., 967 S.W.2d 209 (Mo. Ct. App. 1998).

Mogabgab v. Orleans Parish School Board, 239 So. 2d 456 (La. Ct. App.1970).

Moose v. Massachusetts Inst. of Technology, 43 Mass. App. Ct. 420, 683 N.E.2d 706, 1997 Mass. App. LEXIS 189 (1997).

Motorcoach Enhanced Safety Act of 2012 49 U.S.C. 30101 Pub. L. 112-141, sec 32703.

MU's tab $250,300 in Houston WR suit. (2012). *West Virginia Gazette*. Retrieved from http://www.wvgazette.com /Sports/201204270163

Nabozny v. Barnhill, 334 N.E.2d 258 (Ill. Ct. App. 1975).

New Light Co. v. Wells Fargo Alarm Services, 247 Neb. 57, 525 N.W.2d 25, 1994 Neb. LEXIS 258 (1994).

Osborne, B. (2001). Principles of liability for athletic trainers: Managing sport-related concussion. *Journal of Athletic Training*, 36(3), 316–321.

Owen, D.G. (2007). Idea: The five elements of negligence. *Hofstra Law Review*, 35, 1671–1685.

Pape v. State, 90 A.D.2d 904; 456 N.Y.S.2d 863, 8 Ed. Law Rep. 158 (N.Y. App. Div. 1982).

Pinson v. State, 1995 Tenn. App. LEXIS 807 (Tenn. Ct. App. 1995).

Prejean v. East Baton Rouge Parish School Board, La. App. 98-0063, 729 So. 2d 686, 1999 La. App. LEXIS 412 (La.App. 1 Cir. Feb. 19, 1999).

Roventini v. Pasadena Independent School District, 981 F.Supp. 1013, 1997 U.S. Dist. LEXIS 18805 (S.D. Tex. 1997).

Sanders v. Kuna Joint School District, 876 P.2d 154 (Idaho Ct. App. 1994).

Schubert, G.W., Smith, R.K., & Trentadue, J.C. (1986). *Sports law*. St. Paul, Minn.: West.

Slotnick, D.E. (2011). Orlando Brown, who sued N.F.L. over errant flag, dies at 40. *New York Times*. Retrieved from http://www.nytimes.com/2011/09/24/sports/football /orlando-brown-who-sued-nfl-over-errant-flag -dies-at-40.html?_r=0

Stowers v. Clinton Central School Corporation, 855 N.E.2d 739 (2006).

Thomas v. Wheat, 143 P.3d 767 (Okla. Civ. App. 2006).

Tomjanovich v. California Sports, Inc., 1979 U.S. Dist. LEXIS 9282 (S.D. Tex. Oct. 10, 1979).

United Press International. (1981). Tomjanovich and Lakers reach agreement on suit. *The New York Times*. Retrieved from http://www.nytimes.com/1981/04/21 /sports/tomjanovich-and-lakers-reach-agreement-on -suit.html

United States Football League v. National Football League, 842 F.2d 1335 (2nd Cir. 1988).

USA Today. (March 16, 2013). Pregnant lacrosse coach, driver die in team bus crash. Retrieved from http://www .usatoday.com/story/news/nation/2013/03/16/tour -bus-crashes-in-pa-serious-injuries-reported/1992577/

Wilson, D.P. (2002). Transporting students: Whats, whys, and wherefores. *National Association of Independent Schools*. Retrieved from http://www.nais.org/Articles /Documents/transportation_article_final.pdf

Wolin, M.T., & Lange, R.D. (2013). Legal liability for sports referees in today's litigious world—If you can't kill the ump then sue him. *University of Denver Sports & Entertainment Law Journal*, 15, 83–110.

INTENTIONAL TORTS

LEARNING OBJECTIVES

By the end of the chapter, the reader will be able to:

1. Understand the concept of intentional tort
2. Comprehend and provide examples of assault and aggravated assault that have occurred in sports
3. Comprehend and provide examples of battery and criminal battery that have occurred in sports
4. Comprehend and provide examples of slander and libel that have occurred in sports
5. Analyze the elements of the right to privacy and publicity rights of a sports figure
6. Understand sexual harassment as an intentional tort as it applies to the sports environment
7. Understand hazing as an intentional tort as it applies to the sports environment

RELATED CASES

Case 3.1   Bridges v. City of Carrasco, 982 So.2d 306, 2007-1593 (La.App.c Cir4/30/08)

Case 3.2   O'Connor v. Burningham, 2007 UT 58, 165 P.3d 1214, 2007 Utah LEXIS 139, 583 Utah Adv. 3 (2007)

Case 3.3   Koffman v. Garnett, 265 Va. 12, 574 S.E.2d 258, 2003 Va. Lexis 16 (2003)

INTRODUCTION

Violence in sporting contests have been popular throughout history. In part, spectators may anticipate violence and aggression in sports to occur in order to attain the "thrill" known as the "gladiator syndrome" (Hechter, 1977). Spectators can continue to view violence in such diverse sports as World Wide Entertainment professional wrestling contests and extreme sport competitions to National Football League (NFL) and National Hockey League (NHL) games. The violent actions in these contests may be a primary reason that the sports industry in the United States had an estimated gross revenue of $485 billion dollars in 2014 (Plunkett Research, 2014). The profitability and lenience of violence in sports, however, presents a legal question as to whether athletes are immune from criminal prosecution. Examples of sport-related intentional torts include:

In 1965 San Francisco Giants Hall of Fame pitcher Juan Marichal threw two of these pitches at Los Angeles Dodgers leadoff batter Maury Wills. Later in the bottom of the third inning, when Marichal was at bat, Dodgers catcher Johnny Roseboro returned the second pitch close enough to Marichal's head that it "either nicked his ear or came near enough to make him feel the breeze." What I did was part of being a catcher ... it's retaliation ... The catcher buzzes the guy. It's standard operating procedure (Wilstein, 1990, para. 23). Marichal turned around to question Roseboro who removed his mask and clenched his fist response, Marichal swung his bat and hit Roseboro's unprotected head at least twice, opening a two-inch gash on his head that sent blood streaming down his face (Wilstein, 1990). For hitting Roseboro, Marichal was fined $1750 and was suspended for nine days or eight playing dates (Wilstein, 1990).

During the third round of a 1997 heavyweight championship fight between Evander Holyfield and Mike Tyson, Tyson put Holyfield in a bear hug, spit out his mouthpiece, and bit off a piece of Holyfield's right ear.

In a 1999 National Basketball Association game, All-Star Utah Jazz forward, Karl Malone, elbowed All-Star San Antonio Spurs center, David Robinson with such force that Robinson would fall to the floor, unconscious, suffering both a concussion and a strained knee.

In 2000, a parent of a youth hockey player, Thomas Junta, was convicted of involuntary manslaughter as a result of killing Michael Costin, who was supervising a hockey practice session.

During a regular season National Hockey League game in 2000, Boston Bruins defenseman Marty McSorley hit Vancouver Canucks left wing Donald Brashear in the head with a two-fisted stick attack. Brashear's head hit the ice, he went unconscious, suffered a concussion, and later experienced memory loss (*McSorley, Guilty of Assault, Avoids Jail*, 2000). Although a British Columbia judge found McSorley guilty of assault with a weapon, McSorley was not sent to jail (*McSorley, Guilty of Assault, Avoids Jail*, 2000).

During a National Football League game in 2006, Tennessee Titan defensive lineman Albert Haynesworth kicked and stomped on Dallas Cowboy offensive lineman, Andre Gurode's face that was unguarded due to losing his helmet (Weir, 2006). Gurode's injury resulted in 30 stitches, headaches, and blurred vision.

In a 2011 NFL play-off game, some players from the New Orleans Saints allegedly received $1500 to knock an opposing player out of the game and $1000 for every opposing player who had to carted off the field (Marvez, 2012). Although several players and coaches received various sanctions from the NFL offices for "Bountygate" (Marvez, 2012), none received jail time.

These scenarios are but a few that could be identified in youth, college, and professional sports over the years. Yet, when acts of violence that take place on the playing field are treated in an entirely different manner from the "normal" population (Lassiter, 2007). When a violent sport-related action is committed in a manner as to deliberately injury another person, it is referred to a being an intentional tort.

Intentional Tort

An *intentional tort* is defined as a civil wrong not arising from a breach of contract. The word tort is French for "wrong." Intentional tort law has been described as a vehicle to compensate those who have suffered injuries from wrongful conduct. It covers a wide variety of wrongful conduct and injuries and provides a remedy for acts that may have caused physical injury or that have interfered with physical safety or freedom of movement.

One of the ways to determine if the tort is intentional is by the mental state of the individual who commits the action. In cases in which the individual intends to perform an action with the intent to cause injury to another, it is referred to as an intentional tort. A tort action is typically a civil action brought by a plaintiff to seek compensation for damages incurred by the plaintiff or to seek some other remedy allowed by law. One of the purposes of tort law is to deter or prevent similar conduct by the same party or others in the future. One who commits a tort is referred to as a *tortfeasor*, and an action or conduct that constitutes a tort is referred to as *tortious behavior*. Intent has been defined as "the desire to bring about certain results." According to the court in *Crawn v. Campo* (1994),

> The majority of jurisdictions that have considered the issue of a person's duty to exercise care to avoid injury when engaging in a sports activity have concluded that to constitute a tort, conduct must exceed the level of ordinary negligence. (p. 600)

A wave of tort reform legislation has been passed in the United States. Legislation has been introduced at the state and federal levels to limit the amount of damages a plaintiff may receive for pain and suffering in a tort lawsuit. One of the major purposes of the passage of this type of legislation is to prevent the filing of frivolous lawsuits and to prevent juries from awarding verdicts inconsistent with the evidence. This chapter does not attempt to discuss every tort in the law but only those torts and tort defenses pertinent to the discussion of sports law.

Intentional torts include assault and battery, intentional infliction of emotional distress, defamation, invasion of the right of privacy, misrepresentation, and intentional interference with contractual or business relations. These areas are discussed in this chapter.

Assault

Some torts can be classified as crimes. Although, assault and battery are both considered crimes and are often termed together, they may be separate crimes that can form the basis of a civil action by a plaintiff. If A hits B with a hockey stick without provocation, A could be subject to prosecution by the state and could also be sued by B in a civil action for damages sustained, by A's wrongful conduct, subject to any defense that A might assert against B.

Assault does not refer to the actual violence itself but rather the attempt or threat of violence (*State v. Hayward*, 2014). It is notable that state laws sometimes differ as assault does not require physical contact to have truly happened. Although not all threats are considered assault, assault occurs when an individual threatens bodily harm to another in a compelling way (*State v. Hayward*, 2014). To rise to the level that the offense is significant enough, three main elements must be present: intent to cause apprehension, an apprehension of imminent harm, and the lack of consent of the act by the victim (*Hill v. United States*, 2013). For the *intent to cause apprehension* to occur, the act must be intended to be harmful or offensive contact (Restatement [Second] of Torts § 13, 1965). Additionally, for there to be *imminent apprehension*, the would-be victim must be aware of the threat at the time it is made. This means that there was a deliberate, unjustified interference with the personal right or liberty of another in a way that causes harm (*Nabozny v. Barnhill*, 1975). The *lack of consent* results from circumstances under which the victim clearly expressed that he or she did not consent to the action (*Nabozny v. Barnhill*, 1975).

In the tort of assault, intent is established if a reasonable person is substantially certain that certain consequences will result (*Nabozny v. Barnhill*, 1975). As early as 1905, courts have established the meaning of intent. In *McNeil v. Mullin* (1905), the court stated that "an injury, even in sport, would be an assault, if it went beyond what was admissible in sports of the sort, and was intentional" (p. 170). More recently, assault has been reported as resulting from a person's apprehension of imminent harmful or offensive contact rather than actually being struck (*Etheredge v. District of Columbia*, 1993). Apprehension of imminent harm happens when the possibility of being intentionally hit generates apprehension in the mind of a reasonable person. According to the Restatement (Second) of Torts § 24 (1965):

> In order that the other may be put in the apprehension necessary to make the actor liable for an assault, the other must believe that the act may result in imminent contact unless prevented from so resulting by the other's self-defensive action or by his flight or by the intervention of some outside force.

Thus for assault to exist:

> There must be an intentional, unlawful, offer to touch the person of another in a rude or angry manner under such circumstances as to create in the mind of the party alleging the assault a well-founded fear of an imminent battery, coupled with the apparent present ability to effectuate the attempt, if not prevented. (*Western Union Telegraph Co. v. Hill*, 1933, p. 710)

It is important to note that apprehension is not the same as fear. Apprehension connotes that a person possesses an awareness that an injury or offensive contact is imminent. Therefore, a person who intends to cause apprehension of imminent harm and succeeds in doing so has committed the assault (Restatement [Second] of Torts § 13, 1965). The perception of being the recipient of potential harm in the mind of the victim as a reasonable person is the key.

Aggravated Assault

Aggravated assault occurs when the criminal laws punish more severely due to its seriousness. States classify certain assaults as aggravated assault as well as multiple degrees of criminal charges for aggravated assault under their criminal codes. Factors that raise an assault to an aggravated assault typically include the use of a weapon, the status of the victim, the intent of the perpetrator, and the degree of injury caused. Dave Forbes, a forward for the Boston Bruins, was the first professional athlete to be criminally prosecuted in the United States for assaulting another player during a sporting event. Forbes was charged with aggravated assault with a dangerous weapon after he attacked Henry Boucha of the Minnesota North Stars with his stick during a match, hitting him just above the right eye. However, the charges were dropped after the district attorney determined that the jurors "could not reach unanimity if the case was retried" (Herman, 1975, p. 24). Another example of an aggravated assault case occurred in 1988 when NHL player Minnesota North Star, Dino Ciccarelli, was found guilty of felonious assault and ultimately was sentenced to a fine and a one day jail sentence (Brackin, 1988).

In 2000, Marty McSorley was convicted in a Canadian court of assault with a weapon for striking Donald Brashear in the side of his head causing his helmet to dislodge and his body to hit the ice, unconscious in a puddle of blood (Spousta, 2000). McSorley, who was not aware of the extent of Brashear's injury, skated around and mocked Brashear to stand up and fight (Lapointe, 2000). McSorely, who pled not guilty, received an 18-month conditional discharge, which is similar to probation in the United States, and meant he served no jail time (Hanley, 2000).

As noted previously, in tort law, assault does not require actual touching of the victim. In case in which a person is touched and no consent is provided, the victim may allege that battery has taken place.

Battery

Assault often is followed by battery, which is defined as unlawful physical conduct (often an act of violence, including sexual contact). Battery is defined as the actual "use of force against another, resulting in harmful or offensive conduct" (*Garner*, 2009, p. 173). The concept of battery, as an intentional tort, is sometimes perceived an assault. The confusion between the terms may stem from their association as battery is almost always preceded by an assault. As a result these terms are frequently combined to form assault and battery. However, assault is the act of threatening a violent act or creating an apprehension of imminent harm upon their person without their consent.

A battery is an intentional tort, as opposed to an act that results from negligence, which is considered an unintentional tort. The elements to establish the tort of battery are the same as for *criminal battery* (details below), except that criminal intent need not be present.

The elements of *civil battery* are:

1. Intent—although not criminal intent to cause injury, necessarily, defendant intentionally did an act which resulted in a harmful or offensive contact with the plaintiff's person (*Piedra v. Dugan*, 2004).
2. Contact—contact was made but the plaintiff did not consent to the contact (*Piedra v. Dugan*, 2004).
3. Harm/Damages—the harmful or offensive contact caused injury, damage, loss, or harm to the plaintiff (*Piedra v. Dugan*, 2004).

Damages awarded in battery cases vary widely, depending on the seriousness of the injuries.

Criminal Battery

Within the legal concept of battery, there are two distinct categories: civil battery (tort) and criminal battery. The difference between battery as a crime and battery as a civil tort is merely in the type of intent required. A criminal battery requires the presence of mens rea, or a criminal intent to do wrong, that is to cause a harmful or offensive contact. A criminal battery may be intentional or unintentional. An intentional battery requires "proof that the perpetrator intended to cause harmful or offensive contact against a person without that person's consent and without legal justification" (*Elias v. State*, 1995, p. 183). A reckless battery contains the same elements, but instead of proof of intent, "there must be proof that the perpetrator's misconduct, viewed objectively, was so reckless as to constitute a gross departure from the standard of conduct a law-abiding person would observe" (*Elias v. State*, 1995, p. 184). Battery, as a civil tort, is a non-consensual and intentional contact that is harmful or offensive (*Pritchett v. Heil*, 2001). Non-consensual touching such as directly striking a person's head or face with fists or hockey stick or baseball bat is all that is required for battery to occur. For a tortuous battery to occur, the requisite intent is merely to touch or make contact without consent (*Fugazy v. Corbetta*, 2006).

An example of a situation in which criminal battery may have been construed in a sport was an incident between two intercollegiate football players. After the completion of a televised game an altercation between a University of Oregon player (LaGarrette Blount) and a Boise State University players (Byron Hout) occurred. Although the University of Oregon won the contest, replays showed Hout verbally taunt Blount (presently a professional football player with the New England Patriots). Hout tapped Blount on the shoulder pads, to which Blount reacted by punching Hout in the jaw. Hout, who was not wearing a helmet at the time, went to his knees and became unconscious. It is important to note that the altercation did not occur during the course of play, but rather after the conclusion of the game. If Blount's brutal response to Hout's taunting had taken place in a normal, non-athletic contest public setting, such an eruption would very likely bring about a criminal battery charge, including fines and possible imprisonment.

Defamation

Sports are a topic of conversation for millions of people in the United States every day through a variety of media and electronic outlets. Because sports have become an intrinsic part of the American landscape, individuals think nothing of calling their local sports radio station to praise or berate sports heroes, coaches, referees, broadcasters, or owners. Television and radio sports shows abound, with talking heads, callers, and hosts spouting the latest information concerning the minutiae of each player's performance and sordid details about superstars' personal lives. Could any of these "discussions" ever constitute the tort of defamation? Could a player or coach ever sue a radio talk show host, television anchorperson, journalist, or fan for public remarks made about the athlete?

Abusive or insulting words and threats of future harm may result in a cause of action for the intentional infliction of emotional distress but it does not represent assault (Restatement [Second] of Torts, 1965). If words are accompanied by a threat of physical violence, and conditions indicate a present ability to carry out that threat, an assault may have been committed (*Dahlin v. Fraser*, 1939). However, according to the Restatement (Second) of Torts (1965), "[w]ords do not make the actor liable for assault unless together with other acts or circumstances they put the other in reasonable apprehension of an imminent harmful or offensive contact with his person" (§ 31). As such, words do not represent an assault. If the statement constitutes only opinion, then there is not an actionable tort. However, a difficult question can arise when the statement constitutes a hybrid statement consisting of both fact and opinion. A statement based on false or undisclosed facts can also constitute defamation.

Defamation has been defined as:

> The act of harming the reputation of another by making a false statement [written or oral] to a third person. If the alleged defamation involves a matter of public concern, the plaintiff is constitutionally required to prove both the statement's falsity and the defendant's fault.

It is important to note that the free speech protections of the First Amendment are not absolute in that defamation is not protected speech under the First Amendment. One of the key questions in any defamation case is whether the defendant's statement is one of fact or opinion. *To be held actionable*, a defamatory statement must also be "published." If A tells B that he is a fraud and a thief and it is a false statement but is not communicated to a third party, then the publication requirement has not been met and no defamation has occurred. The defamatory statement must be communicated to a third party to meet the publication requirement.

In 1964, the Supreme Court handed down a landmark defamation decision (*New York Times v. Sullivan*, 1964). The Court in *Sullivan* held that to guarantee certain constitutional protections such as freedom of the press, "actual malice" or "reckless disregard of the truth" by the publisher had to be proven before a "public official" could win damages in a defamation lawsuit (*New York Times v. Sullivan*, 1964). The *Sullivan* decision had an immediate impact on the law which broadened the relative narrow protection that had previous been provided to newspapers that wrote about public officials. In fact, Supreme Court Justice Bryon "Whizzer" White later stated that the *Sullivan* case represented: "first major step in what proved to be a seemingly irreversible process of constitutionalizing the entire law of libel and slander" (*Dun & Bradstreet, Inc. v. Greenmoss Builders, Inc.*, 1985, p. 766).

The Supreme Court later extended concept of "public officials" to "public figures" (*Curtis Publishing Co. v. Butts*, 1967). In *Curtis Publishing Co. v. Butts* (1967), the defendant was a college athletic director accused of fixing one of the school's football games. The Court held that because public figures command similar public interest as well as the same access to the public forum as public officials, public figures should also be held to same standard as public officials in defamation cases (*Curtis Publishing Co. v. Butts*, 1967). The reasoning that Butts was a public figure was predicated his position was of public interest due to its relationship to the university's sports program. Additionally, Butts was deemed to be a public figure based on his access to the media, which supposedly gave him the ability to defend himself against defamation. In reflection of the *Butts* case, Weber stated:

> Ultimately, the policy here [in Butts] is still on the side of the press, it aims to allow the press freedom to purvey news and ideas about public figures without fear, so long as they do not demonstrate an "extreme departure" from responsibility. (p. 492)

In *Gertz v. Welch* (1974), the Court held that the actual malice standard was necessary to protect the press even when the plaintiff was not a public figure. Additionally, the Supreme Court, held that citizens have a basic right to protect their name and reputation (*Gertz v. Welch*, 1974). According to the Supreme Court in *Gertz*,

> Public officials and public figures usually enjoy significantly greater access to the channels of effective communication and hence have a more realistic opportunity to counteract false statements then [*sic*] private individuals normally enjoy. Private individuals are therefore more vulnerable to injury, and the state interest in protecting them is correspondingly greater. (p. 344)

Since this Court examined the difference between private and public figures, *Gertz v. Welch* (1974) has specific application to athletes who choose to pursue defamation litigation. Thus, there are two significant messages from the *New York Times*, *Butts*, and *Gertz* cases. The first is that for a statement to be made with actual malice, it must be made with either knowledge of falsity or a reckless disregard of the truth. Secondly, public figures have a greater burden of proof in defamation cases than private individuals because they must meet the actual malice standard set who is considered a public figure has the burden of proving actual malice by the publisher in a defamation lawsuit. A significant question that must be analyzed in resolving whether the actual malice standard is fitting is why such a burden is "required to guarantee constitutional safeguards." In other words, do athletes, as public figures, actually have to prove actual malice to make sure that a publisher's constitutional right is protected?

In *Cohen v. Marx*, (1949), involving the famous comedian Groucho Marx, a boxer fighting under the nickname of "Canvasback Cohen" sued the entertainer and the American Broadcast Company for statements made by Marx about the boxer. The court discussed the notion that the plaintiff had waived his right to privacy by placing himself in the public light as a professional athlete. The decision gives an early indication that a court will view an athlete as a public figure.

Types of Defamation

There are two types of defamation: *libel* and *slander*. Orally damaging a person's reputation constitutes slander, whereas using the written word involves the tort of libel. At common law, the courts recognized that certain types of statements are defamation per se and therefore need no proof of injury (*Carwile v. Richmond Newspapers*, 1954; *Fleming v. Moore*, 1981). According to an early ruling by the United States Supreme Court in *Pollard v. Lyon* (1876) slander constitutes:

1. Those that impute to a person the commission of some criminal offense involving moral turpitude, for which the party, if the charge is true, may be indicted and punished.
2. Those that impute that a person is infected with some contagious disease, where if the charge is true, it would exclude the party from society.
3. Those that impute to a person unfitness to perform the duties of an office or employment of profit, or want of integrity in the discharge of the duties of such an office or employment.
4. Those that prejudice such person in his or her profession or trade. (p. 255)

Truth is an absolute defense against any defamation claim (Eaton, 1975). A defendant may also assert privilege against a plaintiff's defamation claim under certain circumstances. If false and defamatory statements are made about a public figure, then absent a showing of actual malice, there is no defamation. What constitutes a public figure as defined under defamation law? Public figures are usually individuals who have been placed in the public limelight. The category can include entertainers, politicians, and anybody else who becomes known to the public because of their position or activities in the community.

In *Cobb v. Time, Inc.* (2002), a former professional boxer brought a libel action against *Time* alleging defamation. In reversing a jury verdict of $8.5 million in compensatory damages and $2.2 million in punitive damages, the court found that Cobb was a public figure under the *New York Times* standard and that he had failed to prove "actual malice" on the part of the defendant.

A college track coach who had sued a school magazine for libel based on an article that claimed he had dropped several black athletes from the team for participating in a boycott of a discriminating organization was also held to be a public figure (*Vandenburg v. Newsweek*, 1975). A high school football coach was held to be a public figure for purposes of defamation for actions related to the coach's arrest for bookmaking and alleged grade changes for football players (*Brewer v. Rogers*, 1993). However, the head basketball coach of a small junior college in New Orleans with a largely local student body was declared not to be a public figure under defamation law (*Flose v. Delgado Community College*, 1996).

Courts throughout the United States have labeled athletes as public figures, almost as a per se rule (*Chuy v. Philadelphia Eagles Football Club*, 1979; *Vilma v. Goodell*, 2013). In *Chuy v. Philadelphia Eagles* (1979), held that because Chuy was a professional football player was a public figure for two primary reasons. First, Chuy was a starting player on his team. Second, because he was in the middle of a contract dispute, Chuy was already in the news due to contract issue at the time of the alleged defamatory statement.

In *Vilma v. Goodell* (2013), NFL commissioner, Roger Goodell, was sued by then New Orleans Saints linebacker, Jonathon Vilma, for defamation (Brinson, 2012). Vilma supposedly devised a scheme, otherwise known as Bountygate, in which teammates were financially rewarded for intentionally injuring opposing teams' players (Brinson, 2012). As a result of this accusation, Vilma was suspended for the entire season, and his reputation was tarnished among league officials, fans, and advertising companies (Marvez, 2014). Vilma sued the commissioner to recover damages for allegedly defamatory statements made by Goodell. In the complaint, Vilma alleged that Goodell made public statements which were not in line with National Football League Players Association Collective Bargaining Agreement (*Vilma v. Goodell*, 2013). Vilma stated that the statements were false, defamatory and injurious to his professional and personal reputation (*Vilma v. Goodell*, 2013). According to the District Court, as a public figure, Vilma had the burden of showing that Goodell made the statements with actual malice. Although, Vilma alleged that his suspension was were so procedurally flawed that no reasonable person could have believed the statements were true, the Court related that the statements were based on an extensive investigation (*Vilma v. Goodell*, 2013). Finally, the District Court reported that "while the process was initially procedurally flawed, the statements were ultimately found to have enough support to defeat the defamation claims" (p. 13). Ultimately, it may be perceived that Vilma's defamation case effectively ended because of two words in the District Court's opinion: "public figure."

RIGHT TO PRIVACY AND PUBLICITY RIGHTS

Today's athlete is also a celebrity who has a commercial value in his or her name, likeness, nickname, image, and identity worldwide. An athlete's right of publicity has become a valuable asset to the athlete as well as to his or her team and league. Sports teams and athletes generate millions of dollars each year promoting their products, services, images, and intellectual property rights.

An endorsement by an athlete can be extremely valuable to a company, translating into large commercial gains worldwide. Many companies vie for the right to sign famous athletes to endorsement contracts to promote their products. Over the past few years athletes have endorsed many different types of products, including cars, financial services, food products, and even sexual aids. In 2013, Tiger Woods and Roger Federer are two of the most sought-after athletes with endorsements valued in excess of $65,000 (Lawrence, 2013).

Athletes have become entertainers as well. Many professional sports players have become "actors," thereby increasing their exposure and possible marketability. Chuck Conners of *Rifleman* fame was one of the first athletes to have his own television series. Conners played first base for the Los Angeles Dodgers and also played for the Boston Celtics. Other athletes followed in making appearances on television and in the movies, including Jim Brown (*The Dirty Dozen*), Merlin Olsen (*Little House on the Prairie*), Alex Karras (*Against All Odds*), Bob Uecker (*Mr. Belvedere*), Dan Marino (*Ace Ventura, Pet Detective*), and Shaquille "Shaq" O'Neal (*Blue Chips*).

Many areas of the law come into play when the commercial value of an athlete's name or likeness is at stake. This include the common law right of privacy, the statutory right of publicity, federal and state trademark laws, unfair competition laws, and defamation law. Courts have been willing to extend the right of publicity to names, nicknames, caricatures, and even voices (*Midler v. Ford Motor Co.*, 1988).

The *right of publicity* grants a person the exclusive right to control the commercial value and exploitation of his or her name, likeness, or personality (*Sinker v. Goldsmith*, 1985).The right of publicity protects the commercial interests of athletes and entertainers in their identities (*Carson v. Here's Johnny Portable Toilets, Inc.*, 1983; *White v. Samsung Electronics America, Inc.*, 1992). The tort is derived from the appropriation branch of the right of privacy. Other privacy torts protect primarily personal interests, whereas the right of publicity primarily protects the property interest in the publicity of one's name (*Hirsch v. S.C. Johnson & Son, Inc.*, 1979).

According to Restatement (Second) of Torts 3652A (1971), the right of privacy may be been put into four categories:

1. The use of a person's name, picture, or other likeness for commercial purposes without permission;
2. Intrusion on an individual's affairs or seclusion;
3. Publication of information that places a person in a false light;
4. Public disclosure of private facts about an individual that an ordinary person would find objectionable.

One of the first cases to recognize an athlete's right to his own image was *O'Brien v. Pabst Sales Co.*, (1941). Davey O'Brien sued a beer producer that had used his picture as a football player without his permission. O'Brien had been actively involved in organizations that spoke out against the use of alcohol. He sued Pabst for invasion of privacy. He lost, but Justice Holmes in his now-famous dissent, stated that although there was no controlling authority on the issue, O'Brien still clearly had a property right in his endorsement.

In *Muhammad Ali v. Playgirl* (1978), Ali sued a women's magazine, alleging that it was using his likeness when it published a drawing of an African American boxer sitting in a corner of a boxing ring who had Ali's facial features. The court found in favor of Ali, indicating that the right of publicity is not limited to an actual photograph but could be based merely on the use of the physical characteristics of the individual.

In another case dealing with the right of privacy, Kareem Abdul-Jabbar sued General Motors Corporation (GMC) for its use of his former name, Lewis Alcindor (*Abdul-Jabbar v. General Motors,* 1996). A television commercial played during the 1993 National Collegiate Athletic Association (NCAA) men's basketball tournament stated, "How about some trivia?" Immediately thereafter the words "You're talking to the champ" appeared on the screen. Then a voice asked, "Who holds the record for being voted the most outstanding player of this tournament?" The following words appeared on the screen: "Lewis Alcindor, UCLA, '67, '68, '69." A voice then asked, "Has any car made the *Consumer Digest*'s Best Buy List more than once? The Oldsmobile Eight-Eight has." The commercial then showed the car for several seconds, stated that the '88 had made the list three years in a row, and gave the price. The commercial ended by showing the on-screen message "A Definite First Round Pick," with a voice adding "It's your money" and a final printed message, "Demand Better, '88 by Oldsmobile" (*Abdul-Jabbar v. General Motors*, 1996).

GMC had never obtained consent from Abdul-Jabbar to use his name. After Abdul-Jabbar complained to GMC, the ad was withdrawn. Abdul-Jabbar sued, saying the use of his name was likely to confuse consumers as to his endorsement of the automobile (*Abdul-Jabbar v. General Motors,* 1996). GMC asserted that Abdul-Jabbar had lost the rights to his birth name because he had "abandoned" his former name through nonuse. The court found in favor of Abdul-Jabbar (*Abdul-Jabbar v. General Motors,* 1996).

State Statutes and the Right of Publicity

The majority of states now recognize "the use of a person's name, picture, or other likeness for commercial purposes without permission" as a viable cause of action for infringement of the "right of publicity." Many states have statutes dealing with the right of publicity. For example, California and New York have both seen a great increase in the right of publicity lawsuits. Both states have right of publicity statutes outlining the relevant law. In the California Civil Code § 3344, the California

Right of Publicity Statute contains the following provisions:

(a) Any person who knowingly uses another's name, voice, signature, photograph, or likeness, in any manner, on or in products, merchandise, or goods, or for purposes of advertising or selling, or soliciting purchases of, products, merchandise, goods or services, without such person's prior consent, or, in the case of a minor, the prior consent of his parent or legal guardian, shall be liable for any damages sustained by the person or persons injured as a result thereof. In addition, in any action brought under this section, the person who violated the section shall be liable to the injured party or parties in an amount equal to the greater of seven hundred fifty dollars ($750) or the actual damages suffered by him or her as a result of the unauthorized use, and any profits from the unauthorized use that are attributable to the use and are not taken into account in computing the actual damages. In establishing such profits, the injured party or parties are required to present proof only of the gross revenue attributable to such use, and the person who violated this section is required to prove his or her deductible expenses. Punitive damages may also be awarded to the injured party or parties. The prevailing party in any action under this section shall also be entitled to attorney's fees and costs.

(b) As used in this section, "photograph" means any photograph or photographic reproduction, still or moving, or any videotape or live television transmission, of any person, such that the person is readily identifiable.

1. A person shall be deemed to be readily identifiable from a photograph when one who views the photograph with the naked eye can reasonably determine that the person depicted in the photograph is the same person who is complaining of its unauthorized use.

2. If the photograph includes more than one person so identifiable, then the person or persons complaining of the use shall be represented as individuals rather than solely as members of a definable group represented in the photograph. A definable group includes, but is not limited to, the following examples: a crowd at any sporting event, a crowd in any street or public building, the audience at any theatrical or stage production, a glee club, or a baseball team.

3. A person or persons shall be considered to be represented as members of a definable group if they are represented in the photograph solely as a result of being present at the time the photograph was taken and have not been singled out as individuals in any manner.

(c) Where a photograph or likeness of an employee of the person using the photograph or likeness appearing in the advertisement or other publication prepared by or in behalf of the user is only incidental, and not essential, to the purpose of the publication in which it appears, there shall arise a rebuttable presumption affecting the burden of producing evidence that the failure to obtain the consent of the employee was not a knowing use of the employee's photograph or likeness.

(d) For purposes of this section, a use of a name, voice, signature, photograph, or likeness in connection with any news, public affairs, or sports broadcast or account, or any political campaign, shall not constitute a use for which consent is required under subdivision (a).

(e) The use of a name, voice, signature, photograph, or likeness in a commercial medium shall not constitute a use for which consent is required under subdivision (a) solely because the material containing such use is commercially sponsored or contains paid advertising. Rather it shall be a question of fact whether or not the use of the person's name, voice, signature, photograph, or likeness was so directly connected with the commercial sponsorship or with the paid advertising as to constitute a use for which consent is required under subdivision (a).

(f) Nothing in this section shall apply to the owners or employees of any medium used for advertising, including, but not limited to, newspapers, magazines, radio and television networks and stations, cable television systems, billboards, and transit ads, by whom any advertisement or solicitation in violation of this section is published or disseminated, unless it is established that such owners or employees had knowledge of the unauthorized use of the person's name, voice, signature, photograph, or likeness as prohibited by this section.

(g) The remedies provided for in this section are cumulative and shall be in addition to any others provided for by law.

SOURCE: Courtesy of Westlaw; reprinted with permission.

Sexual Harassment

Sexual harassment has previously involved sports figures such as Isaiah Thomas, Kobe Bryant, Rene Portland, Pokey Chatman, University of Colorado Athletics, University of North Carolina Women's Soccer, and US Olympic Skeleton team. For example, Mauricia Grant's $250 million sexual harassment lawsuit against NASCAR, Inc. was settled for $225 million (Shuster, 2008). This case outlines specific sexual harassments allegations including claims that the plaintiff was subjected to sexual advances from male co-workers, two of whom allegedly exposed themselves to her, and graphic and lewd jokes. In another recent example, former New York Knicks executive Anucha Browne Sanders, filed and subsequently won a $11.6 million in a sexual harassment case against Madison Square Garden and former Knicks coach Isiah Thomas (Schmidt & Newman, 2007). These cases illustrate that sexual harassment occurs in different types of sport organizations. However, these are just a handful of legal cases involving sexual harassment and sport.

Sexual harassment is a legal term that stems from the desire to end discrimination and harassment in the workplace (Clement, Miller, & McGlone, 2010). The term itself has been defined and redefined through both legislation and court decisions. The basic and most accepted definition comes from the United States Equal Employment Opportunity Commission (EEOC). The EEOC defines sexual harassment as:

> Unwelcome sexual advances, requests for sexual favors, and other verbal or physical conduct of a sexual nature constitutes sexual harassment when submission to or rejection of this conduct explicitly or implicitly affects an individual's employment, unreasonably interferes with an individual's work performance or creates an intimidating, hostile or offensive work environment. (29 C.F.R. section 1604.11(a))

Defining sexual harassment is not simple, and often falls upon the subjectivity of the person trying to define it and it appears that there is no universally accepted definition regarding. Sandler and Schoop (1997) described sexual harassment as:

> Unwelcome sexual advances, requests for sexual favors, and other verbal or physical

conduct of a sexual nature constitute sexual harassment when any one of the following is true: (1) submissions to such conduct is made either explicitly or implicitly, a term or condition of a person's employment or academic advancement; (2) submission to or rejection of such conduct by an individual is used as the basis for employment decisions or academic decisions affecting the person; (3) such conduct has the purpose or effect of unreasonably interfering with a person's work or academic performance or creating an intimidation, hostile, or offensive working, learning, or social environment. (p. 4)

Brackenridge (1997) depicted sexual harassment in the following manners:

1. Written or verbal abuses or threats
2. Sexually oriented comments
3. Jokes, lewd comments or sexual innuendoes; taunts about body, dress, marital status or sexuality; shouting and/or bullying
4. Ridiculing or undermining of performance or self-respect
5. Sexual or homophobic graffiti
6. Practical jokes based on sex
7. Intimidating sexual remarks; invitations or familiarity
8. Domination of meetings, training sessions or equipment
9. Condescending or patronizing behavior; physical contact, fondling, pinching or kissing
10. Vandalism related to sex
11. Offensive phone calls or photos
12. Bullying on the basis of sex

Types of Sexual Harassment

The EEOC definition recognizes two types of sexual harassment: (1) quid pro quo and (2) hostile environment. *Quid pro quo* sexual harassment is sometimes described as an exchange of sexual favors in return for some other work related action. This typically occurs when an individual accepts or rejects the sexual advances of a coworker (usually supervisor) as a term of or condition for employment (EEOC, 2000). An example of quid pro quo could include if one's internship supervisor requested a sexual favor and in return, he or she would write the individual (or the victim), a positive letter of recommendation or hire the individual or the victim at the end of the internship.

Hostile environment sexual harassment occurs when unwelcome sexual conduct unreasonably interferes with an individual's job performance or creates a hostile, intimidating, or offensive work environment. According to the EEOC, employers, supervisors, coworkers, customers, or clients can create a hostile work environment ("Harassment," 2000). Hostile environment involves harassing conduct that interferes with the victim's ability to perform his or her job or an environment that is so offensive that an individual becomes uncomfortable. A hostile environment may include either an educational or work setting in which unwelcome behavior or comments of a sexual nature occur including an environment where sexually suggestive pictures, innuendos, comments, jokes or stories are displayed or discussed (Clement, Miller, & McGlone, 2010).

It is important to understand that one does not have to be directly involved to be claim or be affected by sexual harassment. Third party sexual harassment involves unwelcome sexual behavior that is directed at someone else but negatively impacts a different individual's work environment discussed (Clement, Miller, & McGlone, 2010). While third party sexual harassment may occur between co-workers, it is most frequently associated with harassment of employees by people who do not work for the same organization (Aalberts & Seidman, 1994). An example of third party sexual harassment includes if you were working at the ticket office and a season ticket holder made frequent unwanted sexual remarks and told you jokes of a sexual nature when picking up his or her tickets.

Sexual Harassment of Opposite and Same-Sex Members

While sexual harassment most often relates to a male figure harassing a female, it can also occur when a female harasses a male or when the individuals are of the same sex. Title VII of the Civil Rights Act of 1964 prohibits employment discrimination based on "… race, color, religion, sex, or national origin" (42 U.S.C. § 2000(e)-2 (2006)). As such, Title VII protects employees against employment discrimination based the five traits of race, color, religion, sex, and national origin.

According to Title VII of the Civil Rights Act of 1964 (42 U.S.C.S 42 § 2000e-2(a)(1)), an employer's liability for workplace sexual harassment is contingent on the status of the harasser. If the harassing employee is the victim's co-worker, the employer is liable only if it was negligent in controlling working conditions. However, if the harasser is a supervisor and culminates in a tangible employment action, the employer is strictly liable. Thus, a sexual harassment incident relates to whether the harasser is a supervisor or a co-worker. An employee is a supervisor if he or she is empowered by the employer to take tangible employment actions against the victim.

When a sexual harassment claim arises out of a supervisor's conduct, four elements of a hostile working environment claim must be produced:

1. The employee belongs to a protected class
2. The employee was subject to unwelcome sexual harassment
3. The harassment was based on a protected characteristic; and
4. The harassment affected a term, condition, or privilege of employment (*Lauderdale v. Texas Department of Criminal Justice*, 2007).

Further, the harassing conduct must be sufficiently severe or pervasive to change the conditions of the victim's employment and generate an abusive working situation (*Aryain v. Wal-Mart Stores of Texas*, 2008). Courts use an objective reasonable person standard to evaluate severity and pervasiveness (*Meritor Savings Bank, F.S.B. v. Vinson*, 1986; *Oncale v. Sundowner Offshore Services*, 1998). Ultimately, whether an environment is hostile or abusive hangs on the totality of circumstances.

According to Kramer (2012), gender stereotyping may be predicated upon how employees exhibit gender traits, such as masculinity or femininity, and how those traits meet an employer's "expectations about how men and women are supposed to present themselves in the workplace" (p. 297). In 1989, the United States Supreme Court held that a plaintiff may rely on gender-stereotyping evidence to show that discrimination occurred due to the sex of a person (*Price Waterhouse v. Hopkins*, 1989). In *Price Waterhouse*, a woman with a perceived aggressive personality sued after her accounting firm after they did not offer her a partnership in the firm. In the case, the Court viewed,

clear signs … that some of the partners reacted negatively to [the plaintiff's] personality because she was a woman. One partner described her as "macho"; another suggested that she "overcompensated for being a woman"; a third advised her to take "a course at charm school"; she should walk more femininely, talk more femininely, dress more femininely, wear make-up, have her hair styled, and wear jewelry (p. 235).

Although these types of remarks described above may be based on sex stereotypes, they may not absolutely prove that gender was the ultimate condition for continued employment. However, it provides evidence was a keep component in the decision (*Price Waterhouse v. Hopkins*, 1989).

Concerning alleged same-sex harassment, the United States Supreme Court described Title VII's sex provision as protecting men and women from employment discrimination of members from the same gender. The Court stated that no justification existed, "in the statutory language or our precedents for a categorical rule excluding same-sex harassment claims from the coverage of Title VII" (*Oncale v. Sundowner Offshore Services*, 1998, p. 79). In *Oncale v. Sundowner Offshore Services* (1998), a male employee alleged that his employer sexually harassed him. As a result of the alleged harassment, the employee alleged that he was forced to resign after experiencing continuous physical and verbal harassment from other male employees on the basis of sex (*Oncale v. Sundowner Offshore Services*, 1998). The Supreme Court found that an employee claiming gender discrimination and sexual harassment need not prove that instigator was homosexual or heterosexual but merely that employee was subject to discrimination based on their failure to conform to employer's stereotype of gender and allowed a hostile work environment (*Oncale v. Sundowner Offshore Services*, 1998).

Hazing

Hazing has been cited as a serious problem in interscholastic as well as intercollegiate athletics (Crow & Rosner, 2002). Although there are a number of different iterations of hazing, one of the most comprehensive definitions was expressed by Hoover (1999) who stated that *hazing* is "any activity expected of someone joining a group that humiliates, degrades, abuses, or endangers, regardless of the person's willingness to participate." One of the most recent examples of hazing that resulted in the death of sport-related organization occurred when Robert Champion, a member of the Florida A&M University marching band, died as a result of being hazed by other band members. Champion was beaten, kicked and suffocated by fellow band members during a hazing

ritual aboard a bus (Brown, 2012). As a result, 13 individuals were charged with felonies or misdemeanors. According to trial testimony, Champion,

> endured hundreds of blows during a ritual known as "crossing bus c," which required him to run from the front of the bus to the back through a gantlet of band members who blocked his path and battered him with fists, drumsticks and other objects. (Hudak, 2014, ¶ 3)

Champion's death resulted in a season-long suspension of the marching band, the resignations of the band director as well as the university president (Hudak, 2014). Additionally, a former Florida A&M student was sentenced to six years in prison for manslaughter and felony hazing charges (Neuman, 2015).

In another recent hazing case, the criminal trial seven New Jersey high school football players were began in February, 2015. Each of the seven athletes was accused of sexually assaulting for teammates over a 10-day period (Bichao, 2015). Moreover, the long-time head football coach was fired and replaced due to the incident occurring under his tutelage (Bichao, 2015).

The United States Supreme Court has held that a student's right to bodily integrity is a constitutionally protected liberty interest (*Ingraham v. Wright*, 1977). Thus, students who are victims of athletic hazing may contend that they have been denied an existing federal right. To be successful in bringing the claim to the court, a plaintiff is required to show that their constitutional rights have been compromised by the "deliberate indifference" in which the school acted. In order to do so, a hazed athlete would likely have to prove that peer, same-sex hazing attacks were treated differently by the school than peer, opposite-sex hazing attacks. Second, it would be necessary to prove that the hazed athlete was "denied the benefits of" or "excluded from participation" in "any education program or activity." Third, the student-athlete must prove that the hazing was so "severe" and "pervasive" that it constituted a denial of education opportunities. Fourth, the student-athlete must prove that a school official "with authority to take corrective action to end the discrimination" had actual notice of the hazing (*Gebser v. Lago Vista*, 1998). Finally, the student-athlete must prove that the school's response to actual knowledge of the hazing was so "clearly unreasonable" that it reached the required deliberate indifference standard (*Davis v. Monroe County Board of Education*, 1999).

At the time of this writing six states (Alaska, Hawaii, Montana, New Mexico, South Dakota, and Wyoming) do not have anti-hazing laws (Stop Hazing, 2015). Because hazing may be considered potentially perilous, forty-four states (as well as Washington, DC) have enacted or have encouraged the enactment of anti-hazing laws (Stop Hazing, 2015). The majority of these anti-hazing laws are focused address within the educational context. In fact, Indiana, Mississippi, New York, and Utah are the only four states that do not limit the application of hazing laws to student groups (Stop Hazing, 2015).

CONCLUSION

Acts of violence that take place in sports are usually handled in a very different manner from the rest of society (Lassiter, 2007). Actions that could be construed as assaults and batteries that would subject a person to criminal prosecution in normal settings are considered as part of the game when it occurs in an athletic contest. Often, when such acts surpass the accepted standards of play on the field, athletes are sanctioned by fine, suspension, or both. Only in unusual, but not entirely rare, cases does the act of violence on the playing field subject the participant to a risk of criminal prosecution (Weir, 2006). These cases typically involve a rather unusual act of violent assault that gains public notoriety (Hanley, 2000; Lapointe, 2000).

Because of the relative lack of law suits, there may be an implication that players are immune and are treated differently for on-the-field violent activities. However, immunity for athletes for on-the-field play is not absolute. The evolution of civil lawsuits between sports participants for tortious actions has occurred (Jahn, 1988). The success of civil lawsuits, although somewhat limited, represents an encouraging sign that society is willing to hold sports participants accountable for their actions.

In regards to the concept of defamation, the increase of coverage of sports on 24-hour television, the Internet, and social media is changing the professionalism paradigm of sports journalism. Unlike, the case of Roger Clemens, who as a public figure possessed access to the public through media sources to assert his innocence, many others do not have this ability. As a result, almost anyone can become a public figure without meaning to do so. Through social media and websites such as YouTube, anyone has the ability to attain prominence and popularity. With some high school sports now being televised on cable television, could interscholastic athletes as public figures, who can be defamed without a remedy absent proof of actual malice? These are potential situations in which sport administrators may have to tangle with now and in the future.

Sexual harassment in sport can occur between anyone in a sport organization. It is important to understand that sexual exploitation is not just an issue for women. Sexual harassment can occur between two or more people in any organization. We most frequently hear about harassment that is perpetrated by someone who is in an authoritative position or by an individual who others perceive as having some type of power. Individuals in authoritative positions include, but are certainly not limited to: coach-athlete, owner-manager, manager-medical personnel, or administrator-athlete.

When one thinks about sexual harassment it may be assumed that the stereotypical scenario indicates that a male initiated the inappropriate behavior toward a female. Since sport traditionally has been male-dominated, and while progress has been made, there are significantly more males in power positions (administrators, owners, coaches) than women. Research does indicate that men are more likely to harass than women as females are statistically less likely to be identified as the source of sexual harassment (Brackenridge, 2001). It is important to note that both males and females can perpetrate sexual harassment and be on the receiving end. In 1994, Doyle reported that for every 30 male perpetrators there was one female perpetrator. In a meta-analysis of eight studies, it was reported that 97.5% of female victims and 78.7% of male victims were abused by males (Fergusson & Mullen, 1999).

The ritualistic attitude that is pervasive in sports also provides an opportunity for a deeply ingrained acceptance of hazing. Actions that are considered hazing by some are not considered hazing and are not objectionable to others. Athletic hazing can range from comparatively inoffensive initiation rites, such as having rookie team members carry the travel bags of veteran players or sing team songs, to possible hazardous activities such as kidnapping, binge drinking, or sexual harassment (Hoover, 1999). As a result, sports administrators and coaches must be thorough in observing the initiation activities of their athletes. Importantly, they must be mindful of the local, state, and national laws that govern hazing and group initiations.

DISCUSSION QUESTIONS

Aggravated Assault

A professional basketball player was charged with aggravated assault and resisting arrest after allegedly throwing a man through the glass door. Witnesses report that the player continued to punch the victim in the face as he lay on his back, bleeding. The player was suspended from the team and received a reduced charge of disorderly conduct. He was reinstated to the team one month later. Using this case, explain the differences between simple assault and aggravated assault. Discuss why the athlete received a relatively minor sentence.

Battery

A high school assistant football coach was sentenced to 12 months of probation and 250 hours of community service in an assault case resulting from when he punched a player while serving as an assistant football coach. The assistant coach struck a freshman player on the side of his chest with his fist during a spring practice. The blow dropped the 15-year-old to the ground and left a sizeable bruise on his ribs. Discuss what the plaintiff would need to prove in this case. Should more stringent sentences be given to people in youth coaching positions? Explain your answer.

Defamation

A professional baseball player filed a defamation lawsuit against a former player who became a sports radio personality. The radio personality alleged that the baseball player had used

(*continues*)

DISCUSSION QUESTIONS (CONTINUED)

performance enhancing drugs to enhance his playing ability. What publicity rights does a professional baseball player or any well-known athlete have, if any, in a case like this? Discuss the elements that the plaintiff would have to prove for defamation to exist. How would the baseball player's publicity rights impact the defamation allegations?

Hazing

A college team held a party that involved a "keg race," where freshmen were forced to stand in a circle and drink large amounts of beer. The freshmen were tied together with string that passed through their belt loops, and some of the members vomited. Discuss how situations like the one described applied to Hoover's definition of hazing.

Sexual Harassment

A male head coach basketball of a women's college basketball team was sued by a female player. The allegations included the coach sending the player inappropriate messages and picture. The coach alleged told the player that if they did not have sexual relations, she would lose her scholarship. Discuss the elements that the plaintiff would have to establish to be successful in this lawsuit. What are the steps the plaintiff could have employed to halt the alleged actions of the coach?

KEY TERMS

Aggravated assault
Assault
Civil battery
Criminal battery
Defamation
Hazing
Hostile environment
Imminent apprehension
Intent to cause apprehension

Intentional tort
Lack of consent
Libel
Quid pro quo
Right of publicity
Sexual harassment
Slander
Tortfeasor
Tortious behavior

REFERENCES

Aalberts, R.J., & Seidman, L.H. (1994). Sexual harassment by clients, customers and suppliers: How employers should handle an emerging legal problem. *Employee Relations Law Journal, 20*(1), 85–100.

Abdul-Jabbar v. General Motors, 85 F.3d 407 (9th Cir. 1996).

Aryain v. Wal-Mart Stores Tex. LP, 534 F.3d 473, 2008 U.S. App. LEXIS 14324, 91 Empl. Prac. Dec. (CCH) P43246, 103 Fair Empl. Prac. Cas. (BNA) 1360 (5th Cir. Tex. 2008).

Bichao, S. (2015). Sayreville hazing scandal: Court denies media access to trial. MyCentralJersey.com. Retrieved from http://www.mycentraljersey.com/story/news/local/middlesex-county/2015/02/17/sayreville-hazing-scandal-trial-closed-media/23552105/

Brackin, D. (1988, August 25). Convicted of assault, Ciccarelli gets day in jail and $1000 fine. *Minneapolis Star Tribune*, C1.

Brackenridge, C. (1997). "He owned me basically" … Women's experience of sexual abuse in sport. *International Review for the Sociology of Sport*, 32(2), 115–130.

Brackenridge, C. (2001). *Spoilsports: Understanding and preventing sexual exploitation in sport*. New York: Routledge.

Brewer v. Rogers, 439 S.E.2d 77 (Ga. Ct. App. 1993).

Brinson, W. (2012). Jonathan Vilma files defamation lawsuit vs. Roger Goodell in New Orleans court. NFL.com. Retrieved from http://www.cbssports.com/nfl/eye-on-football/19075375/jonathan-vilma-files-defamation-lawsuit-vs-roger-goodell-in-new-orleans-federal-court.

Brown, R. (2012). Criminal charges for 13 in Florida A&M hazing death. *New York Times*. Retrieved from http://www.nytimes.com/2012/05/03/us/13-charged-in-hazing-death-at-florida-am.html

Carson v. Here's Johnny Portable Toilets, Inc., 698 F.2d 831 (6th Cir. 1983).

Carwile v. Richmond Newspapers, 196 Va. 1,7 82 S.E.2d 588, 591 (1954).

Chuy v. Philadelphia Eagles Football Club, 595 F.2d 1265 (3d Cir. 1979).

Clement, A., Miller, J., & McGlone, C. (2010). Sexual harassment issues in internships. In J. Miller & T. Seidler (Eds.), *A Practical Guide to Sport Management Internships* (pp. 193–203). Raleigh, NC: Carolina Academic Press.

Cobb v. Time, Inc., 278 F.3d 629 (6th Cir. 2002).

Cohen v. Marx, 94 Cal. App. 2d 704, 211 P.2d 320, 1949 Cal. App. LEXIS 1593 (Cal. App. 1949)

Crawn v. Campo, 136 N.J. 494, 643 A.2d 600, 1994 N.J. LEXIS 632 (1994)

Crow, R.B., & Rosner, S.R. (2002). Institutional and organizational liability for hazing in intercollegiate and professional team sports. *St. John's Law Review*, 76, 87–114.

Curtis Pub. Co. v. Butts, 389 U.S. 889, 88 S. Ct. 11, 19 L. Ed. 2d 197, 1967 U.S. LEXIS 1069 (1967)

Dahlin v. Fraser, 288 N.W. 851,852 (Minn. 1939).

Davis v. Monroe County Board of Education, 526 U.S. 629 (1999).

Dun & Bradstreet, Inc. v. Greenmoss Builders, Inc., 472 U.S. 749, 765 (1985).

Eaton, J.D. (1975). The American law of defamation Through Gertz v. Robert Welch, Inc. and Beyond: An Analytical Primer. *Virginia Law Review*, 1349–1451.

Elias v. State, 339 Md. 169, 183, 661 A.2d 702 (1995).

Equal Employment Opportunity Commission. (2000). Harassment. Retrieved from http://www.eeoc.gov/laws/types/harassment.cfm.

Etheredge v. District of Columbia, 635 A.2d 908, 1993 D.C. App. LEXIS 325, 33 A.L.R.5th 795 (D.C. 1993).

Fergusson, D.M., & Mullen, P.E. (1999). *Childhood sexual abuse: An evidence-based perspective*. Thousand Oaks, CA: Sage.

Fleming v. Moore, 221 Va. 884, 275 S.E.2d 632 (1981).

Flose v. Delgado Community College, 776 F. Supp. 1133 (E.D. LA 1996).

Fugazy v. Corbetta, 34 AD3d 728, 729, 825 NYS2d 120 [2006].

Garner, B. A. (2009). *Black's law dictionary*. St. Paul, Minn.: Thomson West.

Gebser v. Lago Vista Indep. Sch. Dist., 524 U.S. 274 (1998).

Gertz v. Robert Welch, Inc., 418 U.S. 323, 341 (1974).

Hanley, B. (2000). McSorley guilty: No jail, 18 month's probation for swing at Brashear. *Chicago Sun Times*, 108.

Hechter, W. (1977). The criminal law and violence in sports. *Criminal Law Quarterly*, 19(3/4), 425–453.

Herman, R. (1975, August 12). Charges against Forbes dropped. *New York Times*, 24.

Hill v. United States, 2013 U.S. Dist. LEXIS 68667 (E.D. Pa. May 14, 2013).

Hirsch v. S.C. Johnson & Son, Inc., 280 N.W.2d 129 (Wis. 1979).

Hoover, N.C. (1999). Initiation rites and athletics for NCAA sports teams. Retrieved from http://www.alfred.edu/sports_hazing/docs/hazing.pdf

Hudak, S. (2014). FAMU drummer endured hazing to earn bus 'privileges'. *Orlando Sentinel*. Retrieved from http://touch.orlandosentinel.com/#section/-1/article/p2p-81816512/

Ingraham v. Wright, 430 U.S. 651, 673–74 (1977).

Jahn, G.N. (1988). Civil liability: An alternative to violence in sporting events. *Ohio Northern University Law Review*, 15, 243–261.

Kramer, Z. (2012). Of meat and manhood. *Washington University Law Review*, 89, 287–323.

Lapointe, J. (2000). N.H.L. and Vancouver police are investigating stick attack. *New York Times*, D1.

Lassiter, C. (2007). Lex sportive: Thoughts towards a criminal law of competitive contact sport. *St. John's Journal of Legal Commentary*, 35, 60–68.

Lauderdale v. Texas Department of Criminal Justice, 512 F.3d 157, 162–63 (5th Cir. 2007).

Lawrence, B. (2013). Top 100 highest-paid athlete endorsers of 2013. Opendores.com. Retrieved from http://opendorse.com/blog/top-100-highest-paid-athlete-endorsers-of-2013/

Marvez, A. (2012, May 2). 4 players suspended in bounty scandal. FoxSports.com. Retrived from www.foxsports.com/nfl/story/jonathan-vilma-scott-fujita-anthony-hargrove-will-smith-suspended-in-new-orleans-saints-bounty-scandal-050212.

McNeil v. Mullin, 70 Kan. 634, 79 P. 168, 1905 Kan. LEXIS 21 (1905).

McSorley, guilty of assault, avoids jail. (2000). *New York Times*. Retrieved from http://www.nytimes.com/2000/10/07/sports/07MCSO.html

Meritor Savings Bank, F.S.B v, Vinson, 477 U.S. 57, 64–65, 106 S. Ct. 2399, 91 L. Ed. 2d 49 (1986).

Midler v. Ford Motor Co., 849 F.2d 460 (9th Cir. 1988).

Muhammad Ali v. Playgirl, 447 F. Supp. 723 (S.D.N.Y. 1978).

Nabozny v. Barnhill 31 Ill. App. 3d 212, 334 N.E.2d 258 (1975).

Neuman, S. (2015). Former Florida A&M student sentences to 6 years in hazing death. *NPR The Two Way*. Retrieved from http://www.npr.org/blogs/thetwo-way/2015/01/09/376154171/former-florida-a-m-student-sentenced-to-6-years-in-hazing-death

New York Times Co. v. Sullivan, 376 U.S. 254, 277 (1964).

O'Brien v. Pabst Sales Co., 124 F.2d 167 (5th Cir. 1941).

Oncale v. Sundowner Offshore Services, Inc., 523 U.S. 75, 78, 118 S. Ct. 998, 140 L. Ed. 2d 201 (1998).

Piedra v. Dugan, 123 Cal. App. 4th 1483, 1494, 21 Cal. Rptr. 3d 36 (2004).

Plunkett Research. (2014). Sports industry, teams, leagues & recreation market research. Retrieved from http://www.plunkettresearch.com/industries/sports-recreation-leisure-market-research/

Pollard v. Lyon, 91 U.S. 225, 1 Otto 225, 23 L. Ed. 308, 1875 U.S. LEXIS 1352 (1876).

Price Waterhouse v. Hopkins, 490 U.S. 228, 109 S. Ct. 1775, 104 L. Ed. 2d 268 (1989).

Pritchett v. Heil, 756 N.E.2d 561, 566 (Ind. Ct. App. 2001).

Sandler, B.R., & Shoop, R.J. (1997). *Sexual harassment in higher education: A guide for administrators, faculty and students*. Needham Heights, MA: Allyn & Bacon.

Schmidt, M.S., & Newman, M. (2007). Jury awards $11.6 million to former Knicks executive. *New York Times*. Retrieved from http://www.nytimes.com/2007/10/02/sports/basketball/03garden-cnd.html?_r=0

Shuster, R. (2008). Former official sues NASCAR over harassment claims. *USAToday.com*. Retrieved from http://usatoday30.usatoday.com/sports/motor/nascar/2008-06-10-harassment-suit_N.htm

Sinker v. Goldsmith, 623 F. Supp. 727 (D. Ariz. 1985).

Spousta, T. (2000). McSorely says he wanted to fight, not injure. *New York Times*, D8

State v. Hayward, 166 N.H. 575, 101 A.3d 603, 2014 N.H. LEXIS 94 (2014).

Stop Hazing. (2015). States with anti-hazing laws. Retrieved from http://www.stophazing.org/laws/states-with-anti-hazing-laws/

Vandenburg v. Newsweek, Inc., 507 F.2d 1024 (5th Cir. 1975).

Vilma v. Goodell, 917 F. Supp. 2d 591, 596 (E.D. La. 2013).

Western Union Telegraph Co. v. Hill 150 So. 709 (Ala. Ct. App. 1933).

White v. Samsung Electronics America, Inc., 971 F.2d 1395 (9th Cir. 1992).

Weir, T. (2006). Titans' Haynesworth suspended five games for stomping incident. *USA Today*. Retrieved from http://www.usatoday.com/sports/football/nfl/titans/2006-10-02-haynesworth-suspension_x.htm

Wilstein, T. (1990). Incident forever links Marichal, Roseboro 25 Years after clubbing with baseball bat—former enemies want to forget 1965 clubbing. *Seattle Times*. Retrieved from http://community.seattletimes.nwsource.com/archive/?date=19900909&slug=1092034

TORT DEFENSES

LEARNING OBJECTIVES

By the end of the chapter, the reader will be able to:

1. Understand the concept and types of defenses commonly used in sports litigation
2. Understand the challenges regarding assumption of risk from the viewpoint of the plaintiff as well as the defendant
3. Understand and differentiate between primary assumption of risk and secondary assumption of risk
4. Comprehend and provide examples of the effective use of waivers in a sports setting
5. Comprehend and provide examples of the different types of comparative negligence
6. Analyze the effectiveness of sovereign immunity and its' impact on the states
7. Grasp how workers' compensation may be used in a sports environment

RELATED CASES

Case 4.1   FCH1, LLC v. Rodriguez, 326 P.3d 440, 2014 Nev. LEXIS 55 (Nev. 2014)

Case 4.2   Cousins Club Corp. V. Silva 869 So.2d 719 (Fla. Dist. Ct. App. 2004)

Case 4.3   Avila v. Citrus Community College District 131 P.3d 383 (Cal. 2006)

INTRODUCTION

Generally, laws can be applied to specific situation, or are mainly understood as a matter of court context. However, if not understood, laws are without meaning. As a result, an understanding of tort defense doctrines like assumption of risk, comparative negligence, waivers or releases, or workers' compensation are needed to assist the organization, participants, and spectators in understanding their responsibilities in providing a reasonably safe sports environment. A number of defenses may be employed, but to identify and explain all of them would be overwhelming, or worse, confusing. The defenses discussed in this chapter are among the most used in the sport environment.

ASSUMPTION OF RISK

If a plaintiff voluntarily enters a risky activity and understands that risk, he or she will be barred from recovery in tort (*Grishman v. Porter*, 2006). The basic rule states that a plaintiff who voluntarily enters into a risky situation, knowing the risk involved, will be prevented from recovering in tort for damages. This is commonly referred to as the *assumption of the risk doctrine* (Prosser, Keeton, Dobbs, Keeton, & Owen, 1984).

Athletes assume the risk of injury due to the nature of the game. However, the basic concept of assumption of risk is that if a person voluntarily accepts the danger of a known and appreciated risk, that person may not sue another for failing to protect him from it (Restatement [Second] of Torts, 1965). The assumption of risk doctrine operates as a complete bar to a plaintiff's action only when defendant's conduct did not breach a legal duty of care owed to the plaintiff and the nature of the activity and the parties' involvement in that activity is known (*Ford v. Gouin*, 1992). The defense of assumption of the risk "arises when the plaintiff *knows of and appreciates a risk and voluntarily chooses to encounter it*"

(*Leakas v. Columbia Country Club*, 1993). American Jurisprudence states:

> It is knowledge of the risks involved, rather than knowledge of actual facts, that determines whether such risks have been assumed. In order for a defendant to assert the assumption-of-risk defense, the plaintiff must have actual knowledge of risk, and subjective knowledge of the specific, particular risk of harm associated with the activity or condition that proximately causes injury. The knowledge requirement does not refer to the plaintiff's comprehension of general, nonspecific risks that might be associated with such conditions or activities (*Negligence*, § 775).

A defendant asserting an assumption of the *risk defense must establish* that the plaintiff possessed the following:

1. Actual knowledge of the danger
2. Understood and appreciated the risks associated with such danger
3. Voluntarily exposed himself to those risks (*Vaughn v. Pleasant*, 1996).

In *Louis v. Louis* (2001), the Minnesota Supreme Court dealt with "knowledge" and assumption of risk stating:

> the word "known" denotes not only knowledge of the existence of the condition or activity itself, but also appreciation of the danger it involves. Thus, the condition or activity must not only be known to exist, but it must also be recognized that it is dangerous, and the probability and gravity of the threatened harm must be appreciated.

Do the participants truly know and appreciate the risks? Judge Cardozo explained the concept:

> One who takes part in such a sport accepts the dangers that inhere in it so far as they are obvious and necessary ... The antics

of the clown are not the paces of the cloistered cleric. The rough and boisterous joke, the horseplay of the crowd, evokes its own guffaws, but they are not the pleasures of tranquility... He took the chance of a like fate, with whatever damage to his body might ensue from such a fall. The timorous may stay at home. (*Murphy v. Steeplechase Amusement Co.*, 1929)

According to the court in *Maddox v. City of New York* (1985), the awareness of risks is not determined within a vacuum. Rather, the awareness of risks of an activity may be evaluated as it pertains to the individual's skill and experience. Indeed, an athletic participant with years of experience and high levels of skill may assume a higher degree of awareness and therefore be less successful in employing assumption of risk as a defense strategy.

As mentioned in chapter 2, coaches who act "totally outside the range of the ordinary activity involved in the sport" (*Knight v. Jewett*, 1992, p. 318) may be considered liable. Yet coaches do possess a duty to exercise reasonable care to protect players from "unreasonably increased risks" (*Knight v. Jewett*, 1992). For example, a case revealed that the assumption of risk defense could not be employed because the coaches knew that the player had a concussion, yet they allowed that player to re-enter the game (*Cerny v. Cedar Bluffs Junior/Senior Public Schools*, 2004).

In most cases, the plaintiff's consent cannot be readily proved. For example, the defendant may maintain that the plaintiff's voluntary acceptance of a known and appreciated risk should be inferred from the plaintiff's actions and the present conditions. Assumption of the risk can be express or implied; that is, it can be assumed by express agreement between the parties or implied by the plaintiff's knowledge of the risk involved. An *implied assumption of the risk* states that a defendant does not owe a plaintiff a duty of care for an injury that occurred from an inherent risk of a sport. An *expressed assumption of risk* is enacted when participants in athletic events are required to sign an assumption of risk form before being allowed to practice. If the participants are considered minors, they as well as their parents or legal guardians must often sign the assumption of risk form. Additionally, assumption of the risk includes two very different applications of this doctrine: *primary assumption of the risk* and *secondary assumption of the risk*. The difference between the two types is the origination of the risk.

The definitive case on assumption of risk in a sports setting is *Knight v. Jewett* (1992). *Knight* distinguished between "primary" and "secondary" assumption of the risk. Prior to *Knight* a defendant needed to prove that the plaintiff had knowledge of the risk and chose to voluntarily encounter that risk. However, *Knight* put an end to assumption of risk defense as a complete bar to a plaintiff's recovery. In *Knight v. Jewett* (1992) the emphasis shifted from the plaintiff and whether the plaintiff had consented to the risk, to the defendant and whether the defendant had a duty to use due care. As such, the court recognized two different types of assumption of risk defenses: primary assumption of risk and secondary assumption of risk.

Primary Assumption of Risk

Primary assumption of risk is merely another way of saying no duty of care is owed as to risks inherent in a given sport or activity. An activity falls under the doctrine of primary assumption of risk if it "is done for enjoyment or thrill, requires physical exertion as well as elements of skill, and involves a challenge containing a potential risk of injury" (*Calhoon v. Lewis*, 2000, p. 81). The prevailing thought in the applying primary assumption of risk is to avert the imposition of a duty, which might chill vigorous participation in the sport and thereby alter its fundamental nature (*Wattenbarger v. Cincinnati Reds, Inc.*, 1994).

According to the court in *Knight v. Jewett* (1992), the primary assumption of risk is one in which the defendant owed no duty to the plaintiff.

Regarding primary assumption of risk, the *Knight* court stated that, although the defendant owed no legal duty to the participants for the inherent risks of the sport, the defendant did have a duty not to increase those risks (over and above what was inherent in the sport). The *Knight* court also reported that the primary assumption of risk doctrine applied to co-participants in active sports. In other words, a co-participant defendant is not liable for "ordinary careless conduct committed during the sport" (p. 710).

The primary assumption of risk doctrine has been employed to alleviate both coaches (*Kahn v. East Side Union High School District*, 2003) and owners of facilities (*Nalwa v. Cedar Fair, L. P.*, 2012). For example, the *Kahn* court indicated that a coach breaches his or her duty to his students only if he or she acts recklessly or intentionally. The *Nalwa* court ruled that the owner of a bumper car ride had no duty to protect the plaintiff from risks inherent in bumper cars. It should be noted that the *Nalwa* court stated:

> The primary assumption of risk doctrine is not limited to activities classified as sports, but applies as well to other recreational activities involving an inherent risk of injury to voluntary participants where the risk cannot be eliminated without altering the fundamental nature of the activity. (p. 1163)

Thus, the primary assumption of risk doctrine does not only pertain to sports activities but also recreational activities that concern inherent risks.

Secondary Assumption of Risk

Secondary assumption of risk occurs when the defendant owes the plaintiff a duty, but the plaintiff knowingly encounters a risk created by the breach of that duty. Courts are less willing to bar all recovery in the latter circumstance unless the plaintiff not only knowingly and voluntarily acquiesced in the risk created by the defendant's negligence but

also acted unreasonably in doing so. As such, secondary assumption of risk is not a bar to recovery, but requires the application of comparative fault principles (*Knight v. Jewett*, 1992).

In the secondary assumption the defendant does owe the plaintiff a duty, but the plaintiff knowingly encounters this risk despite the defendant's breach of this duty. Concerning secondary assumption of risk, the *Knight* court held that the defendant owed the plaintiff a duty, but after considering the respective faults of the parties, the judge directed the jury to apportion the damages. In other words, secondary assumption of risk is an assessment of comparative negligence (*Knight v. Jewett*, 1992).

WAIVERS AND RELEASES

Many participants and spectators at sporting and recreation events are required to sign a waiver or release before they are allowed to participate. On college campuses throughout the United States and Canada, students who choose to participate in campus recreational sport activities are often presented with a waiver or release of liability, asked to read it, and sign prior to participating. In exchange for the opportunity to participate, students' signatures indicate their agreement not to sue the organization in the event they are injured. The following is an example of a waiver clause found on the back of a ticket for the Boston Red Sox baseball club:

> The holder assumes all risk and danger incidental to the game of baseball including specifically (but not exclusively) the danger of being injured by thrown bats and thrown or batted balls and agrees that the participant clubs, their agents and players are not liable for injuries resulting from such causes. (*Costa v. The Boston Red Sox Baseball*, 2004)

The release usually requires the participant to waive all rights that he or she has for any claims for damages that may arise from the activity. A valid written release may exonerate a wrongdoer from allegations of negligence or misconduct in the future (*Bennett v. United States Cycling Federation*, 1987). The court in *Bennett* further stated that,

> By an advance waiver of liability, a potential plaintiff promises not to exercise the right to sue for harm caused in the future by the wrongful behavior of a potential defendant, eliminating a remedy for wrongdoing. By an express assumption of risk, the potential plaintiff agrees not to expect the potential defendant to act carefully, thus eliminating the potential defendant's duty of care, and acknowledging the possibility of negligent wrongdoing. Both agreements permit behavior that normally would be actionable as tortious, although an express assumption of risk goes further, more clearly authorizing this behavior. (pp. 7–8)

A *waiver or release* is an attempt by one party to escape liability from another party. For example, service providers owe their participants a duty to conduct themselves as any other reasonable provider would under similar circumstances (*Gossett v. Jackson*, 1995). In instances where service providers do not attain the level of a reasonable standard of care, thus breaching the duty owed, the providers will be considered negligent and therefore liable for the participant's injury (Restatement of Torts, 1965).

Waivers are written articles in which a *party releases or exculpates a second party from possible tort liability*. However, waivers can modify the way liability may be judged. For instance, in situations where the actions or inactions of a service provider obviously caused harm to a participant, the provider may not be held liable if the participant signed a valid exculpatory agreement (i.e., a waiver) and the harm was not intentionally or recklessly inflicted (Keeton & Prosser, 1984; Restatement [Second] of Contracts, 1981).

According to the court in *Leon v. Family Fitness Center* (1998),

> To be effective a liability release or waiver must be clear, unambiguous, and explicit in expressing the intent of the subscribing parties. A release must not be buried in a lengthy document, hidden among other verbiage, or so encumbered with other provisions as to be difficult to find." (p. 9)

The language of the release determines its scope (*Sanchez v. Bally's Total Fitness Corp.*, 1998). When a waiver expressly releases the defendant from any liability, a plaintiff need not have had specific knowledge of the particular risk that ultimately caused the injury (*Paralift, Inc., v. Superior Court*, 1993). Although the express terms must apply to the particular negligence of the defendant, not every possible specific act of negligence of the defendant needs to be identified in the agreement. As such a release or waiver does not need to be perfect nor does the term negligence need to be included to validate it as an exculpatory clause. When a release expressly releases the defendant from any liability, a plaintiff is not required to possess specific knowledge of the particular risk that ultimately caused the injury (*Paralift, Inc., v. Superior Court*, 1993). If all liability is released, the waiver may apply to any negligence on the part of the defendant, and it is only necessary that the act of negligence be reasonably related to reason for which the release was offered (*Paralift, Inc., v. Superior Court*, 1993). The result of an express release of liability is that the defendant owes no duty to protect the plaintiff from injury-causing risk (*Knight v. Jewett*, 1992).

The impact of improperly administering a waiver may be significant especially if the injured party was not aware of what was signed away on their behalf. This practice may negatively affect the power of the waiver for two reasons. First, by having someone read and sign a waiver on another's behalf (a proxy), the informational component of the waiver (designed to inform the participant about the inherent risks involved in the activity *and* the fact that he or she is giving up the right to sue in exchange for participation) is circumvented, diminishing both the deterrent and exculpatory power of the waiver (Miller, Young, & Martin, 2009). Second, and one that subsumes the first reason, a waiver is a contract between the participant and the activity provider. Due to the nature of the agreement, it cannot be considered a contract when a proxy signature is used because no contractual agreement exists (Restatement [Second] of Contracts, 1981). Simply, no one can sign away the individual rights of another, and by allowing a proxy to sign on behalf of another may contractually obligate the proxy, not the participant for whom the proxy is signing (Miller, Young, & Martin, 2009).

Because the waiver serves as a contractual agreement between two parties where the opportunity to participate is exchanged for a promise not to sue, it may serve as an important litigation deterrent. In previous cases, courts usually have held that exculpatory agreements such as waivers are effective when signed before an individual participates in an activity (*Lemoine v. Cornell University*, 2004; *Zollman v. Myers*, 1992). It does this because a well-written waiver informs the participant about the inherent risks of the activity *and* that the provider is not liable for injuries due to ordinary negligence. So, if the waiver is effectively written and administered, an injured participant would recognize that he or she agreed to participate under the waiver's conditions by formally and publicly signing the document. Through this process, the individual may very well not pursue litigation due to his or her understanding of a waiver's legal ramifications. Additionally, a participant may not sue because he or she promised not to, and action that brings a sense of moral accountability to the forefront (Murr, 2002). Thus, the inter- and intra-personal pressure to remain consistent with his or her word reinforces a moral commitment against litigation.

Beyond the morally based deterrent, the protection a waiver provides is further enhanced by its power to provide exculpatory evidence on behalf of the service provider. Simply, if a participant agrees to not sue a provider via a contractually based waiver, that document can be used as evidence that demonstrates the contract consideration elements (what was agreed upon/ exchanged). Waivers make up an exception in which a cumulative good can result in excusing tort liability instead of implementing it (Nelson, 2002). Primarily this may be due to situations where the public safety concerns intersect with the right to contract (*Chumney v. Stott*, 1963). Nelson (2002) clarified this by stating that waivers are hybrids between contract and tort law resulting from the junction of the right to contract and the duty to be accountable for one's actions. This is supported by the courts that have almost unanimously held that the right to contract is slightly more important than upholding tort liability (*Childress v. Madison County*, 1989; *Haines v. St. Charles Speedway, Inc.*, 1989; *Heil Valley Ranch, Inc. v. Simkin*, 1989).

Waivers and releases are generally not favored by the law, and some courts have found them unconscionable and contracts of adhesion and therefore unenforceable. Some have been held to be unenforceable based on public policy grounds (*Wagenblast v. Odessa School District*, 1988). However, releases can be enforceable under certain circumstances if it is clear that the parties intended that the defendant be "held harmless." Waivers may negate the duty element of a negligence action (*Von Beltz v. Stuntman, Inc.*, 1989), but different interpretations of the law may affect the efficacy of a waiver depending on the state where the waiver is administered and the suit is filed. Do releases at sporting events always provide a defense to the defendant? Consider a situation in which a participant fails to sign a release for a particular occurrence of an event but has participated in the event many times before. That was the case in *Beaver v. Grand Prix* (2001). The plaintiff had been kart racing since 1985 and had signed a release many times in the past when participating in races. In 1994, she was injured while racing, and it was discovered that she had not signed a release for that race. More recently, in 2010, Robert Fecteau sued the organizers of a Tough Mudder race saying he was paralyzed after diving headfirst into a muddy pool (Wells & Wood, 2013). However, Fecteau was not registered for the competition but used another person's identification (Wells & Wood, 2013). In 2014, Fecteau settled his lawsuit against the organizers for $300,000 (Walker, 2014).

Comparative Negligence

Comparative negligence is another defense to a tort action and has been recognized as one of the most common responses to negligence claims. In a negligence action, a jury can reduce any damages it finds the plaintiff is entitled to by the percentage of the plaintiff's fault. The doctrine of comparative negligence compares the negligence of the plaintiff with that of the defendant and can sometimes work to reduce the recovery of damages for the plaintiff. Although not technically considered a "defense," comparative negligence may be represented in two forms—"pure" and "modified." It is important to note that as of 2012, 44 states utilized one of the two forms, or a combination of the two.

In *pure comparative negligence*, a plaintiff may be awarded a proportionate allocation of damages unless the negligence was determined to be 100%. For example, should a plaintiff be found to be 80% at fault, the plaintiff would still be able to recover 20% of the award. For instance, if a jury found a stadium owner negligent and returned a verdict for the plaintiff-spectator in the amount of $100,000, but also found that the plaintiff-spectator was 60% negligent, a judgment would be entered for $40,000 for the plaintiff-spectator.

There are *two types of modified comparative negligence*, the 50% form and the 49% form. Some state laws provide for a "fifty percent rule," which prevents a plaintiff who is found to be more than 50% negligent from any recovery whatsoever.[59] In the 49% form, the plaintiff recovers only if his or her percentage of fault is less than the defendant's. As a result, should the plaintiff be found at fault for 49%, he or she may still be awarded 51% of the final judgment.

Sovereign Immunity

Another defense to tort liability is *sovereign immunity*. The doctrine was originally based on the ancient maxim "the king can do no wrong." Unless waived, the doctrine of sovereign immunity shields the state, its agencies, and its officials from lawsuits for damages, absent legislative consent to sue.

The immunity defense differs in every state, and many states have exceptions to this defense. The initial U.S. Supreme Court case in which issues of sovereign immunity received in-depth consideration was in *Chisholm v. Georgia* (1793). The question in this case was whether a South Carolinian could sue the state of Georgia on a contractual debt in the Supreme Court. When the representatives from the state of Georgia refused to appear, the question of jurisdiction was discussed by the justices in several opinions (*Chisholm v. Georgia*, 1793). All but one of the justices resolved that the court had and constitutionally could exercise jurisdiction over the case.

In response to the court's decision in *Chisholm*, the *Eleventh Amendment* was enacted to provide that the judicial power should not "be construed to extend to any suit in law or equity, commenced or prosecuted against one state by Citizens of another State, or by Citizens or Subjects of any Foreign State" (U.S. Const. amend. XI). Although the Eleventh Amendment prevents federal law-based suits against the states, the common law doctrine of state sovereign immunity does not allow plaintiff from alleging any state law claims in a state court against any entity or division of a state government. In *Hans v. State of Louisiana* (1890), the U.S. Supreme Court ruled that a citizen from Louisiana could not sue the state of Louisiana in federal court. As a result, the *Hans* case is "generally used today as the standard citation for the proposition that the Eleventh Amendment forbids citizens from suing states in federal court" (Fletcher, 1983, 1040). Thus, since *Hans*, the U.S. Supreme Court has clung to an interpretation of the Eleventh Amendment that private suits are not allowed irrespective of whether the plaintiff is a citizen of the defendant state. However, it is important to note that in tort cases, damages claims could be brought against individual government officers, though not against the government itself (Jackson, 2003).

In *Bridges v. City of Carrasco* (2008), a participant in a softball game brought a lawsuit after he was injured. The legal issue presented to the court was whether the sports association and its officials who ran the tournament were immune from tort liability under Louisiana law.

WORKERS' COMPENSATION

Workers' compensation laws established an administrative process for compensating injured workers who were injured while doing their jobs. The laws are often deemed *strict liability* because the payment of benefits is not based on any fault of the employer, but rather on the existence of an employment relationship. For the employer to be liable, the employee's injury must be accidental and must have occurred in the course of employment without regard to the question of negligence (*Stringer v. Minnesota Vikings Football Club, Inc.*, 2005).

Workers' compensation provide the following benefits on behalf of covered workers for on the job injuries and occupational diseases:

1. 100% of medical bills related to the injury or occupational disease;

2. A percentage of lost wages as calculated by state statutory Workers' Compensation Law;
3. Lump sum award for certain disabilities;
4. Lump sum for certain disfigurements;
5. Death benefit to beneficiaries (Sadler, 2010).

The original purpose of the Workers' Compensation Law was to provide for the injured worker and to curb lawsuits against the employer for every injury that occurred on the job. The law operates as an exclusive remedy for all injuries sustained by an employee during the scope of employment. Absent an intentional act or gross negligence on the part of the employer, the workers' only remedy against an employer for an injury on the job is the workers' compensation benefits (*Quick v. Meyers Welding Fabricating, Inc.*, 1994). *Workers' compensation* is usually required by the state for every employee, although some state laws have exceptions for certain numbers of workers, small business owners, and other categories. The theory behind Workers' Compensation Law is that the employer has to bear the burden of the cost of the injury.

As mentioned previously, professional athletes usually assume all risks, including injury, inherent to the sport. The collective bargaining agreements of the major sports leagues provide for payment of benefits and some wages to an athlete if he or she sustains a sports-related injury during a sporting event. Professional athletes may also be eligible to receive state workers' compensation benefits for injuries they have sustained from playing a particular sport. In *Palmer v. Kansas City Chiefs* (1981), the workers' compensation claimant was denied benefits for injuries he sustained during a professional football game while executing a block. However, absent a specific exclusion under state law, professional athletes who are injured during the course of their employment might be able to recover workers' compensation benefits. Defenses that are normally available in tort actions, such as assumption of risk, and comparative or contributory negligence, are not available to the employer in a workers' compensation matter.

DISCUSSION QUESTIONS

Assumption of Risk

In *Tilson v. Russo* (2006), the plaintiff was an experienced horse rider who suffered injuries to her left shoulder when a horse named "Lady" bit her. The court of appeals affirmed the lower court's order granting the defendant's motion for summary judgment. The appeals court found that the risk of being bitten was inherent in sporting events that involve horses and that the rider was aware of the risks involved. To what extent should the plaintiff assume the risks described in this scenario?

Primary or Secondary Assumption of Risk

A teenage male enjoys swimming at the local pool. He also enjoys diving in the pool at the shallow as well as the deep end. The shallow end is 3 feet deep. Signage and verbal instructions have been provided and he has been reprimanded several times previously. One day the teenager dives into the shallow end and breaks his neck. Does this scenario fall under primary or secondary assumption of risk? Explain your rationale.

Comparative Negligence

In *Barillari v. Ski Shawnee* (2013), Mrs. Barillari, was not a ticketed skier that day but was there to watch her husband and children take skiing lessons, was generally aware of the risks of collision between skiers. Mrs. Barillari was standing close to tape that divided a ski run from the instruction area where Mr. Barillari was taking a lesson. At the time, however, she was not worried about skiers colliding with her because she believed that she was close enough to the dividing tape and there were other spectators in the area. Unfortunately for Mrs. Barillari, a skier did collide with her and caused an injury to her left leg. What elements of negligence may be used to compare which party is more at fault for the injury to Mrs. Barillari?

Waivers and Releases

In *Tuttle v. TRC Enterprises* (2007), a motorcycle rider sued a cycle park for injuries he sustained when he collided with a utility vehicle driven by one of the park's employees on a "fun day" scheduled by the park. The court held that the release signed by the rider was void against public policy and not enforceable. Explain why you think the court ruled in this fashion.

Sovereign Immunity

In *Hunt v. Central Consolidated School District* (2013), defendants contended that, to the extent that any of the plaintiffs' claims sound in contract, sovereign immunity bars those claims, because "[g]overnmental entities are granted immunity from actions based on contract, except actions

(continues)

DISCUSSION QUESTIONS (CONTINUED)

based on a valid written contract," which the plaintiffs have not alleged. Because the legislature defines "school district" in the New Mexico Statutes Annotated as "a political subdivision of the state," the court concluded that New Mexico school districts, just like any other of the state's political subdivisions, are subject to a private party's lawsuit to the same extent as that to which the law subjects other New Mexico political subdivisions. How does this ruling differ from the traditional employment of sovereign immunity? How does this ruling represent the recent abrogation of sovereign immunity by states?

Workers' Compensation

Is a student-athlete an employee for purpose of Workers' Compensation Law? What about a professional athlete? Suppose a student who is on an academic scholarship is injured on the way to a seminar to present research for the school. Would he or she be entitled to workers' compensation benefits as well?

KEY TERMS

49% modified assumption of risk
50% modified assumption of risk
Assumption of risk
Eleventh Amendment
Expressed assumption of risk
Implied assumption of the risk

Primary assumption of risk
Pure comparative negligence
Secondary assumption of risk
Sovereign immunity
Waiver or releases
Workers' compensation

REFERENCES

American Jurisprudence. 57B Am. Jur. 2d *Negligence* § 775 (2012).

Barillari v. Ski Shawnee, Inc., 986 F. Supp. 2d 555, 2013 U.S. Dist. LEXIS 161029 (M.D. Pa. 2013).

Beaver v. Grand Prix Karting Association, Inc. 246 F.3d 905 (7th Cir. 2001).

Bennett v. United States Cycling Federation, 193 Cal. App. 3d 1485, 1490, 239 Cal. Rptr. 55 (1987).

Bridges v. City of Carrasco, 982 So.2d 306, 2007-1593 (La. App.3 Cir. 4/30/08).

Calhoon v. Lewis, 81 Cal. App. 4th 108, 96 Cal. Rptr. 2d 394, 2000 Cal. App. LEXIS 432, 2000 Cal. Daily Op. Service 4317, 2000 D.A.R. 5769 (Cal. App. 4th Dist. 2000).

Cerny v. Cedar Bluffs Junior/Senior Public Schools, 267 Neb. 958, 679 N. W.2d 198, 2004 Neb. LEXIS 80 (2004).

Childress v. Madison County, 777 S.W.2d 1, 1989 Tenn. App. LEXIS 48 (Tenn. Ct. App. 1989).

Chisholm v. Georgia, 2 U.S. 419, 420, 438 (1793).

Chumney v. Stott, 14 Utah 2d 202, 381 P.2d 84, 1963 Utah LEXIS 180 (1963).

Costa v. The Boston Red Sox Baseball Club, 61 Mass. App. Ct. 299 (2004).

Fletcher, W.A. (1983). A historical interpretation of the Eleventh Amendment: A narrow construction of an affirmative grant of jurisdiction rather than a prohibition against jurisdiction. *Stanford Law Review*, 35, 1033–1131.

Ford v. Gouin, 834 P.2d 724, 734 (Cal. 1992).

Gossett v. Jackson, 249 Va. 549, 457 S.E.2d 97, 1995 Va. LEXIS 62 (1995).

Grishman v. Porter, 2006 WL 1381654 (Cal. Ct. App. 2006).

Haines v. St. Charles Speedway, Inc., 874 F.2d 572, 1989 U.S. App. LEXIS 6576 (8th Cir. Mo. 1989).

Hans v. State of Louisiana, 134 U.S. 1 (1890).

Heil Valley Ranch, Inc. v. Simkin, 784 P.2d 781, 1989 Colo. LEXIS 583, 13 Brief Times Rptr. 1558 (Colo. 1989).

Hunt v. Central Consolidated School District, 951 F. Supp.2d 1136, 2013 U.S. Dist. LEXIS 90275 (D.N.M. 2013).

Jackson, V.C. (2003). Suing the federal government: Sovereignty, immunity, and judicial independence. *George Washington University International Law Review*, 35, 512–609.

Kahn v. E. Side Union High Sch. Dist., 75 P.3d 30 (Cal. 2003).

Keeton, P. & Prosser, W. L. (1984). Prosser and Keeton on the Law of Torts. St. Paul, MN: West Publishing.

Knight v. Jewett, 834 P.2d 701 (Cal. 1992).

Leakas v. Columbia Country Club, 831 F. Supp. 1231, 1993 U.S. Dist. LEXIS 12030 (D. Md. 1993).

Lemoine v. Cornell University, 2 N.Y.3d 701, 810 N.E.2d 912, 2004 N.Y. LEXIS 509, 778 N.Y.S.2d 459 (2004).

Leon v. Family Fitness Center (#107),… , 61 Cal. App. 4th 1227, 71 Cal. Rptr. 2d 923, 1998 Cal. App. LEXIS 170, 98 Cal. Daily Op. Service 1589, 98 D.A.R. 2201 (Cal. App. 4th Dist. 1998).

Louis v. Louis, 636 N.W.2d 314 (Minn. December 6, 2001).

Maddox v. New York, 108 A.D.2d 42, 487 N.Y.S.2d 354, 1985 N.Y. App. Div. LEXIS 48379 (N.Y. App. Div. 2d Dep't 1985).

Miller, J., Young, S., & Martin, N. (2009). To use or not to use? The status of waivers in intramural sports. *Recreational Sports Journal*, 33(2), 129–138.

Murphy v. Steeplechase Amusement Co., 250 N.Y. 479; 166 N.E. 173 250 N.Y. 479; 166 N.E. 173 (1929).

Murr, A. (January, 2002). Sports waivers: An exercise in futility? *Journal of Law and Education,* 31, 114–120.

Nalwa v. Cedar Fair, L.P., 290 P.3d 1158 (Cal. 2012).

Nelson, R.S. (2002). The theory of the waiver scale: An argument why parents should be able to waive their children's tort liability claims. *University of San Francisco Law Review,* 36, 535–569.

Palmer v. Kansas City Chiefs, 621 S.W.2d 350 (Mo. Ct. App. 1981).

Paralift, Inc. v. Superior Court, 23 Cal. App. 4th 748, 755, 29 Cal. Rptr. 2d 177 (1993).

Prosser, W.L., Keeton, W.P., Dobbs, D., Keeton, R.E., & Owen, D.G. (1984). Prosser and Keeton on Torts (5th ed.). St. Paul, Minn.: West Group.

Quick v. Meyers Welding Fabricating, Inc., 649 So.2d 999 (La. Ct. App. 1994).

Restatement (Second) of Contracts. (1981). *Comment a.* St. Paul, Minn.: American Law Institute Publishers.

Restatement (Second) of Torts. (1965). *Comment b.* St. Paul, Minn.: American Law Institute Publishers.

Sadler, J. (2010). Allocation of liability, indemnification/ hold harmless, and insurance. In J. Miller & T. Seidler (Eds.), *A practical guide to sport management internships*, (pp. 176–176). Raleigh, N.C.: Carolina Academic Press Publishers.

Sanchez v. Bally's Total Fitness Corp., 68 Cal. App. 4th 62, 67, 79 Cal. Rptr. 2d 902 (1998).

Stringer v. Minnesota Vikings Football Club, Inc., 705 N.W.2d 746 (Minn. 2005).

Tilson v. Russo, 818 N.Y.S. 2d 311, 2006 N.Y. Slip Op. 05070.

Tuttle v. TRC Enterprises, 2007 WL 610638; 830 N.Y.S.2d 854 (N.Y.A.D. 2007).

Vaughn v. Pleasant, 266 Ga. 862, 864(1), 471 S.E.2d 866 (1996).

Von Beltz v. Stuntman, Inc., 207 Cal. App. 3d 1467, 255 Cal. Rptr. 755, 1989 Cal. App. LEXIS 120 (Cal. App. 2d Dist. 1989).

Wagenblast v. Odessa School District No. 105-157-166J, 758 P.2d 968 (Wash. 1988).

Walker, B. (2014). Mud Run lawsuit settled. LetsRun.com. Retrieved from http://www.letsrun.com/forum /flat_read.php?thread=5629487

Wattenbarger v. Cincinnati Reds, Inc., 28 Cal. App. 4th 746, 33 Cal. Rptr. 2d 732, 1994 Cal. App. LEXIS 963, 94 Cal. Daily Op. Service 7369, 94 D.A.R. 13485 (Cal. App. 3d Dist. 1994).

Wells, C. & Wood, P. (2013). Death and injuries at events like Tough Mudder and Warrior Dash lead to lawsuits. Baltimoresun.com. Retrieved from http://www .baltimoresun.com/news/maryland/bal-with-rise -of-extreme-races-fun-comes- with-serious-risk -20130524-htmlstory.html

Zollman v. Myers, 797 F. Supp. 923, 1992 U.S. Dist. LEXIS 13109 (D. Utah 1992).

RISK MANAGEMENT

LEARNING OBJECTIVES

By the end of the chapter, the reader will be able to:

1. Understand the concept of risks
2. Understand the differences between traditional risk management and modern risk management
3. Understand how risk management is considered a preventative branch of legal theory
4. Comprehend the considerations regarding the probability and severity of a risk
5. Comprehend and provide examples risk assessments
6. Analyze the effectiveness of risk communication
7. Explain how each of the four risk management approaches may be used together in creating an effective risk management program

RELATED CASES

INTRODUCTION

Throughout human history individuals and groups have had to contend with a variety of risks for survival and personal well-being. The origins of structured *risk management* have been traced to the Babylonians in 3200 B.C. (Covello & Mumpower, 1985). In fact, a contention may be made that since human history is very much a story of assessing and adapting to *risks*; risk is inherent to the human condition. Yet if such a tragedy would occur, the impact would be significant. Recent examples include an interscholastic football player such as Max Gilpin (Associated Press, 2009) and an Olympic-caliber open water swimmer such as Fran Crippen (Lord, 2011) who met their demise while participating in supervised competitions. The impact of the Gilpin incident resulted in a head high school football coach facing charges on reckless homicide and wanton-endangerment, of which he was eventually acquitted. After the Crippen incident, the supervising organization was not only fined but banned from hosting open water swimming competitions for the near future.

Neither safety nor risk management are viewed as being overly complicated; yet the specific understanding of safety principles and risk management decisions that assist sport managers to provide athletes with reasonably safe environments may be more problematic. Maslow defined safety as "security, stability, dependency, protection, freedom from fear ... need for structure, order" (1954, p. 39). In many situations most adults and children in sports and recreation activities are largely satisfied regarding their safety needs. In a "good" society, members feel safe enough from the likelihood of being exposed to significantly injurious situations. Thus, an individual participating in or attending supervised sport and recreational activities should no longer have any safety concerns. However, the need for safety at varying levels is still viewed as important in sports as there are growing concerns about the health and safety of athletes, particularly younger ones due to the rising rates of concussions and death from heat. Proof of this need may be seen in the recently passed protocols concerning concussion management in professional, intercollegiate, and interscholastic athletics; lifeguards are required at public pools; and the and athletic administrators must adhere to safety procedures to protect the athletes from unnecessary exposure to harm. In essence, these items identify ways to manage the risks that are inherent in sport and recreational activities on a reactive level. The question is: why aren't risks that could result in significant injury addressed more proactively? Perhaps the reason is the inability of sport managers to foresee areas of possible injury, an issue addressed later in this chapter.

CONCEPT OF RISK

To understand how to manage it, the concept of risk must first be defined. Some have recognized risk as the potential harm of valuable items that result from an individual's actions (Kates & Kasperson, 1983). Slovic and Peters (2006) divided risk into two categories: risk as feelings and risk as analysis. According to Slovic and Peters (2006), risk as feelings links a person's inborn reaction to a harmful situation, whereas risk as analysis includes logic, reason, and scientific considerations to resolve dangerous situations.

Risks can be physical, financial, or ethical. *Physical risks* are those involving personal injuries, environmental and weather conditions and the physical assets of the organization such as property, buildings, equipment, vehicles, stock, and grounds. *Financial risks* are those that involve the assets of the organization and include theft, fraud, loans, license fees, attendances, membership fees, insurance costs, lease payments, payout of damages claims or penalties and fines by the government. *Ethical risks* involve actual or potential harm to the reputation or beliefs of your club, while legal risks consist of responsibilities imposed on providers, participants, and consumers arising from laws made by federal, state and local government authorities. Klinke and Renn (2002) referred to risk as:

> the experience of something that people fear or regard as negative. It is also clear that this fear is extended to an event or situation that has not yet occurred but could occur in the future. (p. 1076)

Risk can also include such items as uncertainty, catastrophic potential, and controllability (Slovic, 2001). *Catastrophic potential* may be perceived as immeasurable in regards to the loss of life and economic consideration (Lerner, & Keltner, 2000). For example, to the extent that an assault is thought to be unique or isolated, the immediate impact may be limited and fleeting (Liesch, Steen, Knight, & Czinkota, 2006). This may result in uncertainty and accompanying fear to be contained at a lesser level (Lerner, Gonzalez, Small, & Fischhoff, 2003). Conversely, if strikes are perceived by fans to be directed toward more vulnerable or "soft targets" such as the sport stadium, the more insidious the uncertainty would be thereby increasing the level of fear among the people (Ip, 2004). Risks, then, may be defined as the possibility or perception that human actions or events lead to consequences that harm others (Hohenenser, Kates, & Slovic, 1983; Kates & Kasperson, 1983). This definition implies that the severity of experienced harm depends on the causal relationship between the stimulus (human activity or event) and the consequences. If we take a nonfatalistic viewpoint, consequences can be altered either by modifying the initiating activity or event or by mitigating the impacts. Therefore, risk is both an analytic and normative concept. If the vast majority of human beings assess potential consequences as unwelcome or undesirable, society is coerced to avoid, to reduce, or at least control risks.

RISK MANAGEMENT AS A PREVENTATIVE LEGAL THEORY

As discussed earlier, there is an increasing application of the law to sport. A primary reason for this application is the increasing number of people involved in sports, including spectators, participants, and coaches. As this book relates, the law is involved in sport in a variety of ways, including civil and criminal negligence, contracts, discrimination and harassment, reputation (defamation), copyright, marketing, drugs testing, among others. The ability to develop, implement, and oversee a method which decreases the impact of the law can provide significant benefits to a sport organization in terms of time, effort and financial cost. Risk management is considered to be within the preventative branch of legal theory (Prairie and Garfield, 2004). It describes a process that is primarily concerned with identifying, measuring, controlling, and minimizing foreseeable risks to protect organizational assets. However, the evaluation of whether a situation is considered a risk and the resulting actions depend on the perception of the risk (Lyytinen, Mathiassen, & Ropponen, 1998). Often these perceptions are dependent on the probability that an incident may occur and the impact that the incident may have on the organization.

Probability is a statistically driven process that often eliminates the intuitive sense that a risk exists (Steele, 2004). Statistical evaluation of probabilities from data, has been an effective cornerstone of risk management for a number of years. This impersonal process is employed to determine a right course of action. In this sense probability provides an organization a basis to make a decision in a limited way. Understanding risk management in its decision-making sense is to understand the probability of a risk occurring may generate an opportunity for action, and to eradicate the reason of indecision. However, it should be clear that simply stating an issue in terms of risk and probability does not in principle lead the organization to 'discover' what to do (Steele, 2004).

Reduced legal risk is a by-product of the implementation of an effective risk management program. It is not a startling concept that risk should be almost universally perceived as important as it has been perceived as a central idea in tort law and tort theory (Perry, 1995). A tort may be defined as "conduct that amounts to a legal wrong and causes harm for which courts will impose civil liability" (Dobbs, 2001, p. 1). Risks develop through human actions and are dangers that could be avoided (Stahl, Lichtenstein, & Mangan, 2003). Luhmann (1990) referred to risk as the form in which the future of decisions are made perceptible and efficient. An accepted approach that can guide an organization's effort to avoid potential dangers and galvanize decision-making process is risk management.

At its center Steele (2004) advocated that legal theory implements approaches in which risk enables decisions and assists to explain the possibility of responsible action. She stated that when affixing responsibility, legal theory tends to employ a prospective decision-making model that is often applied retrospectively. In this case, it identifies a moment of decision that may be completely hypothetical, and uses this hypothesis to come to the right conclusions. In some circumstances, she asserts that these conclusions can be drawn because previous, similar situations may have lent itself to a rational decision through probabilities. Courts traditionally apply a risk-utility analysis that weighs "the risk, in light of the social value of the interest threatened, and the probability and extent of the harm" (*Griggs v. BIC Corp*, 1992). Such application of the risk-utility analyses was famously addressed by Judge Learned Hand, the originator of the "Hand Formula."

The "Hand Formula"

A basic premise of risk management is that individuals, to which there is a duty owed, should expect reasonable standard of care be given. This duty doesn't require that all injuries to others can be avoided but that injuring others as a result of carelessness must be. The reasonable standard of care seems obvious, even elementary. No reasonable person would entertain the idea of purposefully injuring another person. However, the reasonable standard of care is dreadfully fuzzy. How else can it be explained that every year hundreds of millions of dollars turn on such a simple, common sense idea of fault?

While it is useful to attempt to recognize the dynamics the reasonable person considers in pondering an action, it is quite another to detail precisely how he weighs those factors, or what is reasonable on a given set of facts placed before him at the time. Judge Learned Hand attempted to do so in the case of *United States v. Carroll Towing Co.* (1947). Judge Hand proposed that the defendant's duty in controlling the barge was:

> a function of three variables: (1) The probability that the barge will break away; (2) the gravity of the resulting injury, if she does; (3) the burden of adequate precautions. Possibly it serves to bring this notion into relief to state in algebraic terms: if the probability be called P; the injury L; and the burden B; liability depends upon whether B is less than L multiplied by P; i.e., whether B is less than PL. (p. 173)

According to Hand, the reasonable person takes the necessary precaution against the potential injury to others if the burden of doing so is less than the loss due to injury multiplied by the probability the injury will occur. For example, suppose a safety feature costs $100 to install on 100 pieces of athletic equipment, the likelihood of injury is estimated to be one out of 250, and the severity of an injury is not catastrophic. The Hand formula implies that the reasonable person will not connect the safety feature as it will cost $10,000 to put the feature on each of the 100 pieces of athletic equipment, but it will only potentially prevent $1000 in injury costs. Conversely, if the safety feature cost $5 per piece of equipment, the formula would lead to the conclusion that the reasonable person would add it since it would cost less to fix the equipment than the likely damages incurred. If the cost of an accident incurred while using the athletic equipment is multiplied by its probability of occurrence exceeds the cost of untaken precautions, then in the event of a mishap, the defendant should be judged at least negligent. For example, if a respondent estimated the probability of a serious accident to be 0.25, then the cost of the untaken precaution ($10,000 to replace the pieces of athletic equipment) should be less than 0.25 × $50,000 (the loss sustained in the accident) to justify deciding liability. In this example calculation, the expected loss would be $12,500. The precaution should thus be taken (that is, $12,500 is greater than $10,000); a shortcut test is to observe whether the respondent estimates the probability of an accident as greater than 0.20 ($10,000/$50,000).

THE THEORY OF THE THRESHOLD OF EFFECTIVE ZEROHOOD

As addressed in the Hand Formula, the probability of a mishap occurring may be weighed against the cost of safety implementation. Risks may be regarded as the chance of something happening that will have a negative impact on organizational objectives. These risks can be measured in terms of probability and impact. The amount of risk is produced by its impact (e.g., low, medium, high) and the probability of occurrence (e.g., never, sometime, and often). People are often prepared to treat an unimportant possibility as having an effectively zero chance of occurring (Slovic, 1977). In the event that the risk producing harmful incidents are considered improbable, it may be perceived that the management of risks would be

relatively unimportant. When low probability events that have been called to people's attention, people usually overestimate the level of the risk. Small identified risks tend to be overestimated, and large identified risks tend to be underestimated (Slovic, 1987). However, if the risks were considered severe enough in producing events that could negatively impact the organization, the management of such a risk would be significant. Once the likelihood of an eventuation gets to be small enough, the probability of the incident occurring may be seen as no longer possible. This is the *theory of the threshold of effective zerohood* (Rescher, 1983).

Risk management decisions almost invariably involve a generalized risk-reward trade-off (Adams, 2001). It is impossible to drive risks to "zero" without lowering the value (and even then, proximity to "zero" comes only at great expense), so the decision process must follow an optimizing rule, balancing the costs and benefits against overall risk management objectives (Rescher, 1983). If the probability of an incident occurring is considered to be close to zero, the perception may very well be to set aside the need for the assessment or management of risk. However, the assessment of whether a situation is considered a risk and the resulting management of those actions depend on the perception of the risk (Lyytinen, Mathiassen, & Ropponen, 1998).

If the analysis of the impact were the primary concern, the scope of the risk would increase. In other words, if the organization can foresee the realization of a threat occurring as well as negative impact that an incident could create, the level of the management of risks would be elevated. As such, when a plausible danger is multiplied by the potentially harmful impact, the level of risk increases (credible threat × potential negative impact = level of risk increases). For example, since no professional football stadiums have ever been damaged by a terrorist attack, the perceived likelihood of on occurring may be construed as zero.

This perception could lead the football stadium manager, the organization and potentially spectators to fall into the risk of complacency thereby compromising safety and security. According to the Theory of the Threshold of Effective Zerohood it is important to identify the probability of an incident happening (Rescher, 1983). A probability is an absolute value between zero and one. Numbers between zero and one can become very small: as N get larger, $1/N$ grows smaller (Rescher, 1983). In relation to the reasonable standard of care, no one avoids risks that cannot be foreseen as a probability. The reasonable person attends to the kinds of harm that are foreseeable to reasonable people (Dobbs, 2000). Thus, due to the lack of knowledge and/or experience a person may not foresee the likelihood that a harmful situation could occur.

Consider, hypothetically, an injury or situation requiring litigation has never occurred in a physical activity taught at an institution. The department documents that over 5000 individuals have participated in its offerings. The probability of an incident occurring would then be zero (0/5000). Although the possibility of an incident happening *can* occur, it may be viewed as something that no longer presents a realistic prospect to a reasonable person. The theory of the threshold of effective zerohood in regards to risk management, as it appears in the previous paragraph, could mean that the institution has carefully sculpted a safe environment thereby eliminating the likelihood of litigation. However, it could also indicate that the department may not be concerned about litigation since no injuries severe enough to warrant litigation had occurred previously.

To highlight the potential economic impacts, Lee, Gordon, Moore, and Richardson (2008) conducted a case study to ascertain the economic losses as the result of a terrorist strike on a sports stadium. They created a hypothetical situation in which a National Football League stadium seating 75,000 people was the subject of a bioterrorism attack and conducted several computer based simulations to determine economic impacts. The major areas of economic impact were casualties, illnesses, contamination, and business interruption. Casualties were assumed to be 7000 among stadium attendees and an additional 3600 from people within the community. A value of a statistical life computation was used to measure economic impact of lost lives. Lee et al. (2006) estimated that 20,000 attendees and an additional 11,000 people from the community would suffer severe illnesses that would require a hospitalization of seven days as well as follow-up medical appointments. It was estimated that quarantine of the stadium and surrounding area would be required for a month, 50% of the buildings would be uninhabitable for six months, and the entire decontamination process would last approximately a year. The investigators further hypothesized that if a stadium were to be hit and damaged, attendance would drop at least 8% simply due to the cancelling of games for the month of quarantine. Depending on the reaction by the public, attendance levels are estimated to drop anywhere from 15% to 40%. Business would also be affected in the form of lost jobs in the immediate area. Using the attacks of September 11, 2001 as a model, researchers estimated that 3793 jobs would be lost for the first year. Ultimately, economic impacts could be estimated to range anywhere from $62 billion to $73 billion.

RISK MANAGEMENT PROGRAM

The goal of an effective risk management program is to protect the assets and financial resources of the sports organization and its members by reducing risk and the potential for loss. To reduce or control risks, social institutions are formed to evaluate and manage risks. In this context, we understand risk evaluation as the process by which societal institutions such as agencies, social groups within society, or individuals determine the acceptability of a given risk. Effective risk management is predicated on a comprehensive analyses of individual risks. If a risk is judged as unacceptable, adequate measures for risk reduction are required. The process of reducing risks deemed acceptable by society and to assure control, monitoring, and public communication is covered under the term "risk management" (Kolluru, 1995).

The concept of risk management has been advocated as a means to provide; a) safe instructional environments (Miller & Rushing, 2002); b) intramural activities (Miller, Veltri, & Gillentine, 2005); and c) effective sport marketing (Gillentine, Miller, & Calhoun, 2008). Risk management analytically recognizes, evaluates, considers, supervises, and communicates any foreseeable risk, so that negative effects (loss of reputation) and losses (financial) can be decreased. Risk management may be regarded as the ability to foresee circumstances that may expose a person, to whom a duty is owed, to harm (Wendt & Miller, 2010). The consequences of being able to foresee potential harm may cause economic loss as well as negatively impact the reputation of the organization (Wendt & Miller, 2010). At an operational level, effective risk management policies and procedures require a balance between the foreseeable risks to the organization and the costs to protect a particular asset (Cawood, 2002). Effective risk management does not happen automatically as it incorporates several different actions and integrates them into one process of prevention and protection (see Figure 5-1). Risk management should encourage people to take a deliberate, methodical approach to dealing with risks. Thus, they help move risk management from the realm of the accidental to the realm of the proactive.

Foreseeability in Risk Management

Foreseeability may be considered to be the degree to which an organization knew, or should have known, that a participant/spectator/employee may be exposed to harm (Dobbs, 2000). For example, the plaintiff in *Schmidt v. Midwest Sports Events, Inc.* (2010) alleged that the organization generally knew, or should have known, that the swimming phase of a triathlon is the most dangerous for participants because of the risk of drowning. The ability of a sport manager to identify foreseeable risks provides a basis by which the risk of potential injury to a participant and the duty by a sponsoring organization to exercise appropriate care for an injured person exists (American Jurisprudence, 2004).

Judge Oliver Wendell Holmes is credited with saying that the life of the law has not been logic; it has been experience. Holmes (1881/2000) stated: "If a consequence cannot be foreseen, it cannot be avoided. But there is this practical difference that whereas, in most cases, the question of knowledge is a question of the actual condition of the defendant's consciousness, the question of what he might have foreseen is determined by the standard of the prudent man, that is, by general experience" (p. 45).

A sport manager has a legal duty to warn patrons about reasonably foreseeable and credible threats (Dobbs, 2000; Mallen, 2001). If a credible or foreseeable threat exists on a premises and it cannot be corrected, a patron must be warned of such a threat so they may avoid it (Montgomery & Nahrstadt, 2004). Once the priorities have been developed, the sport manager would be able to identify potential targets and implement appropriate risk management measures. Should organizational decision-makers overlook the perceived importance of the contests, lack risk awareness or simply ignore the need to develop, implement and enforce safeguards, it may be only a matter of time before an incident happens (Alston, 2003).

It may be contended that a reasonable person becomes reasonable, primarily, through experience. But what happens if there are no experiences in a person's or institution's past with litigation? Thus, risk management offers the decision-makers an opportunity to advance a

FIGURE 5-1 **Risk Management Processes**

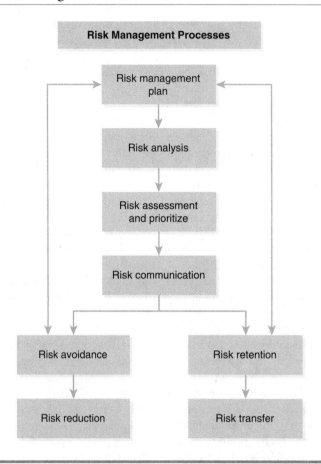

wide-ranging organizational policy for managing risks (Miller, Wendt, & Young, 2010).

MODERN RISK MANAGEMENT PROGRAM

Risk management has evolved rapidly over the past fifteen years, and it is important to emphasize that modern risk management is now structured around a comprehensive process for assessing and addressing risks—a process in which operational risk management is but one part. This approach, frequently labeled *Enterprise Risk Management* (ERM), differs from historical practices in several ways. First, it seeks to identify and assess the widest possible range of risks in organizational or less structured settings. Second, ERM develops a comprehensive organizational policy for managing risks. Third, ERM embeds a process for the ongoing assessment of risks while it ultimately implements a process for the day-to-day management of those risks (Young & Tippins, 2000). Although there is a great deal more that could be said about ERM, most experts would agree that the key characteristics are 1) top management engagement in the establishment of risk policy, and 2) the involvement of all employees in the management of risks that fall within the scope of their general responsibilities (Andersen & Schröder, 2010; Lam, 2003; Slovic & Peters, 2006; Young & Tippins, 2000).

To be effective, risk management must become part of an organization's culture. It should be assimilated into the philosophy, practices, and business plans of the organization. In short, risk management should the major concern of everyone in the organization. By adopting a structured, organization-wide approach to the management of risks several items will emerge. For example, the delivery of sports-related services as well as the potential for increased standards of service may be realized. Increased accountability of employees and supervisors will occur. A rise in creative and innovative management practices may result in morale improvement. Finally, an integrated approach of risk management will augment the understanding of potential legal issues and may assist in the reducing exposure to litigation/penalties. Thematically, ERM approaches risks as a highly interconnected portfolio of risks that need to be managed, not just in response to the individual characteristics of a particular risk, but with a specific eye on understanding the interrelationships of all risks in question (Andersen & Schröder, 2010). This central insight produces a number of effects that extend and frequently challenge thinking about risk management.

It should be noted that the development of an effective risk management policy is not a one-time activity. Rather it should entail a continuous and comprehensive process focused on ascertaining potential problems. The new ISO 31000 guidance produced by the International Organization for Standardization (ISO), is emphatic on this particular point, indicating that the organizations and their environments are dynamic and constantly changing (ISO 31000, 2009). Among other things, ISO's view reflects the fact that traditional risk management does not employ a wide enough lens in looking at risks. Thus, while things like security and public safety might receive attention, other important risks (financial, reputational, supply chain, competitive) have historically failed to receive appropriate attention.

Further, traditional approaches tend to ignore the interconnectivity of most organizational risks. For example, many sport venues have not been designed with security in mind with the ability to control access and visibility (Then & Loosemore, 2006). As such, the security risk in question might be affected not only by stadium design and construction but by marketing policy, general economic considerations, facility maintenance and management, and the managing organization's hiring policy. And, of course, the risk relationship travels in both directions; security can affect many of those risks in return.

It should be noted that the real impact of modern risk management on measures is to add "dimensionality" to the analysis. Any individual measure should be considered in terms of its relationship to overall organizational policy, risk policy, and to the interconnectivity that exists between risks. The temporal dimension must be considered as well—a risk management measure is introduced and it must not only suit its original purpose but must in some way anticipate the responses to that measure over time. Patrons will react, and not always in expected and positive ways. Thus, it is imperative that the risks are analyzed to determine the probability and severity. In other words, any risk management measure must be assessed in terms of the context and in light of its role in assisting the achievement of overall risk goals and objectives. To ensure that risks are properly managed, the organization must have a risk management assessment plan.

RISK MANAGEMENT ASSESSMENTS

A myth about the early development of risk assessment was that it was believed to be completely separate from the risk management process (Goldstein, 2005). However, risk assessment provides a basic tool which may be used to determine the risks to be addressed and communicated (Goldstein, 2005). While creating a risk management plan inherently entails some level of subjectivity, there is little room for variance regarding risk assessment. Risk assessments have three primary mechanisms that need to be fully explored and considered: threat, vulnerability, and criticality (Durling, Price, & Spero, 2005). Once these aspects have been addressed the event organizer may select and communicate risk management strategies, predicated on the magnitude or value of the included characteristics (Kristensen, Aven, & Ford, 2006). Thus, one of the great undertakings of effective risk management is to bridge the gap between assessing the anticipated exposures of harm and communicating them to the public. To accomplish such an undertaking, the event manager should analyze and communicate potential threats, vulnerabilities, and critical aspects as well as strategies to manage the risks.

In order to determine the level of safety and security needed to protect patron life and property, a sport manager should assess a wide number of factors related to the event. Some factors that should be considered are whether the event is open to the public, the number and nature of attendees, whether senior government officials will attend, and specific location of the facility. Additionally, when attaching responsibility to employ a risk management decision-making model, through a blend of several distinct approaches to assess the potential risks. The first approach is to assess the significance of the threat. The second approach is to identify potential vulnerabilities in and around the sport facility. The third approach would be to prioritize critical vulnerabilities and take action to diminish the likelihood of harmful incidences.

Threat Assessment

A *threat assessment* may be used as a decision support tool to assist in creating and prioritizing security-program requirements, planning, and resource allocations (Decker, 2001). When an organization embarks on a risk assessment effort, the team conducting the assessment is searching for potential sources of concern (Frame, 2003). It deals with such issues as how operations might be negatively affected or what weaknesses can be identified.

The threat assessment prepares the organization to provide a better assurance of alertness in case of an incident. One of the significant challenges of appropriately managing risk is to link anticipated events that surfaced through risk assessment and the reality of the situation. In order to answer these questions, a vulnerability assessment should be implemented..

Vulnerability Assessment

Since not every threat might be identified or threat information may be incomplete, vulnerability assessments are crucial in preparing better against possible threats. A *vulnerability assessment* estimates the susceptibility of potential damages by those desiring to create physical or psychological harm to an organization's infrastructure, including employees or patrons. A vulnerability assessment helps in recognizing weaknesses that may be exploited (Decker, 2001). For example, a vulnerability assessment might reveal weaknesses in an organization's security systems, avenues of ingress and egress, or the distance from parking lots to important buildings as being so close that a car bomb detonation would damage or destroy the buildings and the people working in them (Decker, 2001). After all, the bomb that destroyed the Murrah Federal Building in Oklahoma City was detonated in a truck parked next to the building. Additional areas of concern in identifying event vulnerabilities include facility access, food vendor access, areas for concealed threats, security protocol, and access to team locker rooms, as well as lighting and entrance inspections. While results can be produced by risk and vulnerability assessments to truly create effective risk management procedures, a criticality assessment should be conducted.

Criticality Assessment

The *criticality assessment* is essential in actively managing potential risks. A criticality assessment is a practice that recognizes and examines organizationally significant assets, infrastructure, and critical functions based on a variety of factors. These factors include the significance of the event, whether people may be at risk, or the magnitude of a structure or system. Determining the criticality of a target can assist in identifying which potential areas will receive attention first (Decker, 2001).

Criticality assessments are important because they help identify which assets, structures, or functions are relatively more important to protect from an incident. A criticality assessment allows organization decision-makers to prioritize the assets. Once these assessments have been analyzed, a sport event manager will be able to apply appropriate risk management measures. Should organizational decision makers overlook the perceived importance of these assessments, lack risk awareness or simply ignore the need to develop, implement and enforce safeguards, it may be only a matter of time before an incident happens (Alston, 2003).

RISK COMMUNICATION

Scholars have defined *risk communication* as a science-based approach for communicating effectively in a number of different situations. Heath (1994) stated, "Risk communication deals with risk elements, whether they are appropriately tolerable, and risk consequences" (p. 257). Reynolds and Seeger (2005) revealed,

> Risk communication is also grounded in an assumption that the public has a generalized right to know about hazards and risks. The availability of information allows the public to make informed choices regarding risk. In this way risk communication facilitates decision making and risk sharing. (p. 45)

Risk communication is usually entrenched in organizational cultures that take place within the framework of risk management (Jardine, Hrudey, Shortreed, Craig, Krewski, Furgal, & McColl, 2003; Lundgren, 1994). Further, risk communication attempts to understand and manage the value systems of the people from whom a behavioral change is desired (Lundgren, 1994). A limiting factor is that a number of risk managers perceive that the general public tends to react to information that is limited, false, or inadequate (Slovic & Peters, 2006). Thus, members of the affected group may react to such "bad" information that may be inconsistent with the more fully informed conclusions of the policymakers (Plough & Krimsky, 1987). If ineffective or non-existent risk communication exists a significant loss of the trustworthiness of management, clashes with stakeholders, and pointless human distress related to high levels of anxiety and fear may occur (Charnley, 1997; Jardine et al., 2003; Slovic & Peters, 2006). From the risk manager's perspective, the purpose of risk communication is to help residents of affected communities understand the processes of risk management; to form reasonable perceptions of possible hazards;

and allow participants to provide input in making decisions about how risk should be managed (Reckelhoff-Dangel & Petersen, 2007).

THE ROLE OF RISK COMMUNICATION IN THE RISK MANAGEMENT PROCESS

Decker (2001) stated that risk management plans are systematic and analytical processes that consider the possibility that a danger will jeopardize an asset (e.g., a structure, individual, or function). Although, the patron may be responsible for assuming some of the risk inherent in physical activities, Kaplin & Lee (1997) wrote, "risk management can implement the institution's humanistic concern for minimizing and compensating any potential injuries that its operations may cause" (p. 128). Risk management will not work miracles, but it can assist in the preparation to reduce the number of potentially harmful surprises. However, even when serious risk management efforts are employed, it is unlikely that actions that may disrupt events can be accurately predicted.

Risk communication often concentrates on an intentional transfer of information designed to respond to public concerns or public needs related to real or perceived hazards (Plough & Krimsky, 1987). As a result, a common theme by those involved in risk management has been to integrate the role of risk communication into the process (Goldstein, 2005). Correctly used, risk communications involves informing members of a relevant group about the probabilities that some harm may occur as well as the ways for reducing the probability of the harm (Reynolds & Seeger, 2005). Simply stated, risk communication is the process of telling people about a foreseeable danger to their person, property, or community (Reynolds & Seeger, 2005). Thus, the need to integrate risk communication as

a continuous dialogue of information between risk managers and the population they are serving is a fundamental component to the overall risk management process. To ensure that risks are identified and properly communicated to the public, a risk assessment must be conducted.

RISK MANAGEMENT PLANS

A risk management plan should be designed to identify, evaluate the likelihood, plan and deal with foreseeable risks in conducting a sporting event (Miller et al., 2010). Since risk has been cited as the consequences of human actions or events that lead to harming another person, organizations may incorporate various means to classify and manage them (Klinke & Renn, 2002). The main reason for classifying risk is to obtain a general viewpoint, which may assist the managers in recognizing the areas in which significant harm may occur.

Risk management policies should never be thought of as prophetic in nature; however, they can uncover the sources by thoroughly analyzing and classifying possible risks (Miller et al., 2010). In its most basic form, risk classification allows organizational decision makers to identify "effective, efficient, and legally feasible strategies" and measures for *risk reduction* and mitigation (Klinke & Renn, 2002, p. 1085). As previously described, athletes may experience a range of significant medical or environmental problems that must be taken into consideration by triathlon directors. Classifying foreseeable risks is a two-step process in which both the impact and the likelihood of an injury are analyzed to determine the potential risk. The amount of risk is produced by its impact (e.g., low, medium, high) and the likelihood of occurrence (e.g., never, sometime, or often) (see Table 5-1).

Risk classification allows a manager to select or recommend risk management strategies, predicated on the foreseeable magnitude and/or likelihood of harm to which participants are exposed.

TABLE 5-1 **Assessment of Risks**

Frequency of Occurrence	Severity of Occurrence	Method Used
High	High	Avoidance
High	Medium	Retain
High	Low	Retain
Medium	High	Avoid
Medium	Medium	Retain
Medium	Low	Retain
Low	High	Avoid
Low	Medium	Retain
Low	Low	Retain

Regarding the safety of athletic participants, the organization could analyze the likelihood of potential injuries occurring and classify them relative to the severity. The classification may take the form of a numerical scale rating system of 1–5 in which one represents the least assessed frequency and five the most. Generally, there is a relationship between the severity of the risk and the favored strategy. According to Dallam et al. (2005), the rate of occurrence of foreseeable risks and the severity of their potentially negative outcomes are to prevent and respond to the conditions imposed by the conditions presented.

When a foreseeable risk, such as a fatality, is considered unlikely there may be less urgency to manage the risks (Miller & Gillentine, 2006). In this instance, the risk could be assigned a one or two on the frequency and impact scale. Conversely, if the likelihood of an incident occurring is perceived as being probable, the management of such a risk would be important. In this circumstance, the likelihood and impact may receive a classification of four or five. Thus, classifying a risk can enable sport event managers to provide the required level of importance in the risk management process and implement the appropriate

risk management alternative. Depending on the type of risk and its classification, there are three potential courses of action that may be used independently or in combination to retain the event: avoidance, transfer, or reduction. Generally, if the likelihood of an injury may considered to be severe (such as death or paralysis), occurs frequently and the risk cannot be managed due to lack of qualified personnel or money, the sport manager would be wise to avoid offering the activity. If a severe injury occurs occasionally (as it will in sports), the sport manager may elect to retain the activity provided appropriate personnel and supervision are available as risk reduction measures. If a severe injury occurs infrequently, the sport manager should not overlook the potential to manage the risk and provide appropriate measures. For further application, see Table 5-1.

RISK AVOIDANCE

Risk avoidance, as a risk management alternative, reflects the notion that the risk is too great and, therefore, the associated activity with the risk should be eliminated (Klinke & Renn, 2002).

Realizing how and when to properly avoid exposing participants to unnecessary risks is a significant consideration when analyzing and classifying a situation. Because sports events can vary widely in the number of athletes as well as their ability, an organization may elect to avoid a specific portion if it cannot get enough certified personnel. For example, should there be a dearth of certified lifeguards for a triathlon, the organization may sponsor a dualthon in which the participants only compete in the biking and running segments. If avoidance were deemed the most prudent method to treat the risk due to the significant lack of human resources (not enough supervision) or due to environmental conditions (lightning or severe water turbulence), the triathlon race would be cancelled and thereby avoided.

RISK TRANSFER

An alternative in managing risks is *risk transfer*. It should be noted that risk transfer does not mean risk avoidance. Rather, a risk transfer strategy will generate risks that still require proactive management, but reduces the level of risk to an acceptable level. Whereas the avoidance strategy eliminates a risk, the transference strategy often leaves the risk intact but shifts responsibility for it elsewhere. Transfer of risk refers to the notion that the responsibility of a certain risk will be re-allocated to another entity, usually in the form of a waiver (Miller, Young, & Martin, 2009). Because a waiver serves as a contractual agreement between two parties where the opportunity to participate is exchanged for a promise not to sue, it may serve as an important litigation deterrent (Miller et al., 2009).

RISK REDUCTION

Reduction suggests the organization will employ some type of measure to minimize the risk. This technique is usually used when a risk cannot be

avoided and efforts are centered on decreasing damage or loss. Specific to the allegations in both *Moore v. North America Sports* (2010) and *Schmidt v. Midwest Sports Events, Inc.* (2010), there was an alleged failure to provide enough supervision and lifeguards or other persons trained in first aid or cardiopulmonary resuscitation at the swimming portion of those triathlons. To reduce the risk, the organization must ensure that an appropriate number of certified employees are available to supervise (Fenner et al., 1999). Risk reduction could take the form of heightened supervisory procedures, training, lifesaving certifications, or any policies the organization could institute to minimize the likelihood that a participant becomes injured or dies.

Another important process to reduce potential risks is for an organization to be sanctioned, as discussed previously. It was reported in *Schmidt v. Midwest Sports Events, Inc.* (2010), that the triathlon was not sanctioned. Conversely, the triathlon in which Bernard Rice died during the swimming portion of the Ironman Florida competition was sanctioned. In part, because it was not sanctioned event, a settlement of more than $100,000 resulted in *Schmidt*, whereas the court found in favor of the defendant in *Moore*. As a sanctioned event, the participant is assured that the event is conducted professionally and in accordance to the sponsoring organizations safety rules and regulations.

RISK RETENTION

In a broad sense it is a good idea to incorporate and integrate a combination of risk management strategies within a plan, rather than to rely on just one. In retaining the potential risks, the organization assumes responsibility for foreseeable risks that might occur in the event. For example, when the organization chooses to retain and reduce strategies, the foreseeable risks are usually low and moderate such as the occurrence of sprains and strains, which are not usually life-threatening. Alternatively, when the foreseeable risks are high such as life-threatening incidents, the transfer and avoidance strategies may be used. However, in cases that it is not possible to cancel the event (avoidance), the organization must implement methods to reduce the likelihood of a catastrophic incident. Accordingly, the most suitable method to retain the event is to reduce the foreseeable risks as much as possible and then to transfer some portion of the liability.

To provide a balance it is useful to reflect on the relationship between the specific actions and the overall risk management policy as well as other interrelated actions that might be taken (Miller et al., 2010). For example, a risk manager may fashion a risk management policy in the light of (at least) the following questions:

1. What is the organization's overall policy on risk?
2. Does the implementation of the risk management procedures support the goals and objectives articulated in the organizational policy?
3. Is this practice consistent with all other security and safety measures used in the organization?
4. Does the risk management policy achieve the results the organization desires?
5. Does the risk management policy simply move the risk somewhere else (risk avoidance) or in some other way re-assigning the risk (risk transfer) thereby eliminating accountable actions by personnel in the organization?
6. Are foreseeable threats managed in such a way as to harm any of the value-added potential? For example, are draconian safety measures are employed fans could be driven away or diminish their enjoyment of game?

CONCLUSION

Risk is a common item for those participating in sports. As Judge Cardozo explained, "One who takes part in such a sport accepts the dangers that inhere in it so far as they are obvious and necessary ... The timorous may stay at home" (*Murphy v. Steeplechase Amusement Co.*, 1929, p. 174). Since injuries and tort litigation are a ubiquitous presence, those in sport management must be prepared due to the litigious nature of our society. However, the proper understanding of the concept of risk, the probability of a harmful event occurring, risk assessment and risk communication will assist the sport manager to be better prepared in developing, implementing and supervising a risk management plan. This increased comprehension may decrease the likelihood, severity, and impact of injuries thereby potentially reducing lawsuits. Another consideration for the effective employment of risk management plans, beginning with the concept of risk, risk assessment, and risk communication is to prevent, if at all possible, the stress and anxiety a person has to go through when incidents happens and litigation is brought forth. Not only is there the financial consideration in defending oneself and organization but the cost of sustained stress, distraction, and unflattering publicity that could erode the positive contributions may have provided to the community.

DISCUSSION QUESTIONS

Concept of Risk

1. A sport manager must be aware of a number of different types of risk. Discuss these different types of risk and apply how they may be considered as inherent risks, assumed risks, and foreseeable risks.

Modern Risk Management

1. Discuss how modern risk management differs from the traditional risk management.
2. Discuss the importance of creating a culture of safety in the modern iteration of risk management.

Risk Assessments

1. Using your knowledge of the different types of risk assessments, select a sport organization or facility and conduct a threat, vulnerability and criticality assessment.

Risk Communication

1. The communication of risks is a significant component in a risk management plan. Discuss what areas you would communicate to participants and spectators to increase their knowledge of foreseeable risks.

Risk Management Alternatives

1. Four risk management alternatives were highlighted in this chapter. Since each of these alternatives should not be implemented independently, discuss how you would integrate each of these alternatives to fashion an effective risk management plan.

KEY TERMS

Catastrophic potential
Criticality assessment
Enterprise Risk Management
Ethical risks
Financial risks
Foreseeability
Physical risks
Risks
Risk avoidance

Risk communication
Risk management
Risk reduction
Risk retention
Risk transfer
Theory of the Threshold of Effective Zerohood
Threat assessment
Vulnerability assessment

REFERENCES

Adams, J. (2001). *Risk*. London: Routledge.

Alston, G. (2003). *How safe is safe enough?* Burlington, VT: Ashgate.

American Jurisprudence. (2004). *Negligence* (2nd ed.). Eagan, MN: Thomson-West.

Andersen, T.J., & Schröder, P.W. (2010). *Strategic risk management practice*. Cambridge, MA: Cambridge University Press.

Associated Press. (2009). Kentucky coach pleads not guilty in player's death. FOXnews.com. Retrieved from http://www.foxnews.com/story/0%2C2933%2C483027%2C00.html

Cawood, J.S. (2002). Security. In R.W. Lack (Ed.), *Safety, health, and asset protection: Management essentials* (pp. 553–566). New York: Lewis.

Charnley, G. (1997). *The Presidential/Congressional Commission on Risk Assessment and Risk Management: Framework for environmental health and risk* (Vol. 1). Washington, DC: Diane Publishing.

Covell, V., & Mumpower, J. (1985). Risk analysis and risk management: An historical *perspective. Risk Analysis*, 5(2), 103–120.

Dallam, G.M., Jonas, S., & Miller, T.K. (2005). Medical considerations in triathlon competition: Recommendations for triathlon organisers, competitors and coaches. *Sports Medicine*, 35(2), 143–161.

Decker, R.J. (October, 2001). *Homeland security: A risk management approach can guide preparedness efforts*. Retrieved from http://www.gao.gov/cgi-bin/getrpt?GAO-03-102

Dobbs, D.B. (2000). *The law of torts*. St. Paul, Minn.: West Group.

Durling Jr., R.L., Price, D.E., & Spero, K.K. (2005). Vulnerability and risk assessment using the Homeland-Defense Operational Planning System (HOPS), UCRL-CONF-209028. Paper presented at the International Symposium on Systems and Human Science. Retrieved from https://e-reports-ext.llnl.gov/pdf/315115.pdf

Fenner, P., Leahy, S., Buhk, A., & Dawes, P. (1999). Prevention of drowning: Visual scanning and attention span in lifeguards. *The Journal of Occupational Health and Safety—Australia and New Zealand*, 15(1), 61–66.

Frame, J.D. (2003). *Managing risk in organizations*. San Francisco: Jossey-Bass.

Gillentine, A., Miller, J., & Calhoun, A.S. (2008). Negligent marketing: What every sport marketer should know. *Journal of Contemporary Athletics*, 3(2), 161–172.

Goldstein, B.D. (2005). Advances in risk assessment and communication. *Annual Review of Public Health*, 26, 141–163.

Griggs v. BIC Corporation, 981 F.2d 1429, 1435 (3d Cir. 1992).

Heath, R.L. (1994). Environmental risk communication: Cases and practices along the Texas Gulf coast. In B.R. Burelson (Ed.), *Communication yearbook* 18 (pp. 225–277). Newbury Park, Calif.: Sage.

Hohenenser, C., Kates, R.W., & Slovic, P. (1983). The nature of technological hazard. *Science*, 220, 378–384.

Holmes, O.W. (2000). *The common law*. Howe, M.D. (Ed.)., Cambridge, Mass.: Belknap Press of Harvard University Press. (Original work published 1881.)

International Organization for Standardization. (2009). *ISO: 31000: Risk management principles and guidelines*. Final Draft. Geneva: ISO.

Ip, G. (March, 2004). Terror in Madrid: The aftermath: After September 11, the US learned about its economic resilience; attacks shocked markets, but the overall impact was milder than expected. *Wall Street Journal*, A15.

Jardine, J., Hrudey, S., Shortreed, J., Craig, L., Krewski, D., Furgal, C., & McColl, S. (2003). Risk management frameworks for human health and environmental risks. *Journal of Toxicology and Environmental Health Part B Critical Review*, 6(6), 569–720.

Kaplin, W.A., & Lee, B.A. (1997). *A legal guide for student affairs professionals*. San Francisco, Calif.: Jossey-Bass.

Kates, R.W., & Kaperson, J.X. (1983). Comparative risk analysis of technological hazards: A review. *National Academy of Sciences*, 80(22), 7027–7038.

Klinke, A., & Renn, O. (2002). A new approach to risk evaluation and management: Risk-based, precaution-based, and discourse-based strategies. *Risk Analysis*, 22(6), 1071–1094.

Kolluru, R.V. (1995). Risk assessment and management: A unified approach. In R. Kolluru, S. Bartell, R. Pitblado, & S. Stricoff, (Eds.). *Risk assessment and management handbook for environmental, health, and safety professionals* (pp. 1.3–1.4). New York; McGraw-Hill.

Kristensen, V., Aven, T., & Ford, D. (2006). A new perspective on Renn and Klinke's approach to risk evaluation and management. *Reliability Engineering & Safety System*, 91, 421–432.

Lam, J. (2003). *Enterprise risk management: From incentives to controls*. Hoboken, N.J.: Wiley.

Lee, B., Gordon, P., Moore, J., & Richardson, H. (2008). Simulating the economic impacts of a hypothetical bio-terrorist attack: A sports stadium case. *Journal of Homeland Security and Emergency Management*, 5(1), 1–20.

Lerner, J.S., Gonzalez, R.M., Small, D.A., & Fischhoff, B. (2003). Effects of fear and anger on perceived risks of terrorism: A national field experiment. *Psychological Science*, 14, 144–150.

Lerner, J.S., & Keltner, D. (2000). Beyond valence: Toward a model of emotion-specific influences on judgment and choice. *Cognition & Emotion*, 14, 473–493.

Liesch, P., Steen, J., Knight, G., & Czinkota, M.R. (2006). Problematizing the internationalization decision: Terrorism-induced risk. *Management Decision*, 44(6), 809–823.

Lord, C. (2011). *Fran Crippen: The questions facing FINA*. Retrieved from http://www.swimnew.com/new /view/8382

Luhmann, N. (1990). Technology, environment, and social risk. A system perspective. *Industrial Crisis Quarterly*, 4, 223–231.

Lundgren, R.E. (1994). *Risk communication: A handbook for communicating environmental, safety and health risks*. Columbus, Ohio: Battelle Press.

Lyytinen, K., Mathiassen, L., & Ropponen, J. (1998). Attention shaping software risk—A categorical analysis of four classical risk management approaches. *Information Systems Research*, 9(3), 233–255.

Mallen, S.A. (2001). Touchdown! A victory for injured fans at sporting events? *Missouri Law Review*, 66(2), 487–505.

Maslow, A.A. (1954). *Motivation and personality*. New York: Harper.

Miller, J., & Gillentine, A. (2006). An analysis of risk management policies for tailgating activities at selected NCAA Division I football games. *Journal of the Legal Aspects of Sport*, 16(2), 197–215.

Miller, J., & Rushing, G. (Spring/Summer, 2002). Risk management practices of university physical activity supervisors. *Journal of Legal Aspects of Sport*, 12(2), 117–131.

Miller, J., Veltri, F., & Gillentine, A. (Spring/Summer, 2005). Student perspectives of university intramural sport risk management. *Recreation Sports Journal*, 29(1), 23–33.

Miller, J.J., Wendt, J.T., & Young, P.C. (2010). Fourth Amendment considerations and application of risk management principles for pat-down searches at professional football games. *Journal of Legal Aspects of Sport*, 20(2), 108–134.

Miller, J., Young, S., & Martin, N. (2009). To use or not to use? The status of waivers in intramural sports. *Recreational Sports Journal*, 33(2), 129–138.

Moore v. North America Sports, Inc., 623 F.3d 1325 (11th Cir. 2010).

Montgomery, C.B., & Nahrstadt, B.C. (Spring, 2004). A primer for the entertainment community: Legal and practical issues about venue safety—What you should know. *Virginia Sports & Entertainment Law Journal*, 3, 257–283.

Murphy v. Steeplechase Amusement Co., 250 N.Y. 479; 166 N.E. 173 250 N.Y. 479; 166 N.E. 173 (1929).

Perry, S. (1995). Risk, harm, and responsibility. In D. Owen (Ed.), *Philosophical Foundations of Tort Law*. Oxford, UK: Clarendon Press.

Plough, A., & Krimsky, S. (1987). The emergence of risk communication studies: Social and political context. *Science, Technology, & Human Values*, 12, 4–10.

Prairie, M., & Garfield, T. (2004). *Preventative law for schools and colleges*. San Diego, Calif.: School & College Press.

Reckelhoff-Dangel, C., & Petersen, D. (2007). *Risk communication in action: The risk communication workbook*. United States Environmental Protection Agency, Office of Research and Development. Retrieved from http://www.epa.gov/ord/NRMRL /pubs/625r05003/625r05003.pdf

Rescher, N. (1983). *Risk: A philosophical introduction to the theory of risk evaluation and management*. Washington, DC: University Press of America.

Reynolds, B., & Seeger, M.W. (2005). Crisis and emergency risk communication as an integrative model. *Journal of Health Communication*, 10, 43–55.

Schmidt v. Midwest Sports Events, Inc., Complaint and Jury Demand, No. 2010-CV-1509, 2010 WL 8453207 (Wis.Cir. August 4, 2010).

Slovic, P. (1977). Preference for insuring against probable small losses. *Journal of Risk and Insurance*, 44, 237–258.

Slovic, P. (1987). Perception of risk. *Science*, 236, 280–285.

Slovic, P. (September, 2001). The risk game. *Journal of Hazardous Materials*, 86(1), 17–24.

Slovic, P., & Peters, E. (2006). Risk perception and affect. *Psychological Science*, 15(6), 322–325.

Stahl, B.W., Lichtenstein, Y., & Mangan, A. (2003). The limits of risk management—A social construction approach.

Communications of the International Information Management Association, 3(3), 15–22.

Steele, J. (2004). *Risks and legal theory.* Portland, Ore.: Hart.

Then, S.K., & Loosemore, M. (2006). Terrorism prevention, preparedness, and response in built facilities. *Facilities, 24*(5/6), 157–176.

United States v. Carroll Towing Co., 160 F.2d 482, 1947 U.S. App. LEXIS 2626 (2d Cir. N.Y. 1947).

Wendt, J., & Miller, J. (2010). Managing internship risks: Insurance issues. In J. Miller & T. Seidler (Eds.), *A practical guide to sport management internships* (pp. 157–164). Durham, N.C.: Carolina Academic Press.

Young, P.C., & Tippins, S.C. (2000). *Managing business risk: An organization-wide approach to risk management.* New York: AMACOM.

DISCRIMINATION ISSUES

LEARNING OBJECTIVES

By the end of the chapter, the reader will be able to:

1. Identify potential areas of discrimination in sports
2. Explain the potential use of Title VII to prevent discriminatory practice in sport
3. Discuss gender equity in sport, and the use of both Title VII and Title IX to remedy gender discrimination
4. Identify emerging legal protections for transgendered athletes
5. Give examples of the application of the ADEA in sport
6. Identify the ways in which the ADA has been used to remedy and prevent discrimination based on disability in sport
7. Identify generally religious discrimination issues in sport

RELATED CASES

Case 6.1 Class v. Towson University, 806 F.3d 236 (2015)

Case 6.2 Pambianchi v. Arkansas Tech University, 95 F. Supp. 3d 1101 (2015)

INTRODUCTION

Throughout the history of sports, equality has been a topic of much discussion and debate. Discrimination based on race, gender, religion, age, and disability are at the forefront of the sports world today, as they have been for the last century. The unequal treatment of women, racial and religious minorities, and disabled persons in the sports world has been addressed by the court system and legislation in recent years. As such, this chapter focuses on the laws prohibiting discrimination and those who have challenged or used the laws in an attempt to combat discrimination based on gender, race, disability, religion, or age. Specifically, the chapter will address Title VII of the Civil Rights Act of 1964 (Title VII), Title IX, the Age Discrimination in Employment Act of 1967 (ADEA), the Americans with Disabilities Act (ADA), as well as how various laws, including Title VII, are used to combat religious discrimination.

TITLE VII

Title VII of the Civil Rights Act of 1964 prohibits job discrimination against employees and applicants on the basis of race, color, natural origin, religion, and sex; these five categories are called the *protected classes*. A protected class has been defined as a class of persons with identifiable characteristics who historically have been victimized by discriminatory treatment for certain purposes; these characteristics include race, color, national origin, religion and sex (Cross and Miller, 2008). Specifically, Title VII states:

> It shall be an unlawful employment practice for an employer—
>
> (1) to fail or refuse to hire or to discharge any individual, or otherwise to discriminate against any individual with respect to his compensation, terms, conditions, or privileges of employment, because of such individual's race, color, religion, sex, or national origin; or
>
> (2) to limit, segregate, or classify his employees or applicants for employment in any way which would deprive or tend to deprive any individual of employment opportunities or otherwise adversely affect his status as an employee, because of such individual's race, color, religion, sex, or national origin.
>
> (42 U.S.C.A. § 2000e-2(a)1.)

Each of the protected classes is a broad category that prevent discrimination in many circumstances. Race, while not specifically defined in Title VII, encompasses ancestry, physical characteristics, race linked illness, cultural characteristics (such as grooming practices), perception, or association. Discrimination based on color includes complexion, skin tone or shade or pigmentation. There is certainly overlap between race based and color based discrimination, however, there are exclusive protected classes (EEOC Compliance Manual, 2006). National origin discrimination includes treating applicants or employees unfavorably because they are from a certain part of the world or particular country, because of accent or ethnicity, or because they possess certain ethnic traits. Specifically, equal employment opportunity cannot be denied based on birthplace, ancestry, culture, linguistic characteristics or accents (EEOC Facts, 2015). Title VII does provide a definition for religious discrimination: specifically, religion includes "all aspects of religious observance and practice as well as belief" (42 U.S.C. § 2000e (j)). Further, religion includes "not only traditional, organized religions such as Christianity, Judaism, Islam, Hinduism, and Buddhism, but also religious beliefs that are new, uncommon, not part of a formal church or sect, only subscribed to by a small number of people, or that seem illogical or unreasonable to others" (*Thomas v. Review Bd. of the Indiana Employment*

Sec. Div., 1981). Lastly, sex based discrimination includes treating someone unfavorably because of his or her sex, gender identity (including transgender status) or because sexual orientation (as of July 2015). Further, pregnancy and childbirth are also protected (EEOC Enforcement Guidance, 2015).

Title VII applies to employers who have 15 or more employees, labor unions that operate hiring halls, employment agencies, and state and local governments. It has been referred to as "the single most important piece of legislation that has helped to shape and define employment rights in this country" (Bennett-Alexander and Pincus, 1995). The Civil Rights Act of 1991 amended Title VII in many respects, including giving plaintiffs the right to seek compensatory and punitive damages in intentional discrimination cases.

The *Equal Employment Opportunity Commission* (EEOC) is the federal agency that enforces the federal laws prohibiting discrimination and it also provides oversight of all federal and equal employment opportunity regulations, practices, and policies. An individual alleging discrimination under Title VII must file a claim with the EEOC before he or she can bring a lawsuit against his or her employer. The EEOC can investigate the allegations and make an attempt to settle the case between the parties. If no settlement is reached, the EEOC has the authority to file a lawsuit against the employer on the employee's behalf. If the EEOC decides not to bring a lawsuit or decides not to investigate the case, the individual asserting discrimination may file a lawsuit on his or her own initiative against the employer.

Title VII covers both intentional and unintentional discrimination. Intentional discrimination by an employer is commonly referred to as *disparate treatment discrimination* (*Jackson v. University of New Haven*, 2002). Disparate treatment is the most common form of discrimination claim and can be difficult to prove. A typical disparate treatment case could involve an individual's claim that an employer treated him or her less favorably based on membership in a protected class. For an individual to prove a prima facie case of disparate treatment discrimination as either an applicant or an employee, the plaintiff must show the following: (1) he or she is a member of a protected class, (2) he or she applied for or was qualified for the position, (3) he or she suffered an adverse employment decision, and (4) the position remained open and the employer continued to seek applicants or he or she was treated less favorably than other similarly situated employees (*McDonnell Douglas Corp. v. Green*, 1973). Once the plaintiff has established a prima facie case, he or she has met the initial burden of proof. The burden of going forward then shifts to the employer, who must provide a legitimate, nondiscriminatory reason for the employment decision (Cross and Miller, 2008). If the employer meets this burden, then the plaintiff must prove that this stated reason was merely pretext for discrimination. Proving pretext requires the plaintiff to demonstrate that the defendant's reason for taking the adverse employment action is false or a cover up for the employer's discriminatory intent.

Discrimination can also take the form of *disparate impact discrimination*, which occurs when an employer adopts a practice or policy that seems neutral on its face but is shown to have an adverse impact on a protected class. In these types of cases a plaintiff alleges that an employment practice by the defendant "in fact falls more harshly on one group than another and cannot be justified by business necessity" (*International Brotherhood of Teamsters v. U.S.*, 1977). If a person can prove disparate impact discrimination, then it is not necessary to prove intent (*Griggs v. Duke Power*, 1971). Examples of practices that may be subject to a disparate impact challenge include written tests, height and weight requirements, and subjective procedures, such as interviews. Many disparate impact cases are brought as class actions. Most often, proving this form of discrimination involves statistical proof about the employer's practices. The EEOC has promulgated quantitative guidelines to determine if employee selection and promotion rules have a disproportionate impact. These guidelines state that if the observed promotion or selection rate for any group is less than four fifths of the rate for the group with the highest rate, then disproportionate impact will be assumed (29 C.F.R. § 1607.4(d)).

Even if a plaintiff successfully proves his or her burden in a Title VII claim, an employer can assert several defenses to an employment discrimination action. The first defense for the employer is to assert that discrimination did not take place or that the plaintiff has failed to meet the burden of proof. The employer can also attempt to justify discrimination on the basis of business necessity, a *bona fide occupational qualification* (BFOQ), or a seniority system.

The business necessity defense can be a viable defense to disparate impact discrimination if the employer can show that the discriminatory practice is "job-related" (*Griggs v. Duke Power*, 1971). Additionally, sex, national origin, or religious discrimination may be permissible if the employer can show that the discrimination was based on a BFOQ. A BFOQ is "a qualification that is reasonably necessary to the normal operation or essence of an employer's businesses" (*Frank v. United Airlines, Inc.*, 2000) However, race and color based discrimination can never be considered a BFOQ. The BFOQ clause has been narrowly construed by courts, and the burden rests on the employer in asserting such a defense (*Grant v. General Motors*, 1990). An employer may also defend a discrimination case on the basis of a fair seniority system. Differences in employment conditions that result from such a system are permissible as long as there is no intent to discriminate.

Specific applications of Title VII to sport can be found for each of the five protected classes; however, only race and sex will be discussed below. Religious discrimination will be discussed in a later section and include both Title VII and other legal doctrines.

Discrimination Based on Race

Allegations of racial discrimination in employment settings are common, and sport industry employers are not an exception. Plaintiffs can seek to remedy racial discrimination using a myriad of different legal theories, such as the Fourteenth Amendment of the U.S. Constitution, the Civil Rights Act of 1866 (42 U.S.C. § 1981), the Civil Rights Act of 1871 (42 U.S.C. § 1983), state statutes and constitutions, and local legislation. Focus in this section will be given to Title VII (as amended by the Civil Rights Act of 1991 (42 U.S.C. § 2000e)).

In *Moran v. Selig* (2006), a group of Caucasian and Latino ballplayers sued Major League Baseball (MLB), claiming racial discrimination under Title VII. At issue in the case was MLB's exclusion of these players from medical and supplemental income plans devised for former Negro League players. Many African-American ballplayers played in the Negro Leagues before the color barrier in baseball was broken by Jackie Robinson. In 1993, MLB created a plan that provided medical coverage to former Negro League players. In 1997, it adopted a supplemental income plan that provided an annual payment of $10,000 to eligible players (Gould, 2011). Individuals who had played in the Negro Leagues prior to 1948, were eligible for such payments. These two plans are referred to collectively as the "Negro League Plans." To successfully prove a Title VII claim for race based discrimination, the plaintiffs needed to demonstrate membership in a protected class, being qualified for their jobs, being subject to an adverse employment decision or action, and receiving less favorable treatment than similarly situated employees outside the protected class. The court held that the plaintiffs satisfied the first two criteria, but that not being eligible for the Negro League Plans was not an adverse employment decision, and that the plaintiffs were not similarly situated to the employees with whom the plaintiffs chose to equate themselves because the plaintiffs never played in the Negro Leagues.

More recently, Louisiana State University was sued by its former head women's tennis coach, Anthony Minnis, an African-American. The plaintiff, who was the first African-American coach hired by LSU in any sport, alleged that his firing in 2012 (after 21 years at the university) was due in part to racial harassment. Specifically, Minnis alleged that he was subject to race based harassment and discrimination throughout his long tenure as head coach. Further, Minnis alleged *disparate compensation*, given that his replacement, a Caucasian female with no prior collegiate head coaching experience was given a contract with an annual salary $25,000 more than what Minnis had received (*Minnis v. Board of Supervisors*, 2014).

After analyzing his Title VII discriminatory discharge and disparate compensation claims, the court found in favor of LSU. With regard to the discriminatory discharge claim, Minnis was required to prove the four part plaintiff's burden discussed earlier. There was no question that Minnis was a member of a protected class, qualified for the position, and subject to an adverse employment action. However, the court found that Minnis failed to demonstrate that he was treated less favorably than other similarly situated employees. Minnis was compared to the head men's tennis coach, Jeff Brown, a white male, and it was determined that Brown and Minnis were treated differently because Brown had a superior win-loss record. Further, the court held that even if Minnis had established his case, the claim still would have failed because he was unable to rebut the non-discriminatory reasons that LSU advanced for the terminating Minnis: (1) his failure to meet established goals, (2) his losing record, and (3) morale issues (*Minnis v. Board of Supervisors*, 2014).

Minnis also failed on the disparate compensation claim. To succeed, Minnis needed to show that his circumstances were nearly identical to those of a better paid employee who was not a member of the protected class (*Taylor v. United Parcel Service, Inc.*, 2008). When analyzing whether Minnis was paid less than white employees for substantially the same job responsibilities, the court found that none of the other head coaches, including Minnis's replacement, were proper comparisons, and that Minnis was unable to rebut LSU's legitimate, non-discriminatory reasons for the disparity in pay. Specifically, LSU asserted that: (1) Minnis's competitive record did not justify merit increases, (2) Minnis's salary was set by comparing his performance to that of SEC women's tennis coaches, and (3) Minnis's salary was calculated based on the market for the position at the time of hiring. (*Minnis v. Board of Supervisors*, 2014).

Discrimination Based on Sex

Title VII also prohibits discrimination based on sex, which as noted includes sexual orientation (as of July 2015), gender identity, pregnancy, and childbirth. To establish a prima facie case of sex discrimination under Title VII, a plaintiff must prove that he or she (1) was a member of a protected class; (2) was qualified for the position; (3) was discharged or otherwise subjected to an adverse employment action; and (4) others (similarly situated but not of the protected class) were treated more favorably (*Peirick v. Indiana University-Purdue University Indianapolis Athletics Dept.*, 2005).

In *Perdue v. City University of New York* (1998) Molly Perdue, the former women's basketball coach and women's sports administrator at Brooklyn College, filed a Title VII intentional sex discrimination claim against Brooklyn College, in addition to claims filed under the Equal Pay Act (29 U.S.C. § 206(d)) and Title IX of the Education Amendments of 1972 (20 U.S.C. § 1681 et seq.). Perdue alleged that she was subject to a lesser salary, worse employment conditions, and demeaning job responsibilities, in contrast to her male coach counterparts. Specifically, as evidence of sex discrimination, Perdue cited that she received less than half the average salary of her two male counterparts (although she did work that was comparable), had to clean the gym for her games, had to launder her team uniforms, had a significantly smaller office, had worse game times and practice times, had fewer assistant coaches who worked only part-time as opposed to the full-time assistant coaches for the men's team, and had no team locker room, and an overall smaller budget. The federal jury returned a verdict and damage award in favor of Perdue, which was upheld by appellate courts.

There can also be cases of *reverse sex discrimination* as well. For instance, in *Medcalf v. Trustees of University of Pennsylvania* (2003), a male assistant crew coach alleged he had been the subject of reverse discrimination when the university would not allow him to apply to be the head coach of the women's crew team. A federal jury returned a verdict in his favor, and a federal appellate court affirmed the verdict when the University of Pennsylvania appealed.

In a more recent reverse discrimination case, *Mollaghan v. Varnell* (2012), two male soccer coaches sued the University of Southern Mississippi, senior somen's administrator Sonya Varnell and athletic director Richard Giannini, alleging sex discrimination, in addition to other claims (a third coach also filed a sexual harassment claim). Specifically, the coaches claimed that the administrators stated they preferred women to coach women's teams, and that the administrators had engaged in conduct that undermined the coaches' ability to coach the women's team, including taking over scholarship decisions and traveling with the team, with the intent to diminish the coaches' authority, giving cause for replacement with female coaches. After over ten years of trials and subsequent appeals, the Mississippi Supreme Court held in favor of the university on all claims, including the gender discrimination claim.

Specifically, the court reasoned that there was insufficient evidence to demonstrate that either coach was discharged based on gender. Neither coach had actually been discharged (one failed to have his contract renewed and one accepted another position before his contract expired) and neither was replaced with a female coach.

Sexual Harassment

Title VII also protects employees against sexual harassment in the workplace. *Sexual harassment* consists of unwelcomed sexual advances, requests for sexual favors, and other physical and verbal conduct of a sexual nature when the conduct affects an individual's employment, unreasonably interferes with an individual's work performance, or creates an intimidating, hostile, or offensive work environment (EEOC Enforcement Guidance, 1990). There are two types of sexual harassment: *quid pro quo* harassment, and *hostile work environment* sexual harassment. When a tangible negative employment action results from a refusal to submit to a supervisor's sexual demands, quid pro quo sexual harassment exists. Where, however, a claim targets a supervisor's 'severe and pervasive' sexually demeaning behavior rather than a fulfilled threat, the claim is properly characterized as a hostile work environment sexual harassment (*Alwine v. Buzas*, 2004).

For a plaintiff to establish a claim for quid pro quo sexual harassment, he or she must prove that (1) the employee belongs to a protected group, (2) the employee was subject to unwelcome sexual harassment, (3) the harassment complained of was based on sex, (4) the employee's reaction to the harassment complained of affected a tangible employment action, and (5) the harasser was the employee's supervisor (*Burlington Industries, Inc. v. Ellerth*, 1998).

To establish a claim for hostile work environment sexual harassment, the plaintiff must prove that (1) the employee was a member of a protected group, (2) the employee was subject to unwelcome harassment that was sufficiently severe or pervasive to create a hostile work environment, (3) the harassment complained of was based on the employee's sex, (4) the harassment resulted in a tangible employment action, and (5) the harasser was the employee's supervisor, although a hostile environment can arise from someone other than the employee's supervisor (*Jew v. University of Iowa*, 1990). Although the phrase "hostile work environment" is not specifically mentioned in Title VII, a viable cause of action still exists under the statute (*Clarke v. Bank of Commerce*, 2007).

There have been many sexual harassment lawsuits involving athletes, coaches, school administrators, and others who are involved in sport or recreation; several of the cases already discussed in this chapter also included sexual harassment claims. Most prominent is *Faragher v. City of Boca Raton* (1998), in which a city lifeguard filed a Title VII sexual harassment claim after resigning from her job as a lifeguard, a position she held for five years. Beth Ann Faragher claimed that throughout her employment, two of her immediate supervisors subjected her to sexual remarks, uninvited offensive touching, and vulgar speech, creating a sexually hostile work environment. The city did have a sexual harassment policy, however it was never discussed with the lifeguards. Further, Faragher never reported any of the alleged conduct to managers above her supervisors. The district court held that the criteria for hostile work environment (as listed above) were met; specifically, they found the supervisors conduct sufficiently severe or pervasive to create a hostile work environment. Also, the court held that because the supervisors were acting within the scope of their job responsibility when they created the hostile work environment, the city of Boca Raton was liable under the theory of *respondeat superior*. On appeal, the 11th Circuit Court affirmed the hostile work environment, but reversed the ruling regarding liability to the city. The United States Supreme Court granted certiorari and reinstated the ruling of the district

court finding that a hostile work environment did exist, and that because the city failed to disseminate its sexual harassment policy or keep track of supervisor conduct, the city was in fact liable. This case is important not only for the precedent regarding hostile work environment sexual harassment claims under Title VII, but also for the precedent regarding vicarious liability of the employer for supervisor misconduct.

TITLE IX

Historically, women have been discriminated against in sports and have not been provided with the same opportunities for participation as men. A vast disparity has existed between men's and women's sports in the provision of participation opportunities, training facilities, adequate equipment, coaching staff, trainers, playing fields, recruitment for the sport, and adequate funding. Opportunities for girls at the interscholastic level were curtailed because of an overall attitude that girls could not play or had no desire to participate in sports at the same competitive level as boys. Female amateur athletes have also experienced much discrimination and harassment, which has limited their opportunities in athletics over a long period of time. Fortunately, this has begun to change. Girls and women are now participating in sports at the interscholastic and intercollegiate levels in record numbers, which are still increasing. More females are now participating in what were once all-male sports. Girls now participate on boys' high school football, baseball, and even wrestling teams. The gap in opportunities between boys and girls has begun to shrink because of laws such as Title IX, as well as attitude changes in our society about the role of girls and women and their ability to participate and compete in the sports world. Further, more women are coaching at the collegiate level, and some strides are being made by women in athletic administration as well. Many of the archaic notions about women participating in sports have been discarded as women achieve greatness and notoriety in both amateur and professional sports.

History and Overview of Title IX

Prior to 1970 there had been very few legal challenges addressing sex discrimination in athletics. In the early 1970s, women began using the Fourteenth Amendment for sex discrimination claims. But in 1972, Title IX was passed, federal legislation that gave women the statutory remedy needed to address problems dealing with sex discrimination; its purpose was to eliminate discrimination in federally funded activities. The statute states in part, "No person in the United States shall, on the basis of sex, be excluded from participation in, be denied the benefits of, or be subjected to discrimination under any education program or activity receiving Federal financial assistance" (20 U.S.C. § 1681 (a)). While Title IX was not originally intended specifically as a remedy for gender inequity in athletics, the passage and implementation of Title IX has done more to advance women's rights in sports than any other piece of legislation.

The Department of Health, Education, and Welfare (HEW) was given the task of implementing Title IX. Approximately three years after Title IX was passed, regulatory guidance became effective (45 C.F.R. Part 86). The Office of Civil Rights (OCR) under the Department of Education is responsible for enforcing Title IX. The OCR's job is to ensure that universities that receive federal funds are in compliance with the requirements of Title IX. However, determining the scope of the federal fund requirement presented challenges in the early history of the legislation. *Grove City College v. Bell* (1984), was a landmark case in which the court ruled that only programs that received *direct* financial assistance were subject to Title IX. However, the holding of *Grove City* was not the intent of Congress when it passed Title IX, so the Civil Rights Restoration Act of 1987 was subsequently passed, which further clarified the applicability of Title IX to athletes. Based on the broader interpretation of federal funding included in the Civil Rights Restoration Act, almost all colleges, universities, secondary, and elementary school districts are covered under Title IX. The Civil Rights Restoration Act further supported congressional intent to protect against sex discrimination in institutions receiving federal funds by indicating that a "program" or "activity" includes the entire range of programs in a federally funded institution, not just specifically funded programs as set forth in *Grove City College*.

The OCR also has a compliance review program for selected recipients. During the review process the OCR is able to identify and resolve sex discrimination issues that may not have been addressed through the compliance process. Many universities and colleges have established guidelines for the development of a Title IX action plan, and many will provide their gender equity plan if requested. Universities and colleges have committees that work directly with athletes in addressing issues of gender equity. Some even will invite OCR representatives or Title IX consultants to visit the campus and assist them in the evaluation and development of policies intended to ensure gender equity.

Compliance with Title IX is further broken down into three areas: effective accommodation (participation opportunities), financial assistance, and equality in other program areas. Title IX plaintiffs have filed claims against university, interscholastic, and recreational athletic programs in all three areas; as such, each will be discussed.

Effective Accommodation

Equal provision of participation opportunities, or *effective accommodation*, is most often evaluated using a three-prong test established in 1979 by the Department of Civil Rights. The test was later clarified in 1996 and again in 2005. A school can comply with Title IX by meeting the requirements of any one of the three prongs (*Pederson v. La. State University*, 2000). Specifically, the test indicates that a school will be compliant:

1. Where intercollegiate level participation opportunities for male and female students are provided in numbers substantially proportionate to their respective enrollment (the *substantial proportionality* prong); or
2. Where the members of one sex have been and are underrepresented among intercollegiate athletics, where the institution can show a *history and continuing practice* of program expansion which is demonstrably responsive to the developing interest and abilities of the members of that sex (the history of continuing expansion prong); or
3. Where the members of one sex are underrepresented among intercollegiate athletes, and the institution cannot show a continuing practice of program expansion such as cited above, where it can be demonstrated that the interests and abilities of the members of the sex have been fully and effectively accommodated by the present program (the full and effective accommodation prong).

Each of the prongs is intended to offer a way for an educational institution (or other recipient of federal funds) to demonstrate that they are providing playing opportunities in an equitable manner. The first prong, substantial proportionality, is widely sought after because if an institution is substantially proportionate, it is also Title IX compliant. In simple terms, if an institution has an overall enrollment of 48% females and 52% males, the athletic participation opportunities must be substantially proportionate to those percentages. However, given the vast demographic diversity of educational institutions, substantial proportionality is not possible in many educational institutions; thus, history and continuing expansion or effective accommodation can also be used by institutions to demonstrate Title IX compliance. History and continuing expansion evaluates whether an institution has continuously expanded participation opportunities (or has plans to do so) to meet the interest and abilities of the underrepresented sex (most often women). Full and effective accommodation considers whether participation opportunities offered are meeting the full needs of all interested participants at an institution.

The necessity of institutions to be compliant regarding effective accommodation has had a major effect on colleges and universities. Many have made substantial changes within their athletic programs to ensure compliance with this provision of Title IX. In 2006, for example, James Madison University (JMU) voted to dismantle ten athletic teams to achieve substantial proportionality. Seven men's varsity teams (outdoor and indoor track, cross country, archery, gymnastics, swimming, and wrestling) and three women's varsity teams (archery, fencing, and gymnastics) were discontinued to comply with Title IX. JMU had been out of compliance with federal law because women made up 61% of enrolled students, whereas female athletic participation was only 50%. With the new plan in place, female athletic participation was predicted to increase to 61% (JMU Enacts Proportionality Plan, 2006).

James Madison University made the staggering cuts to its athletic program in 2006 to avoid liability for Title IX non-compliance. Given that as early as ten years prior, universities were being found liable for Title IX violations, JMU made what it thought was a prudent decision. Specifically, *Cohen v. Brown University* (1996), Title IX was used successfully by the plaintiffs to obtain remedy for gender inequity.

Cohen v. Brown (1996) may be the most significant case ever decided under Title IX. After the Ivy League university announced that it was going to eliminate two women's sports, but stated that the teams could still qualify as unfunded club sports, the university was sued for failure to comply with Title IX's requirement of effective accommodation. The court analyzed all three prongs of the effective accommodation test, and found that under the first prong, Brown was not substantially proportionate. The Brown student body was 52% male and 47% female, however 63% of its student-athletes were male. For the second prong analysis, the court found that because Brown had not added a women's sport team since 1977 (14 years prior to the lawsuit filing), there could be no history or continuing practice of effective accommodation. Lastly, the court also found Brown did not fully and effectively accommodate the interests of the underrepresented sex because they were cutting women's sports teams. Given that none of the three prongs could be used to demonstrate Title IX compliance, the district court held that Brown was in violation of Title IX, and ordered the women's teams restored, with funding. On appeal, The Court of Appeals for the First Circuit ruled against Brown again, stating that the university was not in compliance with Title IX and that a university must fully and effectively accommodate the interests of women students to ensure Title IX compliance.

As a result of litigation and feared litigation, many athletic administrators began to cut men's sports teams as a way to become compliant (using the substantial proportionality prong). As such, men began to file lawsuits under Title IX, citing a form of reverse discrimination under the law. In *Kelly v. Board of Trustees of the University of Illinois* (1994), the court ruled that the university did not violate Title IX when it eliminated the men's swimming team and not the women's. The university cited budget constraints along with the need for compliance with Title IX and the gender equity policy of the Big Ten Conference. The court found that Illinois could do away with men's programs

without violating Title IX because men's interests are permanently met when substantial proportionalities exist. Men's participation in athletics at the University of Illinois was at 76.6%, which was more than substantially proportional to their enrollment (56%).

After numerous cases like *Kelly v. Board of Trustees of the University of Illinois* (1994), the fairness of having to cut certain sports programs to comply with Title IX came under debate (Klinker, 2003). In a July 2003 memo, Assistant Secretary of Civil Rights Gerald Reynolds wrote regarding the compliance of intercollegiate athletics with Title IX, "OCR hereby clarifies that nothing in Title IX requires the cutting or reduction of teams in order to demonstrate compliance with Title IX, and that the elimination of teams is a disfavored practice." However, courts continued to hold that eliminating men's sports to achieve substantial proportionality was a legally permissible practice under Title IX.

One other distinction that has been made in Title IX case law regarding participation is that of contact and non-contact sports. Women will usually be allowed to participate on men's teams if the sport is deemed a non-contact sport and no women's team is available. If there is no team for one sex in a particular sport, and the excluded sex has had a history of limited opportunity, then the excluded sex must be allowed to try out for the existing team. If women have the opportunity to compete, then courts are usually less willing to allow them to participate on men's teams. The HEW regulations under Title IX allow athletic departments that receive federal funding to establish separate teams if the sport is deemed a contact sport or is based on competitive skill (45 C.F.R. § 86.41(b)).

In *Mercer v. Duke University* (1999), Heather Mercer, a placekicker, sued the university under Title IX for discriminating against her on the basis of sex when denying her an equal opportunity to earn a roster spot on the Duke football team. Prior to enrolling at Duke, Mercer was an all-state high school kicker. After arriving at Duke in the fall of 1994, Mercer tried out for the Duke Football team as a walk-on kicker. Although Mercer did not initially make the team, she did serve as a manager during the 1994 season. She also regularly attended fall practices and participated in conditioning drills the following spring.

In April 1995, Mercer was selected to participate in an intra-squad scrimmage by team seniors. In that game, Mercer kicked the winning 28-yard field goal. Shortly after the game, Duke Football coaches told both the news media and Mercer that she had made the team. Mercer did not play in any games during the 1995 season, however, she again attended practices in the fall and spring. Further, Mercer was officially listed on the team roster filed with the National Collegiate Athletic Association (NCAA).

Mercer alleged that during the latter period of her tenure "on the team," she was the subject of discriminatory treatment. Specifically, she claimed that the coach "did not permit her to attend summer camp, refused to allow her to dress for games or sit on the sidelines during games, and gave her fewer opportunities to participate in practices than other walk-on kickers" (p. 2). In addition, Mercer claimed that the coach made many offensive comments to her, asking why she "did not prefer to participate in beauty pageants rather than football, and suggesting that she sit in the stands with her boyfriend rather than on the sidelines" (p. 2).

Just prior to the start of the 1996 season, the coach informed Mercer that he was dropping her from the team. Mercer alleged that this decision was based on of her sex because the coach "allowed other, less qualified walk-on kickers to remain on the team" (p. 3). When Mercer attempted to participate in spring drills, she was asked to leave because the drills were only for members of the team.

In the lawsuit, the university argued that a correct reading and interpretation of Title IX does not include coverage of contact sports, and that because football is a contact sport, the school wasn't required to allow the plaintiff to try out for the team. However, the court found that once the plaintiff was allowed to try out and actually made a member of the team (per the coaches own admission), she should not have been discriminated against on the basis of sex. The trial court awarded her $1 in compensatory damages and $2 million in punitive damages, finding that Duke had engaged in intentional discrimination. However, the punitive damages award was vacated by the Fourth Circuit Court of Appeals. Mercer was awarded $1 in compensatory damages, and on subsequent appeal, the plaintiff was awarded $349,243 in attorneys' fees.

Financial Assistance and Other Benefits

Aside from equality regarding participation opportunities, Title IX also requires equitable allocation of financial assistance; male and female student-athletes must receive athletics scholarship dollars proportional to their participation. Further, equal treatment of male and female student-athletes is necessary regarding the provision of (a) equipment and supplies; (b) scheduling of games and practice times; (c) travel and daily allowance/per diem; (d) access to tutoring; (e) coaching; (f) locker rooms, practice and competitive facilities; (g) medical and training facilities and services; (h) housing and dining facilities and services; (i) publicity and promotions; (j) support services; and (k) recruitment of student-athletes (20 U.S.C. § 106.41 (c)). The Equity Athletics Disclosure Act (EADA), passed in 1994, requires public disclosure of financial records relating to athletic expenditures by universities and colleges. The Department of Education is required to report to Congress on gender equity in college athletics; it relies on information received through the EADA in making that report. The university or college must list all participants in athletics, the operating expenses for men's and women's programs, the number of scholarships awarded, the revenue received, coaches' salaries, and recruiting expenses. This statute allows the NCAA and the public to closely monitor gender equity issues and graduation rates for student athletes.

Although the EADA provides for reporting and monitoring of expenditures, alleged violations of Title IX still exist. Specifically, there have been numerous cases alleging that the distribution of benefits and services amongst athletic teams violates Title IX. In *Daniels v. School Bd. of Brevard County, Fla.* (1997), disparity existed between the high school programs for girls' softball and boys' baseball. Specifically, the female plaintiffs claimed that the boys baseball field had an electronic scoreboard while the girls softball field had no scoreboard at all; the boys had a batting cage while the girls did not; the bleachers at the girls softball field were in worse condition and allowed for fewer spectators than those at the baseball field; the baseball team had promotional signage on the school grounds, while the softball team did not; there were no available restrooms at the softball field, while restrooms were part of the baseball facility; concessions and a press box were available at the baseball field while the softball field contained neither amenity; maintenance of the baseball field was more routine, leaving the baseball field in better condition that the softball field; and the baseball field was lighted for nighttime play while the softball field was not. The initial court found that the school board was in violation of Title IX, and that the inequities posed a risk that the plaintiffs would suffer an irreparable threat of injury from the inequalities, namely the daily perception within the student body, faculty and community that girls are not as important as boys. The court afforded the school board an opportunity to submit a remedial plan to the court; however, the plan proposed that to achieve equity, the boys baseball facility would be modified or restricted.

The school board contended that funding did not exist to improve the girls softball facility, thus the solution was to dismantle the boys baseball field. The court made clear that this approach was not within the spirit of the law, and ordered the school board to make several improvements to the girls' softball field, including the installation of lighting, promotional signage and restrooms.

The *Daniels* case presents one of the most glaring examples of unequal provision of benefits. While not all cases present such clear violations of Title IX, many cases have been filed challenging the equitable provision of access and services across all categories listed above. A reading of this case law indicates that Title IX requires male and female athletes to receive equitable benefits; however, male and female athletes do not need to receive the exact same benefits. Title IX has been interpreted by the courts to allow for variations in the benefits based on legitimate and justifiable discrepancies for non-gender related differences in sports, such as the differing costs of equipment or event management expenditures (NCAA Title IX, 2015).

Finally, discussion of a lawsuit filed against Quinnipiac University in 2009, and settled in 2013, demonstrates the overall breadth of issues that are covered by Title IX, and the changes this legislation is capable of producing. Specifically, in 2009, five volleyball players filed a lawsuit against Quinnipiac University after the school announced its intent to eliminate the women's volleyball team. The lawsuit claimed that Quinnipiac violated Title IX with regard to participation opportunities and equitable provision of benefit. Between 2010 and 2013, the plaintiff athletes won multiple decisions against the school in both the United States District Court of Connecticut and the United States Court of Appeals in the Second Circuit. After subsequent appeals, the two sides settled the case, and Quinnipiac agreed to make many sweeping changes regarding both participation opportunities and provision of benefits. Regarding participation opportunities, Quinnipiac agreed to maintain all women's sports teams including volleyball, and continue its expansion by offering women's rugby, golf, and an enlarged track program. Regarding benefits, Quinnipiac agreed to increase scholarship allocation to female teams, spend $5 million dollars renovating and improving facilities for female teams, spend $450,000 on coaching salary increases, and provide greater access to academic support staff and training/conditioning staff, and allocate an additional $175,000 per year for three years to general improvements of the women's sport program (Court Approves Settlement, 2013).

TRANSGENDER DISCRIMINATION

An emerging area in sport law is transgender equality. Athletic participation by transgendered athletes is rising, due in part to the increasing visibility of transgendered athletes in multiple sports. Specifically, successful athletes Renee Richards (tennis), Jaiyah Saelua (soccer), Mianne Bagger (golf), and Kye Allums (basketball) are all transgendered (Mahoney, Dodds, & Polasek, 2015). As discussed, discrimination against transgendered individuals in the employment setting is actionable under Title VII. However, there are additional legal standards emerging at the state level aimed to protect transgendered individuals from discrimination (beyond the employee-employer relationship).

In 2013, California passed the School Success and Opportunity Act (California Education Code § 220). The law was intended to allow students to "remain consistent with their gender choice throughout the school day" including allowing transgendered students to participate on sports teams based on their gender identities (Mahoney et al., 2015). Specifically, the law states that students should be allowed to participate in sex-segregated activities, such as restroom use and athletic teams, based on their gender identity and not the gender listed on their school record (California Education Code, § 221.5). Additionally, as of 2014, high school athletic associations in several states have rules that allow students to participate on athletic teams based on gender identity (California, Colorado, Connecticut, Florida, Maryland, Massachusetts, Minnesota, Nevada, New Hampshire, Rhode Island, South Dakota, Vermont, , and Wyoming). While these athletic association policies are certainly not law, they do demonstrate a transition toward inclusion of transgendered athletes.

AGE DISCRIMINATION IN EMPLOYMENT ACT (ADEA)

The Age Discrimination in Employment Act (ADEA) of 1967 protects individuals who are 40 years of age or older from employment discrimination based on age. The ADEA's protections apply to both employees and job applicants. Under the ADEA, it is unlawful to discriminate against a person because of his or her age with respect to any term, condition, or privilege of employment, including hiring, firing, promotion, layoff, compensation, benefits, job assignments, and training.

The courts have interpreted the ADEA to permit employers to favor older workers based on age, even when doing so adversely affects a younger worker who is 40 or older. The ADEA applies to employers with 20 or more employees, including state and local governments, employment agencies, labor organizations, as well as the federal government. In order to establish a prima facie case of age discrimination, a plaintiff must prove the following four elements: (1) he or she suffered an adverse employment decision; (2) he or she was at least 40 years old at that time; (3) he or she was performing his or her job duties, or capable of performing job duties, at a level that met the employer's legitimate expectations; and (4) he or she was treated more harshly than other similarly situated younger employees (*Alba v. Merrill Lynch and Co.*, 2006). Similar to Title VII, employers may assert defenses such as business necessity or BFOQ to the lawsuit and demonstrate that age was not a determining factor in any adverse employment decision made by the employer.

In *Moore v. University of Notre Dame* (1998), the court was called on to determine the damages that should be awarded to the plaintiff under the ADEA after a jury found in favor of the plaintiff on his claim for age discrimination. Joe Moore was the offensive line coach at the University of Notre Dame from 1988 to 1996. In December of 1996, Moore was terminated; he claimed that he was fired because he was "too old." By contrast, Notre Dame claimed that Moore had intimidated, abused, and made offensive remarks to players. In his lawsuit, Moore alleged that the reasons given for his firing were pretext for discrimination and that, in fact, he was discriminated against due to his age. Based on evidence that the head coach considered Moore's age to be a strong factor in the firing decision, a jury agreed with Moore and awarded him back pay in the amount of $42,935.28. Additionally, the jury determined that Notre Dame's violation of ADEA was willful; thus, Moore was awarded additional liquidated damages in the amount of $42,935.28.

By contrast, the plaintiff in *Raineri v. Highland Falls-Fort Montgomery School District* (2002) did not win his ADEA claim. Raineri was the high school boys varsity basketball coach from 1996-2000; when he was terminated, the school hired a coach ten years younger than him (Raineri was 53, the new coach was 43) with less coaching experience. The court granted summary judgment for the school district, citing lack of evidence of any age discrimination. Although the replacement employee was significantly younger, age was not found to be a factor in the employment decision; rather, Raineri was fired for reasons related to team success.

AMERICANS WITH DISABILITIES ACT (ADA)

The Americans with Disabilities Act (ADA) of 1990 was passed into law to prohibit discrimination against individuals with a disability. The precursor to the ADA was the Rehabilitation Act of 1973, which prohibited discrimination because of disability by federal government contractors and by those who receive federal financial assistance. Many disabled athletes asserted Section 504 of the Rehabilitation Act to establish their right to participate in collegiate athletics. However, the ADA is more extensive than the Rehabilitation Act. According to the ADA, "individuals with disabilities continually encounter various forms of discrimination, including outright intentional exclusion, the discriminatory effects of architectural, transportation, and communication barriers, overprotective rules and policies, failure to make modifications to existing facilities and practices, exclusionary qualification standards and criteria, segregation, and relegation to lesser services, programs, activities, benefits, jobs, or other opportunities" (42 U.S.C. § 12101(a)(5)). The ADA is designed to remedy that situation.

The ADA is divided into four major sections: Title I–Employment, Title II–Public Services, Title III–Public Accommodations and Services by Private Entities, and Title IV–Telecommunications and Common Carriers; Title I and Title III are the most commonly applied to sport and recreation. Each section contains its own specific definitions and applications, however, the definition of a disabled individual remains constant. Specifically, the ADA's definition of disability reads, in part, "disability means, with respect to an individual . . . (a) a physical or mental impairment that substantially limits one or more of the major life activities of such individual; (b) a record of such an impairment; or (c) being regarded as having such an impairment" (42 U.S.C. § 12103 (3)). Disabilities have been defined under the ADA to include blindness, alcoholism, morbid obesity, muscular dystrophy, and being HIV positive.

In 2008, the ADA was amended to further clarify who is covered by the law's protections. The "ADA Amendments Act of 2008" revises the definition of "disability" to more broadly encompass impairments that substantially limit a major life activity. The amended language also states that mitigating measures, including assistive devices, auxiliary aids, accommodations, medical therapies and supplies (other than eyeglasses and contact lenses) have no bearing in determining whether a disability qualifies under the law. Changes also clarify coverage of impairments that are episodic or in remission that substantially limit a major life activity when active, such as epilepsy or post-traumatic stress disorder.

As noted, Title I covers discrimination in an employment setting. The term employer means "a person engaged in an industry affecting commerce who has 15 or more employees for each working day in each of 20 or more calendar weeks in the current or preceding year" (42 U.S.C. § 12111(5)(a)). Further, the ADA defines a "*qualified individual with a disability*" as an individual with a disability who, with or without reasonable accommodations, can perform the essential functions of the employment that such individual holds or desires (42 U.S.C. § 12131(2)). An employer is not required to hire a disabled person who is not capable of performing the duties of the job; however, the ADA does require the employer to make a *reasonable accommodation* for the disabled individual. According to the ADA, a reasonable accommodation may include (but not be limited to) making existing facilities accessible, job restructuring, reassignment, modified work schedules, acquisition of assistive devices, or appropriate modification of training materials or policies (42 U.S.C. § 12111(9)). An employer is not required to make an accommodation for an individual if that accommodation would impose undue hardship on the operation of the employer's business. An undue hardship is defined as an action requiring significant difficulty or expense when considered in light of the nature and cost of the accommodation and the overall financial resources of the employer (42 U.S.C. § 12111(10)(a)).

Title III of the ADA requires owners and operators of *places of public accommodation* to allow disabled individuals to participate equally in the goods, services, and accommodations provided by the establishment. Specifically, disabled individuals must have "full and equal enjoyment of the goods, services, facilities, privileges, advantages or accommodations of any place of public accommodation by any person who owns, leases or operates a place of public accommodation" (42 U.S.C. § 12182 (a)). Title III specifically includes 12 categories of places of public accommodation; including over five million private establishments, such as restaurants, hotels, convention centers, retail stores, hospitals, museums, parks, zoos, private schools, health spas, gymnasiums, golf courses, and bowling alleys (to name a few). However, entities controlled by religious organizations, including places of worship, are not covered; nor are private clubs, except to the extent that the facilities of the private club are made available to customers or patrons as of a place of public accommodation (Title III Highlights, n.d.). Owners and operators of public accommodations are required under Title III to make reasonable accommodations for disabled patrons, assuming those accommodations don't fundamentally alter the nature of the goods or service provided; as with Title I, owner operators of public accommodations must make reasonable modifications in their policies to enable this goal to be achieved.

In *Anderson v. Little League Baseball, Inc.* (1992), a wheelchair-bound Little League coach, Lawrence Anderson, wanted to continue as an on-field base coach, a position he successfully held for three years. However, just prior to the 1991 post-season, Little League adopted a policy banning wheelchair-bound individuals from coaching from anywhere other than the dugout. Specifically, Little League argued that this policy was necessary to ensure the health and safety of the players. Anderson, however, contended that the policy was created specifically to keep him from coaching, and that the policy was in violation of the ADA. Anderson asserted that as a wheelchair-bound individual, he was significantly limited in the major life function of walking, and thus disabled under the ADA. Further, he asserted that a Title III public accommodation includes Little League Baseball and its games and that defendants are subject to the provisions of the Americans with Disabilities Act because they own, lease (or lease to), or operate a place of public accommodation within the meaning of the ADA. Little League argued that while the ADA does require equal access to participation and enjoyment of activities, it does not require owner/operators of public accommodations to provide modifications that create a direct threat to the health and safety of other participants. The court discussed the issue of whether a wheelchair-bound coach in the first or third base coaches' box was a direct threat to the safety of the players, and concluded there was insufficient evidence to support this claim. Specifically, the court found that the blanket policy restricting on-field coaching by wheelchair-bound participants was a violation of the ADA because public accommodation owner/operators are required to make a case-by-case assessment of whether a direct threat to other participant health and safety exists.

Many Title III cases in sport law focus on participation; however, the law requires full and effective enjoyment, which does not always mean as a participant. An emerging application of Title III in sport focuses on spectators, not participants. Aside from spectator access issues that impact sport facilities, there is a recent history of case law that focuses on whether the live in-game experience is equal for all attendees. In *Feldman v. Pro Football Inc.* (2011), the United States Court

of Appeals for the Fourth Circuit upheld a grant of summary judgment in favor of two Washington Redskins fans who challenged the adequacy of captioning as an auxiliary aid; the fans alleged that in-game entertainment features were inaccessible to them as deaf patrons, thus their ability to fully and effectively enjoy the experience was compromised, a violation of Title III of the ADA. Prior to the lawsuit, the Redskins provided little to no captioning on stadium video boards, opting instead to offer handheld captioning devices. After the plaintiff's filed suit, the Redskins significantly increased captioning to include a "considerable amount of game information and other announcements."

Specifically, the Redskins used stadium video boards to (1) caption public service announcements, including pregame information; (2) make announcements detailing each play; (3) provide referee penalty explanations; (4) make in-game entertainment announcements; (5) advertise; and (6) make end-of-the-game announcements, and announcements regarding the final score and information regarding the next home game. This captioning was provided in the seating bowl, and in the stadium concourse areas. Additionally, the Redskins captioned the emergency evacuation video on the stadium video board. While this captioning was a significant improvement over the Redskins' past practice, the plaintiffs contested the failure to caption additional aural programming, including lyrics to songs played for entertainment and a radio program that was broadcast in the concourse areas separate from the public address system broadcast was a violation of Title III of the ADA.

The court determined that Title III of the ADA required the defendants to provide equal enjoyment of aural information, including music with lyrics. As a result, the lower court's grant of summary judgment to the plaintiffs was withheld. This case is one example of several cases that have been filed regarding stadium captioning, and compliance with the ADA. Many lawsuits are filed under Title III, however, if the facility in question is government owned/operated, the same claim would be filed under Title II.

Last but certainly not least, the preeminent ADA case in sport and recreation, which included both Title I and Title III (when filed) is *PGA Tour, Inc. v. Martin* (2001). Casey Martin has a rare medical disorder, a degenerative muscle condition that results in severe pain when he walks for extended periods of time. Martin entered the Professional Golfers' Association's (PGA's) qualifying tournament to earn his PGA tour card, and was allowed to use a cart for the first two rounds. In the third round, carts were not permitted, and Martin petitioned the PGA to allow him to use a cart in both that third qualifying round and in subsequent PGA sanctioned activities. Martin asserted that making the cart allowable was a reasonable accommodation for his disability under the ADA. The PGA denied his request, stating it would fundamentally alter the game of golf. Martin then requested injunctive relief from the court, and was granted an injunction, which allowed him to use a cart in the third qualifying round. However, after Martin earned his tour card, the PGA restricted his cart use again, and Martin filed an ADA lawsuit. Specifically, Martin claimed that as a PGA employee, he was entitled to reasonable accommodation under Title I, and that as a participant he was entitled to reasonable accommodation under Title III because by definition, a golf course is a place of public accommodation. The Title I claim did not survive because the court determined that Martin was not in fact an employee of the PGA; however, the Title III claim survived and was ultimately decided by the United States Supreme Court.

Before the Supreme Court rendered a final decision, both the district and appellate courts found in favor of Casey Martin; however, the PGA made two specific arguments in attempting to win its case. First, the PGA claimed that it was not subject to Title III because during a golf tournament, the area of the golf course used by the tournament players is roped off and restricted, therefore it does not qualify as a place of public accommodation. The court disagreed, noting that even if an owner/operator selectively decides to restrict access, the facility as a whole is still a place of public accommodation. Next, and more significant, the PGA argued that allowing a tour player to use a cart would fundamentally alter the sport of golf because the walking rule was essential to the game. While the PGA presented support for its arguments from many former golfers and industry experts, none of the courts were persuaded. The Supreme Court upheld the findings of the lower courts and ruled that allowing Martin to use a cart during PGA events increased his access, as required by the ADA, but did not fundamentally alter the game of golf.

RELIGIOUS DISCRIMINATION

As noted at the beginning of the chapter, religion is a protected class under Title VII; religious discrimination in the workplace is remedied using this law. Specifically, employers must reasonably accommodate the religious practices of employees, unless the employer can demonstrate doing such would cause an undue hardship. Further, employers cannot intentionally discriminate against employers based on religion. In *Johnson v. National Football League* (1999), the plaintiff, a converted Muslim, contended that the National Football League (NFL), among others, discriminated against him because of his race and religion. In particular, J. Edwards Johnson asserted that the NFL violated his rights under Title VII by refusing to "employ" him as a football player in the NFL.

Johnson, an African-American, played offensive tackle as well as defensive lineman for the University of Miami for five years. While in school, Johnson converted to Islam as a religion and became a Muslim. Johnson published two articles about race and religion in the university newspaper; his coaches did not respond well to the articles, and a controversy ensued. Johnson claims that this controversy, along with a mistaken media report regarding his draft status, prevented NFL teams from drafting him. He specifically alleged that the league and certain NFL teams "blackballed" him because of his religion and the controversy at the University of Miami.

J. Edwards Johnson eventually filed a charge of discrimination with the EEOC. The EEOC did not address the charge on the merits, but issued Johnson a right-to-sue letter in 1999. The NFL moved to dismiss the lawsuit, but did not succeed; the court found that Johnson sufficiently alleged a claim of discrimination. However, Johnson later filed a voluntary motion to dismiss the case, as the parties likely settled.

Additionally, the NCAA clashed with a member institution regarding religious discrimination. In 1992, the NCAA proposed Rule 9.2 as an attempt to do away with religious displays by players such as kneeling, removing their helmets, and crossing themselves in the end zone following a score. In 1995, Liberty University, its football coach, and four of its players filed a lawsuit against the NCAA (School Sues over Game Prayer, 1995). The lawsuit alleged that banning players from kneeling constituted religious discrimination, and

violated the 1964 Civil Rights Act. However, the plaintiff dismissed the lawsuit after the NCAA stated that students were still permitted to pray under the rules.

There are many other areas where religion and sport intersect; specifically student athletes often challenge freedom of religion using the First Amendment of the United States Constitution. Freedom of religion guaranteed by the Constitution is discussed in Chapter 12.

CONCLUSION

The state and federal legislation discussed in this chapter aim to provide a remedy for the inequalities that are present at all levels of sport. Barriers still exist based on race, gender, religion, sexual orientation, age, and disability, but progress has been made in each of these areas as unequal treatment has been addressed by the court system and legislation in recent years. There is an established body of common law precedent in each of these areas, and guiding principles have been established regarding what conduct constitutes discrimination: sport managers and athletic administrators must be mindful of conduct that is potentially discriminatory so it can be avoided. Thoughtful consideration of policies and practices is essential to avoid discrimination and ensure compliance with the law.

DISCUSSION QUESTIONS

Title VII

1. Mary Johnson has loved hockey all of her life. She has been a hockey referee in many semi-professional leagues for the past seven years. She has received outstanding performance reviews for her work as a referee in the leagues she has worked. She now desires to be a referee in the Instructional Hockey League (IHL). She has filed an application for employment but the league has a rule that it does not allow women referees due to safety concerns for players

and referees alike. Ms. Johnson is 5 feet 2 inches and weighs 105 pounds. Johnson filed a lawsuit against the IHL based on discrimination seeking employment with the league. What defenses does the league have against the lawsuit? How would a court rule in this case?

2. Sex discrimination under Title VII has only recently been interpreted by the courts to include sexual orientation and gender identity. Discuss the potential impact of this expanded interpretation on athletic programs.

3. What racial issues do you believe are facing sports today? Do you believe Title VII has resulted in progress regarding racial discrimination in sports?

4. Does Title VII require that all sport organizations be accessible by both genders? In *Graves v. Women's Professional Rodeo Association, Inc.* (1990), a male barrel racer sued the Women's Professional Rodeo Association (WPRA) alleging that it denied him membership on the basis of his gender in violation of Title VII of the Civil Rights Act of 1964. The court found against Graves and discussed the following relating to the concept of BFOQ:

> Although WPRA raised no defense beyond its failure to qualify as an "employer" under Title VII, we note that under the bona fide occupational qualification (BFOQ) exception the organization probably would not have to admit males even if it had the requisite fifteen employees. The legislative history offers as an example of legitimate discrimination under the BFOQ exception to the proscriptions of Title VII "a professional baseball team for male players" 110 Cong.Rec. 7213 (1964). Presumably, being female would similarly constitute a BFOQ for competing in women's professional rodeo, in the same way that being female would constitute a BFOQ for competing in women's professional tennis or for membership in the Ladies' Professional Golf Association. In short, we do not believe that Title VII mandates the admission of men as competitors in women's professional sports.

Title IX

1. Consider what Title IX requires regarding provision of benefits and services; what are some of the practical challenges in this area? How do athletic administrators balance the benefits and services provided to revenue and non-revenue sports, assuming there is a gender difference?

2. Mary Williams was an outstanding placekicker for her high school football team. She wants to try out for her college football team but is not allowed to do so. The university cites federal law that states that educational institutions are allowed to maintain separate teams in contact sports. Mary argues that because she is a placekicker only, a non-contact position, she should therefore be allowed to try out. Is she correct? Does the school have to let her try out for the team? Should rules be different for placekickers as opposed to other players?

3. You have recently been named Title IX coordinator for a Division I athletic program. The athletic director has asked you to draft a two-page summary outlining a Title IX compliance

(continues)

DISCUSSION QUESTIONS (CONTINUED)

plan. Draft a short memorandum highlighting the significant portions of a Title IX plan that will withstand scrutiny. What information do you need to draft such a plan? What will be your major concerns and the focus and goals of the plan?

ADEA

1. Wilson Miller was an eight-time Pro-Bowl quarterback. At age 43 he still is able to play quarterback in the NFL. He is signed by the Denver Broncos to a contract and participates in the training camp. He is competing for the third-team quarterback position with Rusty Johnson, a 22-year-old rookie. Miller is cut from the team at the end of the camp in favor of Johnson. Miller was told by the head coach that although he had more experience reading defenses the owner wanted to go with the "new kid." He was also told by the head coach that Johnson had less propensity to get injured than Miller because of Miller's age. The assistant coach told Miller that the owner told the head coach to keep the rookie over Miller because the Broncos have a very young fan base and the head coach wanted to "make his roster as young as possible," in order to attract more fans to the game. Miller files an age discrimination case against the Broncos. The Broncos admit that both quarterbacks are of the same level of skill and both fill the team's offensive scheme. The Broncos argue that keeping Johnson over Miller was a business necessity because more fans will buy season tickets as a result of Johnson's presence on the team. Johnson's hometown is Denver, Colorado, and he played his college football for the University of Colorado. Can Miller prevail in his age discrimination lawsuit? Is the business necessity defense a valid defense to an age discrimination case?

2. Do you agree with the law in setting 40 as the age at which discrimination can occur under the ADEA?

ADA

1. Cynthia Jones is an outstanding basketball player for the Women's Maryland Wheelchair Scholastic League. She believes she could also play and compete in a non-wheelchair league with footed players. She makes a request of her local city league that she be allowed to participate in a footed league. The league turns her down, citing safety concerns. She has told the league she will only compete outside the three-point line on the court and never go inside of that line. Does the league have a right to refuse her request? What reasonable accommodations could be made for her? See *Kuketz v. MDC Fitness Corp.*, 13 Mass. L. Rptr. 511 (Mass. Super. Ct. 2001).

2. In *PGA v. Martin*, the court found that walking is not an essential part of the game of golf. Do you agree? How far do PGA golfers walk during a PGA event?

3. What reasonable accommodations could be made for Jim Abbott, former California Angels pitcher? Abbott was born without a right hand but overcame his disability by becoming the collegiate player of the year at the University of Michigan and even tossed a no-hitter with the

DISCUSSION QUESTIONS (CONTINUED)

New York Yankees in 1993. Abbott pitched ten years in the major leagues. Could he argue he was entitled to a "special fielder" as a reasonable accommodation due to his disability?

Sexual Harassment

1. You have just been named the new athletic director at your alma mater. You are concerned about some statements that have been made to women trainers for the football team. It has been brought to your attention that student-athletes have made sexually explicit remarks to women trainers at practice and during games. You have scheduled a meeting with the university's general counsel about your concerns. What policies or procedures would you put into place to prevent sexual harassment from occurring in the future? Would you provide sexual harassment training to all student-athletes and staff? If so, what would the training consist of? Could the university be held liable for sexual harassment of a university employee by student-athletes?

KEY TERMS

Bona fide occupational qualification
Disparate compensation
Disparate impact discrimination
Disparate treatment discrimination
Effective accommodation
Equal Employment Opportunity Commission
History and continuing practice
Hostile work environment
Places of public accommodation

Protected classes
Qualified individual with a disability
Quid pro quo
Reasonable accommodation
Respondeat superior
Reverse sex discrimination
Sexual harassment
Substantial proportionality

REFERENCES

20 U.S.C. § 106.41(c).
20 U.S.C. § 1681(a).
29 U.S.C. § 206(d).
29 C.F.R. § 1607.4(d).
42 U.S.C. § 1981.
42 U.S.C. § 1983.
42 U.S.C. § 2000e (j).
42 U.S.C.A. § 2000e-2(a)1.
42 U.S.C.A. § 2000e-2(e).

42 U.S.C. § 12101(a)(5).
42 U.S.C. § 12103(3).
42 U.S.C. § 12111(5)(a).
42 U.S.C. § 12111(9).
42 U.S.C. § 12111(10)(a).
42 U.S.C. § 12131(2).
42 U.S.C. § 12182(a).
45 C.F.R. Part 86.
45 C.F.R. § 86.41(b).

Alba v. Merrill Lynch and Co., 198 Fed. App. 294 (Va. Ct. App. 2006).

Alwine v. Buzas, 89 Fed. Appx. 196 (10th Cir. 2004).

Anderson v. Little League Baseball, Inc., 794 F. Supp. 342 (D. Ariz. 1992).

Bennett-Alexander, D., & Pincus, L. (1995). *Employment Law for Business* (5th ed.). New York: McGraw-Hill.

Burlington Industries, Inc. v. Ellerth, 524 U.S. 742 (1998).

California Education Code §220.

California Education Code §221.5.

Clarke v. Bank of Commerce, 2007 WL 1072212 (N.D. Okla. 2007) (slip opinion).

Cohen v. Brown University, 101 F.3d 155 (1st Cir. 1996).

Court approves settlement in historic Title IX case: Quinnipiac makes major commitment to women's sports, 2013. Retrieved from http://www.pullcom .com/news-listings-402.html

Cross, F., & Miller, R.M. (2008). *The Legal Environment of Business: Text and Cases, Ethical, Regulatory, Global and E-Commerce Issues* (7th ed.). South-Western College/West Mason, OH.

Daniels v. School Bd. of Brevard County, Fla., 995 F. Supp. 1394 (M.D. Fla. 1997).

EEOC Compliance Manual, Section 15: Race and Color Discrimination, 2006. Retrieved from http://www .eeoc.gov/policy/docs/race-color.html#II

EEOC Enforcement Guidance, 1990. Retrieved from http://www.eeoc.gov/eeoc/publications/upload /currentissues.pdf

EEOC Enforcement Guidance, 2015. Retrieved from http:// www.eeoc.gov/laws/guidance/pregnancy_guidance .cfm

EEOC Facts About National Origin Discrimination, 2015. Retrieved from http://www.eeoc.gov/eeoc /publications/fs-nator.cfm

Faragher v. City of Boca Raton, 524 U.S. 775 (1998).

Feldman v. Pro Football Inc. (2011 U.S. App. LEXIS 6188).

Frank v. United Airlines, Inc., 216 F.3d 845 (9th Cir. 2000).

Gould, W.B. (2011). *Bargaining with baseball: Labor relations in the age of turmoil*. Jefferson, N.C.: McFarland.

Grant v. General Motors, 908 F.2d 1303 (6th Cir. 1990).

Graves v. Women's Professional Rodeo Association, Inc., 907 F.2d 71 (1990).

Griggs v. Duke Power, 401 U.S. 424 (1971).

Grove City College v. Bell, 46 U.S. 555 (1984).

International Brotherhood of Teamsters v. U.S., 97 S. Ct. 1843 (1977).

Jackson v. University of New Haven, 228 F. Supp. 2d 156 (D.Conn. 2002).

Jew v. University of Iowa, 749 F. Supp. 946 (S.D. Iowa 1990).

Johnson v. National Football League 1999 WL 892938 (S.D.N.Y. 1999).

JMU Enacts Proportionality Plan to Comply with Title IX, James Madison Media Relations, 2006. Retrieved from http://www.jmu.edu/jmuweb/general/news2 /general7490.shtml

Kelly v. Board of Trustees of the University of Illinois, 35 F.3d 265 (7th Cir. 1994).

Klinker, D. (2003). Why conforming with Title IX hurts men's collegiate sports. *Seton Hall Journal of Sport Law*, 13, 73–96.

Kuketz v. MDC Fitness Corp., 13 Mass. L. Rptr. 511 (Mass. Super. Ct. 2001).

McDonnell Douglas Corp. v. Green, 411 U.S. 792 (1973).

Mahoney, T.Q., Dodds, M.A., & Polasek, K.M. (2015). Progress for transgender athletes: Analysis of the school success and opportunity act. *Journal of Physical Education Recreation and Dance*, 86, 45–47.

Medcalf v. Trustees of University of Pennsylvania, 71 Fed. App. 924 (3rd Cir. 2003).

Mercer v. Duke University, 190 F.3d 643 (4th Cir. 1999).

Minnis v. Bd. Of Sup'rs of La. State Univ. and Agric. and Mech. College, 2014 WL 5364049 (M.D. La. Oct. 21, 2014).

Mollaghan v. Varnell, 105 So. 3d 291 (Miss. 2012).

Moore v. University of Notre Dame, 22 F. Supp. 2d 896 (N.D. Ind. 1998).

Moran v. Selig, 447 F.3d 748 (9th Cir. 2006).

NCAA Title IX Frequently Asked Questions, 2015. Retrieved from http://www.ncaa.org/about/resources/inclusion /title-ix-frequently-asked-questions#dollars

PGA Tour, Inc. v. Martin, 532 U.S. 661 (2001).

Pederson v. La. State University, 213 F.3d 858 (2000).

Peirick v. Indiana University-Purdue University Indianapolis Athletics Department, 2005 WL 1518663 (S.D. Ind. 2005).

Perdue v. City University of New York, 13 F. Supp.2d 326 (1998).

Raineri v. Highland Falls-Fort Montgomery School District, 198 F. Supp 2d. 542 (S.D.N.Y.2002).

School sues over game prayer. (1995). *New York Times*. Retrieved from http://www.nytimes.com/1995/09/01 /sports/sports-people-college-football-school-sues -over game-prayer.html

Taylor v. United Parcel Serv., Inc., 554 F.3d 510 (5th Cir. 2008).

Thomas v. Review Bd. of the Indiana Employment Sec. Div., 450 U.S. 707 (1981).

Title III Highlights, United States Department of Justice, n.d. Retrieved from http://www.ada.gov/t3hilght.htm

CHAPTER 7

DRUG TESTING IN SPORTS

LEARNING OBJECTIVES

By the end of this chapter, the reader will be able to:

1. Identify drug use and drug testing issues in professional sports
2. Consider the role of collective bargaining in professional sport drug prevention policies
3. Recognize the considerable variations in collectively bargained drug policies across the four primary professional sport leagues in the United States
4. Consider key provisions of the NCAA drug testing policy
5. Identify the state constitutional issues presented by the NCAA drug testing policies
6. Identify the federal constitutional issues presented by interscholastic drug testing policies
7. Consider search and seizure issues within interscholastic drug testing policies
8. Consider the implication of constitutionally permissible drug testing policies within interscholastic athletics
9. Consider the differences between federal and state constitutional protections for privacy and against unreasonable search and seizure

RELATED CASE

Case 7.1   State v. Lindsey, 881 N.W.2d 411 (2016)

INTRODUCTION

The use of drugs in sports, and the drug testing procedures that have been instituted as a result, have been a major focus at the professional and amateur levels in recent years. Many episodes of drug use in sports have brought attention to this issue, involving both performance-enhancing drugs and recreational drugs. Every professional sport has instituted some form of drug testing and monitoring program. Heavily regulated sports such as horse racing and boxing can require mandatory drug testing without much debate. In sports that engage in *collective bargaining*, such as football, hockey, baseball, and basketball, drug testing programs are the result of the combined inputs of management and labor through the process of collective bargaining. The regulation of drug testing and drug use in professional sports is quite different from amateur sports. Both, however, present unique legal issues.

The National Collegiate Athletic Association (NCAA) has a vested interest in ensuring that competition is drug free and has instituted its own drug testing policies. The NCAA requires all student-athletes to sign a consent form to retain their eligibility to participate in sports. The NCAA has been forceful in administering its drug policy for both street drugs and performance-enhancing substances. Additionally, the association has dealt with constitutional challenges to its policies.

Drug use has also increased at the interscholastic level, becoming a concern for high schools and even for middle schools. Schools and school districts have instituted drug policies for student-athletes and those participating in extracurricular activities. Constitutional challenges have been raised to many schools' drug testing schemes, and several of those challenges have reached the United States Supreme Court. Drug testing policies at the high school level have led to a myriad of constitutional challenges relating to equal protection rights and the Fourth and Fourteenth Amendments. The Supreme Court has attempted to fashion the law by balancing the constitutional rights of individuals against concerns regarding drug use by students.

Many studies have shown that athletes at all levels are using performance-enhancing drugs at a very high rate; some experts believe that a doping problem exists at all levels of sports competition (Wick, 2014). Professional and amateur sports associations have taken different approaches in trying to combat the problem of doping in sports. This chapter presents an overview of drug use in sports and what has been done at the professional and amateur levels to control it.

PROFESSIONAL SPORTS

Professional athletes are usually deemed employees of the team or league. When professional athletes organize in labor unions, they receive protection under the *National Labor Relations Act* (see Chapter 10). Any drug testing program implemented in professional sports must therefore be agreed to by management and labor through the collective bargaining process (Rabuano, 2000). The National Labor Relations Act requires that owners and unions "meet at reasonable times and confer in good faith with respect to wages, hours, and other terms and conditions of employment." The National Labor Relations Board (NLRB) determined in *Johnson-Bateman Co.* (1989), that drug testing is a subject of mandatory bargaining between management and labor. For example, Major League Baseball (MLB) owners could not impose a drug testing policy on players without first entering into good-faith negotiations with the MLB Players Association. Because drug programs are mandatory subjects of collective bargaining, teams or leagues cannot unilaterally institute a drug testing program.

A drug testing scheme at the professional level generally sets forth, among other policies, what players can be tested, the procedure by which the testing is done, what substances are banned by the league, and the discipline imposed for a violation of the drug testing policy. In any drug testing policy for professional leagues, several matters need to be considered by both parties:

- What drugs are prohibited under the policy? Who makes the decision about which drugs are prohibited? How can a drug become prohibited by the league?
- Will random testing of all players occur? If not, how does one determine who is to be tested? Will probable cause be used as a standard for testing?
- What disciplinary measures are to be taken if an athlete is found to be in violation of the league policy? What are the penalties for repeat offenders of the league's drug policy? What are the appropriate fines and suspensions for violations of the policy?
- How are the tests conducted and by whom? What are the procedures for maintaining the integrity of the samples?
- What are the procedures for challenging the test results?

Professional athletes have a great deal at stake in a short professional career. A career can be cut short by a positive drug test, which may subsequently result in discipline by the team or commissioner, or in suspension from the league. The league or team is also concerned about the overall image of the league and wants to assure its fans and the public that the players do not use drugs. That is a conflict that is not easily resolved but has to be hammered out through collective bargaining. *Players unions* are concerned about the image of players as well as the effect that suspensions might have on a player's career. Unions have argued for a "stair-step" approach to player discipline, in which discipline ranges from rehabilitation to suspension from the league.

The four major sports in the United States have instituted policies regarding performance-enhancing drugs. The following presents a summary of each league policy, and where applicable, a summary of recent issues.

Major League Baseball

The past decade has been one of heighted scrutiny and significant progress regarding drug use and drug prevention in Major League Baseball. On March 30, 2006, MLB commissioner Bud Selig requested George Mitchell, a former senator from Maine, to investigate the allegations that many MLB players had used steroids or other performance-enhancing drugs. Mitchell's charge from the commissioner was to determine whether any MLB players used steroids or other illegal performance-enhancing substances at any point after the substances were banned by the 2002–2006 collective bargaining agreement. Senator Mitchell accepted the charge of Commissioner Selig on the condition that he be given independence both during the investigation and in compiling the report. The commissioner agreed to this condition. Selig also agreed that the Mitchell Report would be made public when it was completed.

Senator Mitchell's investigation was thorough. He and his team sifted through over 115,000 pages of documents that had been provided to them by a variety of sources, including the Office of the Commissioner of Major League Baseball and all the MLB teams. Approximately 20,000 other electronic documents from these sources were also reviewed by Mitchell and his legal team. Over 700 witnesses were interviewed during the investigation including then current or former club officials, managers, coaches, team physicians, athletic trainers or resident security agents. Additionally, 16 individuals from the commissioner's Office were interviewed, including Commissioner Bud Selig and Chief Operating Officer Robert DuPuy. Further, Senator Mitchell and his staff attempted to contact almost 500 former players for the investigation, but only 68 agreed to be interviewed. Mitchell also attempted to contact the Players Association during his investigation, but stated in his report that the Players Association was uncooperative (Mitchell, 2007).

Senator Mitchell's investigation led him to conclude that the use of anabolic steroids and other performance-enhancing substances was widespread in Major League Baseball and threatened the integrity of the game. Senator Mitchell further found that all 30 MLB teams had players involved with performance-enhancing substances at some point. The report named 78 players, most notably baseball's all-time home run leader Barry Bonds, star pitcher Roger Clemens, and Clemens's former teammate Andy Pettitte. However, the report recommended that the commissioner take no action against players who were found to have used steroids in the past (Mitchell, 2007).

The Mitchell Report contained many recommendations aimed to prevent the illegal use of performance-enhancing substances. Specifically, the Mitchell Report stated that there should be a higher priority on aggressive investigation, enhanced educational programs, and continued drug testing. Senator Mitchell was uncertain how this would actually happen, considering the combative relationship between management and the players union; however, in the collective bargaining agreement that took effect in 2007, enhanced measures to control drug use were present. Most recently, the collectively bargained Joint Drug Agreement (JDA) went into effect in December 2011 and is scheduled to terminate Dec. 1, 2016; the list of banned substances is updated annually (Joint Drug Agreement, 2011). The JDA is over sixty pages long and provides regulations regarding oversight and administration, prohibited substances, drug testing, discipline, appeals and educational programs. A few key provisions from the JDA include:

Player Tests Positive for a Performance Enhancing Substance
1. First positive test result: a 50-game suspension;

2. Second positive test result: a 100-game suspension; and
3. Third positive test result: permanent suspension from Major League and Minor League Baseball; provided, however, that a Player so suspended may apply, no earlier than one year following the imposition of the suspension, to the Commissioner for discretionary reinstatement after a minimum period of two years.

Player Tests Positive for a Stimulant
1. First positive test result: follow-up testing . . .;
2. Second positive test result: a 25-game suspension;
3. Third positive test result: an 80-game suspension; and
4. Fourth and subsequent positive test result: a suspension for just cause by the Commissioner, up to permanent suspension from Major League and Minor League Baseball, which penalty shall be subject to challenge before the Arbitration Panel.

Conviction for the Possession or Use of Prohibited Substance
1. For a first offense: at least a 60-game but not more than an 80-game suspension, if the Prohibited Substance is a Performance Enhancing Substance, or at least a 15-game but not more than a 30-game suspension, if the Prohibited Substance is a Drug of Abuse (including a Stimulant);
2. For a second offense: at least a 120-game but not more than a one-year suspension, if the Prohibited Substance is a Performance Enhancing Substance, or at least a 30-game but not more than a 90-game suspension, if the Prohibited Substance is a Drug of Abuse (including a Stimulant);

3. For a third offense involving a Performance Enhancing Substance: permanent suspension from Major League and Minor League Baseball; provided, however, that a Player so suspended may apply, no earlier than one year following the imposition of the suspension, to the Commissioner for discretionary reinstatement after a minimum period of two years;

4. If the Prohibited Substance is a Drug of Abuse (including a Stimulant), a third offense shall result in a one-year suspension, and any subsequent offense shall result in a suspension for just cause by the Commissioner, up to permanent suspension from Major League and Minor League Baseball, which penalty shall be subject to challenge before the Arbitration Panel (Joint Drug Agreement, 2011).

National Football League

Similar to MLB, the National Football League (NFL) has a collectively bargained drug policy that governs aspects such as administration, testing and discipline. In 2014, the NFL and the NFL Players Association (NFLPA) implemented revisions to its then existing drug policy; the revisions were in response to some high profile NFL players having issues with banned substances. As of 2014, a first violation of the policy will result in a suspension of up to six games, depending on the nature of the violation. Specifically, using diuretics or masking agents will result in a two-game suspension, using steroids, stimulants, human growth hormone, or other banned substances will result in a four-game suspension and, attempting to manipulate a test will result in a six-game suspension. A second violation will result in a 10-game suspension and a third violation will result in a two-year minimum banishment (Brinson, 2014). Further, testing positive for

banned stimulants in the off-season will not result in a suspension; rather, the player will be put into the substance abuse program (Brinson, 2014).

National Basketball Association

The National Basketball Association (NBA) and the National Basketball Players Association have jointly maintained a drug prevention and education program since 1983 (CBA 101, 2014). Although the policy is longstanding, it has been critiqued for over a decade. In 2005, the NBA's anti-doping testing program was called inadequate, pathetic, and a joke (Abbott, 2013). Although the league has made the drug program more stringent, most recently updating it in the 2011 collectively bargained agreement, the policy overall is still criticized, specifically regarding its lenient penalties for marijuana use, and its harsher punishment of street drugs than performance enhancing drugs.

The NBA's list of prohibited drugs includes amphetamines, cocaine, LSD, opiates, and PCP; these drugs are classified as "Drugs of Abuse." Also prohibited are marijuana, steroids, performance enhancing drugs and masking agents; these drugs are classified as SPEDs (CBA 101, 2014). Further, NBA players are subject to random drug testing six times during each season and off-season. In addition, if there is *reasonable cause* to believe a player is using drugs, the league or the Players Association can request a conference with the player and an independent expert to implement reasonable cause testing. The independent expert will determine whether reasonable cause exists for testing and will authorize testing if appropriate (CBA 101, 2014). Discipline under the NBA policy varies depending on the type of drug used; as mentioned, positive tests for "Drugs of Abuse" incur a far harsher penalty than performance enhancing drugs. Specifically, a positive test for a "Drug of Abuse" constitutes dismissal and disqualification from the NBA, whereas "if a player tests positive for a SPED, he will be suspended for 20 games for his first violation and 45 games for his second violation, and will be dismissed and disqualified from the NBA for his third violation" (CBA 101, 2014). Regarding marijuana, a first positive test results in mandatory treatment, a second positive test results in a $25,000 fine, and any subsequent positive tests result in game suspensions in multiples of five games (CBA 101, 2014).

National Hockey League

The National Hockey League (NHL) and NHL Players Association (NHLPA) first established the Performance Enhancing Substances Program to test for performance enhancing drugs in 2005; that policy was revised in 2012 as part of the new NHL/NHLPA collective bargaining agreement. Similar to the NBA, the NHL policy has been criticized as being exceptionally weak; in the first eight years after its inception, only two players were disciplined for violations. The 2012 agreement, which is good for 10 years, included enhancements to the previous drug policy, partially in response to such critiques. Under the 2012 policy, each Ccub will be: (1) subject to team-wide no-notice testing once during Training Camp (commencing with the start of the 2013–2014 League Year); (2) selected at random for team-wide no-notice testing once during the Regular Season; and (3) Individual Players will be randomly selected for no-notice testing during the regular Season and playoffs (Collective Bargaining Agreement, NHL, 2012). Further, the 2012 agreement added reasonable cause testing to the policy, modeling such policy after the MLB.

If a player tests positive, a 20-game suspension without pay results. The player can also be referred to the league's substance abuse/behavioral health program for evaluation, education, and further possible treatment. A second positive offense results in a 60-game suspension. The player is suspended permanently for a third positive test, and the player can apply for reinstatement after two years if suspended for a third time.

Legal Challenges to Drug Testing

Fewer challenges have been made to drug testing at the professional level than at the amateur level, mainly because many drug testing procedures in professional sports have been agreed to during the collective bargaining process. While *grievances* and appeals have been filed in all four professional leagues, those procedures are also governed by the collective bargaining agreements (CBA); as such, most outcomes in drug policy violation cases are based on the entirety of the CBA. However, there are instances where the policies themselves have been challenged. In *Long v. National Football League* (1994), an NFL player challenged the league's anabolic steroid policy on constitutional grounds. He sued several defendants, including the NFL and the NFL commissioner, in his failed attempt to challenge the policy. Additionally, in *Williams v. National Football League and John Lombardo, M.D.* (2009), two NFL players who had been suspended after testing positive for a banned supplement challenged the enforceability of the NFL/NFLPA collectively bargained drug policy. The players argued that as employees of a Minnesota-based company, they were governed by state drug policies, and not those of the NFL/NFLPA (Belson, 2011). In the 2009 case, the United States Court of Appeals for the eighth circuit did uphold a lower court ruling prohibiting the NFL from suspending the players; however, in 2011, a Minnesota state appellate court held that the NFL did not violate state law because Minnesota's workplace drug testing policy did not include the supplement the players took. This decision effectively upheld the structure and enforceability of the NFL/NFLPA drug policy (Belson, 2011).

AMATEUR SPORTS

Professional sport organizations and professional athletes are not the only entities subject to scrutiny regarding drug use and regulation; these issues are also prevalent in both collegiate and interscholastic athletics. While professional sport issues are handled through *arbitration* and collective bargaining, there are constitutional considerations at issue in the drug testing of athletes involved in amateur sports. These issues will be discussed separately as they impact the NCAA and member institutions, and high school athletic programs.

Constitutional Protections: Privacy, Search, and Seizure

The United States, as well as each of the 50 states, has a constitution that sets forth the principles known as constitutional law. Some state constitutions are modeled after the United States Constitution, but each constitution is unique to the jurisdiction that created it. Among the similarities are the state action requirement, privacy protections, and/or protections against unreasonable search and seizure.

State action will be fully addressed in Chapter 12; however, an introduction to the concept is required to understand how constitutional protections may impact drug testing policies of the NCAA, NCAA member institutions, and interscholastic sport programs. Under constitutional law, the plaintiff must first demonstrate that the defendant is a state actor, meaning the challenged action (in this case a drug testing) was done on behalf of the government. Only state actors (not private entities) are required to ensure that citizens are afforded their constitutional rights; thus, state action is necessary to successfully challenge a practice as unconstitutional. If the defendant is a public college, university, middle or high school, the state action requirement is met. However, the question becomes more difficult when the defendant is a *private entity*. A private entity may be engaging in conduct that has the characteristics of a "state actor" or is actually a de facto *state actor*. Courts have applied certain tests to determine whether the defendant is a state actor; if there is a

close nexus between the state and the challenged action, the defendants may be treated as a state actor.

Privacy protections, and/or protections against unreasonable *search and seizure* may vary slightly in language and application, but they are found in all state and federal constitutions. Specifically, the Fourth Amendment of the United States Constitution states that people have a right to be secure in their persons, houses, papers, and effects against *unreasonable* searches and seizures, and that this right shall not be violated but upon probable cause (United States Constitution, Amendment IV). Additionally, state constitutions use language that affords state citizens privacy rights that cannot be violated by the state actor. In cases discussed below, student athletes at all levels have challenged that drug testing policies and programs violated these varying constitutional protections. In determining whether a drug test is in fact a violation of a student athletes constitutional rights, courts have attempted to determine whether there was state action, whether the drug test (most often urinalysis) constitutes a search, whether the search was reasonable, and whether the search was based on reasonable suspicion. These criteria evolved from a series of cases on this issue, several of which are discussed in this chapter.

The National Collegiate Athletic Association

In 1986, the NCAA began a drug testing program for all student-athletes as a response to evidence of drug use amongst athletes competing in NCAA sanctioned activities. The program was created to ensure that all participants in collegiate athletics were on a level playing field and were healthy and safe. Originally, the NCAA tested student athletes at 73 post-season events, as well as at 18 post-season football bowl games (Roshkoff, 1996). The program has undergone modification and revision since its inception, including the implementation of year round testing; the policy is still very much in use today. Specifically, NCAA bylaws require student-athletes to sign a consent form demonstrating their understanding of the drug testing program and their willingness to participate in the program. Each student athlete must sign the consent form before the school year or he or she cannot participate in intercollegiate competition. Notable provisions from the consent form include the following:

1. A student-athlete who tests positive shall be withheld from competition in all sports for a minimum of 365 days from the drug test collection date and shall lose a year of eligibility;
2. A student-athlete who tests positive has an opportunity to appeal the positive drug test;
3. A student-athlete who tests positive a second time for the use of any drug, other than a "street drug" shall lose all remaining regular-season and postseason eligibility in all sports. A combination of two positive tests involving street drugs (marijuana, THC, or heroin) in whatever order, will result in the loss of an additional year of eligibility;
4. The penalty for missing a scheduled drug test is the same as the penalty for testing positive for the use of a banned drug other than a street drug; and
5. If a student-athlete immediately transfers to a non-NCAA institution while ineligible and competes in collegiate competition within the 365 day period at a non-NCAA institution, the student-athlete will be ineligible for all NCAA regular-season and postseason competition until the student-athlete does not compete in collegiate competition for a 365 day period. (NCAA Manual, 2015–2016)

Further, the NCAA policy includes information regarding the test procedure itself, stating that student athletes must be notified of selection to be tested, must appear for NCAA testing (or be sanctioned for a positive drug test), will be observed by a person of the athletes same gender while producing the sample, must accept the consequences of a positive drug test, must allow the drug test sample to be used by the NCAA drug testing laboratories for research purposes to improve drug testing detection, and must allow disclosure of the drug testing results only for purposes related to eligibility for participation in NCAA competition (NCAA Manual 2015–2016).

Although student athletes are voluntary participants in intercollegiate athletics and consent to the drug testing policy, the constitutionality of the NCAA policy has been challenged in the courts on numerous occasions. Specifically, student athletes have asserted that the NCAA drug test policy violates privacy laws and search and seizure protections found in state constitutions. The NCAA is not a state actor, as is required for scrutiny under the United States Constitution; however, there are examples of cases where state courts have found the NCAA subject to scrutiny under state constitutional protections.

Hill v. National Collegiate Athletic Ass'n (1994), upheld the NCAA drug testing policy as constitutionally permissible. In *Hill*, student athletes attending Stanford University sued the NCAA, contending its drug testing program violated their right to privacy, as secured by the California Constitution (p. 633). The original court found in favor of the student-athletes, stating that the NCAA drug testing violated their constitutionally protected right of privacy. Further, the Superior Court of California permanently enjoined the NCAA from enforcing its policy against the plaintiffs and other Stanford athletes. However, on appeal, the California Supreme Court held that the NCAA had not violated the privacy rights of student-athletes with its mandatory drug testing program. In arguing its case to the California Supreme Court, the NCAA stated that its program was justified because it was protecting the health and safety of the athletes as well as safeguarding the integrity of intercollegiate athletic competition (p. 659). The court agreed with the NCAA, reversing the lower court's decision and upholding its drug testing program (p. 661). Specifically, the court reasoned that the NCAA has an interest in protecting the health and safety of student athletes who are involved in NCAA-regulated competition, which may involve risks of physical injury to athletes, spectators, and others, effectively creating occasions for potential injury resulting from the use of drugs. The court found that as a result, the NCAA may concern itself with the task of protecting the safety of those involved in intercollegiate athletic competition (p. 661).

Regarding the integrity of the game argument, the court reasoned that "the practical realities of NCAA-sponsored athletic competition cannot be ignored. Intercollegiate sports is, at least in part, a business founded upon offering for public entertainment athletic contests conducted under a rule of fair and rigorous competition. Scandals involving drug use, like those involving improper financial incentives or other forms of corruption, impair the NCAA's reputation in the eyes of the sports-viewing public" (p. 661). The court found that a vigorously pursued drug testing program provides a significant deterrent to would-be violators, and assures student athletes, their schools, and the public that fair competition remains the overriding principle in athletic events (p. 661).

The Hill case was determinative in California, however, other states have dealt with similar challenges. Notably, in almost all other cases, the NCAA member institution was the defendant, (not the NCAA) given that only state actors are required to adhere to privacy protections afforded by state and federal constitutions.

NCAA Member Institutions

College and universities that are members of the NCAA are required to administer the NCAA drug policy or one similar; as such, many student athletes have filed lawsuits against the educational institution for violation of constitutional protections. Specifically, athletes have argued that the passing of urine is a deeply private act, and that urinalysis violates medical confidentiality because of the results it can yield. In contrast, educational institutions have argued that protecting student athlete welfare, health and safety is a compelling enough government interest to outweigh the privacy concerns.

In *University of Colorado v. Derdeyn* (1993), a class of current and prospective student athletes filed a lawsuit against the University of Colorado (UC), claiming that the drug testing policy violated privacy protections in the Colorado Constitution and search and seizure protections found in the Fourth Amendment of the United States Constitution. The policy, which had been revised numerous times, included monitored urination for sample acquisition, penalties for positive test results, and mandatory communication of the results to multiple parties, including athletic trainers, coaches, the athletic director, the athlete's parents/legal guardian and the UC Student Health Center. Additionally, the UC policy required student athletes to sign a consent form submitting to random, suspicionless urinalysis testing; students who did not sign the form were not eligible to participate as student athletes.

The Boulder County District Court found in favor of the student athletes, holding that "obtaining a monitored urine sample from a student athlete is a substantial invasion of privacy" (p. 933). UC argued a governmental interest of "compliance with NCAA required tests, a concern for the students' health and safety, and a need to promote fair competition" (p. 933). Although the district court agreed that these interests were commendable and valid, the court ruled that "they were not sufficiently compelling as governmental interests to outweigh an intrusion on the reasonable privacy expectations of students that is "clearly significant" (p. 934). As such, the district court found the testing unconstitutional under both the federal and state constitutions. Regarding the consent form, the trial court reasoned that because participation and potential scholarships were at risk if students failed to sign, the consent was not obtained voluntarily, and was therefore invalid. Accordingly, the district court permanently enjoined (prevented) UC from administering the policy. On appeal, both the Colorado Court of Appeals and the Supreme Court of Colorado affirmed the lower court's ruling.

In *Brennan v. Bd. of Trustees for Univ. of Louisiana Systems* (1997), the court rendered a contrary decision. Specifically, a student at the University of Southwestern Louisiana filed a lawsuit after testing positive for drug use. The student claimed that the result was impacted by heavy drinking and sexual activity the night before the test; however, the University denied his appeals and complied with NCAA regulations, suspending the student for one year.

In finding against the plaintiff student, the court was influenced by the decision of the *Hill* court in California. Specifically, the court held that the student privacy interest was not violated because the student athletes (in both cases) had a diminished expectation of privacy. The court acknowledged that the urine test was an invasion of privacy, but reasoned that the University's desire to protect the integrity of the game, as well as the health and safety of student athletes (by enforcing the NCAA policy) outweighed any intrusion on privacy interests.

Clearly, there was ample case law regarding whether the NCAA drug testing policies or policies at NCAA member institutions were constitutional. State courts were making a range of decisions on this issue, while at the same time, decisions were also being rendered regarding policies for interscholastic athletes. Ultimately, the constitutionality of drug testing programs for college (and high school) athletes was decided by

Vernonia School District v. Acton (1995), discussed later in this chapter.

INTERSCHOLASTIC DRUG TESTING

The *interscholastic* education level is generally understood to include students from grades 6 through 12; this covers middle school and high school students. Interscholastic athletics are governed by state level high school activity associations, as well as the National Federation of State High School Associations. While these organizations do not require a high school to have a drug testing program, many school districts have implemented a drug testing policy for athletes and other students who participate in extracurricular activities. These policies vary from testing for marijuana to testing specifically for performance-enhancing drugs.

As noted in the previous section, the primary issue when implementing drug testing programs for middle and high school age students is whether the privacy protections afforded by state and federal constitutions are compromised (assuming the educational institution is a state actor, or classified as such). However, the broader issue of whether students in the interscholastic education level are protected by the constitutional law generally has also been challenged. In *Tinker v. Des Moines* (1969), the United States Supreme Court held that in light of the special characteristics of the school environment, constitutional rights (*Tinker* addressed the First Amendment specifically) are available to teachers and students. Specifically, the court stated that neither students nor teachers shed their constitutional rights at the schoolhouse gate (see Chapter 12 for a full discussion of *Tinker*). Although the court made clear that school students are entitled to constitutional protections in school, this idea has deteriorated somewhat with subsequent legal challenges and court decisions.

For some issues, the recent trend in the common law is an erosion of student constitutional rights.

As discussed in this chapter, prior to 1995, lower federal courts were split on the issue of drug testing in college (and in high schools); there were conflicting ideas regarding whether such policies violated student constitutional rights. However, clarity was provided in the United States Supreme Court case, *Vernonia School District v. Acton* (1995). In 1989, the Vernonia School District (the District) approved a district wide policy, expressly purposed to prevent student athlete drug use and protect the health and safety of student athletes. Prior to passage of the policy, the District was experiencing significant discipline issues and rebellion, much of which was attributed to a drug culture in the schools, and drug use by student-athletes. The policy required students to consent to random urinalysis testing as a condition of participation on any athletic team. The plaintiff, James Acton (as represented by his parents), was a seventh grade middle school student who wanted to join the football team. Acton's parents refused to sign the consent form, and Acton was not allowed membership on the team. The Actons filed a lawsuit alleging that the policy violated their son's constitutional rights under the Oregon and United States Constitutions. Specifically, they claimed that the Fourth Amendment rights protecting against unreasonable search and seizure were being violated, and that the school could not require consent to drug testing as a condition of participation. The District Court entered an order denying the claims and dismissing the action; however, the United States Court of Appeals for the Ninth Circuit reserved that decision and found that the policy violated James Acton's constitutional rights. Given the litany of cases in both the federal and state courts on the same issue, the United States Supreme Court granted certiorari and issued a ruling that the drug testing policy was constitutional.

In reaching its decision, the United States Supreme Court considered the factors identified earlier; whether the activity constituted a search, and whether the search was reasonable. Relying on case law precedent, the court easily determined that urinalysis constitutes a search for constitutional purposes. The Supreme Court has succinctly held: "Urination is 'an excretory function' traditionally shielded by great privacy" (*Skinner v. Railway Labor Executives Association*, 1989). As such, the court addressed the appropriate standard for determining whether the search was reasonable. Although the Fourth Amendment requires "probable cause" for a search to be justified, the *Vernonia* court applied the "special needs" doctrine; this doctrine was first explained in *Griffin v. Wisconsin* (1987), and provided that a search not supported by a warrant or *probable cause* can still be constitutional if special needs arise that make the probable cause standard impracticable. In applying the special needs doctrine to the facts of the *Vernonia* case, the Supreme Court stated that special needs exist in the public school context; the warrant requirement would unduly interfere with the maintenance of the swift and informal disciplinary procedures, and the requirement that searches be based upon probable cause would undercut the substantial need of teachers and administrators freedom to maintain order in the schools (*Vernonia*, p. 653). This application also aligned with United States Supreme Court cases that precede *Vernonia*; specifically, in *New Jersey v. T.L.O.* (1985) the court's holding purported a reasonable cause standard, and not a *probable cause* standard, for students in school. The *T.L.O.* court stated it "[A] school official may properly conduct a search of a student's person if the official has a reasonable suspicion that a crime has been or is in the process of being committed or reasonable cause to believe that the search is necessary to maintain school discipline or enforce school policies (*New Jersey v. T.L.O.*, p. 329).

After determining that the probable cause standard was not appropriate, and that the District only needed reasonable cause to justify a search (drug test), the court evaluated three other factors; in doing so, they applied a balancing test. Specifically, the court compared the legitimate privacy expectation that James Acton had as a potential student athlete and the character of the intrusion (invasiveness of the test) to the nature and immediacy of the governments concern in drug testing students. When considering the privacy interest of the plaintiff and the potential intrusion on that privacy, the court addressed how much privacy students should expect in school. The court's opinion only considered the privacy expectation of student athletes, not the general student body, and found that a student-athlete does have a diminished expectation of privacy. The court reasoned that student-athletes are sometimes required to submit to physical examinations as well as disrobe in front of other student-athletes when participating in athletics in school. Students also use public restrooms and communal locker rooms when they participate in physical education classes. Thus, courts have reasoned that a student who chooses to participate in sports has a diminished expectation of privacy.

The court also carefully considered whether the testing protocols were overly invasive, and whether the urinalysis results were revealed to inappropriate parties; these considerations are called character of the intrusion. Regarding sample collection, the degree of privacy intrusion is linked to the manner in which production of the sample is monitored. The District's drug test protocol required male students to provide samples at a urinal, while fully clothed and minimally observed; female students were asked to produce a sample in a closed restroom stall. Given that these protocol are near identical to conditions found in public restrooms, which are used by school students daily, the court did not find the monitoring of sample production to be overly invasive. Regarding test result distribution, the court also found the limited group of individuals to be reasonable. Specifically, the court found that

because the urinalysis included in the District policy only screened for prohibited substances, and not for evidence of other medical conditions, the information obtained was reasonable. The court did have some concern about the District policy requirement that students disclose in advance any medications they were taking, however, after consideration that practice was considered reasonable as well.

After considering James Acton's legitimate privacy expectation and the character of intrusion of the District's specific policy, the court compared these variables to the nature and immediacy of the state actors concern (the District). Given that students were asked to consent to random testing, and not testing based on individual suspicion, the court looked for evidence of compelling need for the drug test policy. The court defined "compelling need" as "an interest that appears important enough to justify the particular search at hand, in light of other factors that show the search to be relatively intrusive upon a genuine expectation of privacy" (*Vernonia*, p. 657). When considering whether the nature of the District's concern was compelling, the court found that deterring drug use among school children was undoubtedly compelling. Regarding immediacy of the concern, the court found the evidence of the rebellion in the Vernonia school district, coupled with discipline problems that had reached epidemic proportions, to be sufficient proof of an immediate concern.

After comparison of all the above factors, the court concluded that requiring *student athletes* to consent to random suspicionless drug testing as a condition of participation is constitutional; neither James Acton's right to privacy or protection against unreasonable search and seizure were violated. However, that rule of law was very much based on the extraordinary discipline issues present in the District, and the fact that student athletes have a diminished expectation of privacy given locker room conditions and expectations of heightened regulation. The court was clear that the holding was narrow in scope, and the outcome was based on case specific factors.

After *Vernonia*, courts had guidance regarding legal challenges to drug test policies by students (high school and college). In particular, student athletes were increasingly susceptible to constitutionally permissible drug testing, assuming the test itself was not overly invasive. However, there was less clarity regarding the constitutionality of drug tests for the general student population, or students participating in other non-athletic activities. In *Board of Education of Ind. Sch. Dist. No. 92 of Pottawatomie County v. Earls* (2002), the Supreme Court allowed urinalysis drug testing of all students who participated in extracurricular activities. Consequently, *Earls* expanded the decision of *Vernonia* by allowing a school district to test more students with less of a basis than that set forth in *Vernonia*. The court reasoned that given the nationwide epidemic of drug use, and the evidence of increased drug use in the school implicated in the case, it was entirely reasonable for the school district to enact this particular drug testing policy that included all students wishing to participate in any extra-curricular activity. The court considered the drug test a reasonably effective means of addressing the school's legitimate concerns in preventing, deterring, and detecting drug use. Further, the court made comparisons to *Vernonia*, stating that while the testing of athletes may have been central to the outcome of that case, such a factor was not essential to find a drug test policy constitutional. Specifically, the *Earls* court reasoned that *Vernonia* considered the constitutionality of the program in the context of the public school's custodial responsibilities, and that the scope of the holding was not nearly as narrow at Earls argued (*Earls*, pp. 836–838).

While the *Vernonia* and *Earls* cases significantly lessened the constitutional protections afforded to school students regarding random suspicionless drug testing, the cases only applied and interpreted federal constitutional law. As discussed, state constitutions also afford privacy protections to students, and many cases have challenged the constitutionality of drug testing policies at the state level since *Earls* was decided in 2002. Specifically, in *York v. Wahkiakum School District* (2008), the Washington Supreme Court struck down a random suspicionless drug testing policy as unconstitutional; the court found that the students' rights under Article I, Section 7 of the Washington State Constitution were violated. In rendering its opinion, the court distinguished its analysis from the analysis of federal constitutional law in *Vernonia* and *Earls*, stating that the Washington State Constitution afforded students in that state greater constitutional protections. Where the United States Supreme Court allowed the "special needs" exception to impact the analysis and allow suspicionless testing, the Washington Supreme Court stated that the exceptions are far more limited in that state (*York*, p. 1003). In addition, Washington State has a long line of case law precedent striking down suspicionless testing, and found this case was not an exception (Young, 2010, p. 181).

CONCLUSION

The issue of drugs in sports calls into question the integrity of sports, and certainly presents ample ground for both legal and ethical challenges. Players at the professional level understand that the better they perform, the more money they will make. In today's commercial sports market, players have a huge incentive to hit more home runs, score more touchdowns, or jump higher than the next athlete because their next contract will be directly tied to their performance. In amateur sports, there are equal pressures to perform and advance to the next level, be that college or professional leagues. In addition to performance enhancing drugs, both professional and amateur athletes use common street drugs, which can impact their health and safety and the health and safety of other athletes. While at the professional level, monitoring drug use and providing penalties is handled more easily due to collectively bargained agreements, the appropriate level of monitoring and testing at the amateur levels still causes some concern. There is ample case law precedent at both the state and federal level, but challenges still exist today. Understanding the various implications of drug testing at any level of sport is essential for a sport administrator.

DISCUSSION QUESTIONS

1.   Generally speaking, should there be different rules and penalties for the use of illegal street drugs as opposed to performance-enhancing drugs? If so, what should be the standard? Should it differ with regard to amateur and professional sports?
2.   Do you believe that the use of performance-enhancing drugs should be legalized? If such drugs were legal, would that not place all athletes on the same competitive level?

Professional Sports

1.   Compare and contrast the drug policies in the four major professional leagues. If you were drafting a drug policy for professional sports league, what would you include? Do you think that the drug testing programs are harsh enough for its violators? If not, what is the appropriate discipline for violations of the policy?
2.   Running back Onterrio Smith had a history of violating the NFL's drug policy. In May 2005 while traveling through Minneapolis–St. Paul International Airport, he was briefly detained by authorities after a search of his belongings revealed a device called "The Original Whizzinator." The "Whizzinator," named for obvious reasons, is a device used to beat drug tests. Should Smith have suffered any consequences from the NFL as a result of this incident (Littman, 2009)?
3.   Do you believe Congress should be involved in setting regulations for drug testing in professional sports? What role does collective bargaining play with regard to any bill that would be passed by Congress? (See Chapter 10.)
4.   The sanction for violation of anti-doping rules in the Australian Football League is the loss of two years of eligibility and a lifetime ban for a second violation. Do you agree with this penalty? Should American sports institute the same provisions for violations?
5.   Do you believe that players who take performance-enhancing drugs are "cheating"? Who is actually hurt by a player taking performance-enhancing drugs? What ethical issues do drugs in sports present?

Amateur Sports: NCAA

1.   Discuss the relevance of the NCAA not being a state actor for constitutional law purposes. If the NCAA was classified as such, do you think the courts would apply the same balancing test set forth in *Vernonia* to cases where the NCAA was the defendant?

DISCUSSION QUESTIONS (CONTINUED)

2. Marijuana is a banned substance per NCAA regulations; however, marijuana is legal in a few states. Should the NCAA be able to ban student athletes from using a substance that state law says is legal? What comparisons can you draw to other banned substances?
3. Consider the penalties included in the NCAA drug test policy. Are they adequate? Too harsh? What level of penalty do you think is appropriate?

Amateur Sports: NCAA Member Institutions

1. College and universities that are NCAA members implement drug testing policies and procedures because they are required to do so. Do you think colleges and universities would uphold this practice absent the requirement? Are there arguments that can be made against drug test policies in college sports?
2. Should colleges and universities be given the latitude to restrict more substances than the NCAA list? What concerns might this practice create?

Amateur Sports: Interscholastic

1. What factors must be taken into consideration when drafting a drug testing policy for a public high school?
2. At what age or grade should drug testing start?
3. The decision in the *Earls* case expands the decision of *Vernonia* by allowing school districts to test more students with no direct evidence of drug use by students present. Under what circumstances should schools be allowed to test student-athletes? What about those who participate in "competitive" extracurricular activities? How would you define extracurricular activity? How would you treat members of the school's debate team?
4. The Supreme Court's decision in *Earls* mentions that a study shows that students who engage in extracurricular activities at schools are less likely to have substance abuse problems. Do you agree with this proposition? If you do agree, wouldn't the proper course of action be to test all students who are not involved in extracurricular activities? What would be the effect of that? What legal ramifications might result?
5. In between the Vernonia and Earls cases, state courts have found that drug testing of student-athletes without any suspicion of the use of drugs was unconstitutional. In *Trinidad School District No. 1 v. Lopez* (1998), a band member challenged the school board's policy of suspicionless urinalysis drug tests for 6 through 12 grade students participating in extracurricular activities. In finding that the policy was unconstitutional, the court stated: "Although band members wear uniforms, they do not undergo the type of public undressing and communal showers required of students athletes. The court here finds this fact significant. Furthermore, the court holds that 'the type of voluntariness to which the *Vernonia* Court referred does not apply to students who want to enroll in a for-credit class that is part of the school's

(continues)

DISCUSSION QUESTIONS (CONTINUED)

curriculum.'" See also *Gardner ex rel. Gardner v. Tulia Independent School District* (2000), in which a policy mandating suspicionless drug testing for all students in grades 7 through 12 who were engaged in extracurricular activity was considered in violation of the Fourth Amendment. Do you agree more with the state level interpretations or the federal interpretations? Why?

6.   Victoria Dixon is an honor student and member of the ninth-grade chess team at her high school. The school district has recently instituted a drug testing procedure whereby "all students involved in extracurricular activities in school will be subject to random drug testing throughout the year." The first draft of the policy included only athletic teams, but after the parents of some of the football team members complained, the board changed the policy to include all students in extracurricular activities. The board stated, "There is no rampant drug use in high schools in the district at the current time but this policy is instituted to ensure that drug use does not occur." Victoria and her parents refuse to sign a drug testing consent form, and she is removed from the team. She and her parents file a lawsuit in federal court challenging the policy. What legal considerations are present? What defenses does the school district have in implementing such a policy?

KEY TERMS

Arbitration

Collective bargaining

Grievance

Interscholastic

National Labor Relations Act

Players unions

Private entity

Probable cause

Reasonable cause

Search and seizure

State actor

REFERENCES

Abbott, H. (2013). Gaps in the NBA drug testing program. Retrieved from http://espn.go.com/blog/truehoop/post/_/id/51305/gaps-in-nba-drug-testing

Belson, K. (2011). Judge rules for NFL in supplement case. Retrieved from http://www.nytimes.com/2011/02/09/sports/football/09starcap.html?_r=0

Board of Education of Ind. Sch. Dist. No. 92 of Pottawatomie County v. Earls, 536 U.S. 822 (2002).

Brennan v. Bd. of Trustees for Univ. of Louisiana Systems, 691 So.2d 324 (La. Ct. App. 1997).

Brinson, W. (2014). NFL, NFLPA finalize updated drug testing program. Retrieved from http://www.cbssports.com/nfl/eye-on-football/24712879/nfl-nflpa-finalize-drug-testing-program

CBA 101: Highlights of the collectively bargained agreement between the National Basketball Association and the National Basketball Players Association (2014). Retrieved from http://www.nba.com/media/CBA101.pdf

Collective bargaining agreement between the National Hockey League and the National Hockey League

Players Association (2012). Retrieved from http://www.nhl.com/nhl/en/v3/ext/CBA2012/NHL_NHLPA_2013_CBA.pdf

Gardner ex rel. Gardner v. Tulia Independent School District, 183 F. Supp. 2d 854 (N. D. Tex. 2000).

Griffin v. Wisconsin, 107 S. Ct. 3164 (1987).

Hill v. National Collegiate Athletic Association, 865 P.2d 633 (Cal. 1994).

Johnson-Bateman Co., 295 N.L.R.B. 180, 182 (1989).

Joint Drug Agreement, 2011. Retrieved from http://mlb.mlb.com/pa/pdf/jda.pdf

Littman, C. (2009). Onterrio Smith's Whizzinator on the auction block. SBNation. Retrieved from http://www.sbnation.com/2009/8/28/1644527/onterrio-smiths-whizzinator-on-the

Long v. National Football League, 870 F. Supp. 101 (W.D. Pa. 1994).

Mitchell, G.J. (2007). Report to the Commissioner of Baseball of an independent investigation into the illegal use of steroids and other performance enhancing substances by players in Major League Baseball. Retrieved from http://files.mlb.com/mitchrpt.pdf

National Collegiate Athletic Association, NCAA Division I Manual 1 (2015).

New Jersey v. T.L.O., 469 U.S. 325, 329 (1985).

Rabuano, M.M. (2000). An examination of drug-testing as a mandatory subject of collective bargaining in Major League Baseball. *University of Pennsylvania Journal of Labor and Employment Law*, 4(2), 439–461.

Roshkoff, R.L. (1996). University of Colorado v. Derdeyn: The constitutionality of random, suspicionless urinalysis drug-testing of college athletes. *Jeffrey S. Moorad Sports Law Journal*, 3(1), Article 10.

Skinner v. Railway Labor Executives' Ass'n, 489 U.S. 602, 626 (1989).

Tinker v. Des Moines, 393 U.S. 503 (1969).

Trinidad School District No. 1 v. Lopez, 963 P. 2d 1095 (Colo. 1998).

United States Constitution, Amendment IV.

United States v. Jacobsen, 466 U.S. 109, 113 (1984).

University of Colorado v. Derdeyn, 863 P.2d 929 (Colo. 1993).

Vernonia School District v. Acton, 515 U.S. 646, 653 (1995).

Wick, J.Y. (2014). Performance-enhancing drugs: A new reality in sports? *Pharmacy Times*, Retrieved from http://www.pharmacytimes.com/publications/issue/2014/march2014/performance-enhancing-drugs-a-new-reality-in-sports

Williams v. National Football League and John Lombardo, M.D., 582 F.3d 863 (2009).

York v. Wahkiakum School District, 178 P.3rd 995 (2008).

Young, S. (2010). PIAC (Pee in a cup): The new standardized test for student athletes. *BYU Education and Law Journal*, 10, 163–190.

CONTRACTS

CHAPTER

8

LEARNING OBJECTIVES

By the end of the chapter, the reader will be able to:

1. Identify the uniqueness of sports contracts and how they are used and interpreted within the sports industry
2. Identify the elements of a valid and legally enforceable contract
3. Identify the remedies available when a breach of contract occurs
4. Recognize the key provisions present in sport employment contracts
5. Identify the unique characteristics of coaching contracts and standard player contracts
6. Recognize the varying types of non-employment contracts that are common in the sport industry

RELATED CASES

Case 8.1   Summey v. Monroe County Department of Education, Tenn. Court of Appeals (2012)

Case 8.2   Spears v. Grambling State University, 111 So. 3d 392 (2012)

INTRODUCTION

Contracts are formed in every area of the sports industry; the majority of sport enterprises are operated as businesses, and contracts are the foundation of any business relationship. There are contracts for broadcasting deals, sponsorships, ticket sales, facility leases, merchandising and licensing, and players and coaches. The law of contracts emanates from several sources, such as the common law, the Uniform Commercial Code (UCC), and federal and state statutes. The common law principles of contract law apply to sports contracts. The UCC has been enacted in every state and governs commercial transactions between merchants. It is applicable to many contracts in sports as well.

Contracts play a pivotal role in the job responsibilities of many sports industry professionals. Specifically, lawyers, agents, and executives are called on to examine, draft, and interpret contracts frequently as part of their job. A player's agent must be familiar with the terms of the standard player contract as well as other supporting documents to properly represent his or her client. A management executive must understand how salary caps and a luxury tax operate and how they interact with the standard player contract and the collective bargaining process as a whole to properly represent management interests. Facility managers must understand the concept of risk and contract provisions dealing with risk and insurance. Those involved in the marketing and sponsorship areas must grasp the specific provisions that deal with issues such as the right of publicity of athletes, morals clauses, specific uses of the product, territorial rights, and termination. Those working with a college or university may be called on to interpret the National Letter of Intent (NLI), sponsorship contracts, or facility leases in the course of their employment.

Given the many ways contracts impact the sport industry, professionals in all areas of sport must understand the general tenets of contract law. A basic understanding of contract law allows sport industry professionals to determine how contracts function and how they can be interpreted. As contract law is quite in-depth, this chapter will not provide a treatise on contracts; rather, the chapter will provide an overview of contract law so the reader may have the necessary background to understand contracts in the context of sports law.

CONTRACT LAW

Contracts dominate daily business dealings in America. Parties enter into contracts to gain a better understanding of the rights and responsibilities of each party to the agreement. Contracts should clearly state the obligations of each party to the contract and also state the repercussions if a party fails to fulfill those obligations. Parties exchange goods and services in the stream of commerce on an everyday basis through written or oral contracts. Some contracts are more detailed than others, but it is wise for all parties to an agreement to fully understand the terms of a contract before reaching an agreement. Sports contracts are governed by the basics of contract law but possess some unique features as well; contract clauses unique to sport will be discussed later in this chapter.

Contract Defined

The Restatement (Second) of Contracts §1 defines a contract as "a promise or set of promises for the breach of which the law gives a remedy, or the performance of which the law in some way recognizes as a duty" (1981). Contracts create agreements between parties and provide stability to the marketplace so that businesspersons are able to rely on the good faith of others when planning and engaging in business (Niland, 2013). However, as will be discussed, not all promises are enforceable contracts.

CONTRACT ELEMENTS

A contract must meet several criteria to be considered valid and enforceable, or legally binding. Specifically, a contract must contain: (1) agreement between the parties (mutual assent) demonstrated by offer and acceptance of the offer; (2) exchange of consideration between the parties; (3) proper subject matter (legality); and, (4) competence of the parties (capacity).

Mutual Assent

The first requirement of contract formation is agreement, or mutual assent. A valid contract exists after the parties have agreed to all material facts of the contract and a meeting of the minds has occurred. A contract comes into being once the parties have "reached a meeting of the minds, on the essential terms and have manifested the intent to be bound by those terms" (*Schulz v. U.S. Boxing Ass'n*, 1997, p. 136). Parties to a contract obligate themselves to the terms of the contract through offer and acceptance.

An *offer* is a conditional promise made by an offeror to an offeree; an offer occurs when one party presents terms of an agreement to another party, and the other party is in a position to respond (Restatement (Second) of Contracts § 24, 1981). *Acceptance* is defined as a willingness to be bound by the terms of the offer and must contain an assent—or meeting of the minds—to the essential terms contained in the offer (*Gillespie v. Budkin*, 2005). The essential terms of the contract must be definite enough to provide a basis for enforcement of the agreement. Further, acceptance can be verbal, signatory, or otherwise performed as permitted by the contract. Occasionally, contracts are created after acceptance of the initial offer; however, many contracts are entered into through a negotiating process where an offer by one party is countered by the opposing party. Negotiations may continue until the parties reach an agreement and have a meeting of the minds, thereby creating a binding and enforceable contract.

Consideration

Beyond offer and acceptance, a contract must also have consideration to be valid; these three elements work together as a contract is formed. *Consideration* is the value given in exchange for a promise (the promise made when the offer was accepted). Consideration is the thing of value that has been bargained for in exchange for a promise. No contract is enforceable until both parties receive something of value out of the exchange (*Schulz v. U.S. Boxing Ass'n.*, 1997). In *Philadelphia v. Lajoie* (1902), a player argued that he was allowed to abandon his contract because it lacked consideration, but the court disagreed. Courts will not question the adequacy of consideration exchanged between the parties, only that consideration has in fact been exchanged. Further, consideration can be either a promise to give something of legal value or a promise to refrain from doing something. For example, if John's Sporting Goods store offers Jared $50,000 to stop using a trademark similar to John's store, a valid agreement has been formed between the parties. The consideration between the parties is the money John is giving to Jared and Jared's forbearance to not use the trademark.

Capacity

Aside from offer, acceptance and consideration, another requirement for contract validity is *capacity*; this requires parties to the contract to be competent to enter into the contract. A contract is not valid unless all parties to the contract are competent and are able to bind themselves to the contract. A party might lack the necessary capacity if he or she is a minor (under 18), under the care of a guardian, or intoxicated at the time the party enters into the contract. Disputes can arise over capacity, and whether a contract is voidable because capacity was absent. For example, in *Central Army Sports Club v. Arena Ass'n.* (1997), the court found a Russian hockey player's signature on a standard player contract voidable because he signed it before he was 18 years of age.

Capacity is of particular concern in collegiate sport, given that many high school athletes commit to play for colleges and universities using the NLI, a legally binding agreement between a prospective student-athlete and institution. Since prospective college athletes may not have reached majority age by the signing period for their sport, the National Collegiate Athletic Association (NCAA) and Collegiate Commissioners Association, who administer the NLI program, require that the NLI be signed by either a parent or a legal guardian if the athlete is under 21 years old. Such language is intended to insure that lack of capacity does not render the NLI voidable.

Legality

A contract must also be for a legal purpose to be enforceable. A court will not enforce an illegal contract. Likewise, a court will not enforce a contract that violates a statute or is against public policy. For example, a contract between an agent and student-athlete that violates NCAA rules is considered against public policy and is not enforceable.

ADDITIONAL CONTRACT LAW DOCTRINES

Beyond the four contract elements, additional doctrines and theories can impact contract validity and enforceability. Specifically, sport professionals must be mindful of the statute of frauds, the parol evidence rule, and promissory estoppel, as well as how interpretation can impact an agreement.

Statute of Frauds

As stated above, acceptance of contract terms can occur verbally, in writing, or through performance of certain criteria. However, the *statute of frauds* dictates that certain contracts must be in writing to be enforceable; such circumstances include contracts for the sale or lease of land, contracts that cannot be performed in one year, and contracts for the sale of goods that exceed $500. For example, employment contracts such as coaching contracts are typically multi-year contracts, and will not be fully performed within one year from the signing; these contracts must be in writing. Similarly, facility lease agreements are typically for multiple years, and must too be in writing (Wong, 1988).

Parol Evidence Rule

The *parol evidence rule* provides that a valid contract is the final statement of agreement between the parties and that no prior or subsequent statements, oral or written, can be considered if a contract dispute arises. For example, in *Taylor v. Wake Forest University* (1972), plaintiff student-athlete Gregg Taylor and the University differed on whether Taylor's refusal to participate in football for poor academic performance was reasonable grounds to constitute revocation of the scholarship. The court deferred to the written provision governing academic performance in the scholarship agreement (the contract), and refused to accept oral statements allegedly made by representatives of Wake Forest that differed from the contract language. In *Yocca v. Pittsburgh Steelers Sports Inc.* (2004), season ticket holders sued the team after purchasing seat licenses. The ticket holders alleged that the brochure for the seat license promised tickets at the 20-yard line, and the seats received were at the 18-yard line. The court dismissed the case holding that the contract for the seat license represented the full and final contract between the parties, and that the brochure was not sufficient to alter the terms therein.

The parol evidence rule makes it very challenging for a party to a contract dispute to impose obligations "different from or in addition to those expressly delineated in the contract documents" (Mitten et al., 2009, p. 116).

Promissory Estoppel

The basis of any contract is an agreement between two or more parties; this agreement is a promise that is then bound by consideration. The doctrine of *promissory estoppel* recognizes that individuals may rely on promises to their detriment absent consideration, and allows individuals to recover the benefit of a promise made even if all required elements of a contract don't exist (Restatement (Second) of Contracts § 90 (1981)). If a promise made by a promisor to a promisee was significant enough to move the promisee to act on it, promissory estoppel may allow for a legal remedy. A plaintiff asserting they are owed such legal remedy must prove: (1) existence of a promise between parties; (2) reasonableness that the promise could be relied upon; (3) the promise relied upon to promisees detriment; and (4) failure of the court to enforce the promise would result in an injustice. In *Fortay v. University of Miami* (1994), Brian Fortay alleged that he based his decision to attend the University of Miami (instead of other highly recognized Division I football programs) on promises made by the coaching staff during the recruiting process. Specifically, Fortay alleged that Miami promised not to recruit other quarterbacks, that Fortay would be the starting quarterback by his third year, and that Miami would provide specific player development opportunities to improve his skill at the quarterback position. When Fortay was not given the starting job, he filed a lawsuit to recover damages for the broken promise. In stark contrast to other similar cases brought by student athletes, the *Fortay* court ruled that Fortay alleged facts sufficient to support a breach of oral contract claim; subsequently, the parties settled.

Promissory Estoppel is not a doctrine commonly accepted by courts, especially in cases brought by student athletes; however, the *Fortay* case illustrates the elements of the doctrine.

OTHER CONTRACT LAW ISSUES

A valid contract that meets all required elements may still be unenforceable if genuineness of assent between the parties is absent. A party to the contract may assert that contract terms were misrepresented or that the contract contains a mistake and thus no true meeting of the minds has occurred. Additionally, a party to a contract may claim that a contract is unconscionable. Lastly, a party to a contract may claim that there are issues regarding how the contract is interpreted. If a party to the contract successfully asserts any of the above conditions, the contract may be rendered unenforceable.

Misrepresentation

A *misrepresentation* is a false assertion, or "an assertion that is not in accord with the facts" (Restatement (Second) § 159). If one party to a contract makes a false assertion that induces another party to enter into a contract, the innocent party may be able to rescind the contract or file a claim for damages. To be actionable, misrepresentation must be a false assertion of a fact, not an expression of an opinion. Further, the misrepresentation may be unintentional or intentional. Unintentional misrepresentation (innocent) results in contract rescission while intentional misrepresentation (fraudulent) often results in damages (Murphy et al., 1997).

Mistake

Mistakes in contracts can create issues as well. There are two types of mistakes: unilateral and mutual. A *unilateral mistake* occurs when one of the parties to the contract makes a mistake as to some material fact contained in the contract, and it has an adverse effect on the performance of the contract. The adversely affected party may be able to void the contract, assuming they can prove the other party knew of the mistake or was at fault for causing the mistake (Wong, 2010). A *mutual mistake* occurs when "both parties, at the time of contracting, share a misconception about a basic assumption of vital fact upon which they base their bargain." (*Alea London, Ltd. v. Bono Soltysiak Enterprises*, 2006, p. 415). A mutual mistake in a contract might lead to a rescission of that contract.

Unconscionability

Unconscionability can also create problems in the formation of contracts. A case dealing with this concept in the sports context was *Connecticut Professional Sports Corp. v. Heyman* (1967), in which a player contract was deemed unconscionable and therefore unenforceable. To determine unconscionability, "[t]he basic test is whether, in the light of the general commercial background and the commercial needs of the particular trade or case, the clauses involved are so one-sided as to be unconscionable under the circumstances existing at the time of the making of the contract. . . . The principle is one of the prevention of oppression and unfair surprise . . . and not of disturbance of allocation of risks because of superior bargaining power" (U.C.C. § 2-302, 1977).

Interpretation

Issues relating to the interpretation of a contract can be essential to a contract dispute. The parties may believe they are entering into a contract and that they have reached a meeting of the minds on all essential terms of the contract, but they may be operating under different assumptions as a result of the parties' differing interpretation of a word or phrase found in the contract. When interpreting a contract, the court gives effect to the intent of the parties involved in the contract. "When the words of a contract are clear and explicit and lead to no absurd consequences, no further interpretation may be made in search of the parties' intent" (*Sports Tech, Inc. v. SFI Manufacturing, Inc*, 2003, p. 807). Any ambiguity in a contract will be construed against the drafter of the contract.

BREACH OF CONTRACT REMEDIES

A breach of contract results when one party to the contract (or both) fail to fulfill the obligations they agreed to when executing the contract. Several remedies may be available to the non-breaching party, including various types of damages and an equitable remedy called *specific performance*.

Damages

The purpose of awarding *damages* to the non-breaching party is to make that party whole under the contract. A non-breaching party can receive "benefit of the bargain" damages, which place the injured party in the same position they would have been had the contract not been breached. *Compensatory damages* are damages available to the non-breaching party to recover direct losses and costs. *Consequential damages* are losses caused indirectly by a breach of contract. These damages, which are also referred to as "special" damages, attempt to compensate the non-breaching party for any additional losses they may have incurred as a result of the defendant's breach of contract. *Punitive damages*, also referred to as "exemplary" damages, are designed to punish a defendant for improper conduct. Parties may also agree to the damages that will be caused in the case of a breach of the contract in the form of a *liquidated damages clause*. A liquidated damages clause includes in the contract itself a predetermined damage award should the contract be breached. Based on the freedom of contract, this clause will be upheld as long as the amount is not unconscionable, does not operate as a penalty, and does not offend public policy (Murphy et al., 1997).

Equitable Remedy

Specific performance of a contract is an equitable remedy available to the non-breaching party that calls upon the opposing party to perform the contract. It will not usually be granted unless monetary damages are inadequate (Restatement (Second) of Contracts § 356). Specific performance is a remedy reserved for when the subject matter of the contract is unique. For example, if A proposed to sell B a 1952 Topps Mickey Mantle baseball card and then refused to perform, thus breaching the contract, the appropriate remedy for A would be specific performance because the card is unique. Specific performance of a contract is an order by a court to require a breaching party to perform obligations under the contract.

Lastly, when a breach of contract occurs, the injured party must take reasonable steps to lessen or mitigate the damages incurred; this is called the *duty to mitigate* (Murphy et al., 1997). For example, if an employee is terminated in the third month of a 12-month employment contract, he or she must mitigate the damages by attempting to find a new job; he or she cannot stay unemployed for nine months and then claim damages for that time period. This principle is further discussed in *Baldwin v. Board of Supervisors for the University of Louisiana System* (2014), a case available in the online course supplement.

APPLICATION OF CONTRACT LAW TO SPORTS

Contracts govern most aspects of the sport industry including coach and player employment, broadcasting deals, sponsorships, ticket sales, facility leases, endorsements, merchandising and licensing. These contract types can be categorized as employment contracts and non-employment contracts. While each individual contract is unique, contracts within each category are likely to contain common provisions or clauses.

Employment Contracts

Employment contracts typically contain *clauses* or *provisions* that govern the employment relationship; many of these provisions are standard, setting forth the nature and duration of the contract, employment terms and compensation, and any other relevant employment conditions (Wong, 1988). While all employment contracts contain provisions that govern the relationship between employer and employee, employment contracts are also industry specific. To demonstrate the varying types of clauses and provisions contained in a sport employment contract, coaching contracts (collegiate head coach) and a standard player contract (professional athlete) will be discussed.

Coaches' Contracts

At the collegiate (and professional) levels, coaches are being given contracts with large financial commitments over long periods of time. For example, Nick Saban, the head football coach at the University of Alabama is currently under an eight-year contract with guaranteed compensation of over $55 million ("College Football Coaches," n.d.). Oklahoma State head men's basketball coach, Travis Ford, is under a 10-year, $24.5 million contract, which is actually lower than many other prominent college basketball coaches (Baumbach, 2015).

The specific clauses of a collegiate head coaching contract are impacted by the level of sport and the responsibilities required of the position. Perhaps most important are the contract provisions related to *term* and *compensation*: the length of the contract and the financial obligations contained within. The term of the contract is calculated in a specific number of years, typically ranging between three to five (Lopiano, 2008). In addition to the initial term, many coaching contracts also contain a *rollover provision* that specifies the agreement will automatically extend for a new term, or rollover, if certain conditions are met.

Compensation is typically composed of a base salary, paid in annual installments, and other performance based earnings or deferred compensation incentives (discussed below). Coaches' total earnings often include far more than a base salary; other components may include payments for personal services such as participation in fundraising initiatives, conducting camps or clinics, endorsing team sponsors, making speeches or appearances, appearing on television or radio programs, and participating in social media or other public relations initiatives. Also, a coach may receive benefits that are paid for by the institution such as a car, family travel, private club memberships, insurance policies, or event tickets (Lopiano, 2008).

In addition to the term and compensation clauses, the contract must outline the job responsibilities under; the *duties and responsibilities clause*. As noted above, a college coach is called on to function in many capacities in today's competitive coaching market. He or she has to serve as coach, recruiter, counselor, event scheduler, budget analyst, fundraiser, and sometimes public relations expert as well. One of the most emphasized responsibilities of a head coach is the mandate to comply with NCAA and other governing body regulations. Given the strict oversight of college athletics at both the national and conference level, compliance with the rules and regulations is of particular importance, and often described in detail within a college coaching contract. Additional duties and responsibilities may be mandated by conference or NCAA membership.

Further, college coaching contracts may also contain multiple *incentive* clauses; these clauses monetize achievements related to a coach's duties

and responsibilities. For example, a coach may receive bonus compensation for accomplishing objectives such as increased ticket revenue, post-season or championship appearances, meeting or surpassing graduation rate targets, winning rivalry games, or receiving coaching honors (Lopiano, 2008). *Incentive clauses* are typically very specific and tied to quantifiable benchmarks. Further, incentive clauses can contain other items such as travel expenses, automobiles, and private memberships. For example, Dabo Swinney, the head football coach at Clemson University receives the following incentives (among others): (1) $1,720,024 for media work, public appearance and an apparel/shoe deal; (2) $37,500 for an Atlantic Coast Conference (ACC) title game appearance; (3) $75,000 for an ACC Championship; (4) $56,250 for a Bowl Championship Series (BCS) bowl bid; (5) $75,000 for a BCS bowl win; (6) $150,000 for a national championship win; (7) $50,000–$100,000 for conference or national coach of the year; (8) two automobiles, replaced every year, with paid insurance; (9) 10 tickets and a 22 person suite to each Clemson home football game, along with other Clemson sporting event tickets; and (10) use of the Clemson University plane and a country club membership ("College Football Coaches," n.d.).

Given the transitional nature of the coaching profession, the *termination clause* is a particularly important component of a coaching contract; as in all employment contracts, coaches can be dismissed with or without cause. *With cause termination* occurs when the employer terminates the contract prior to its term expiring for reasons such as breach of the contract, criminal conduct, improper behavior, or violation of team rules. For example, Larry Eustachy, an Iowa State basketball coach, was terminated with cause after he was photographed at a student party holding a beer can and kissing young women on the cheek. The photograph appeared in the *Des Moines Register*, and Eustachy later admitted he had made poor decisions (Witosky, 2003). The following is a standard clause in a coach's contract dealing with termination for cause.

Termination by university with cause. University shall have the right to terminate this Agreement for just cause prior to its normal expiration. The term "just cause" shall include, in addition to and as examples of its normally understood meaning in employment contracts, any of the following:

a. Violation by Employee of any of the material provisions of this Agreement not corrected by Employee within twenty (20) days following receipt of notification of such violation from the University.
b. Refusal or unwillingness by Employee to perform his duties hereunder in good faith to the best of Employee's abilities.
c. Any serious act of misconduct by Employee, including but not limited to an act of dishonesty, theft or misappropriation of University property, moral turpitude, insubordination, or act injuring, abusing, or endangering others.
d. A serious or intentional violation of any law, rule, regulation, constitutional provision, by-law, or interpretation of the University, the state of _____, conference, or the NCAA, which violation may, in the sole discretion of the University, reflect adversely upon the University or its athletic program in a material way.
e. Any other conduct of Employee seriously and materially prejudicial to the best interests of the University or its athletic program.

Termination without cause is best defined as "a premature termination of a contract prior to the end term date, and it normally involves payment of compensation to the coach who was prematurely

terminated" (Greenberg, 2006, p. 205). Termination without cause occurs when the employer wishes to end the employment relationship prior to the term expiring, but does not have a "with cause" option to do so per the contract provisions. "In most contracts the university has the right at any time to terminate the coach's contract without cause or reason and for the university's own convenience prior to its normal expiration" (Greenberg, 2006, p. 205). Such cases are complex and often result in significant financial repercussions for the university, as it will likely be obligated to pay a portion of the remaining compensation owed for the initial term of the contract, the entirety of the remaining compensation owed, or other liquidated damages. For example, the following clause is found in Sean Miller's head basketball coaching contract with the University of Arizona:

University shall pay to Coach an amount equal to one half of the sum of his then current annual Program Salary and Related Compensation for the remainder of the Contract Year in which such termination occurred plus (i) $4.8 million if the termination occurred in the first Contract Year, (ii) $4.0 million if the termination occurred in the second Contract Year; (iii) $3.2 million if the termination occurred in the third Contract Year, or (iv) $1.6 million if the termination occurred in the fourth Contract Year. In the event of such termination after the fourth Contract Year, University shall pay to Coach an amount equal to one half of the sum of his then current annual Program Salary and Related Compensation per year, multiplied by the number of full and fractional years remaining on the Term. (Greenberg and Paul, 2013, p. 343)

A liquidated damages clause is a provision in an employment contract that stipulates the amount of money to be recovered if the contract is breached by either party (Greenberg and Paul,

2013). "Damages for breach by either party may be liquidated in the agreement but only at an amount that is reasonable in the light of the anticipated or actual loss caused by the breach" (Restatement (Second) of Contracts § 356, 1981). In a coaching contract, the employer university and the coach "will stipulate that the payments received for termination without cause are agreed upon payments that constitute liquidated damages" (Greenberg and Paul, 2013, p. 348). A *buyout clause* lists the damages that the coach will pay back to the school, should the coach choose to end the contract early. The transitional and competitive nature of coaching makes these clauses standard in coaching contracts. The Dabo Swinney contract referenced earlier contains a buyout provision that obligates Swinney to pay amounts ranging from $750,000 to $3,000,000 in damages depending on the year of the buyout ("-College Football Coaches," n.d.).

PROFESSIONAL ATHLETES (THE STANDARD PLAYER CONTRACT)

All major sports leagues use standard player contracts to convey the essential terms of the employment relationship. The standard player contract is a product of the collective bargaining process (see Chapter 10). Management and labor have negotiated what they have deemed to be a contract suitable for both parties, each arguing for provisions that support the best interests of either labor or management. Standard player contracts are typically brief; the National Football League's (NFL's) is just 25 paragraphs. However, even though all athletes are bound by the same standard terms, many athletes are able to modify the standard player contract through the negotiation process by adding incentives and bonus clauses unique to their unique contract terms.

The standard player contract is similar to other employment contracts in that it governs the employee-employer relationship. However, given the uniqueness of professional sport teams and leagues as the employer, the standard player contract contains provisions not found in other employment contracts; some of the provisions are discussed below.

Compensation Structure

The standard player contract and addendums include the compensation structure for professional athletes. Specifically, an athlete's total compensation includes negotiated amounts such as base salary, signing bonuses, option bonuses, incentive clauses, and roster bonuses, as well as non-negotiated achievement based earnings such as playoff or Pro Bowl appearances (Deubert and Wong, 2009). The complexities of professional athlete compensation structures cannot be understated. Some monies, such as a signing bonus, are considered "guaranteed," whereas other monies are not. Specifically, the base salary offered to a player in Section 5 of the NFL standard player contract can be guaranteed, but this does not happen often. Players who do not earn a roster spot on the team for the contracted season are not owed the base salary if Section 5 is non-guaranteed (Deubert and Wong, 2009). For example, prior to the 2011 NFL season, David Akers signed a three-year, $9 million contract with the San Francisco 49ers. The team paid Akers a $1.7 million signing bonus that was guaranteed. In 2011, Akers was paid the remaining $1.3 million in salary and in 2012, the team paid him another $3 million in salary. Akers was scheduled to earn the remaining $3 million in salary for the 2013 season, but he did not get that money because the 49ers released him (Sando, 2013).

Bonus and Addendum Clauses

Professional athletes in all major leagues are able to negotiate bonus clauses to the standard player contract. *Bonus clauses* can include performance bonuses based on statistics compiled by the player or team or bonuses based on awards given by the team or league.

Bonus clauses are not a new invention. In 1919, Chicago White Sox pitcher Eddie Cicotte had a $10,000 bonus in his contract payable to him if he won 30 games. According to the book *Eight Men Out* by Eliot Asinof (1963), Cicotte was benched late in the season so that Charles Comisky would not have to pay the bonus; he finished with a win-loss record of 28 and 12. In 1959, slugger Rocky Colavito was apparently going to receive a bonus for not hitting 40 home runs, because the Indians wanted him to strike out less. He didn't try hard enough, however, and finished the 1959 season with 42 home runs and 86 strikeouts (Light, 2005). In 1972, Oakland Athletics owner Charlie Finley inserted a clause in each player's contract offering $300 if he grew a mustache. Many players on the team took him up on the offer. More recently, outfielder Carlos Beltran negotiated a private suite while traveling on the road for the New York Mets, and Padres outfielder Phil Nevin's contract indicated that he could become a free agent if the construction of the Padres new ballpark ever stopped and did not resume within one year. Nevin's agent wanted the clause in the contract because he believed the team could not be a contender without a new stadium.

Some players have been able to negotiate attendance clauses in their contracts. Hall of Fame pitcher Bob Feller had an attendance clause in his contract with the Cleveland Indians in the 1940s. Roger Clemens's contract contained a clause that paid him a bonus if the Astros drew 2.8 million fans in 2005 and also provided that for each 100,000 fans that attended, he could earn up to an additional $3.4 million.

The *signing bonus* is perhaps one of the most customary and often used bonuses; many players will receive a one-time bonus for merely signing the contract. Joe Namath received the largest bonuses of his era when the New York Jets of the AFL gave him a record $427,000 and a new Lincoln Continental in 1967. Signing bonuses have continued to increase over the years, and often exceed million dollar amounts. For example, in 2013 Aaron Rodgers, quarterback of the Green Bay Packers signed a contract that included a $35 million signing bonus (Badenhausen, 2013).

Although the signing bonus is typically thought of as "guaranteed money," they are not without controversy. NFL teams have attempted to retrieve all or part of signing bonuses paid to players for various reasons. The Miami Dolphins prevailed at arbitration against Ricky Williams for the return of his signing bonus. Arbitrator Richard Bloch awarded the Dolphins $8,616,373 from Williams, who announced in July 2004 that he was retiring. The $8.6 million award included $5.3 million in contract incentives as well as a $3.3 million portion of a signing bonus paid to Williams by the New Orleans Saints in 1999. The Dolphins asserted that because Williams had retired and failed three drug tests, they were entitled to recoup bonuses paid to him (Cole, 2004). The New England Patriots withheld $8.75 million of Terry Glenn's $11.5 million bonus, stating he violated the morals clause in his contract when he tested positive under the NFL Substance Abuse Policy. In a rare situation, Chris Borland, formerly of the San Francisco 49ers, returned three quarters of his signing bonus after only playing out one year of his four year contract. Borland initially received $617,436, and returned $463,077 back to the team (Brinson, 2015).

Interpretation of Bonus Clause

Signing bonuses are not the only type of bonus subject to dispute; issues can arise over bonus provisions in contracts if they are not drafted carefully. Former Minnesota Vikings Hall of Famer Alan Page had a dispute with the Vikings over a provision in his contract that stated "said player shall receive a bonus in the amount of $2500 if he is selected 'All Pro' by any of the following: AP, UPI, PFW, or the *Sporting News*." He was chosen as one of the defensive tackles on the "All-NFL" team selected by UPI and the *Sporting News* as well as being named to the AP's second-team "All-NFL" squad. He subsequently requested payment of the bonus from the Vikings. The issue was how to define "All-Pro." Jim Finks of the Vikings testified that to him, "All-Pro" meant that the player was selected as the top player at the position in the entire league. Finks had drafted the clauses in question on behalf of the Vikings. NFL commissioner Pete Rozelle ruled in favor of Page, finding he was entitled to the $2500 bonus. The team had specifically stated that the UPI and the *Sporting News* would serve to determine if Page were entitled to the bonus. The problem was that neither of those entities used the term "All-Pro" but instead chose two All-Conference Teams, AFC, and NFC. Page had been named to the "All-NFC" team, which was the highest designation he *could* receive because there was no "All-Pro" team chosen.

Option Clauses

An *option* contract is an offer that is considered irrevocable for a specific period of time (*George v. Schuman*, 1918). A player and team may agree to a particular length of a contract, but they can also give each party an option to extend the contract; this is similar to the rollover provision discussed in coaching contracts. Player contracts have contained option clauses in which the team retains the right to a player at a certain salary. In today's sporting world, option contracts are usually negotiated as an addendum to the standard player contract.

Teams or players can agree to option clauses, and they can appear in all forms. Former Houston Texans quarterback David Carr signed a seven-year, $46.75 million contract as a rookie. The final three years of the contract were voidable if he reached certain performance incentives. Therefore, his contract would have expired on March 3, 2006. However, the Texans had the option to "buy back" the voidable years. The first option was that

the team could pay Carr a bonus of $5.5 million to buy back two seasons, with base salaries of $5 million for 2006 and $5.25 million for 2007. The second option was for the Texans to pay an $8 million bonus to buy back three seasons, with base salaries of $5.25 million in 2006 and 2007 and a salary of $6 million in 2008. The Texans exercised the second option, retaining Carr for three more seasons.

Other Significant Clauses in Player Contracts

A variety of other specialty clauses can be inserted into players' contracts. They are too numerous to name here, but a few deserve special attention: the no-trade clause, the skills clause, and a clause regulating off-season activities.

Most standard player contracts include an "assignment clause" that allows the team to trade a player without the player's consent; however, some players are able to negotiate a *no-trade clause* as an addendum to their contracts. Typically, no-trade clauses provide that the player cannot be traded without the player's consent. Similarly, no-trade clauses may allow a player to list teams to which the player cannot be traded or specify a specific division or conference to which the player can or cannot be traded.

All standard player contracts in sports have a skills clause that allows the team to cut a player from a team if the player fails to possess the requisite skill to continue to be on the team. Paragraph 11 of the NFL's standard player contract allows a team to terminate a player's contract if the team determines there are better players on the squad. The NFL's standard player contract includes the following provision:

1.   SKILL, PERFORMANCE AND CONDUCT.

Player understands that he is competing with other players for a position on Club's roster within the applicable player limits. If at any time, in the sole judgment of Club, Player's skill or performance has been unsatisfactory as compared with that of other players competing for positions on Club's roster, or if Player has engaged in personal conduct reasonably judged by Club to adversely affect or reflect on Club, then Club may terminate this contract. In addition, during the period any salary cap is legally in effect, this contract may be terminated if, in Club's opinion, Player is anticipated to make less of a contribution to Club's ability to compete on the playing field than another player or players whom Club intends to sign or attempts to sign, or another player or players who is or are already on Club's roster, and for whom Club needs room.

(NFL CBA Standard Player Agreement, 2011)

A standard player contract will also typically include obligations on the part of the player to keep him or herself in good physical condition to be able to perform services on behalf of the team. The standard player contract for the NHL states the following with regard to physical condition of the player:

2. The Player agrees to give his services and to play hockey in all League Championship, All Star, International, Exhibition, Play-Off and Stanley Cup games to the best of his ability under the direction and control of the Club in accordance with the provisions hereof. The Player further agrees,

   a. To report to the Club training camp at the time and place fixed by the Club, in good physical condition,
   b. To keep himself in good physical condition at all times during the season . . . (Weiler, 1992)

Teams have a major stake in ensuring that players are kept in good physical condition, especially if they have signed the player to a guaranteed contract. They do not want to assume the risk that a player will get injured participating in another sport. Therefore, a player's extracurricular activities are also addressed in the standard player contract.

Many players have been subjected to scrutiny for their off-season activities. For example, the Atlanta Hawks attempted to suspend Michael Sojourner without pay based on Paragraph 17 of the Uniform Player Contract because of an off-season injury he sustained. Sojourner broke his kneecap when executing a slam dunk while he was practicing at the University of Utah. The arbitrator found in favor of Sojourner, stating that slam dunking was not a "dangerous activity" and that the injury did not occur while he was playing for another team or exhibition game (Greenberg and Gray, 1998).

Non-Employment Contracts

Sport is a business; as such, most transactions related to sport are governed by contracts. Think about a charity basketball tournament: for just that one time event, there is likely to be a facility lease agreement, a sponsorship agreement, an event management agreement, a food vendor or concessions agreement, etc. Each of these agreements is a contract, and subject to the same principles of contract law discussed earlier in this chapter. The primary difference between service contracts and employment contracts is the subject matter and the parties involved. These parties may include vendors, officials, security staff, concessionaires, mascots, facility owners and/or media partners; as such, the specific terms and content of the contract will vary from agreement to agreement (Greenwell, Danzey-Bussell, & Shonk, 2014).

Event Contracts

Sporting events range from large scale and complex to small and relatively simple. Regardless of event size, event contracts always contain standard contract inclusions such as parties, term, responsibilities, and termination. In addition, event contracts may include other unique provisions related to event staffing, security deposits, signage, payment terms, event security, food and beverage, and other clauses for ancillary events such as banquets, awards presentations, and autograph signings (Greenwell, Danzey-Bussell, & Shonk, 2014). Each sport event requires a carefully constructed contract that clearly delineates the promises made, responsibilities assigned, and terms of compensation.

Sponsorship and Endorsement Contracts

Sport is a billion dollar business, and sponsorship opportunities are plentiful. Many non-sport businesses invest significant financial resources sponsoring sporting events, teams, or individual athletes as a way to market their own goods and services. Given that sponsorship deals are often multi-year, multi-million dollar agreements, the contracts tend to be lengthy and complex. A *sponsorship contract* ensures that companies and either athletes or sporting events fulfill obligations agreed to as part of the sponsorship negotiations (Wong, 2010).

One of the key factors considered in any sponsorship contract is whether the sponsor is entitled to *exclusivity*, meaning the sponsor is the only business in the product or service category with the ability sponsor the event. Businesses desire exclusivity, and are often willing to pay a premium to get it. When contracting for exclusivity, the parties must be certain to specifically define the exclusive product categories. For example, if a bank sponsors a tennis tournament, the product category will be payment services, and can include ancillary services such as credit cards, ATM cards, traveler's checks, and money wire transfers. The sponsorship contract must specifically define the meaning of the product category and all covered

inclusions as to avoid misunderstandings regarding intent. This same principle is true regarding all other provisions of a sponsorship contract.

Parties to a sponsorship contract must also be aware of policies articulated in the respective Standard Player Contract, Collective Bargaining Agreement, or other governing documents as these policies may impact what sponsorship categories or activities are permissible. While most athletes and teams are free to negotiate sponsorship deals as they deem appropriate, restrictions do exist. For example, per the league Collective Bargaining Agreement, NHL players are not allowed to endorse alcohol or tobacco products.

Sponsorship contracts also contain provisions that grant or restrict use of the sport organization's intellectual property by the sponsoring organization. Frequently, team, league, or event sponsors will be given permission to use an official mark, logo, or slogan from the sport entity, but such use is dictated by *licenses* or clauses written into the contract that define allowable use. Similarly, an emerging area regarding sponsorship contracts is the inclusion of provisions that dictate the permissible use of social media. Digital and social media present sponsors with many new opportunities, but to optimize them they need to be identified and negotiated up front (Ukman, 2013). The list of potential digital and/or social media rights that are available to be sponsored is growing exponentially. The intricacies present in social and digital media, coupled with ever-present emerging technologies, makes this area of primary importance in any sponsorship contract. Specifically, sponsorship contracts may include the following rights: to host live (and/or on-demand) stream on sponsor web site and/or social media channels; to use/sponsor images and video; category exclusivity to property web site; sponsorship of rightsholder's social media account(s); category exclusivity to property's social media account(s); sponsor ID, ads, links and/or features in property's official app; and/or sponsor to conduct property-themed campaign via sponsor's social media accounts (Ukman, 2013).

Similar to sponsorship contracts, *endorsement contracts* have become standard fare for many athletes. Professional athletes can makes millions of dollars if they acquire corporate sponsorship or endorsement deals. The negotiation of such deals can be crucial to the player's livelihood and future. Endorsers desire athletes who present a clean, wholesome image for their products. Corporations thus require athletes to sign a contract that contains a *morals clause*, whereby the company can terminate the agreement if the player places the company in a bad light or brings harm to the company's reputation.

Corporations that retain athletes to represent the company take the risk that the athletes might tarnish the reputation of the product by involvement in off-the-field conduct that is inappropriate. Because so much is at stake, corporations are now taking more precautions to ensure that they have the ability to terminate a contract if an athlete places the corporation in a bad light. For example, in 2014 when Minnesota Viking Adrian Peterson was accused of child abuse, the three companies with which he had endorsement deals either terminated or suspended the contract.

Tortious Interference with a Contract

One last contract law principle that warrants discussion is tortious interference with a contract. This occurs when a third party (not a party to the contract) "knowingly interferes in a contract already in place between two parties" (Wong, 2010). Tortious interference can occur with any contract, and certainly with the sport industry examples discussed thus far. Specifically, tortious interference can occur between agents and athletes, between leagues and other corporations, and between sport sponsors and sport organizations or when a team pursues a head coach already under contract with another university. To prove tortious interference, a plaintiff would need to demonstrate: (1) the existence of a contractual or prospective contractual relation between the complainant and a third party; (2) purposeful action on the part of the defendant specifically intended to harm the existing relation or to prevent a prospective relation from occurring; (3) the absence of privilege or justification on the part of the defendant; and (4) the occasioning of actual legal damage as a result of the defendant's conduct (*Milicic v. Basketball Marketing Co., Inc.*, 2004).

There are many examples of tortious interference claims related to sport contracts. In 2009, Marist University filed a lawsuit against Matt Brady, its former men's basketball coach, and James Madison University (JMU), his new employer. The claims against JMU were for tortious interference with a contract and alleged that JMU knowingly enticed Brady to breach his employment contract with Marist (*Marist College v. Matt Brady et al.*, 2009). Similarly, in 2010, the Tennessee Titans filed a lawsuit claiming that the University of Southern California (USC) and its head football coach Lane Kiffin tortuously interfered with the contract of Kennedy Pola, the Titans running backs coach, when Pola was hired by USC. More recently, Major League Baseball (MLB) filed a tortious interference claim against Biogenesis, a health clinic specializing in hormone therapy and weight loss. The MLB alleged that Biogenesis employees were specifically targeting MLB players to purchase and use performance enhancing drugs known to be banned MLB contracts (Thompson et al., 2013).

CONCLUSION

Contracts govern most business relationships, employment and otherwise. Given the business like nature of sport at all levels, contract law is likely to impact all sport organizations. Well-drafted contracts adhere to the general contract law principles discussed, and include provisions that clearly and specifically dictate the many terms of the promise between parties. Sport managers and administrators must understand the terms of any individual contract, as well as the general legal theories that are present in contract law.

DISCUSSION QUESTIONS

Elements of a Contract

1. In 2001, Jamil Blakmon filed a lawsuit against Allen Iverson alleging breach of contract (among other claims). Blakmon asserted that Iverson breached a promise to pay Blackmon 25% of all earnings from use of the nickname/logo "The Answer," which Blakmon claimed to have created. In ruling for Iverson, the court found no evidence of an agreement where both parties show intent to be bound to definite terms; meaning there was no specific offer, acceptance, and consideration. Blackmon did create the logo, however Iverson's promise to pay was made after the nickname was created; the court considered this a form of past consideration. A promise made in return for actions that have already occurred is unenforceable and is not adequate consideration to form a contract because there is no bargained-for exchange (*Blackmon v. Iverson*, 2003). How should Blackmon have handled this situation initially? As a sport manager, what lessons are learned from this case? Which additional contract law claim may Blackmon have filed?

Additional Contract Law Doctrines

1. In *Jackson v. Drake University* (1991), the plaintiff, Terrell Jackson, was recruited to attend and play basketball at Drake University. During the recruiting process, a Drake coach told Jackson that he would receive a high quality education, and be the star of the basketball team. In both 1988 and 1989, Drake and Jackson signed financial aid agreements related to his sport participation; these agreements were the only written agreements that existed between the parties. During Jackson's time on the basketball team, he was forced to attend practices that interfered with his class and tutoring schedule, was expected to turn in assignments for his classes that were prepared by coaching staff, and advised to take easy courses, instead of courses required to graduate. Jackson also claimed that coaches were emotionally abusive to him during practices. In January 1990, Jackson quit the basketball team and subsequently filed a breach of contract lawsuit alleging that the right to play basketball and the right to an uncompromised educational opportunity were implicit in the financial aid agreements. Drake claimed that all of its obligations under the financial aid agreements were met. The court sided with Drake and held that because the language of the financial aid agreements was clear and unambiguous, no additional rights were implicitly contained. Which contract law doctrine prevented Jackson from succeeding in his claim? Are there any other additional contract law doctrines that may have helped him make his case?

DISCUSSION QUESTIONS (CONTINUED)

2. *Jackson v. Drake University* was decided 25 years ago; however, the issues in that case are still present today. College coaches often make promises to prospective athletes during recruiting visits that are not contained in the NLI; further, if a student is recruited by a coach who then leaves for a different university, the student athlete is still contractually bound to attend the school to which they committed. Should student athletes have recourse when promises made are not kept? Should addendums to the NLI be allowed, as they are to standard player contracts for professional athletes? How would collegiate athletics be impacted if student athletes successfully used promissory estoppel in legal challenges?

Breach of Contract Remedies

1. The calculation of damages in a breach of contract lawsuit is impacted by the plaintiff's duty to mitigate. In 1995, Michael Jordan entered into a 10-year endorsement contract with MCI, a communications company. The agreement gave MCI the right to use Jordan's name, image, and likeness to promote its products. Additionally, the deal was exclusive in its product category; under the contract, Jordan was not permitted to endorse any other communications related products. After the first five years of the contract, MCI filed for bankruptcy, and ceased payment to Jordan; a breach of contract lawsuit was filed. Jordan claimed he was entitled to damages; MCI argued that Jordan had a duty to mitigate the damages, and that he did not adequately do so. Jordan asserted that there was no evidence he could have entered into a substantially similar agreement, and that his business strategy at the time of the bankruptcy had shifted to future NBA ownership and away from endorsements. Ultimately, after consideration of many factors, the court concluded that Jordan did not fulfill his duty to mitigate (*In re Worldcom, Inc.,* 2007). The duty to mitigate places the burden on the plaintiff in a breach of contract lawsuit; does this seem fair? Given the current economic climate, coupled with the advent of social media and public scrutiny, do long-term endorsement deals make sense for either the athlete or the business entity?

Employment Contracts

1. James Kason is an outfielder with the Oakland Athletics. His contract prohibits him from engaging in dangerous off-season activities. While on vacation with his family, he attended a minor league baseball game in which his college roommate was the starting pitcher. The manager of the minor league team asked him to throw out the first pitch. He did not warm up, and during the throw to the plate he suffered a dislocated shoulder. He subsequently missed the first 35 games of the season with the A's. His contract specifically provided the following: "Player shall not play baseball for any other team during the off-season nor shall the player engage in any of the following activities during the off-season, including but not limited to football, or any impromptu or competitive game of football, baseball or softball, lacrosse, lawn

(continues)

DISCUSSION QUESTIONS (CONTINUED)

bowling, bowling, horseback riding, car racing, parachuting, basketball, ice or field hockey, track and field activities, table tennis, tennis, polo, karate, cricket, badminton or any other form of martial arts." Does the team have the legal right to terminate the player's contract? How do you anticipate each party would interpret the relevant clause?

Non-Employment Contracts

1. Your client had recently signed an endorsement agreement with Adidas Corporation. The contract states the following: "Company may revoke this agreement if player commits any act of moral turpitude which reflects poorly on the Company's reputation or diminishes the Company's good will in the marketplace." Your client was arrested for allegedly assaulting a fellow patron in a bar fight. He was shown on television in handcuffs, wearing a hat bearing the company's logo. This picture was displayed on television many times for the next several weeks. The player claimed he was innocent. The company invoked the clause and sent the player a notice that it was terminating the contract. Six months after the player received the termination notice, the local prosecutor dismissed all charges against the player. The player now wants to sue the company for breach of contract. Was the company's position legally sound when it terminated the contract? How could the morals clause be drafted better?

Contract Law Principles Applied

1. Assume you are responsible for planning a golf tournament to raise funds for a charity. Which aspects of the event might require contracts? After considering the collective list of contracts that might be needed, focus on one, and consider what you might include as important terms of the contract.
2. Consider the benefits and burdens of exclusivity in sponsorship contracts. As a sport manager, would you rather negotiate a contract with one sponsor per product category and be compensated for exclusive rights? Or, would you rather have the flexibility to negotiate with multiple companies per category? Regardless of your choice, how important is specifically defining the inclusions of a product category? Can you think of product categories that may seem straightforward but actually aren't?

KEY TERMS

Acceptance	Clause
Bonus clause	Compensation
Buyout clause	Compensatory damages
Capacity	Consequential damages

Consideration
Damages
Duties and responsibilities clause
Duty to mitigate
Endorsement contract
Exclusivity
Incentive clause
Licenses
Liquidated damages clause
Misrepresentation
Morals clause
Mutual mistake
No-trade clause

Offer
Parol evidence rule
Punitive damages
Rollover provision
Signing bonus
Specific performance
Sponsorship contract
Statute of frauds
Term
Termination clause
Termination without cause
Unilateral mistake
With cause termination

REFERENCES

Alea London, Ltd. v. Bono-Soltysiak Enterprises, 186 S.W.3d 403, 415 (Mo. App. E.D. 2006).

Asinof, E. (1963). *Eight Men Out*. New York: Henry Holt.

Badenhausen, K. (2013). The NFL's highest paid players in 2013. Forbes. Retrieved from http://www.forbes.com/sites/kurtbadenhausen/2013/08/14/the-nfls-highest-paid-players-2013/

Baldwin v. Board of Supervisors for the University of Louisiana System et al., No. 2014-C-0827 (La. Sup. Ct. 2014).

Baumbach, J. (2015). Huge performance bonuses commonplace for NCAA basketball coaches. Newsday. Retrieved from http://www.newsday.com/sports/college/college-basketball/huge-performance-bonuses-commonplace-for-ncaa-basketball-coaches-1.10095574

Blackmon v. Iverson, 324 F. Supp. 2d 602 (2003).

Brinson, W. (2015). Chris Borland says he's returning most of signing bonus to 49ers. CBS Sports. Retrieved from http://www.cbssports.com/nfl/eye-on-football/25118370/chris-borland-tells-face-the-nation-he-returned-his-signing-bonus

Central Army Sports Club v. Arena Ass'n., 952 F. Supp. 181 (S.D.N.Y. 1997).

Cole, J. (2004). Ruling: Williams owes Dolphins 8.6 million. *San Diego Union-Tribune*. Retrieved from http://www.utsandiego.com/uniontrib/20040925/news_1s25ricky.html

College football coaches salaries in NCAA FBS. (n.d.). Retrieved from http://sports.newsday.com/long-island/data/college/college-football-coaches-salaries/

Connecticut Professional Sports Corp. v. Heyman, 276 F. Supp. 618 (1967).

Deubert, C., & Wong, G.M. (2009). Understanding the evolution of signing bonuses and guaranteed money in the National Football League: Preparing for the 2011 collective bargaining negotiations. *UCLA Entertainment Law Review*, 16, 179–204.

Fortay v. University of Miami. (1994). U.S. Dist. LEXIS 1865 (D.N.J. 1994).

George v. Schuman, 168 N.W. 486 (Mich. 1918).

Gillespie v. Budkin, 902 So.2d 849 (Fla. 2005).

Greenberg, M.J. (2006). Termination of college coaching contracts: When does adequate cause to terminate exist and who determines its existence? *Marquette Sports Law Review*, 17, 197–224.

Greenberg, M.J., & Gray, J.T. (1998). *Sports Law Practice* (2nd ed.). Charlottesville, Va.: Lexis Law Publishing.

Greenberg, M.J., & Paul, D. (2013). Coaches' contracts termination: Terminating a coach without cause and the obligation to mitigate damages. *Marquette Sports Law Review*, 23, 339–391.

Greenwell, T.C., Danzey-Bussell, L.A., & Shonk, D. (2014). *Managing sport events*. Champaign, Ill.: Human Kinetics.

In re Worldcom, Inc., 20067 WL 446735 (Bkrtcy. S.D.N.Y. 2007).

Jackson v. Drake University, 778 F. Supp. 1490 (S.D. Iowa 1991).

Light, J.F. (2005). *The Cultural Encyclopedia of Baseball* (2nd ed.). Jefferson, N.C.: McFarland.

Lopiano, D.A. (2008). Key elements of coaches' contracts. Sport Management Resources. Retrieved from http://www.sportsmanagementresources.com/library/coach-contract-elements

Marist College v. Matt Brady et al., No.: 709CV07262 at ¶ 13 (S.D.N.Y. 2009).

Milicic v. Basketball Marketing Co., Inc. 857 A.2d 689 (Pa. Super. Ct. 2004).

Mitten, M., Davis, T., Smith, R., & Berry, R. (2009). *Sports law and regulation: Cases, materials, and problems* (2nd ed.). New York: Aspen.

Murphy, E., Spiedel, R., & Ayres, I. (1997) *Studies in Contract Law* (5th ed.). Westbury, N.Y.: Foundation Press.

NFL Collective Bargaining Agreement, Standard Player Contract. (2011). Retrieved from https://nfllabor.files.wordpress.com/2010/01/collective-bargaining-agreement-2011-2020.pdf

Niland, B. (2013). Contract essentials. In J. Wolohan and D. Cotton (Eds.), *Law for recreation and sport mangers* (pp. 362–373). Dubuque, Iowa: Kendall Hunt.

Philadelphia v. Lajoie, 51 A. 973 (Pa. 1902).

Restatement (Second) of Contracts § 1 (1981).

Restatement (Second) of Contracts § 24 (1981).

Restatement (Second) of Contracts § 90 (1981).

Restatement (Second) of Contracts § 159 (1981).

Restatement (Second) of Contracts § 356 (1981).

Sando, M. (2013). How do contracts work? ESPN Retrieved from http://espn.go.com/blog/nflnation/post/_/id/73449/how-do-contracts-work-glad-you-asked

Schulz v. U.S. Boxing Ass'n., 105 F.3d 12, 136 (3d Cir. 1997).

Sports Tech, Inc. v. SFI Manufacturing, Inc., 838 So.2d 807 (2003).

Taylor v. Wake Forest University, 191 S.E.2d 379 (1972).

Thompson, T., Red, C., Madden, B., & O'Keefe, M. (2013). MLB files lawsuit against Anthony Bosch accusing the owner of Biogenisis Clinic of intentional interference. *New York Daily News.* Retrieved from http://www.nydailynews.com/sports/baseball/mlb-files-suit-bosch-interference-article-1.1296024

U.C.C. § 2-302 cmt. 1 (1977).

Ukman, L. (2013). Sponsorship related social and digital rights to negotiate. IEG Sponsorship Blog. Retrieved from http://www.sponsorship.com/About-IEG/Sponsorship-Blogs/Lesa-Ukman/July-2013/Sponsorship-Related-Social—Digital-Rights-To-Neg.aspx

Weiler, Joseph M. (Fall 1992). Legal analysis of the NHL player's contract. *Marquette Sports Law Journal* 3, 59–83.

Witosky, T. (May 2003). Eustachy's party behavior called "Poor judgment." *Des Moines Register,* 62.

Wong, G.M. (1988). *Essentials of amateur sports law.* Dover, Mass.: Auburn House.

Wong, G.M. (2010). *Essentials of sports law* (4th ed.). Santa Barbara, Calif.: ABC-CLIO.

Yocca v. Pittsburgh Steelers Sports, Inc., 854 A.2d 425 (Pa. 2004).

ANTITRUST LAW

LEARNING OBJECTIVES

By the end of the chapter, the reader will be able to:

1. Comprehend the sections of the Sherman Anti-Trust Act
2. Understand how the Sherman Anti-Trust Act has affected sports in the United States
3. Understand the importance of the outcome of *Flood v. Kuhn* on professional sports
4. Understand and differentiate between the three standards used to evaluate an antitrust issues: rule of reason, per se, or a quick look test
5. Analyze the Rozelle Rule
6. Comprehend the impact that the Curt Flood Act had on professional sports

RELATED CASES

Case 9.1   Mackey v. National Football League 543 F.2d 606 (8th Cir. 1976)

Case 9.2   Clarett v. National Football League 369 F.3d 124 (2nd Cir. 2004)

INTRODUCTION

In the 1970s professional athletes began using antitrust laws to challenge restraints such as player drafts, restrictions on player movement, standard player contracts, player corporations, and salary caps. Leagues began to assert the *nonstatutory labor exemption* as a defense to antitrust lawsuits, arguing that any antitrust lawsuits brought on behalf of players should be dismissed based on labor law. The nonstatutory labor exemption has become an extremely effective tool in the defense of antitrust claims and is discussed fully later in this chapter.

SHERMAN ANTITRUST ACT

The Sherman Antitrust Act has shaped the structure of professional and amateur sports for the past 40 years. It has been used by a variety of entities to effect change in the sports world. Players, colleges and universities, owners, alumni, business owners, and even cheerleaders have attempted to use the antitrust laws to strike down what they perceived to be anticompetitive rules and regulations. Professional sports leagues institute regulations so they can operate smoothly and efficiently. Some of the regulations have been challenged as anticompetitive under the Sherman Antitrust Act. Individual sports have also seen their share of antitrust challenges.

The *Sherman Act* was passed by Congress in 1890 with the overall goal of protecting fair competition in the marketplace and preventing monopolies. The act exists to promote customer welfare, protect individuals against the corruptive practices of big business, and offer individuals protection from monopolistic and anticompetitive behavior. Starting in the early 1900s, employers in a variety of industries sued under the Sherman Act to prevent unions from organizing (*Loene v. Lalor*, 1908). In response, the Clayton Act was passed by Congress in 1914. In 1934, the Norris–LaGuardia Act, 29 U.S.C. §§ 101–105, was enacted because courts had been narrowly construing the scope of union activity that was immune from antitrust liability. The two statutes created a statutory exemption, providing labor unions with immunity from antitrust liability for their efforts to further their members' economic interests.

Sherman Antitrust Act and Sports

Because of the unique nature of sports, courts have sought to apply federal antitrust laws in a consistent fashion while addressing individual rules from a variety of leagues. In *St. Louis Convention & Visitors Commission v. National Football League* (1998), the court discussed antitrust laws in the context of a sports league:

> Section 1 of the Sherman Antitrust act makes it unlawful to form a conspiracy in restraint of trade. 15 U.S.C. § 1. Restraints which have 'pernicious virtue' are illegal per se under Section 1 without inquiry into the reasonableness of the restraint of trade. . . . Analysis of whether a restriction's harm to competition outweighs any procompetitive effects is necessary if the anticompetitive impact of a restraint is less clear or the restraint is necessary for a product to exist at all. . . . Some trade restrictions by sports leagues have been held to fall into this category. (*St. Louis Convention & Visitors Commission v. National Football League* (1998) p. 861)

Professional sports teams and organizations are unique under antitrust laws. The court in the seminal case of *Flood v. Kuhn* (1972) noted that,

> [t]he importance of the antitrust laws to every citizen must not be minimalized. They are as important to baseball players as they are to football players, lawyers, doctors, or members of any other class of workers.

Baseball players cannot be denied the benefits of competition merely because club owners view other economic interests as being more important.

As in any other business, teams desire to ensure a maximum profit. However, unlike other entities that sell the same product and compete for the same customer base, clubs in professional sports leagues have no desire to drive other member clubs out of the marketplace. All clubs have an interest in ensuring that all teams in the league are competitive ongoing ventures so as to maintain the league's success. Each club depends on the other for success while at the same time competing for an individual customer base. The Detroit Lions of the National Football League clearly have an interest in selling more team merchandise than their division rival, the Chicago Bears, but they have no interest in seeing the Chicago Bears franchise fold. The Lions' success as a franchise is dependent on their competitor's success as well. In describing this unique relationship in the NFL, one federal district court stated:

[T]he NFL clubs which have 'combined' to implement the draft are not competitors in any economic sense. The clubs operate basically as a joint venture in producing an entertainment product—football games and telecasts. No NFL club can produce this product without agreements and joint action with every other team. To this end, the League not only determines franchise locations, playing schedules, and broadcast terms, but also ensures that the clubs receive equal shares of telecast and ticket revenues. These economic joint venturers "compete" on the playing field, to be sure, but here as well cooperation is essential if the entertainment product is to attain a high quality: only if the teams are "competitively balanced" will spectator interest be maintained at a high pitch. No NFL team, in short, is

interested in driving another team out of business, whether in the counting-house or on the football field, for if the League fails, no one team can survive. (*Smith v. Pro Football, Inc.*, 1979)

Sherman Antitrust Act and Restraint of Trade

A defendant's business activities or anticompetitive conduct must be connected to interstate commerce to be subject to scrutiny under federal antitrust laws (*Summit Health, Ltd. v. Pinhas*, 1991). If Section 1 of the Sherman Act were read literally, it would strike down every contract as illegal (*National Bancard Corporation v. Visa*, 1986). Section 1 of the Sherman Act prohibits agreements and collective action that unreasonably restrain trade:

Every contract, combination in the form of trust or otherwise, or conspiracy, in restraint of trade or commerce among the several States, or with foreign nations, is declared to be illegal. Every person who shall make any contract or engage in any combination or conspiracy hereby declared to be illegal shall be deemed guilty of a felony, and, on conviction thereof, shall be punished by fine not exceeding $10,000,000 if a corporation or, if any other person, $350,000, or by imprisonment not exceeding three years, or by both said punishments, in the discretion of the court. (15 U.S.C. § 1)

Elements of the Section 1 Violations

A plaintiff must prove *three elements* for an activity to be deemed in violation of Section 1 of the Sherman Act. It must be proven that:

1. there was an agreement among the league and member teams in restraint of trade;

2. it was injured as a direct and proximate result; and

3. its damages are capable of ascertainment and not speculative. (St. Louis Convention, citing *Admiral Theatre Corp. v. Douglas Theatre*, 585 F.2d 877, pp. 883–884 (8th Cir. 1978)).

A plaintiff must show that two or more persons acted in concert to restrain trade (*Brenner v. World Boxing Council*, 1982). The first requirement of a Section 1 antitrust claim is to prove "concerted activity." Section 1 of the Sherman Act "does not prohibit independent business decisions but only prohibit[s] concerted action" (*JES Properties, Inc. v. USA Equestrian, Inc.*, 2005). There does not have to be direct evidence of concerted action; it can be inferred from the words and conduct of the parties (*JES Properties*). The alleged conspiracy must have a unity of purpose or common design and understanding (*JES Properties*, citing *Michelman v. Clark-Schwebel Fiber Glass Corp.*, 534 F.2d 1036, 1043 (2nd Cir.)).

Sherman Antitrust Act and Section 2 (Monoplization)

Under Section 1 antitrust cases, courts are generally looking for an agreement between parties that results in a restraint of trade which may be considered unreasonable in situations in which the anticompetitive effects overshadow its procompetitive effects, whereas Section 2 antitrust cases are concerned with the operations of a *monopoly*. A monopoly has been defined as "the power to control prices or exclude competition" (USCS § 2). *Section 2 of the Sherman Antitrust Act* guards against attempted monopolization (15 U.S.C. § 2). Whereas Section 1 requires two or more persons to engage in the illegal activity, Section 2 applies to one or more persons. Section 2 reads as follows:

Every person who shall monopolize, or attempt to monopolize, or combine or conspire with any other person or persons, to monopolize any part of the trade or commerce among the several States, or with foreign nations, shall be deemed guilty of a felony [and shall be punished].

Every contract can be viewed as a restraint; therefore, the United States Supreme Court has held that only restraints that are deemed "unreasonable" will be actionable under the Sherman Antitrust Act (*National Hockey League Players Association (NHLPA) v. Plymouth Whalers Hockey Club*, 2005, citing *NCAA v. Bd. of Regents of Univ. of Okla.*, 468 U.S. 85, 98 (1984)). In *Chicago Board of Trade v. United States* (1918), Justice Louis Brandeis stated the following with regard to antitrust laws:

Every agreement concerning trade, every regulation of trade, restrains. To bind, to restrain is of their very essence. The true test of legality is whether the restraint imposed is such as merely regulates and perhaps thereby promotes competition or whether it is such as may suppress or even destroy competition.

EVALUATING ANTITRUST ISSUES

Courts have used three standards to evaluate an antitrust problem: *rule of reason*, per se, and a quick look test. Most sports antitrust problems today are evaluated by the rule of reason standard (*Bryant v. United States Polo Ass'n*, 1986). Under a rule of reason analysis, the plaintiff must show "significant anticompetitive effects within a relevant market" (*NHLPA v. Plymouth Whalers*, p. 469). If the plaintiff is able to meet this burden, then the defendant must present evidence of any procompetitive effect of the restraint justifying the anticompetitive injuries (*NHLPA v. Plymouth Whalers*). If the defendant succeeds, the burden then shifts back to the plaintiff to show that any legitimate objectives can be achieved in a substantially less restrictive manner (*Worldwide Basketball and Sports Tours, Inc. v. Nat'l Collegiate Athletic Ass'n*, 2004). This test has been described as follows:

> Under the rule of reason, a restraint must be evaluated to determine whether it is significantly anticompetitive in purpose or effect. . . . If, on analysis, the restraint is found to have legitimate business purposes whose realization serves to promote competition, the 'anticompetitive evils' of the challenged practice must be carefully balanced against its 'procompetitive virtues' to ascertain whether the former outweigh the latter. A restraint is unreasonable if it has the 'net effect' of substantially impeding competition. (*Smith v. Pro Football*, p. 1183)

If an activity is anticompetitive on its face, then it will be deemed a per se violation under the Sherman Act. The *per se test* is reserved for restraints that have a very clear antitrust effect. It is applied when the challenged restraint is "entirely void of redeeming competitive rationale" (*NHLPA v. Plymouth Whalers*). Under a per se analysis, the court will not examine the practice's impact on the market or the procompetitive justifications for the restraint (*NHLPA v. Plymouth Whalers*). This standard is applied only in clear-cut cases (*Continental T.V., Inc. v. GTE Sylvania Inc.*, 1977, pp. 49–50).

In *Eureka Urethane, Inc. v. PBA, Inc.* (1990), the court summarized the per se rule as follows:

> There are certain business combinations and practices which are so pernicious and devoid of redeeming attributes that they are considered to be unreasonable restraints on interstate or foreign commerce per se. If a party is injured as a result of a per se violation of § 1 of the Sherman Act, he need not allege or prove any particular effect or

impact of the violation on interstate or foreign commerce; the existence of such an effect or impact is conclusively presumed.

The *quick look test* is applied when the practice has obvious anticompetitive effects, such as price fixing. Under the quick look, it is unnecessary to examine whether the defendant possessed market power. Relating to sports, the Supreme Court's decision in *National Collegiate Athletic Association v. Board of Regents of the University of Oklahoma* (1984) was significant in elaborating the quick look standard. This case involved the ability of the National Collegiate Athletic Association (NCAA) and its television partners regarding the number of intercollegiate football games that could be shown on a weekly basis as well as the number of games that schools televise in a season. To counteract this ability and to increase their opportunity to develop lucrative contracts of their own, a number of Division I schools with significant football teams brought an antitrust lawsuit against the NCAA under Section 1 (*National Collegiate Athletic Association v. Board of Regents of the University of Oklahoma*, 1984).

The schools were able to convince the Supreme Court that the NCAA decreased output, made broadcasts that were indifferent to consumer preferences, and fixed the prices of network bids. As a result, the Supreme Court found that a comprehensive industry analysis was not needed to conclude that such a restraint was net anticompetitive. However, because neither the rule of reason or per se rule were applicable in evaluating the restraint, the Supreme Court provided the NCAA an opportunity to develop procompetitive justifications.

PROFESSIONAL SPORTS

Player Restraints

Starting in the 1970s, professional athletes began using the antitrust laws to challenge restraints instituted by leagues through league rules. Federal antitrust laws have been used to defeat rules instituted by leagues dealing with a player's ability to play for the club of his or her own choosing as well as rules limiting the amount of money a player can earn. All professional sports leagues' collective bargaining agreements (CBAs) contain player movement systems dictating the requirements a player must attain to achieve free agency. Antitrust laws have been used to challenge player restraints; however, not all restraints are illegal—only those that are deemed unreasonable (*Standard Oil v. United States,* 1911).

Restraints could be in the form of a specific player movement system dealing with a player's right to market his or her services on the open market to several teams, or a particular rule that may limit a player's salary, such as a salary cap or luxury tax. Restraints can also come in the form of standard player contracts or a draft system of players (*Smith v. Pro Football,* p. 1188) (striking down the NFL draft as an illegal restraint of trade under the Sherman Act). Although all players in major sports leagues are required to sign the standard player contract, that contract can be modified to a certain extent. Therefore, the standard player contract cannot be considered a true restraint because if a player has enough negotiating power he can force the team to add addenda to the standard player contract to obtain a more favorable contract. All these restraints and a few others have been challenged by professional players using antitrust laws.

Leagues, players, and clubs have actually agreed to a variety of restraints through the collective bargaining process, including annual player drafts, restrictive player movement systems, salary caps, standard player contracts, and different salaries for players on developmental squads. Both parties have agreed to these restraints after determining they are necessary for the functioning of the league.

Professional leagues and member clubs have asserted that the nonstatutory labor exemption prevents antitrust lawsuits by the players. NFL players challenged the draft and free agency rules on antitrust grounds since the 1970s (*Smith v. Pro Football; Kapp v. National Football League,* 1978). Players in the NBA were successful in challenging player restraints on antitrust grounds (*Robertson v. Nat'l Basketball Ass'n,* 1975). Baseball players were unsuccessful in their antitrust challenge against the reserve clause. The Supreme Court relied on the doctrine of stare decisis in upholding baseball's antitrust exemption to antitrust laws (*Flood v. Kuhn,* p. 258). Players have also challenged salary caps as antitrust violations (*Wood v. National Basketball Association,* 1984). Salary caps have been instituted by most professional leagues. The National Hockey League instituted a salary cap after the 2004 NHL season was canceled. The National Football League and the National Basketball Association both have salary caps. The NBA's cap has been referred to as a "soft cap."

KAPP v. NATIONAL FOOTBALL LEAGUE (1974)

In one of the first cases involving player restraints, Joe Kapp, a former Most Valuable Player in the Canadian Football League, alleged that certain NFL rules violated the antitrust laws and caused his expulsion from the National Football League (*Kapp v. National Football League,* 1974). Kapp alleged that league tampering rules, the standard player contract, and the NFL's *Rozelle Rule* were all unreasonable restraints of trade. In defense, the league argued as follows:

> [D]efendants argue that professional league sport activities, such as football, must be distinguished from other kinds of business activities which have been held to be per se antitrust violations; that league sports activities are so unique that the per se rule is inapplicable; that, although club teams compete on the playing field, the clubs are not, and indeed cannot be, competitors with one

another in a business way because the very purpose of a professional sports league is to provide reasonably matched teams for field competition to attract and sustain the interest and patronage of the fans; that the success of the league as a joint venture of its clubs depends upon the ability of each club to do this; that, if each member club were allowed by the league to engage in free-for-all competition for the best or better players, then the most strongly financed or otherwise better advantaged clubs would be able to sign up and monopolize the best or better players, leaving only average or mediocre players for the other clubs with the effect of destroying the evenly matched field competition that brings fans to the games. (*Kapp v. NFL*, 1974)

A jury found in favor of Kapp. On appeal, the Ninth Circuit found in favor of the league.

MACKEY v. NATIONAL FOOTBALL LEAGUE (1976)

In *Mackey v. National Football League* (1976), the NFL's Rozelle Rule was challenged by NFL players and determined to be an antitrust violation. The rule stated that when a player's contract ended and he switched teams, the new team was required to compensate the former team by way of draft choices, current players, or cash. If the structure of the transaction could not be worked out between the teams, then the commissioner would make the decision or the award. This system restricted player movement and was challenged in *Mackey* as an antitrust violation. In *Mackey v. National Football League* (1976), sixteen NFL players took on the NFL's Rozelle Rule, which had been named after the NFL commissioner, Pete Rozelle. The Mackey case was decided a few years after the first collective bargaining agreement had been entered into in professional sports. It was a significant case in that it analyzed the relationship between antitrust law and labor law in the context of a collective bargaining agreement. The NFL's Rozelle Rule stated:

> Any player, whose contract with a League club has expired, shall thereupon become a free agent and shall no longer be considered a member of the team of that club following the expiration date of such contract. Whenever a player, becoming a free agent in such manner, thereafter signed a contract with a different club in the League, then, unless mutually satisfactory arrangements have been to the former club one or more players, from the Active, Reserve, or Selection List (including future selection choices) of the acquiring club as the Commissioner shall be final and conclusive. (NFL Constitution § 12.1(H)).

Numerous NFL players challenged the NFL's Rozelle Rule on the basis that the rule kept players' salaries low and prevented players from marketing their services to the highest bidder. Players who were free agents were having difficulty finding teams to sign them to a new contract. The *Mackey v. NFL* (1976) made an effort to ascertain the boundaries regarding the nonstatutory labor exemption in a sports environment. The Rozelle Rule restricted the ability of a player to sign with a different team when the player's contract expired. In *Mackey v. NFL* (1976), the Eighth Circuit ruled that the nonstatutory labor exemption protects the terms of a collective bargaining agreement when the agreement meets three specific requirements:

1. The *restraint of trade* primarily affects only the parties to the collective bargaining agreement;
2. The agreement concerns a mandatory subject of collective bargaining; and
3. The agreement is a product of bona fide arm's-length bargaining (pp. 609–610).

By applying the three-part test, the *Mackey* court determined that the Rozelle Rule was a mandatory subject of bargaining that affected only the parties involved with the collective bargaining agreement. It was against that background that Mackey was decided.

McCourt v. CALIFORNIA SPORTS, INC. (1979)

After *Mackey v. NFL*, players began challenging terms that were in existing CBAs. In *McCourt v. California Sports, Inc.* (1979), the plaintiff, Dale McCourt, was the Red Wings leading scorer as a rookie. McCourt was awarded to the Los Angeles Kings as compensation for the Red Wings signing the Kings goaltender, Rogatien Vachon. The 1976 collective bargaining agreement of the NHL required that an "equalization payment" be made by the signing team to the team losing the player under NHL Bylaw 9A. McCourt refused to play for the Kings and instead filed a lawsuit challenging the restraint as an unreasonable restraint under the Sherman Act. The Sixth Circuit Court for the Federal Court of Appeals found in favor of the NHL, stating:

> [I]t is apparent that the inclusion of the reserve system in the collective bargaining agreement was the product of good faith, arm's-length bargaining, and that what the trial court saw as a failure to negotiate was in fact simply the failure to succeed, after the most intensive negotiations, in keeping an unwanted provision out of the contract. This failure was a part of and not apart from the collective bargaining process, a process which achieved its ultimate objective of an agreement accepted by the parties. . . .
>
> Assuming without deciding that the reserve system incorporated in the collective bargaining agreement was otherwise subject to the antitrust laws, whether the good faith, arm's-length requirement necessary to entitle it to the nonstatutory labor exemption from the antitrust laws applies is to be governed by the developed standards

of law applicable elsewhere in the field of labor law and as set forth in Mackey, supra. So viewed, the evidence here, as credited by the trial court, compels the conclusion that the reserve system was incorporated in the agreement as a result of good faith, arm's-length bargaining between the parties. As such it is entitled to the exemption. (*McCourt,* 1979)

SMITH v. PRO FOOTBALL INC. (1979)

In another case dealing with player restraint, *Smith v. Pro Football, Inc.* (1979), the court held that the NFL's draft of college players was in violation of antitrust laws. James "Yazoo" Smith was an All-American defensive back at the University of Oregon and was drafted by the Washington Redskins in the first round of the 1968 NFL draft. He signed a one-year contract for $50,000, which included a $20,000 signing bonus. In the last game of the 1968 season, he suffered a career-ending neck injury. Washington paid him an additional $19,800, which was the amount he would have received had he played out his option year. Two years later Smith filed a lawsuit alleging that the NFL rookie draft was in violation of antitrust laws. He argued that if not for the draft, he would have received a more lucrative contract from the Redskins. The court in Smith found the draft in violation of antitrust laws:

> Many of the player restraints that once existed are now in effect and found in collective bargaining agreements in a revised form, agreeable to both management and labor. These restraints have now been agreed to by players and management through the collective bargaining process and can no longer be challenged as antitrust violations. Once the parties have agreed to a "restraint" through the collective bargaining process, and the negotiations have in fact taken place in good faith and occurred at arm's length, then the nonstatutory labor exemption prevents a successful antitrust challenge.

The current NFL draft is composed of seven rounds with 32 teams selecting players, with supplemental draft picks awarded each year to NFL clubs. Prior to 1993 the NFL draft could consist of more than seven rounds with numerous teams selecting. The reduction of draft rounds creates more free agents. However, statistically, the chances are less than 15% that an undrafted rookie will earn a roster spot on an NFL club. Is it more advantageous for the players' union that the draft be seven rounds or more than seven rounds?

LEON WOOD v. NBA (1987)

In *Leon Wood v. National Basketball Association* (1987), Wood alleged he had been a victim of the NBA's salary cap because he was offered only the league minimum salary when he entered the NBA draft. A salary cap operates to limit a team's payroll within a league. The salary cap could, under certain circumstances, restrain the amount a particular player could earn in a year. For instance, if a player were a free agent and wanted to play for a certain team, a scenario could exist whereby the team could not afford to sign that player if the team did not have enough money under the salary cap of the league to pay the free agent. Wood asserted that the college draft and the salary cap were in violation of antitrust laws and that the NBA was not shielded by the nonstatutory labor exemption. The salary cap had been negotiated by management and labor and became a part of the NBA's collective bargaining agreement, therefore Wood's case was dismissed.

SPENCER HAYWOOD AND THE NATIONAL BASKETBALL ASSOCIATION (1971)

Players have also challenged eligibility restrictions dealing with regulations on when they could become a professional. Former American Basketball Association (ABA) and NBA star Spencer Haywood challenged the NBA's draft eligibility rule in a case that made it to the Supreme Court (*Haywood v. National Basketball Association, 1971*). The NBA draft rule stated that a player could not enter the NBA draft until four years after the date of his high school graduation. Haywood had won All-American honors in college and also won an Olympic medal in the 1968 Summer Games. After one year at the University of Detroit, he signed a contract with the Denver Rockets of the ABA and received Rookie of the Year honors. Haywood eventually left the Rockets in a contract dispute. He then agreed to a six-year contract with the Seattle SuperSonics of the NBA. The NBA commissioner disapproved the contract based on Haywood's ineligibility. Haywood sued, and the Federal District Court found in his favor, holding the four-year rule as per se illegal as a "group boycott" under the Sherman Antitrust Act. The ruling in Haywood stated the following:

> Section 2.05 of the bylaws of the NBA provides as follows:
> High School Graduate, etc. A person who has not completed high school or who has completed high school but has not entered college, shall not be eligible to be drafted or to be a player until four years after he has been graduated or four years after his original high school class has been graduated, as the case may be, nor may the future services of any such person be negotiated or contracted for, or otherwise reserved. Similarly, a person who has entered college but is no longer enrolled, shall not be eligible to be drafted or to be a Player until the time when he would have first become eligible had he remained enrolled in college. Any negotiations or agreements with any such person during such period shall be null and void and shall confer no rights whatsoever; nor shall a Member violating the provisions of this paragraph be permitted to acquire the rights to the services of such person at any time thereafter.

Section 6.03, while included in the bylaws as a part of the draft provisions, further defines eligibility for the NBA and reinforces the rule that a player cannot sign with an NBA team prior to four years after the graduation of his high school class. Section 6.03 provides as follows:

Persons Eligible for Draft. The following classes of persons shall be eligible for the annual draft:

(a) Students in four-year colleges whose classes are to be graduated during the June following the holding of the draft;

(b) Students in four-year colleges whose original classes have already been graduated, and who do not choose to exercise remaining collegiate basketball eligibility;

(c) Students in four-year colleges whose original classes have already been graduated if such students have no remaining collegiate basketball eligibility;

(d) Persons who become eligible pursuant to the provisions of Section 2.05 of these bylaws. (*Denver Rockets v. All-Pro Management,* 1971)

The NBA asserted its reasons for the rule:

Three reasons have been suggested for having the four-year college rule. First, the NBA has suggested that it is financially necessary to professional basketball as a business enterprise. It seems clear . . . that this does not provide a basis for exemption from the antitrust laws with regard to group boycotts, unless it qualifies under the [exception]. As discussed earlier, Silver does not exempt the present rules from illegality.

A second reason given by the NBA is that this type of regulation is necessary to guarantee that each prospective professional basketball player will be given the opportunity to complete four years of college prior to beginning his professional basketball

career. However commendable this desire may be, this court is not in a position to say that this consideration should override the objective of fostering economic competition which is embodied in the antitrust laws. If such a determination is to be made, it must be made by Congress and not the courts.

Finally, Haywood has suggested that at least one of the reasons for the four-year college rule is that collegiate athletics provides a more efficient and less expensive way of training young professional basketball players than the so-called "farm team" system, which is the primary alternative. Even if this were true, it would not, of course, provide a basis for antitrust exemption. (*Denver Rockets v. All-Pro Management,* 1971)

The court found in favor of Haywood, stating that the rule constituted a group boycott under the antitrust laws. Do the reasons set forth by the NBA in Haywood still exist today? The current eligibility rule found in the 2011 NBA's CBA states:

Article X: Player Eligibility and NBA DRAFT

Section 1. Player Eligibility. . . .

(b) A player shall be eligible for selection in the first NBA draft with respect to which he has satisfied all applicable requirements of Section 1(b)(i) below . . .:

(i) The player (A) is or will be at least 19 years of age during the calendar year in which the Draft is held, and (B) with respect to a player who is not an international player (defined below), at least one (1) NBA Season has elapsed since the player's graduation from high school (or, if the player did not graduate from high school, since the graduation of the class with which the player would have graduated had he graduated from high school); and

(ii) (A) The player has graduated from a four-year college or university in the United States (or is to graduate in the calendar year in which the Draft is held) and has no remaining intercollegiate basketball eligibility; or

(B) The player is attending or previously attended a four-year college or university in the United States, his original class in such college or university has graduated (or is to graduate in the calendar year in which the Draft is held), and he has no remaining intercollegiate basketball eligibility; or

(C) The player has graduated from high school in the United States, did not enroll in a four-year college or university in the United States, and four calendar years have elapsed since such player's high school graduation; or

(D) The player did not graduate from high school in the United States, and four calendar years have elapsed since the graduation of the class with which the player would have graduated had he graduated from high school; or

(E) The player has signed a player contract with a "professional basketball team not in the NBA" (defined below) that is located anywhere in the world, and has rendered services under such contract prior to the Draft; or

(F) The player has expressed his desire to be selected in the Draft in a writing received by the NBA at least sixty (60) days prior to such Draft (an "Early Entry" player); or

(G) If the player is an "international player" (defined below), and notwithstanding anything contained in subsections (A) through (F) above:

(1) The player is or will be twenty-two (22) years of age during the calendar year of the Draft; or

(2) The player has signed a player contract with a "professional basketball team not in the NBA" (defined below) that is located in the United States, and has rendered services under such contract prior to the Draft; or

(3) The player has expressed his desire to be selected in the Draft in a writing received by the NBA at least sixty (60) days prior to such Draft (an "Early Entry" player).

Source: National Basketball Association 2011 Collective Bargaining Agreement. Retrieved from http://nbpa.com/cba/

MAURICE CLARETT AND THE NATIONAL FOOTBALL LEAGUE (2003; 2004)

Compare those to the rationale by the league set forth in *Clarett v. National Football League* (2004), Maurice Clarett, a former Ohio State student-athlete, challenged the NFL's eligibility rules on antitrust grounds, claiming they constituted an unreasonable restraint upon his ability to market his services in the NFL. NFL bylaws prohibited member clubs from selecting any college football player through the draft who had not first exhausted all college football eligibility, graduated from college, or been out of high school for three football seasons. In 1990 the NFL had changed the league policy relating to entering the NFL draft by allowing any player who was more than three years out of high school to apply for "special eligibility" to enter its amateur draft. Many college players took advantage of this year and applied for the NFL draft; however, the league would strictly enforce its policy regarding being three years out of high school. Prior to the implementation of that rule, the NFL would typically deny eligibility to anyone who applied who had not completed four years of college.

Maurice Clarett believed he was ready to make the transition to the NFL from Ohio State, but NFL draft eligibility rules prevented him from playing in the NFL. As a freshman he played on the Ohio State National Championship team that went 14–0, culminating in a double-overtime victory over the University of Miami in the Fiesta Bowl. He was awarded for his outstanding play as a freshman when he was voted the best running back in college football by the Sporting News. He was also named Big Ten Freshman of the Year.

Clarett was six feet tall and 230 pounds, and many teams and scouts indicated they believed he could play in the NFL after his freshman season. Clarett was eventually drafted in the 2005 NFL as the 101st pick in the third round of the NFL draft by the Denver Broncos. He was later released by the Denver Broncos during training camp.

In August of 2003, Clarett requested the NFL grant him a hardship exemption for the 2004 draft under the "special eligibility" application. The NFL denied his application. Clarett eventually filed a federal lawsuit, and the federal district court granted Clarett's motion for summary judgment, which prevented the NFL from refusing his entry into the 2004 NFL draft (*Clarett v. National Football League,* 2003). The NFL appealed, and the Second Circuit found in favor of the NFL, stating that the nonstatutory labor agreement protected the NFL's eligibility rules *Clarett v. National Football League, 2003*). Even though the collective bargaining agreement between the NFL and the Players Association failed to include any specific reference outlining the three-year eligibility rule, the executive director of the NFL Players Association (NFLPA) had given his approval for the draft rules, and that was enough for the court to allow the rule to be shielded by the nonstatutory labor exemption. The Second Circuit did not address the application of the draft rule to the antitrust laws, even though the federal district court did analyze the draft rules pursuant to the antitrust laws.

After the federal district court found in favor of Clarett, several college football students declared for the 2005 NFL draft. The most notable was Mike Williams, an All-American wide receiver from the University of Southern California. He would most likely have been picked in the first round of the 2004 NFL draft, but when the NFL prevailed on appeal, Williams was ruled ineligible for the 2004 draft. When he had declared his eligibility for the 2004 NFL draft, he had also retained an agent and received financial benefits based on his athletic ability. The NCAA subsequently declared him ineligible to play at USC. Williams terminated the relationship with his agent and repaid the financial benefits he had received, but the NCAA still declared him ineligible. He was forced to sit out the entire 2004 college football season but was selected as the tenth overall pick in the 2005 NFL draft by the Detroit Lions.

ANTITRUST EXEMPTIONS

The law has carved out multiple exemptions to antitrust law. Many regulations and policies of sports would seem to violate antitrust law but are not deemed in violation of the Sherman Act because they fall under certain exemptions. Baseball, for example, has had a longtime historical exemption to antitrust laws. The NFL has several exemptions which in some respects excludes it from antitrust scrutiny. Finally, the nonstatutory labor exemption protects union–management agreements that have been entered into after good-faith bargaining by the parties from any antitrust violations.

Baseball

Baseball is unique in its exemption from antitrust laws. It has been described as a "narrow application of stare decisis" (*Flood v. Kuhn, 1972*). Football, basketball, hockey, boxing, professional bowling, golf, tennis, and even wrestling are all subject to antitrust scrutiny. Baseball's exemption, although largely historical, has been kept mostly intact since *Federal Baseball v. National League of Professional Baseball Clubs* (1922).

In *Federal Baseball,* the Supreme Court first considered the applicability of the federal antitrust laws to baseball. In that case, Justice Holmes declared that professional baseball was not a business that was involved in interstate commerce (*Federal Baseball,* 1922, p. 209). Subsequently, in *Toolson v. New York Yankees* (1953), the Supreme

Court upheld Federal Baseball, stating that any decision that allowed the application of the antitrust laws to baseball should be addressed by the legislature. Conversely, in other cases the Supreme Court has determined that particular sports are subject to antitrust laws, such as basketball in *Robertson v. National Basketball Association* (1980), football in *Radovich v. National Football League* (1957), and boxing in *United States v. International Boxing Club* (1955). These sports are all subject to antitrust laws because of business activity occurring in "interstate commerce."

FLOOD v. KUHN (1972)

Baseball's exemption from antitrust laws was once again challenged in *Flood v. Kuhn* (1972). Prior to the free agency era in sports, all baseball players were bound by a clause in their contract known as the reserve clause. The *reserve clause* essentially stated that teams had the right to unilaterally renew a player's contract following each season. In essence, the reserve clause allowed teams to retain all rights to a player and thereby prevented a player from seeking contract offers from other teams for his services. The club could buy, sell, or trade a player without the player's input into the decision. It was against this background that Curt Flood brought his case to the United States Supreme Court in 1972.

Flood was the co-captain of the 1967 World Series champion St. Louis Cardinals and was one of the best center fielders in baseball. He won seven Gold Glove Awards for his outstanding play in center field. In 1968, the cover of Sports Illustrated touted Flood as "the best center fielder in baseball," quite an honor considering Hall of Famer Willie Mays was the center fielder at the time for the San Francisco Giants.

At the beginning of the season, with the reserve clause still in place, Flood had sought a raise from the Cardinals. The Cardinals' owner, August Bush, was well known for quashing attempts at labor organizing at his breweries and had very

little sympathy for ballplayers. He did not give Flood the raise he requested. The next season Flood once again asked for a raise and was turned down. In October 1969, Flood was informed he was being traded to the Philadelphia Phillies as part of a seven-player deal. Even though he was not allowed to refuse the trade, on Christmas Eve 1969 he sent the following letter to Commissioner of Baseball, Bowie Kuhn:

> Dear Mr. Kuhn:
> After 12 years in the Major Leagues, I do not feel that I am a piece of property to be bought and sold irrespective of my wishes. I believe that any system which produces that result violates my basic rights as a citizen and is inconsistent to laws of the United States and of the several states. It is my desire to play baseball in 1970, and I am capable of playing. I received a contract from the Philadelphia club, but I believe I have the right to consider offers from other clubs before making any decision. I therefore request that you make known to all Major League clubs my feelings in this matter and advise them of my availability for the 1970 season.
> Sincerely,
> Curt Flood

Source: Courtesy of www.bizofbaseball.com.

After reading the letter, Kuhn refused Flood's request. Flood refused to play for the Philadelphia ball club, gave up a $90,000-per-year salary, and retired from baseball. Later, Flood did play 13 games for the Washington Senators in 1971 but retired immediately thereafter. On July 16, 1970, Flood filed an antitrust lawsuit challenging the century-old reserve clause. Even though Flood lost his antitrust challenge at the Supreme Court, baseball players were able to achieve free agency status through labor arbitration. It could be argued that Curt Flood is one of the reasons baseball players enjoy the large salaries they do today. He took a chance in challenging the reserve clause, and it essentially ended his baseball playing days. Flood, a native Houstonian, passed away in 1997.

The Curt Flood Act of 1998

The *Curt Flood Act of 1998* was the end result of many bills that had been placed before Congress in an attempt to dismantle with or block baseball's historical antitrust exemption. The act modified the Sherman Antitrust Act to allow Major League Baseball players the same rights and remedies as some other professional athletes. The act allows antitrust challenges only to conduct or agreements by those persons "in the business of organized professional Major League Baseball directly relating to or affecting employment of Major League Baseball players to play baseball at the Major League level" (15 U.S.C. § 526b(a)). It specifically denies any remedy to a player for terms and conditions of his employment arising out of the collective bargaining process. Furthermore, the act does not affect the application of the nonstatutory labor exemption (15 U.S.C. § 26b(d)(4)).

Curt Flood Act of 1998 (15 U.S.C. § 27)
Section 1. Short Title.
　　This Act may be cited as the "Curt Flood Act of 1998."
Section 2. Purpose.
　　It is the purpose of this legislation to state that major league baseball players are covered under the antitrust laws (i.e., that major league baseball players will have the same rights under the antitrust laws as do other professional athletes, e.g., football and basketball players), along with a provision that makes it clear that the passage of this Act does not change the application of the antitrust laws in any other context or with respect to any other person or entity.
Section 3. Application of the Antitrust Laws to Professional Major League Baseball.

The Clayton Act (15 U.S.C. §§ 12 et seq.) is amended by adding at the end the following new section:
Section 27 (a) Subject to subsections (b) through (d), the conduct, acts, practices, or agreements of persons in the business of organized professional major league baseball directly relating to or affecting employment of major league baseball players to play baseball at the major league level are subject to the antitrust laws if engaged in by the person in any other professional sports business affecting interstate commerce.
(b) No court shall rely on the enactment of this section as a basis for changing the application of the antitrust laws to any conduct, acts, practices, or agreements other than those set forth in subsection (a). This section does not create, permit, or imply a cause of action by which to challenge under the antitrust laws, or otherwise apply the antitrust laws to, any conduct, acts, practices, or agreements that do not directly relate to or affect employment of major league baseball players to play baseball players to play baseball at the major league level.

Source: Courtesy of Westlaw; reprinted with permission.

PIAZZA v. MAJOR LEAGUE BASEBALL (1993)

Baseball's antitrust exemption has been narrowed by later decisions. In *Piazza v. Major League Baseball* (1993), the court held that the proposed sale and relocation of a baseball team was not protected by baseball's exemption. The court stated:

Applying these principles of stare decisis here, it becomes clear that, before Flood, lower courts were bound by both the rule of Federal Baseball and Toolson (that the business of baseball is not interstate commerce and thus not within the Sherman Act) and the result of those decisions (that baseball's reserve system is exempt from the antitrust laws). The Court's decision in *Flood*, however, effectively created the circumstance referred to by the Third Circuit as "result stare decisis," from the English system. In *Flood*, the Supreme Court exercised its discretion to invalidate the rule of *Federal Baseball* and *Toolson*. Thus no rule from those cases binds the lower courts as a matter of stare decisis. The only aspect of *Federal Baseball* and *Toolson* that remains to be followed is the result or disposition based upon the facts there involved, which the Court in *Flood* determined to be the exemption of the reserve system from the antitrust laws. . . For these reasons, I conclude that the antitrust exemption created by *Federal Baseball* is limited to baseball's reserve system, and because the parties agree that the reserve system is not at issue in this case, I reject Baseball's argument that it is exempt from antitrust liability in this case. (*Federal Baseball*, p. 209)

In examining the prior decisions involving baseball and the antitrust laws, the court found that when the United States Supreme Court directly addressed baseball's antitrust exemption, it was only in the context of the reserve clause.

NONSTATUTORY LABOR EXEMPTION

The United States Supreme Court established the nonstatutory labor exemption in *Allen Bradley Co. v. Local Union No. 3* (1945). The nonstatutory labor exemption flows from the statutory labor exemption and protects from antitrust scrutiny unionmanagement agreements that result from good-faith negotiations. It is based on the premise that the law favors collective bargaining over antitrust laws. One of the more difficult questions that

has arisen in this area is the extent management can claim the protection of the nonstatutory labor exemption. What happens if the parties cannot agree during the collective bargaining process as to the terms and conditions of employment? How far does the nonstatutory labor exemption go to protect management from antitrust lawsuits?

The labor exemption will protect management from antitrust challenges even after a CBA has expired. Labor law requires parties to the CBA to maintain the status quo and make efforts to enter into a new agreement until they reach an impasse. Only when there is a total breakdown of negotiations between union and management will an impasse be declared. Strikes or lockouts might follow an impasse. The duty to maintain the status quo expires once an impasse is reached and the employer has bargained in good faith. The employer may then unilaterally impose changes to mandatory subjects of collective bargaining without fear of antitrust scrutiny.

The terms of collective bargaining continue after expiration because labor law requires all parties to maintain the status quo and engage in continued bargaining in an attempt to reach a new agreement until they reach an impasse (National Labor Relations Act, 1982). This creates an environment that furthers the policy of collective bargaining and hopefully leads to stable labor relations. Sometimes an impasse can be temporary; therefore, the process of collective bargaining is not over until the first impasse occurs.

In *Powell v. National Football League* (1991), the court considered whether the terms of an expired collective bargaining agreement lose their antitrust immunity if the parties reached an impasse in their efforts to negotiate a new agreement. *Powell v. National Football League* (1991) held that the exemption continues even after the parties have reached an impasse. The federal district court in *Powell* found as follows:

> Our reading of the authorities leads us to conclude that the League and the Players

have not yet reached the point in negotiations where it would be appropriate to permit an action under the Sherman Act. The district court's impasse standard treats a lawful stage of the collective bargaining process as misconduct by defendants, and in this way conflicts with federal labor laws that establish the collective bargaining process, under the supervision of the National Labor Relations Board, as the method for resolution of labor disputes.

In particular, the federal labor laws provide the opposing parties to a labor dispute with offsetting tools, both economic and legal, through which they may seek resolution of their dispute. A union may choose to strike the employer . . . and the employer may in turn opt to lock out its employees. . . . Further, either side may petition the National Labor Relations Board and seek, for example, a cease-and-desist order prohibiting conduct constituting an unfair labor practice. . . . To now allow the Players to pursue an action for treble damages under the Sherman Act would, we conclude, improperly upset the careful balance established by Congress through the labor law.

. . . After a collective bargaining agreement has expired, an employer is under an obligation to bargain with the union before it may permissibly make any unilateral change in terms and conditions of employment which constitute mandatory subjects of collective bargaining. After impasse, an employer may make unilateral changes that are reasonably comprehended within its pre-impasse proposals.

. . . Following the expiration of the 1982 Agreement, the challenged restraints were imposed by the League only after they had been forwarded in negotiations and subsequently rejected by the Players. The Players do not contend that these proposals were

put forward by the League in bad faith. We therefore hold that the present lawsuit cannot be maintained under the Sherman Act. Importantly, this does not entail that once a union and management enter into collective bargaining, management is forever exempt from the antitrust laws, and we do not hold that restraints on player services can never offend the Sherman Act. We believe, however, that the nonstatutory labor exemption protects agreements conceived in an ongoing collective bargaining relationship from challenges under the antitrust laws. "[N]ational labor policy should sometimes override antitrust policy," and we believe that this case presents just such an occasion. . . .

. . . In sum, we hold that the antitrust laws are inapplicable under the circumstances of this case as the nonstatutory labor exemption extends beyond impasse. We reverse the order of the district court. (*Powell v. National Football League*, 1991, pp. 1301–1304)

Source: Courtesy of Westlaw; reprinted with permission.

BROWN v. PRO FOOTBALL INC. (1996)

The only Supreme Court decision in a sports labor antitrust case is *Brown v. Pro Football Inc.* (1996). The *Brown* case dealt with the issue of developmental squad players in the NFL. The developmental squad would consist of first- and second-year NFL players who failed to make the roster but whom teams needed for practice purposes and as possible replacements for injured players. The NFLPA wanted developmental squad contracts to be negotiated in the same manner as NFL player contracts. The NFL had unilaterally created these squads, and instead of engaging in negotiations with the NFLPA about salaries for developmental squad players, the league unilaterally implemented its own salary, starting at

$1,000 a week for each player. This salary was well below the minimum salary for roster players. The NFLPA filed an antitrust lawsuit against the NFL over the issue of the developmental players' salaries.

The federal district court found that the labor exemption expired when the collective bargaining agreement expired. The case went to trial in the fall of 1992, and a jury awarded $10 million to 235 developmental squad players. The case was reversed on appeal, holding that the nonstatutory labor exemption protected the league from all antitrust lawsuits brought by players or their representatives relating to conduct that occurred during the collective bargaining process.

AMERICAN NEEDLE, INC. v. NATIONAL FOOTBALL LEAGUE (2010)

For the past several decades professional sports leagues have often asserted that they should be perceived as a single economic enterprise. Such a perception would render them incapable of conspiring as depicted in *Section 1 of the Sherman Antitrust Act* (15 U.S.C. § 1, 2012). For example, the "single entity" defense claims that a league, as well as its members, should be conceived of as a partnership with offices spread out in different locations. Similarly, because a professional sports league is made up of separately owned teams, they must cooperate as if they were a single economic undertaking for the league to operate effectively.

The result of permitting the single entity defense would be that the contract, combination, or conspiracy under Section 1 would not be present (15 U.S.C. § 1, 2012). Instead, rules governing sale and relocation of franchises, would be perceived as the internal regulations of a single legal and economic body. Thus, such league arrangements would be immune from analysis under Section 1. In *American Needle, Inc. v. National Football League* (2010), the United States Supreme Court noted that there was significant evidence that NFL teams had long acted as one source of economic

power to license their intellectual property collectively and to promote league football. As such, the teams were depicted as a single source of economic command when promoting itself through the licensing of intellectual property. As a result, the Supreme Court ruled that there was no basis for a claim under Section 1 of the Sherman Act. Before the *American Needle* case, the lower federal courts usually rejected the single entity defense (*Sullivan v. National Football League*, 1994). The primary response was to view the league as a kind of joint venture with numerous companies which would allow the rule of reason to evaluate the antitrust legality of agreements between league members (*Clarett v. National Football League*, 2004).

CALDWELL v. AMERICAN BASKETBALL ASSOCIATION (1991)

The nonstatutory labor exemption was expanded onto the basketball context in *Caldwell v. American Basketball Association*, (1991). In that case a former basketball player who had been suspended from the league brought an antitrust lawsuit. The issue before the court was whether the suspension flowed from the collective bargaining agreement and was then subject to the nonstatutory labor exemption. The court found that the suspension arose from the CBA and not the particular terms of Caldwell's player contract. On appeal, Caldwell lost at the Second Circuit Court of Appeals, which held that his antitrust claims were barred by the nonstatutory labor exemption.

SPORTS BROADCASTING EXEMPTION

Congress has created various antitrust *sports broadcasting exemptions* for professional football. For instance the NFL and TV networks are allowed to sell a unitary television package. Additionally, "blackouts" for home games in the home territory are also exempted from antitrust scrutiny. Finally, the combined merger of the AFL and NFL draft systems are also exempt as well. The exemption for sports broadcasting reads as follows:

> § 1291. Exemption from antitrust laws of agreements covering the telecasting of sports contests and the combining of professional football leagues
>
> The antitrust laws . . . shall not apply to any joint agreement by or among persons engaging in or conducting the organized professional team sports of football, baseball, basketball, or hockey, by which any league of clubs participating in professional football, baseball, basketball, or hockey contests sells or otherwise transfers all or any part of the rights of such league's member clubs in the sponsored telecasting of the games of football, baseball, basketball, or hockey, as the case may be, engaged in or conducted by such clubs. In addition, such laws shall not apply to a joint agreement by which the member clubs of two or more professional football leagues, which are exempt from income tax under section 501(c)(6) of the Internal Revenue Code of 1986 [26 U.S.C.A. 501(c)(6)], combine their operations in expanded single league so exempt from income tax, if such agreement increases rather than decreases the number of professional football clubs so operating, and the provisions of which are directly relevant thereto (15 U.S.C. § 1291).

League Versus League

There has been much litigation in the antitrust area dealing with disputes between rival leagues. Start-up leagues have sued established leagues, arguing that the practice of the established league constitutes a monopoly and that it is in violation of antitrust laws. The NFL has seen its share of rival leagues appear on the horizon. The World Football League (WFL), the American Football League (AFL), the United States Football League (USFL) and the XFL have all attempted to compete against the NFL. Some had more success than others.

In *American Football League v. National Football League* (1962), the burgeoning American Football League and its franchise owners brought an antitrust action against the owners of the NFL franchises. The court ruled in favor of the NFL finding it was not a monopoly as alleged by the AFL. In 1960 the AFL started with eight teams. The AFL and the NFL began playing one another in the 1966 Super Bowl. The NFL was thought to be the dominant league; however, the first two Super Bowls were split between the two leagues. The New York Jets, under the leadership of Joe Namath, knocked off the heavily favored Baltimore Colts and their Hall of Fame quarterback, Johnny Unitas, 16–7. The 1967 Super Bowl victory for the Jets was also a victory for the AFL and a major breakthrough for the league. The AFL signed and produced great stars such as George Blanda, Lance Alworth, Daryle "Mad Bomber" Lamonica, Mike Garrett (USC Heisman Trophy winner), Billy Cannon (Heisman Trophy winner), Bubba Smith, George Webster, Len Dawson, Charlie Hennigan, Jan Stenerud, Jim Nance, Babe Parilli, Otis Taylor, Jim Ringo, and Matt Snell, to name a few.

FRANCHISE RELOCATION

Antitrust laws have also been at issue when franchises relocate. Numerous franchises have been added to professional sports leagues in the past 40 years, while others have relocated. Owners may have different reasons to move a professional sports franchise to a new city. Many cities attempt to lure a professional franchise with the promise of a new facility. Franchises must provide fans with a first-class facility in which to watch the sport. A facility must also provide all the comforts that go along with watching a sport. Gone are the days when a hot dog and a beer were the only choices at the national pastime. Owners must provide fans with a myriad of food and entertainment choices while at the park.

In the NFL, there has been significant franchise movement since 1984:

- Cleveland Browns to the Baltimore Ravens
- Houston Oilers to the Tennessee Titans
- Los Angeles Rams to the St. Louis Rams
- Los Angeles Raiders to the Oakland Raiders
- Baltimore Colts to the Indianapolis Colts
- St. Louis Cardinals to Phoenix Cardinals

The following franchises were added to the NFL since 1995:

- Cleveland Browns (1999)
- Houston Texans (2002)
- Jacksonville Jaguars (1995)
- Carolina Panthers (1995)

In *Los Angeles Memorial Coliseum Commission v. National Football League* (1984), the issue facing the court was whether the Oakland Raiders could move to Los Angeles. After the Raiders' lease expired with the Oakland Coliseum in 1978, the club's managing partner, Al Davis, signed an agreement with Los Angeles Coliseum officials outlining the terms of the Raiders' proposed move to Los Angeles. The Raiders had to overcome Rule 4.3 of Article IV of the NFL Constitution, which stated:

> The League shall have exclusive control of the exhibition of football games by member clubs within the home territory of each member. No member club shall have the right to transfer its franchise or playing site to a different city, either within or outside its home territory, without prior approval by the affirmative vote of three-fourths of the existing member clubs of the League.

Other NFL teams voted 22–0 against the move by the Raiders, with five teams abstaining. The Raiders subsequently filed an antitrust action against the NFL and its member clubs. A jury returned a verdict for the Raiders for $11.55 million in damages, which was trebled because the team was the prevailing party in an antitrust lawsuit. The Ninth Circuit Court of Appeals affirmed the jury's verdict.

The court found that the NFL's three-fourths rule was a violation of antitrust law partly based on the fact that the regulation was an unreasonable restraint of trade.

In *Minnesota Twins Partnership v. State* (1999), a court was called on once again to deal with baseball's antitrust exemption when the league attempted to disband the Minnesota Twins. The court found that the sale and relocation of the Twins was exempted from antitrust scrutiny because it was an integral part of the business of baseball. The court found that the number of teams allowed to compete in the league was a decision that was integral to the game of baseball. The court stated:

> The *Piazza* opinion is a skillful attempt to make sense of the Supreme Court's refusal to overrule *Federal Baseball*, an opinion generally regarded as "not one of Mr. Justice Holmes' happiest days." But *Piazza* ignores what is clear about *Flood*—that the Supreme Court had no intention of overruling *Federal Baseball* or *Toolson* despite acknowledging that professional baseball involves interstate commerce. Although the facts of *Flood* deal only with baseball's reserve system, the Court's conclusion in *Flood* is unequivocal. . . .
>
> As intellectually attractive as the *Piazza* alternative is, we are compelled to accept the paradox the Supreme Court acknowledged in *Flood* when it declined to overrule *Federal Baseball*. . . . We choose to follow the lead of those courts that conclude the business of professional baseball is exempt from

federal antitrust laws. Further, we conclude that the sale and relocation of a baseball franchise, like the reserve clause discussed in *Flood*, is an integral part of the business of professional baseball and falls within the exemption. (*Federal Baseball*, p. 209)

AMATEUR ATHLETICS AND ANTITRUST

Antitrust law has had a major impact on amateur sports as well. Alleged illegal restraints have been challenged at the amateur level as well as at the professional level The same legal analysis is applied for antitrust cases at both levels. The majority of courts have given deference to amateur sports associations to preserve the integrity and character of amateur athletics. In *Hairston v. Pacific 10 Conference* (1996), several collegiate athletes sued their conference, alleging antitrust violations after the conference suspended them for recruiting violations.

MISCELLANEOUS ANTITRUST ISSUES

Antitrust laws have been applied to many sports. In *Elliott v. United Center* (1997), a regulation that prohibited fans from entering an area with food that was purchased outside the arena was challenged. Independent peanut vendors sued, claiming the center monopolized the market for food sales at and around the arena in violation of the Sherman Act. The court disagreed, ruling that the United Center's rule did not violate antitrust law. In *Fieldturf Inc. v. Southwest Recreational Industries, Inc.* (2002), a company that manufactured Astroturf sued its competitors on antitrust grounds, but the court found that the plaintiff failed to establish the existence of a monopoly. One of the significant issues in addressing an antitrust

problem is defining the relevant geographic and product market. The broader a market is defined, the smaller the market share will be for the entity alleged to be monopolizing.

There have been many antitrust lawsuits dealing with equipment use. In *In re Baseball Bat Antitrust Litigation* (1999), a manufacturer of wooden baseball bats sued a manufacturer of aluminum bats. The court held that no antitrust injury was present. In *Eureka Urethane, Inc. v. PBA, Inc.*, (1990), a manufacturer of bowling balls brought an antitrust action against a bowling association when the association refused to sanction one of its balls for tournament play. The defendant, the Professional Bowlers Association (PBA), refused to allow the plaintiff to manufacture the "Bud Ball." The plaintiff had obtained a license from Anheuser Busch for the use of the Budweiser bow tie logo. The bow tie was placed on a bowling ball colored in Budweiser red. PBA rules stated the following:

> Rule VII, Section A [before any bowler can use any new equipment in PBA competition it must have PBA clearance].
> Rule VII, Section E [prohibits logos on bowling balls other than the original under which they were manufactured].
> Rule XI, Section I and J [before any bowler can avail himself of an incentive offer, the offer must have PBA approval].
> Rule XVIII, Section D [proscribes speech by PBA bowlers during interviews of the name of a commercial organization or product unless it relates to the tournament's title sponsor].
> Rule XX, Section A [logos competitive with a title sponsor are precluded from appearing on a player's shirt].

Source: Courtesy of Westlaw.

The court granted summary judgment in favor of the defendant, finding that the association did not engage in anticompetitive behavior when it prohibited the use of the ball.

DISCUSSION QUESTIONS

Professional Sports

1. In *Salvino v. MLBPA*, why did the court select the rule of reason standard instead of the per se standard argued by the plaintiffs? What procompetitive effects did the Major League Baseball Players Association's expert note? Do you agree with the expert's opinions?

2. How does the application of antitrust law differ within the context of the sports world? How does it differ with regard to professional versus amateur sports?

3. Would you consider a professional draft an unreasonable restraint of trade? If so, why does every professional league have a draft? Do you believe the drafts fulfill the purpose as set forth in *Smith v. Pro Football*? Is it true that if no draft existed, all draftees would want to play for the New York Yankees, the Los Angeles Lakers, or the Detroit Red Wings?

4. What is the rationale behind baseball's exemption from antitrust law? How has baseball's exemption been narrowed since *Flood v. Kuhn*? What was the historical basis for the exemption?

5. What antitrust challenges are left for professional players after *Clarett v. NFL*? The nonstatutory labor exemption seems to be expanding. This will make it difficult for any professional player to bring a successful antitrust lawsuit arising from a labor dispute with a team. The nonstatutory labor exemption would most likely not apply to individual sports such as golf, track and field, boxing, or tennis. Usually, these athletes are not organized and do not engage in a collective bargaining process.

Amateur Athletics and Antitrust

1. Is the restriction on 18-year-olds in the NBA an antitrust violation? If so, how? What defenses can be asserted in its defense?

2. Could a plaintiff contest the age requirements for the NBA on antitrust grounds? The league now requires a potential player to be at least 19 years old before he can enter the NBA draft and be at least one year removed from graduating from high school. Are the arguments for the age requirement different from other sports?

3. Why do the MLB and NHL allow players to come into the league directly out of high school, but the NFL does not? Do you agree with the argument that football players coming right out of high school are not physically ready to play in the NFL? What other reasons could the NFL argue in support of the regulation?

KEY TERMS

Curt Flood Act of 1998
Federal Baseball v. National League of Professional Baseball Clubs (1922)

Mackey v. NFL
Monopoly
Nonstatutory labor exemption

Per se test
Quick look test
Reserve clause
Restraint of trade
Rozelle Rule

Rule of reason
Section 1 of the Sherman Antitrust Act
Section 2 of the Sherman Antitrust Act
Sherman Antitrust Act
Sports broadcasting exemption

REFERENCES

Allen Bradley Co. v. Local Union No. 3, International Brotherhood of Electrical Workers, 325 U.S. 797, 65 S.Ct. 1533 (1945).

American Football League v. National Football League, 323 F.2d 124 (4th Cir. 1962).

Brenner v. World Boxing Council, 675 F.2d 445 (1982).

Brown v. Pro Football Inc., 518 U.S. 231 (1996).

Bryant v. United States Polo Ass'n, 631 F. Supp. 71 (1986).

Caldwell v. American Basketball Ass'n Inc., 1991 WL 270473 (S.D.N.Y. 1991).

Chicago Board of Trade v. United States, 246 U.S. 231 (1918).

Clarett v. National Football League, Inc., 2003 WL 22469936 (2003).

Continental T.V., Inc. v. GTE Sylvania Inc., 433 U.S. 36, 49–50 (1977).

Denver Rockets v. All-Pro Management, Inc., 325 F. Supp. 1049 (D.C. Cal. 1971).

Elliott v. United Center, 126 F.3d 1003 (7th Cir. 1997).

Eureka Urethane, Inc. v. PBA, Inc., 746 F. Supp. 915 (E.D. Mo. 1990).

Federal Baseball v. National League of Professional Baseball Clubs, 259 U.S. 200 (1922)

Fieldturf Inc. v. Southwest Recreational Industries, Inc., 235 F. Supp. 2d 708 (E.D. Ky. 2002).

Flood v. Kuhn, 402 US 528 (1972).

Hairston v. Pacific 10 Conference, 101 F.3d 1315 (1996).

Haywood v. National Basketball Ass'n, 401 U.S. 1204 (1971).

In re Baseball Bat Antitrust Litigation, 75 F. Supp. 2d 1189 (D. Kan. 1999).

JES Properties, Inc. v. USA Equestrian, Inc., 2005 WL 112665 (M.D. Fla.).

Kapp v. National Football League, 390 F. Supp. 79 (N.D. Cal. 1974).

Loene v. Lalor, 208 U.S. 274 (1908).

Los Angeles Memorial Coliseum Commission v. National Football League, 726 F.2d 1381 (1984).

Mackey v. NFL, 543 F.2d 606 (8th Cir. 1976).

McCourt v. California Sports, Inc., 600 F.2d 1193 (6th Cir. 1979).

Minnesota Twins Partnership v. State, 592 N.W. 847 (Minn. 1999).

National Bancard Corporation (NaBanco) v. Visa U.S.A., 779 F.2d 592, 597 (11th Cir. 1986).

National Collegiate Athletic Association v. Board of the University of Oklahoma, 468 U.S. 85 (1984).

National Labor Relations Act § 8(9)(5), (d), 29 U.S.C. § 158 (a)(5), (d) (1982).

National Hockey League Players Association v. Plymouth Whalers Hockey Club, 419 F.3d 462, 469 (6th Cir. 2005).

Piazza v. Major League Baseball, 831 F. Supp. 420 (E.D. Penn. 1993).

Powell v. National Football League, 930 F.2d 1293 (8th Cir. 1989) cert. denied, 498 U.S. 1040 (1991).

Radivich v. National Football League, 352 U.S. 445 (1957).

Robertson v. National Basketball Ass'n., 622 F.2d 34 (2nd Cir. 1980).

Smith v. Pro Football, Inc., 593 F.2d 1173 (D.C. Cir. 1979).

St. Louis Convention & Visitors Commission v. National Football League, 154 F.3d 851 (8th Cir. 1998).

Standard Oil v. United States, 221 U.S. 1, 31 S.Ct. 502, 55 L.Ed. 619 (1911).

Summit Health, Ltd. v. Pinhas, 500 U.S. 322 (1991).

Toolson v. New York Yankees, 346 U.S. 356 (1953).

United States v. International Boxing Club, Inc., 348 U.S. 236 (1955).

Wood v. National Basketball Association, 809 F.2d 954 (2nd Cir. 1987).

Worldwide Basketball and Sports Tours, Inc. v. Nat'l Collegiate Athletic Ass'n, 388 F.3d 955, 959 (6th Cir. 2004).

LABOR RELATIONS IN SPORTS

LEARNING OBJECTIVES

By the end of the chapter, the reader will be able to:

1. Understand the unique characteristics of labor law in sport
2. Understand the importance of the National Labor Relations Act and the National Labor Board in sports
3. Comprehend collective bargaining agreements as applied to sports
4. Recognize the typical collective bargaining agreement topics in sports
5. Analyze the effects of professional sports lockouts and/or holdouts
6. Examine how different court cases preceded free agency of professional athletes
7. Explain how arbitration has been used in the sports setting
8. Analyze the duty for fair representation as well as unfair labor practices in sports

RELATED CASES

Case 10.1   White v. National Football League 149 F. Supp2d 858 (D. Minn. 2001)

Case 10.2   North American Soccer League v. N.L.R.B. 613 F.2d 1379 (5th Cir. 1980)

INTRODUCTION

Conflict between players and management has led to strikes and lockouts in professional sports. The players run the risk of fans becoming disengaged or apathetic after they see multi million-dollar ballplayers complaining about their salaries and working conditions. Owners run the risk of a shutdown of the sport and of being perceived as greedy by fans, which could turn into a public relations nightmare. The players and owners know all too well the repercussions of a "work stoppage," whether that occurs by way of strike or lockout. It has been estimated that the 1994 players' strike in baseball cost both parties approximately $1 billion. The players lost approximately $243 million in wages, and the owners lost approximately $376 million in attendance and television revenues in 1994 and $326 million in revenue for lost attendance in 1995. Certainly, damage is done to the reputation of the sport, which must be remedied by the goodwill of the players and management after a work stoppage. After the 2004 players' strike in the National Hockey League, fans returned to hockey with a slight increase in attendance.

Labor law has become a mainstay in the sports industry and has now taken precedence over antitrust law in resolving disputes between management and labor. Labor law as applied to professional sports presents some unique characteristics. For example, the typical professional athlete is not the typical worker in the context of a labor issue. Clearly, the average salary of a professional football player separates him from the auto worker or the teamster. So too does the very public nature of the business. Very few workers, aside from professional athletes, have detailed accounts of their on the job performances replayed on television networks or in the print media on a daily or weekly basis. Additionally, the professional athletes have relatively short careers. Thus, unlike most other union situations, the composition of the union rank and file is constantly changing (Berry, Gould, & Staudohar, 1986). There are also several classes of athletes within the union: superstar, rookie, journeyman player, and role player. It is a multi-employer bargaining unit, with each team having a player representative to the union. In addition, beyond league minimum salaries and other basic conditions of employment, individual contract negotiations occur within the context of a collective bargaining unit.

Management is also a unique group in professional sports. Typically, management of professional teams consists of extremely wealthy individuals or groups of individuals with relatively minimal knowledge of the game or its history and culture. In many situations the franchise has been purchased not as the individual's sole business. For example, Jerry Jones, owner of the Dallas Cowboys became a multi-millionaire in the oil business; George Steinbrenner, owner of the New York Yankees, made millions in the ship-building industry; and Mark Cuban, owner of the Dallas Mavericks, made billions in the computer industry. However, most owners assert that because they have taken the risk of investing their money into the team, they should be able to control the destiny of the franchise. They also assert that a larger payroll does not always guarantee success on the court, field, or ice. Owners have historically stated that they are losing money and that the sport will not be able to survive if players' salaries continue to rise. Both sides have valid points, and both have fought hard through the collective bargaining process to make headway in creating a collective bargaining agreement that all parties can live with.

This chapter explores labor relations between players and management, examining the rights and responsibilities of each party under federal law as well as significant provisions of the collective bargaining agreements of professional leagues. The duty of unions to fairly represent members is also reviewed, as well as issues relating to the arbitration process between management and labor.

NATIONAL LABOR RELATIONS ACT

Federal antitrust and labor law have a strained relationship (Yoffie, 2015). While federal antitrust supports the development of competition by barring "restraints of trade or commerce" labor law urges parties to collaborate that often leads to such restraints (Feldman, 2012). Accordingly, Congress passed the Norris-LaGuardia Act (29 U.S.C. §§ 101–115 (2013)) as well as § 6 and § 20 of the Clayton Act, which jointly established the "statutory labor exemption" which eradicated unionized activity from antitrust claims under Section 1 of the Sherman Act (Feldman, 2012). The Norris LaGuardia Act created the "non-statutory labor exemption" and limited the ability of federal courts to enjoin certain labor-related activities (Krueger-Wyman, 2012). This exemption allows employees to organize as a collective bargaining unit and negotiate with *employers* over a contract that covers all *employees* within that unit (29 U.S.C. § 101) Professional athletes have used the exemption to form players' unions and negotiate collective bargaining agreements (CBAs) with their specific sport's league and owners (Krueger-Wyman, 2012). The Clayton Act is designed "to protect trade and commerce against unlawful restraints and monopolies" (15 U.S.C § 12, 2002). To accomplish such a protection, the Clayton Act offered more specific "provisions to prohibit anticompetitive price discrimination, kept corporations from making exclusive dealing practices, and expanded the ability for individuals to sue for damages" (15 U.S.C. § 12, 2002).

Once unionized the employees need to reach agreements with their employers (Krueger-Wyman, 2012; *N.L.R.B. v. Allis-Chamlers Mfg. Co.*, 1967). To provide a framework for such negotiations, the Supreme Court developed the non-statutory labor exemption, which similarly removes collective bargaining from the purview

of Section 1 (Shapiro, 1993). Under the National Labor Relations Act (NLRA), an employer (i.e., the National Basketball Association [NBA] Board of Governors, National Football League [NFL] Executive Board, Major League Baseball [MLB] Board of Directors) and the employee-selected representative (i.e., the NBA Players Association [NBPA], NFL Players Association [NFLPA], or MLB Players Association [MLBPA]) are obligated to bargain collectively (29 U.S.C. § 158(d)).

Professional sports are governed by the NLRA (29 U.S.C. §§ 151–166). Baseball received the protection of the NLRA in 1969 (American League of Professional Baseball Clubs, 1969). The National Labor Relations Board (NLRB) enforces the NLRA—an act created to protect the rights of employees and employers, encourage collective bargaining, promote the free flow of commerce, and restore bargaining equality between employees and employers (29 U.S.C. § 151 (2012)). The NLRB asserted jurisdiction over football in *National Football League Management Council* (1973). Once professional sports came under the jurisdiction of the NLRA, labor and management became subject to the act and all parties were given all the rights set forth in the act. At one time, sports were not viewed as a business and therefore were not subject to the protection of the NLRA. However, it is now well settled that the NLRA and its corresponding protections apply to professional sports.

Labor laws govern professional sports league CBAs; therefore, any dispute between a players' union and a league falls within the jurisdiction of the NLRB (*Brown v. Pro Football*, 1996). One of the NLRB's first duties was to determine the appropriate bargaining unit for a sport. The bargaining unit is usually the sport as a whole instead of individual teams or certain positions (such as a union for quarterbacks only). Once recognized, the designated union becomes the sole bargaining representative for all members. For example, the CBA of the Women's National Basketball Association (WNBA) acknowledges the Women's National

Basketball Players Association as the appropriate bargaining unit for labor in the WNBA.

In *North American Soccer League v. N.L.R.B.* (1980), the question of what the "appropriate unit" is for collective bargaining purposes was examined. In the majority of sports, the sport as a whole is determined to be the bargaining unit, as opposed to a particular position on a team or the team itself. The union desires the largest unit possible, whereas management wants a "divide and conquer" strategy to be able to put itself in a better bargaining position. In *North American Soccer League v. NLRB*, the court held the league and its member clubs to be "joint employers." The North American Soccer League (NASL) disputed the NLRB's certification of "all NASL players of clubs based in the United States" as the appropriate bargaining unit.

The NLRB may decline jurisdiction over an industry if its impact on interstate commerce is not substantial enough. For example, the NLRB refused to exercise jurisdiction over the thoroughbred horse racing industry, finding it to be only a local activity. It is the policy of the NLRB to encourage parties to engage in collective bargaining. The following are significant excerpts from the NLRA that outline the act's policies, relevant findings and declaration of policy, definitions, and rights of employees to organize.

FINDINGS AND DECLARATION OF POLICY

Strikes and lockouts have been common since the institution of player unions as both players and management have used the tools available to them in attempts to force their will on the other party during labor negotiations. According to the National Labor Relations Act § 151, the Findings and Declaration of Policy states,

the denial by some employers of the right of employees to organize and the refusal by some employers to accept the procedure of collective bargaining lead to strikes and other forms of industrial strife or unrest, which have the intent or the necessary effect of burdening or obstructing commerce.

The inequality of bargaining power between employees who do not possess full freedom of association or actual liberty of contract, and employers who are organized in the corporate or other forms of ownership association substantially burdens and affects the flow of commerce, and tends to aggravate recurrent business depressions, by depressing wage rate and the purchasing power of wage earners in industry and by preventing the stabilization of competitive wage rates and working conditions within and between industries.

Experience has proved that protection by law of the right of employees to organize and bargain collectively safeguards commerce from injury, impairment, or interruption, and promotes the flow of commerce by removing certain recognized sources of industrial strife and unrest, by encouraging practices fundamental to the friendly adjustment of industrial disputes arising out of difference as to wages, hours, or other working conditions, and by restoring equality of bargaining power between employers and employees.

It is hereby declared to be the policy of the United States to eliminate the causes of certain substantial obstructions to the free flow of commerce and to mitigate and eliminate these obstructions when they have occurred by encouraging the practice and procedure of collective bargaining and by protecting the exercise by workers of full freedom of association, self-organization, and designation of representatives of their own choosing, for the purpose of negotiating the terms and conditions of their employment or other mutual aid or protection (29 U.S.C. 151).

RIGHT OF EMPLOYEES AS TO COLLECTIVE BARGAINING

Collective Bargaining

Collective bargaining is the staple of labor relations. CBAs, which govern the complicated relationship among players, teams, and leagues, can be the result of protracted negotiations between management and labor. Each party has duties and responsibilities that arise from the collective bargaining agreement. All major sports leagues now have CBAs that govern the relationship between the parties. Through the collective bargaining process, management and labor have attempted to arrive at an agreement that satisfies both parties. They must form a partnership that will govern their relationship for an extended period of time and maximize benefits and revenues for both management and labor. Each party wants to negotiate the best terms it can and wants to avoid any possible labor strife. Under the collective bargaining requirements of the NLRA, the parties must "meet at reasonable times and confer in good faith with respect to wages, hours, and other terms and conditions of employment" (29 U.S.C. § 158(d) (2013)). It has been the vague phrasing of the "other terms and conditions of employment" has given rise to extensive litigation between owners and players across the major sports leagues.

Given the huge increase in the popularity of sports in the last 40 years, owners and players arrive at the negotiating table with their own interests in mind along with the added incentive of dividing up the pie of revenues generated by the particular sport. Players are concerned with items such as salaries, injury protection, job security, free agency, pension benefits, and the vast realm of licensing and marketing opportunities for professional players. Owners have some of the same concerns but from a different perspective. Their concerns can include stadium issues, team payroll, guaranteed contracts for players, and revenue streams, with the primary purpose of attracting fans to the stadium.

Professional sports CBAs allow sports leagues and owners to avoid antitrust liability and simultaneously give players more bargaining power (Krueger-Wyman, 2012). Many of the standard practices used by professional sports leagues in America today would be considered illegal because, without the presence of CBAs, these standard practices would violate antitrust laws (Krueger-Wyman, 2012). Collective bargaining is the process by which a group of workers negotiates as a collective unit with management to establish the working conditions, salaries, and benefits for all employees. Both parties must negotiate in good faith or the proceedings can be considered an *unfair labor practice* (29 U.S.C. § 158(b)). Management cannot unilaterally impose its will upon the union for new terms that relate to subjects of mandatory collective bargaining until the parties have reached an impasse in negotiations. It would be an unfair labor practice to do so before impasse. The parties' labor negotiations will, it is hoped, produce a collective bargaining agreement that outlines the compromise agreement. The CBA takes precedent over league rules, bylaws, and individual agreements between players and teams.

A CBA can be a lengthy, comprehensive document. It is developed by labor law experts and covers almost every conceivable issue that might arise between the parties. Courts recognize the CBA as an enforceable contract; any material breach will give a cause of action to a party to the CBA. The CBA establishes the individual rights of the parties and also implements federal labor policy. Courts use the traditional rules of contract interpretation to determine whether the CBA has been breached. Section 301 of the Labor Management Relations Act provides parties with the power to file a federal lawsuit for violations of the CBA (29 U.S.C.A. § 185).

In the sports context, individual players still have the authority to negotiate certain aspects of their employment contract even though the union is considered the sole representative for union members during the collective bargaining process. Players and their agents are able to negotiate their own salaries in excess of the league minimum, as well as bonus clauses, without the assistance of the union as long as they are not in violation of the CBA. A typical collective bargaining agreement in sports addresses the following topics:

- *Free agency and player mobility systems.* How can players move within the league? How many years do they have to be in the league before they can declare free agency?
- *Salary caps and luxury taxes.* What is the amount of the cap and how long does it last? How is the cap or luxury tax number determined? Is there a minimum amount teams must spend on payroll?
- *Standard player contracts.* What terms make up the standard player contract? To what extent can this standard contract be revised through collective bargaining?
- *Revenue sharing.* What constitutes "revenue" for the league? How are the revenues to be divided?
- *Grievance and arbitration procedures.* When can a player go to arbitration? How does the arbitration process work? Can a party still pursue a remedy through the court system if arbitration is agreed to in the CBA?
- *Player agents.* Who can be a player agent? Is an examination required? What qualifications must an agent have to be approved as an agent? To what extent can an agent be disciplined by the union for poor representation?

- *Off-season workouts, medical examinations, and physical conditions of players.* Who determines whether a player is physically fit to play? Can a player have a second medical opinion if he or she suffers an injury?
- *Player drafts.* How are players drafted into a league? How does the draft function? How many draft rounds are there?
- *Drug testing programs.* Who can be tested and how frequently? What drugs are included in the testing program? What happens if a player tests positive? How does the drug program treat multiple offenders?
- *Player salaries and benefits.* What are the minimum salaries for players? Are veterans and rookies treated differently? Who is entitled to a pension and benefits?
- *Licensing and marketing of players.* Who owns the publicity rights of players? Can players opt out of such a program? How are licensing revenues determined and divided?
- *Player conduct and discipline.* What player conduct can be regulated? What about off-field or off-season misconduct? What fines can be levied? Can a player be fined by both a team and the league?

This list is not exhaustive but rather presents a general overview of the issues that can be negotiated between management and labor.

Collective bargaining requires a lot of give and take from both sides. Historically, the parties have been willing to sacrifice the game itself to push their point. Each side presents different arguments. The players argue that their services are unique and that without them the sport could not exist. That is certainly a valid point in light of the owners' attempt in 1987 to play NFL games with replacement players. The players also argue that their careers are short and thus they need to achieve their earning power in a very short period of time. Players argue that they are the ones taking the risks of career-ending injuries and that they are the reason the fans attend games. As fans flock to concerts with their favorite entertainers so to do sports fans watch their favorite entertainers in sports competitions.

Collective bargaining in professional sports is a relatively new concept. It has only been a factor in professional team sports for about the 40 years. During this short time period, a turbulent history ensued with the promise of additional controversy in the future. To gain a thorough appreciation of the current issues within the collective bargaining context of professional sports, it is important to understand some historical aspects of the major professional sports in North America, including the National Football League (NFL), National Hockey League (NHL), National Basketball Association (NBA), and MLB.

NATIONAL FOOTBALL LEAGUE AND COLLECTIVE BARGAINING

The National Football League Players Association (NFLPA) was first formed in 1956, but it was not recognized until two years later when passing reference was made to the union in congressional testimony by Commissioner Bert Bell (Berry et al., 1986). Despite the existence and some recognition of the association, there was not actually a collective bargaining agreement between the players and owners until 1968 (Berry et al., 1995). At approximately this same time, professional baseball and basketball were beginning to organize (Berry et al., 1995). Despite the existence and recognition of players associations, none were particularly strong nor well accepted by management. Finally, in 1969, the NLRB indicated that it would accept jurisdiction over professional sports (Wiestart & Lowell, 1979).

The first major strike in professional sports occurred in 1974 in the NFL (Berry et al., 1986). It was a catastrophic failure. The strike lasted forty-four days and left the union badly split and seriously underfunded. The key focus of the strike was the Rozelle Rule pertaining to player free agency. The rule allowed a player to change teams at the conclusion of his contract if he could negotiate a new deal with a new club; however, the new club was required to compensate the old club for the loss of the player. Adequate compensation in the form of players or cash was to be negotiated between the two teams. If the teams could not reach an agreement, the compensation was to be set by the Commissioner of the NFL, Pete Rozelle (Berry et al., 1986). There were no guidelines for awarding compensation and, ultimately, there was very little player movement.

Previous cases had established that professional baseball was exempt from the antitrust laws on grounds unique to the times and to the treatment of the sport by Congress and the American public (*Federal Baseball Club v. National League*, 1922; *Radovich v. NFL*, 1957; *Toolson v. New York Yankees, Inc.*, 1953). The first significant litigation focusing on the NFL collective bargaining process was *Mackey v. NFL* (1976), in which the Eighth Circuit was called upon to evaluate the validity of the Rozelle Rule. Such evaluation was necessary because of the failure of the bargaining process and the strike to effectively represent the players' interests, thus leaving the antitrust laws as the only vehicle for challenging the owners' actions. The basic complaint of the players was that the Rozelle Rule amounted to an "illegal combination and conspiracy in restraint of trade denying professional football players the right to freely contract for their services" (*Mackey v. NFL*, 1976, p. 609).

The 32 clubs of the National Football League are generally exempt from antitrust laws while there is a CBA in effect (*Powell v. National Football League*, 1989). This policy is known as the non-statutory labor exemption (*Powell v. National Football League*, 1989). In *Mackey*, the court initially assessed the various factors to be considered in applying the non-statutory exemption to a particular case. Essentially, the analysis is whether the relevant federal labor policy is deserving of pre-eminence over the federal antitrust policy given the particular circumstances of the case at hand. According to the *Mackey* court, three factors must be present for the labor exemption to apply:

1. the restraint on trade must primarily effect only the parties to the collective bargaining agreement;
2. the agreement sought to be protected must concern a mandatory subject of collective bargaining; and
3. the agreement sought to be protected must be the product of bona fide arm's length bargaining (p. 614).

Because the third element could not be upheld, the court found that the non-statutory labor exemption did not apply.

A new CBA was reached in 1977, following the *Mackey* ruling, which replaced the Rozelle Rule with a right of first refusal system and agreed upon compensation for the club losing the player (Wong, 2010). However, the players did not gain the right to unrestricted free agency in the 1977 CBA even though players in MLB, the NBA, and the NHL now enjoyed this right due to a variety of legal proceedings (Deubert & Wong, 2009). The players instead agreed to increased minimum salaries and benefits (Wong, 2010).

During the 1982 season, the players conducted a 57-day strike that resulted in the cancelling of several games. However, while the 1982 CBA increased salaries, benefits, and pensions, it is most noteworthy as it is the first time a drug testing program was instituted (Wong, 2010). In 1987, labor relations between the players and owners were significantly strained as when the players went on strike, the owners used replacements players in the games. One year later, the players asserted that the collective bargaining system at the time violated Section 1 of the Sherman Anti-Trust Act (*Powell v. National Football League*, 1988). The NFL owners argued that the system was protected by the non-statutory labor exemption. Judge David Doty ruled that the labor exemption persisted since the terms and conditions of the

1982 CBA were still in effect (*Powell v. National Football League*, 1988). On appeal, the Eighth Circuit court reversed Doty's decision stating that the labor exemption would exist as long as a collective bargaining relationship was being continued (*Powell v. National Football League*, 1989).

As a result of the reversal, the players decided to decertify the National Football League Player Association (Wong, 2010). By decertifying the Association, the players essentially renounced the union's authority to act as their bargaining unit and subsequently sought the court's endorsement of this action as well as a ruling that the nonstatutory labor exemption had ended. The court found that the NFLPA was no longer engaged in any collective bargaining and was not representing players in grievances. It also found that the players had paid a price for the decertification of the union in that the League had unilaterally, without notice, changed insurance benefits and lengthened the playing season. It also held that with the demise of the union as a bargaining unit, the nonstatutory labor exemption was no longer available and the players' antitrust action could proceed on the merits (*Powell v. National Football League*, 1991).

One year later, the jury in *McNeil v. National Football League* (1992) ruled that the Right of First Refusal/Compensation Rules in Plan B had a significantly detrimental effect on the competition for the services of professional football players. Ultimately, the jury found that the rules caused economic harm to the plaintiffs. Following the *McNeil* case, a class action case, *White v. National Football League* (1993) ensued. As a result of this case, the NFLPA and the NFL entered into a new collective bargaining agreement. Among the items within the new collective bargaining agreement allowed for unrestricted free agency to players who had completed five years of service in the league and restricted free agency to players with three years of service. However, teams could still retain restricted free agents by matching offers received by other teams. These two pieces as part of the collective bargaining process, could arguably be considered as literal game changers of professional football in the United States.

NATIONAL HOCKY LEAGUE AND COLLECTIVE BARGAINING

The NHL Collective Bargaining Agreement contains provisions governing rules, arbitration and grievance procedures, along with minimum player salaries and working conditions (Mirtle, 2012). The NHL's role in the collective bargaining process is to represent the collective interests of all thirty NHL franchises and owners (Mirtle, 2012). As the NHL's hockey-related revenue has steadily increased over the past couple of decades conflicts between the NHL and the NHLPA have dramatically increased as well.

1994–1995 Lockout

On the day the 1994–1995 season was set to begin, the owners locked out the players. The primary issue was the owners' insistence on implementing salary caps that would limit how much teams were allowed to pay their players. Owners felt the salary cap system would help equalize costs throughout the league, but the players preferred the implementation of a revenue sharing scheme. Only 48 games, as opposed to the typically scheduled of eighty-two games, were played that season (Allen & Brehm, 2005). In addition, the Collective Bargaining Agreement that was put in place after months of negotiations between the players and owners failed to adequately resolve the salary cap issue, which led to the infamous lockout during the 2004–2005 season (Baumann, 2012).

2004–2005 Lockout

The 2004–2005 *labor dispute* resulted in the cancellation of the entire NHL season (Allen & Brehm, 2005). In 2003, with eleven and one-half months remaining on the then-current Collective Bargaining Agreement, the NHL and NHLPA attempted to negotiate a new agreement (Shaw, 2014). The owners insisted on implementing a $31 million team salary cap into the Collective Bargaining

Agreement in order to control player salaries (Baumann, 2012). In October of 2003, the players offered a slight reduction in their salaries, but the owners sought larger reductions (Baumann, 2012). With no process of arbitration included in the Collective Bargaining Agreement, the parties had no incentive to negotiate with one another in good faith (Shaw, 2014). Despite ongoing negotiations and the use of federal mediators, the NHL canceled the entire 2004–2005 season (Baumann, 2012). This was the first time a labor dispute forced a North American sport to cancel an entire season (Yoost, 2006). Ultimately, the NHL lost an estimated $2 billion in revenue and the players lost roughly $1 billion in salaries as a result of the entire season being canceled (Staudohar, 2006).

2012–2013 Lockout

The NHL endured another lockout during the 2012–2013 season. The primary issue why this lockout occurred was how the players and owners would share hockey-related revenue (Mirtle, 2012). Due to an annual revenue increase of slightly more than 7% after the 2004–2005 lockout, the owners demanded a higher percentage of the revenue (Mirtle, 2012). Shortly after the parties reached an agreement, the NHL announced that a forty-eight game season would be played (Strang, 2013). Each team held a brief one-week training camp before beginning a season in which each team played an average of three and one-half games per week. As a result of the lockout, a total of 625 games were canceled, which cost the league an estimated billion dollars in revenues (Strang, 2013).

MAJOR LEAGUE BASEBALL AND COLLECTIVE BARGAINING

MLB players have attempted to unionize for many years. John Montgomery Ward (a Columbia Law School graduate) was both an outstanding ballplayer (he was selected to baseball's Hall of Fame in 1964) and a labor organizer. Ward organized the Brotherhood of National League Players in the late 1880s and continued to represent professional baseball players against management after he left baseball as a player (Stevens, 1988). Marvin Miller was named executive director of the MLBPA in 1966 and was instrumental in the players' making great strides toward bigger salaries and more benefits for players. Miller once stated that "[t]he essential dignity of equals sitting down together just can't be overemphasized." Miller was a noted labor organizer and assisted players in eventually gaining free agency and striking down baseball's reserve clause, which had prevented players from declaring free agency and gaining economic freedom.

After Curt Flood's challenge to baseball's reserve clause was defeated at the U.S. Supreme Court in *Flood v. Kuhn*, free agency for baseball players was eventually achieved through the Messersmith/McNally labor arbitration decision and its subsequent appeals through the courts (*Kansas City Royals v. Major League Baseball Players' Ass'n.*, 1976). The labor arbitration decision forced management to the bargaining table and resulted in an increase in player's rights under a new Basic Agreement.

The MLBPA and MLB negotiated the first collective bargaining agreement in any professional sport in 1968. Two years later, the players and owners sign their second collective bargaining agreement. Additionally, the owners agreed to grievance arbitration possibly due to concern of the Curt Flood lawsuit which challenged MLB's antitrust exemption (Snyder, 2006). Since this time there have been several work stoppages, either by way of strike or lockout. Most notably, in 1975 the arbitrator interpreted the reserve clause as major league player contract to permit only a single one-year renewal, rather than an unending series of one-year renewals. Federal trial and appellate courts upheld the interpretation against challenges by the owners, who choose not to appeal to the Supreme Court. The result is free agency for pitchers Dave McNally and Andy Messersmith, as well as the same status in the very near future

for all major league players. The MLBPA and the major leagues negotiated through much of the first half of the 1976 season before signing their fourth collective bargaining agreement which featured a radically restructured reserve system (really a free agency management system).

The 1994–1995 strike was the longest in baseball history, resulting in the cancellation of the 1994 World Series. Many baseball fans said they would never return to the sport because of the work stoppage and the subsequent cancellation of the World Series, but attendance figures since then have shown otherwise. Fans continue to flock to the ballpark in record numbers.

After almost nine decades of unsuccessfully tackling professional baseball's antitrust exemption, Congress enacted the Curt Flood Act in 1998 (Curt Flood Act of 1998). The Act made clear that:

> major league baseball players are covered under the antitrust laws (i.e., that major league baseball players will have the same rights under the antitrust laws as do other professional athletes, e.g., football and basketball players), along with a provision that makes it clear that the passage of this Act does not change the application of the antitrust laws in any other context or with respect to any other person or entity. (15 USC 27 § 2)

NATIONAL BASKETBALL ASSOCIATION AND COLLECTIVE BARGAINING

According to Krueger-Wyman (2012) the ability to collectively bargain benefits NBA players in the following ways:

1. Collective bargaining gives the players leverage when negotiating with the owners. Without collective bargaining most individual players would have no leverage in negotiations with the owners without the presence of CBAs because the owners would be able to drive down

the price of compensation and threaten to replace existing players with new ones willing to accept worse contract terms.

2. Collective bargaining allows a perponderance of players in the league to collect appreciably higher guaranteed salaries than they would otherwise. This aspect prevents perception that only "superstars" have enough leverage to demand and negotiate for higher salaries on an individual bargaining basis.

3. Collective bargaining permits the players to command a share of the owner's profits. Under the 2011 CBA, profits from a wide variety of areas, including luxury suites, arena naming rights, and premium seat licenses, are shared between the owners and the players.

Collective bargaining also provides several benefits to the owners in the following ways (Krueger-Wyman, 2012).

1. Through collective bargaining the owners can exert exercise more control over player salary, movement, and entry into the league. Under this condition NBA players cannot demand a longer contract or higher salary than the CBA allows and that the NBA draft includes a designated rookie pay scale with pre-determined contract lengths and amounts.

2. The owners of less-popular, small-market teams are guaranteed a certain degree of parity, which increases the NBA's overall popularity and makes these small-market teams more attractive destinations for players. This condition prevents teams with bigger budgets to outspend small-market teams and acquire all the top talent.

3. The collective bargaining agreements as well as the the non-statutory labor exemption offers the NBA with the flexibility to establish the terms and conditions for the successful operation of the entire league.

Before the 2011–2012 season, the NBPA and the NBA began negotiations to avert the potential of cancellation of the season. In May 2011, the NBPA alleged that the league negotiated in bad faith by withholding critical financial data, engaging in surface bargaining, and repeatedly threatening to lockout the players. The complaint alleged violations of several NLRA sections: 8(a)(1), interfering with rights of employees; 8(a)(5), refusing to bargain in good faith; and 8(d), obliging parties to bargain in good faith in regards to wages, hours, and other terms and conditions of employment (National Basketball Players Ass'n Charge Against Employer, 2011). Utlimately, the basic changes could not be reached which lead to the lockout in July 2011. The NBA filed a counter complaint with the NLRB against the NBPA (Carpenter, 2013). The NBA alleged that the NBPA had failed to bargain in good faith with the NBA in regards to wages, hours, and other terms and conditions; therefore violating section 8(d) of the NLRA (Carpenter, 2013). Eventually the lockout ended on November 26, 2011, as the NBPA and the NBA came to a tentative agreement on the terms of a new CBA. The agreement took place prior to the NLRB had an opportunity to make a ruling on the NBA's bargaining practices. The current CBA runs through the 2020–2121 season, but either party may opt out following the 2016–2017 season, as long as notice is given by December 15, 2016.

COLLECTIVE BARGAINING IN INTERCOLLEGIATE SPORTS

In *Northwestern University* (2014), it was contended that scholarship football players were "employees" within the meaning of the NLRA. As a result, they should be able to choose whether or not to be represented for the purposes of collective-bargaining. Northwestern University maintained that its football players receiving grant-in-aid scholarships are not "employees" under the NLRA.

The first question to answer in deciding whether the Northwestern University football players have the right to unionize was: Are the employees of the university? Under the common law, an employee is one who performs services for another, under the other's control or right of control, and does so in return for payment agency (*NLRB v. Town & Country Electric*, 1995). This definition of employee has served as the foundation for NLRB decisions, and has been cited in law for cases concerning college graduate students (*Brown University*, 2004).

The primary factor in the *Brown University* (2004) case was the source of the relationship between the graduate students and the university. In *Brown University*, the Board found that graduate assistants were not employees as:

the role of graduate student assistantships in graduate education, the graduate student assistants' relationship with the faculty, and the financial support they receive to attend Brown, we conclude that the overall relationship between the graduate student assistants and Brown is primarily an educational one, rather than an economic one. (p. 30)

Thus, the NLRB stated that Brown University graduate student assistants primary relationship with their university was educational in nature which is significantly different from economically-based relationships. However, Regional Director Peter Sung Ohr of the National Labor Relations Board indicated that Brown University was not applicable because ""the players" football related duties [were] unrelated to their academic studies" (p. 53).

In March 2014, Ohr ruled that the Division I scholarship football players at Northwestern University were employees pursuant to the NLRA, and that they had the right to unionize and collective

bargaining (*Northwestern University*, 2014). Ohr based his analysis in Northwestern University on the definition provided in *NLRB v. Town & Country Electric*, (1995). The first item of the agency test, "performing services under a contract for hire," "the Northwestern scholarship players all signed tenders (binding letters of intent) with the school when they decided to attend Northwestern and perform football-related services for the benefit of the university" (*Northwestern University*, 2014). By signing the tender and participating in football related activities, the players fulfilled this part of the agency test. For the second item, "subject to the other's control," the Northwestern players were subjected to the control of their football coaches and other athletic department officials throughout the football season, and the offseason (*Northwestern University*, 2014). The third item in which the players must have received compensation for their work which was in the form of their grant-in-aid scholarships, adequately achieved the compensation requirement of the agency test. Considering all three items of the common law agency test, Ohr ruled that the Northwestern players fulfilled all of the requirements of the test, and that they were entitled to the "twin rights" of unionization and collective bargaining under the NLRA (*Northwestern University*, 2014). It is also important to note that since walk-on players did not sign a tender with the university, thereby entering into an employment contract, they were excluded from joining with the scholarship players' union (*Northwestern University*, 2014).

Sixteen months later on August 17, 2015 the NLRB choose not to assert jurisdiction in the Northwestern University case (Office of Public Affairs, 2015). Interestingly, the NLRB did not indicate if the scholarship football players were statutory employees under the National Labor Relations Act (NLRA). In addition, the Board noted that Northwestern was the only private institution in the Big 10. As the National Collegiate Athletic Association and conferences continue to have significant control conference teams, the Board held that affirming jurisdiction over one team would not encourage stability in labor relations across the league. Finally, the Board focused this ruling only the players in this case and did not rule out a future reconsideration (Office of Public Affairs, 2015).

THE UNION'S DUTY OF FAIR REPRESENTATION

A players' union is called on to represent a diverse group of individuals who have individual interests but essentially the same goal—to maximize their revenues and improve working conditions for all players. The union has an obligation to its members to represent and serve their interests. It must represent equally both the superstar and the proverbial clipboard-holding quarterback. A union must listen to all its members, evaluate all essential data, and attempt to obtain the most favorable CBA it can for its members. Although it is true that some members may not be satisfied with any deal that is negotiated, it is difficult to prevail in a lawsuit against a union for a breach of its duty of fair representation. The NLRA grants exclusive authority to the union to handle all negotiations on behalf of the bargaining unit. Many times a union must sacrifice certain individual rights to achieve the common goal. They must take into consideration the bargaining unit as a whole rather than a few individual superstars when trying to gain the upper hand on management.

The phrase "duty of fair representation" is incapable of a precise definition (*Clair v. Local 515, Int'l Bhd. of Teamsters*, 1969). There is no code that explicitly prescribes the standards that govern unions in representing their members in processing grievances. Furthermore, whether a union has breached its duty of fair representation depends on the facts of each case (*Griffin v. International Union, United Automobile, Aerospace,*

and Agricultural Implement Workers of America, 1972; *Thompson v. Brotherhood of Sleeping Car Porters*, 1963; *Trotter v. Amalgamated Ass'n of Street Railway Employees*, 1963). The NLRA requires a union to fairly represent all members of the bargaining unit (*Steele v. Louisville & N.R. Co.*, 1944). It has been determined that any breach of a union's duty of fair representation is considered an unfair labor practice (*National Labor Relations Board v. Miranda Fuel Company*, 1962). However, mere negligence on the part of a union does not establish a breach of the duty of fair representation (*Peterson v. Burlington Northern Railroad Co.*, 1990). It is essential that unions be given discretion to act on what they believe to be the best interests of their members (*Herring v. Delta Airlines, Inc.*, 1990). If a union proceeds on some reasoned basis, then it will not breach its duty of fair representation (*Eichelberger v. NLRB*, 1985). Unions are therefore given much leeway to make decisions regarding what they believe to be in the best interests of union members.

Player Salaries and Team Payrolls

One of the results of the increased power of the major league sports in North America, particularly in MLB, has been the huge increase in player salaries. Salaries have risen extravagantly since the institution of free agency and collective bargaining. Baseball's salary arbitration process has also been a factor in increasing players' salaries. For example, there is a wide discrepancy among the payrolls of the Major League teams, with the New York Yankees having a larger payroll than other teams. It is clear that the owner of the Yankees wants to win the World Series every year. It is understandable that ballplayers with the Yankees may thus feel a little more pressure to perform than players in some other franchises do. However, if baseball is interested in achieving competitive balance, how can that goal be achieved given the wide discrepancy in team payrolls? Does the gap in payroll affect the overall competition of the league?

Salary Caps and Luxury Taxes

Because of the continuing increase in player salaries, owners have argued that some limit on player salaries should be introduced to allow professional sports to function competitively. The increase in baseball salaries has been a perennial concern for baseball. Albert Goodwill Spalding expressed apprehension about the issue in 1881, stating, "Professional baseball is on the wane. Salaries must come down or the interest of the public must be increased in some way. If one or the other does not happen, bankruptcy stares every team in the face." (Antitrust quotes, 2001). One of the ways owners have attempted to decrease or hold down salaries of players is through the implementation of salary caps or luxury taxes.

Unions and management in all major sports, have battled over limiting player salaries through these methods over the last 20 years. In the early 1980s, NBA management and the players union agreed to a salary cap. In 1981, 16 of the 23 NBA teams showed losses, and the league had rumors of rampant drug usage. Television ratings were low and so was game attendance. By the end of the 1980s, the NBA was a successful and growing league. Many factors contributed to the rise of the NBA, including marquee players such as Michael Jordan, Larry Bird, and Magic Johnson. In 1993, the NFL instituted its salary cap.

The operation of a salary cap is an extremely complicated calculation and will only be addressed in summary here. Major League Baseball does not have a salary cap but rather a luxury tax. The WNBA also has a salary cap.

The NHL salary cap was set at $56 million per team for the 2009–2010 season. NHL teams were required to spend at least $40 million on player salaries for 2009–2010. The cap figure includes salary and bonuses. All leagues have certain limits on player salaries.

The NBA's salary cap is often referred to as a "soft cap," whereas the NFL's has been referred to as a "hard cap." NBA teams can exceed the cap on a regular basis because of the "Larry Bird exception." The NBA allows teams to exceed the salary cap by resigning their own free agents at an amount up to the maximum salary.

The most common way NFL teams attempt to circumvent the salary cap is by extrapolating guaranteed signing bonuses over the life of the contract. The NFL salary cap has grown from approximately $34 million in 1993 to $128 million for the 2009 season. Internationally, Australian Rules Football has had a salary cap since the 1980s.

Does a salary cap create competitive balance or mediocrity? Do you believe that fans would rather see one dominating team in a sport or different teams competing for the title every year? If all teams in the NFL have the same amount of money to spend on payroll, then all teams should be able to compete for the NFL title every year. Among the MLB teams, the Yankees outdistanced the second-biggest spender in 2009 by a large margin. In baseball, the teams with the largest payroll generally make it to the playoffs. Do owners generally get what they pay for with regard to sports salaries?

Player Mobility and Free Agency

For many years players had no ability to change teams because of the reserve clause or other contractual restrictions, and as a result players' salaries basically stayed relatively dormant. One of the results of collective bargaining has been the increase of players moving from team to team, increasing the amount of salary offers players receive. Major League Baseball achieved free agency through the labor arbitration process, whereas other sports used the antitrust laws to strike down what they perceived to be as unreasonable restraints on player movement.

Since the implementation of the NFL's Rozelle Rule and its subsequent demise, players have fought for free agency, that is, the ability to market themselves in the open market to receive their fair market value. *Free agent* (FA) has become a well-known term in team sports. Leagues have established different categories of free agency. Each major sports league has different rules on how a player achieves free agency status. If a player is able to achieve full free agency status, then that player may be able to command substantial offers from several clubs, thereby driving up the player's negotiation price.

Unrestricted free agency (UFA) is the most valued type of free agency in any player movement system. It is usually given to a player who has achieved a certain level of service within the league and whose contract has expired with his or her present team. These players are then able to enter the market with an opportunity to receive offers from several teams in an attempt to receive fair market value for their services. *Restricted free agency* (RFA) means a player can market his or her services to other clubs but that the player's current team holds a right of first refusal or some other mechanism to restrict a player's movement. A restricted free agent can receive offers from competing clubs, but the player's current team might have the opportunity to match that offer. The restricted free agent may be able to garner an increase in salary but may not be able to move to another team.

The NFL provides for "franchise players" and "transition players" in its CBA. After an NFL player reaches the pinnacle of unrestricted free agency, an NFL club may still retain his rights through the designation of that player as the team's "franchise player" under the CBA. In MLB, players can achieve free agency status after six years of Major League service.

ARBITRATION

Through collective bargaining, management and labor have agreed to avoid the litigation process by resolving their disputes through binding arbitration, with certain exceptions. Arbitration cases in professional sports can involve salary disputes, discipline of players, injury grievances, and contractual disputes, among other matters. If an arbitration clause is present in the CBA, arbitration will usually be the sole remedy for a player to pursue a grievance. Courts give great deference to an arbitrator's ruling and are therefore hesitant to overrule an arbitrator's decision.

The first legal issue to be addressed in an arbitration case is whether the claim is arbitrable under the CBA. Is it one of the matters that was contemplated by the parties to be subject to the arbitration process when they entered into the CBA? Arbitration is usually less expensive and quicker than litigation, and can also be confidential under certain circumstances. Lawsuits can be costly and time-consuming. Arbitration is an alternative dispute resolution method that all parties can agree to and hope to abide by in resolving a dispute. Most standard player contracts in professional sport leagues contain a very broad arbitration clause describing all matters that are subject to arbitration. Parties can also agree who will arbitrate the matter as well.

Salary

After the 1976 basic agreement was signed, the MLBPA wanted free agency but not for all players every year. The MLBPA believed that if players were able to declare themselves free agents every year of their career, the free agent market would become saturated and result in a decrease of players' salaries. Because of that belief, the players association entered into a deal that allowed players to achieve free agency after six years of service in the Major Leagues. The MLB salary arbitration system was implemented in the 1976 basic agreement.

The salary arbitration system was seen as a compromise between the reserve clause and unrestricted free agency. Salary arbitration is available to those players in MLB who have three or more years but less than six years of service at the Major League level. If a player has between two and three years of service, he can qualify for salary arbitration if he has 86 days of service at the Major League level for the previous season and also ranks in the top 17 of all Major League players who are eligible for arbitration for the same reasons. These players are commonly known as "super two" players.

Baseball's arbitration process began in 1976 and presents a unique dispute resolution system. Each party presents a confidential offer to the arbitrator, and the arbitrator is required to select from the proposed offers presented by the parties. This is commonly referred to as "final offer" arbitration. Each party presents arguments in support of its position to a single arbitrator. It is fundamental to say that arbitration in baseball has increased salaries. Alfonso Soriano "lost" his arbitration case with the Washington Nationals and had to settle for the losing figure of $10 million per season. He had requested $12 million at arbitration. To date it was the highest salary ever awarded in arbitration. In 2006 Alfonso Soriano had a batting average of 0.277 while hitting 46 home runs, knocking in 95 runs batted in, and stealing 41 bases. Despite his contributions, the Washington Nationals finished the season with a 71–91 record, in last place in the National League Eastern Division.

Many players settle their case prior to arbitration so they can avoid the adversarial arbitration process. At the arbitration hearing, clubs will argue that the player is not worth as much as he is claiming with the player arguing he is worth the claimed amount. Arbitrations are statistically driven, with experts testifying on both sides about the player's performance in different situations. The arbitration hearing will go far beyond the wins and losses for pitchers and batting averages for hitters. The arbitration will explore in detail how the player performs and contributes to the club's success.

Baseball's collective bargaining agreement outlines the criteria and procedure of baseball's arbitration process. The MLB Basic Agreement sets forth the following arbitration provisions:

F. Salary Arbitration . . .

(12) Criteria

(a) The criteria will be the quality of the Player's contribution to his Club during the past season (including but not limited to his overall performance, special qualities of leadership and public appeal), the length and consistency of his career contribution, the record of the Player's past compensation, comparative baseball salaries (see paragraph (13) below for confidential salary data), the existence of any physical or mental defects on the part of the Player, and the recent performance record of the Club including but not limited to its League standing and attendance as an indication of public acceptance (subject to the exclusion stated in (12) subparagraph (b)(i) below). Any evidence may be submitted which is relevant to the above criteria, and the arbitration panel shall assign such weight to the evidence as shall appear appropriate under the circumstances. The arbitration panel shall, except for a Player with five or more years of Major League service, give particular attention, for comparative salary purposes, to the contracts of Players with Major League service not exceeding one annual service group above the Player's annual service group. This shall not limit the ability of a Player or his representative, because of special accomplishment, to argue the equal relevance of salaries of Players without regard to service, and the arbitration panel shall give whatever weight to such argument as is deemed appropriate.

(b) Evidence of the following shall not be admissible:

(i) The financial position of the Player and the Club;

(ii) Press comments, testimonials or similar material bearing on the performance of either the Player or the Club, except that recognized annual Player awards for playing excellence shall not be excluded;

(iii) Offers made by either Player or Club prior to arbitration;

(iv) The cost to the parties of their representatives, attorneys, etc.;

(v) Salaries in other sports or occupations.

Grievances

Numerous grievance arbitrations have been asserted, ranging from discipline of players to uniform issues, disputes over ownership of balls, off-field activities, and contract disputes (*Sprewell v. Golden State Warriors*, 2001). Grievance arbitration functions to handle a variety of disputes and provides an expedient manner to resolve them. For example, Latrell Sprewell became involved in a scuffle with his coach, P.J. Carlesimo, in 1997. While the team was practicing, Carlesimo and Sprewell began yelling profanities at each other, and then Sprewell grabbed Carlesimo around the neck and began choking him. Sprewell was suspended 68 games for his conduct, with a loss of pay of $6.4 million. He appealed the decision of the arbitrator and lost.

UNFAIR LABOR PRACTICES

The National Labor Relations Board enforces the NLRA regarding unfair labor practices. Section 8(d) of the NLRA requires management and labor to "meet at reasonable times and confer in good faith with respect to wages, hours, and other terms and conditions of employment." If either side fails to do so, it can be considered an unfair labor practice. The National Labor Relations Board cannot coerce or force either the union or employer to agree to a specific proposal or to make any concessions (*United Steelworkers of America, AFL-CIO v. N.L.R.B., C.A.D.C.,* 1970). The NLRA describes unfair labor practices as follows.

§ 158. Unfair Labor Practices

(a) Unfair labor practices by employer It shall be an unfair labor practice for an employer—

(1) to interfere with, restrain, or coerce employees in the exercise of the rights guaranteed in Section 157 of this title;

(2) to dominate or interfere with the formation or administration of any labor organization or contribute financial or other support to it. . . .

(3) by discrimination in regard to hire or tenure of employment or any term or condition of employment to encourage or discourage membership in any labor organization. . . .

(4) to discharge or otherwise discriminate against an employee because he has filed charges or given testimony under this subchapter;

(5) to refuse to bargain collectively with the representatives of his employees.

An unfair labor practice can arise in a variety of situations. For instance, it is considered an unfair labor practice for an employer to promote decertification of a union (*N.L.R.B. v. Birmingham Publishing Company*, 1958). The NLRA promotes the freedom of employees to select a bargaining representative, and it would be considered an unfair labor practice for an employer to encourage or discourage employees from joining a bona fide union (*N.L.R.B. v. Stowe Spinning Co.*, 1949). An employer cannot attempt to influence employees to join one union over another (*N.L.R.B. v. Fotochrome, Inc.*, 1965). If an employer uses threats and coercion to interfere with an employee's right of organization under the act, it is considered an unfair labor practice (*N.L.R.B. v. Coast Delivery Service, Inc.*, 1971). In the context of sports, labor relations issues have arisen regarding leagues interfering with the players' right to unionize, leagues refusing to recognize players' unions as the exclusive bargaining representatives, and employers retaliating against players for engaging in union activity.

If a team releases a player because of union activity, that can constitute an unfair labor practice. In *N.L.R.B. v. Nordstrom d/b/a Seattle Seahawks* (1985), wide receiver Sam McCullum alleged that the Seahawks cut him because of his union activity. McCullum had been selected as the team's union representative. He implemented a "solidarity handshake" that he engaged in with his teammates and opposing players prior to the first preseason games of the 1982 season. This did not win favor with the coaching staff of the Seahawks. McCullum started every preseason game for the Seahawks but was cut from the team after the Seahawks acquired another wide receiver. The NFLPA and McCullum alleged that his union activities had cost him his job. The Seahawks defended, stating that McCullum was cut based on lack of skill. The Seattle Seahawks sought a review of the NLRB's ruling that McCullum had been released by the team for engaging in union-related activities. Eleven years after his release, McCullum was vindicated when a federal court affirmed the NLRB's proceeding and affirmed an award of $301,000 in back pay to the wide receiver.

After the signing of the 1985 basic agreement, baseball owners began to conspire with one another on how to hold down salaries in baseball. The owners entered into an unspoken gentlemen's agreement to attempt to drive down the market price for star players by failing to offer free agents a significant contract. The owners as a collective group refused to sign star free agents. Kirk Gibson was the 1984 World Series Most Valuable Player (MVP) for the Detroit Tigers, who beat the San Diego Padres. Gibson was unable to attract any offers whatsoever from other clubs after his great season and showing in the World Series. The National League MVP for the 1984 season was Andre Dawson, "the Hawk." He was forced to sign a blank contract with the Cubs that paid him less than he had earned the previous season. The Players Association filed a grievance in 1985 and filed a second grievance in 1986 after more free agents were not able to receive their full market value. After the 1987 season, the owners began using an information bank when they traded offers about players. The Players Association filed a third grievance, asserting that this practice was collusion among owners. The average salary for a Major League Baseball player declined from 1986 to 1987. The players' challenge to the owners' collusion was upheld through the arbitration process, and the three cases were eventually settled for $280 million, with funds being distributed to individual players through the MLBPA.

NOTES AND DISCUSSION QUESTIONS

Collective Bargaining

1. What is required of management and labor during the collective bargaining process? Under what circumstances could management or labor be considered to be acting in "bad faith" during labor negotiations?
2. Do you agree with the operation of baseball's luxury tax system? Should owners be required to spend a minimum amount for payroll to keep their team competitive? The NBA's luxury tax has a "floor" requiring owners to keep a minimum payroll. If a team owner wants to spend as much money as he or she can to produce a winner, why shouldn't the owner be allowed to do so?
3. Do you believe professional athletes make too much money? Examine the pay scale for "The Celebrity 100" list published by *Forbes* magazine for details of the salaries of famous people. Are professional athletes also entertainers? The average career for an NFL players is less than four years.
4. After cancellation of the 1994 World Series, many fans swore they would never again attend a baseball game. In 2009, Major League Baseball drew 73.4 million spectators while 73,739,622 went through the turnstiles in 2014 (MLB.com, 2014) A person could argue based on these figures that no one person can ruin the game of baseball. It is, in essence, the national pastime.
5. In October 2006, MLB and the players union extended their CBA for five more years, through 2011. The majority of the key points of the former CBA were kept intact, including revenue sharing and the luxury tax. The deal was the longest in baseball history (five years). If a strike or lockout does not occur during the term of the basic agreement, baseball would experience 16 consecutive years without a concerted action by union or management. Management wanted to get a deal done so the luxury tax would remain in place for the 2007 season. The threshold for the luxury tax was set at $136.5 million, rising continuously until 2011, when it is set to be $178 million. The minimum salary increased from $327,000 to $380,000. It will be $390,000 for 2008, $400,000 in 2009, and adjusted for the cost of living in 2011 (MLB, MLBPA reportedly reach tentative deal, 2006).
6. In terms of baseball economics, when a star free agent becomes available, only a few teams in Major League Baseball are able to make offers to the free agent. In recent years the majority of MLB teams were unable to compete for superstar free agents. How can a professional sports league operate competitively if a majority of the teams cannot compete in the open market for the best players? How can owners draw fans to the stadium if the team does not have a realistic chance of winning before the season starts?
7. Professional leagues have taken action against teams that have exceeded the salary cap. The NFL fined 49ers' executives Carmen Policy and Dwight Clark $400,000 and $200,000, respectively, for salary cap violations. The 49'ers were required to pay a $300,000 team fine and also gave up a fifth round draft choice in 2001 and a third round draft choice in 2002. What should the penalty be if a team exceeds salary cap restrictions? Fines? Draft picks? Forfeits? A combination of these? Was the penalty meted out to Policy and Clark too harsh?

(continues)

NOTES AND DISCUSSION QUESTIONS (CONTINUED)

Arbitration

1. Do you approve of baseball's arbitration process? Would it operate more fairly for the owners if the arbitrator could negotiate a settlement between the two numbers instead of being required to choose between two numbers? How do you view the adversarial process of arbitration? Is it harmful to the relationship between the parties that the team is required to demean the player's accomplishments during the hearing?

2. Grievances come in all shapes and forms. In 2006 the NBPA filed a grievance over the length of shorts worn by players. League rules provided that players' shorts could not be below 0.1 inch above the knee. Over $10,000 in fines were given to several players, and NBA teams were fined $50,000 for each violation. The NBA deputy commissioner stated, "These are rules, just as there are rules with other parts of the game." The union argued during the grievance that players were being unfairly penalized for wearing uniforms made by Reebok. Billy Hunter, head of the NBPA, stated, "I understand the need to appeal to a fan base who buy tickets, but sometimes I think it's like throwing the baby out with the bath water." He further stated, "Too much scrutiny is going on, and what it's doing is interfering with the play." Do you believe this is the type of issue that should be subject to labor arbitration?

3. In 2006, an arbitrator ruled that the Tennessee Titans could not prevent quarterback Steve McNair from using their training facility while he was under contract with the team. The Titans were attempting to renegotiate McNair's contract to reduce the salary cap impact before training camp so they could pursue other free agents. During a contract dispute with the Titans, McNair was asked to conduct his training away from the team's complex. The Titans were concerned that if McNair were injured while working out with the team, the team might be responsible for the "cap figure" if he were unable to play. The NFLPA argued that as long as McNair was under contract he had a right to be on the premises. The NFLPA prevailed through the arbitration process.

4. Barry Bonds was fined $5,000 by Major League Baseball for wearing wristbands that violated baseball uniform rules. His wristbands were larger than allowed and also contained a logo design not allowed by Major League Baseball rules (Bloom, 2006).

5. In *Major League Baseball Players Association v. Garvey* (2001), former MLB star Steve Garvey argued at the Supreme Court that an arbitration decision regarding his claim for damages arising from collusion should be vacated. The Court was called upon to determine the scope of an arbitration decision. Garvey had alleged that his contract with the San Diego Padres had not been extended because of collusion and made a claim for $3 million. The arbitrator denied his claim, expressing doubt as to the veracity of a letter from Ballard Smith, the Padres' president and CEO from 1979 to 1987, in support of Garvey's claims. The U.S. Supreme Court affirmed the arbitration decision, denying Garvey's claims for damages due to collusion.

6. Arbitration in sports can cover a variety of topics. In *Allen v. McCall* (1988), a dispute arose concerning the amount an agent was entitled to for negotiating a contract. The agent invoked

NOTES AND DISCUSSION QUESTIONS (CONTINUED)

the arbitration provisions under the NFLPA regulations that governed contract advisors. The court of appeals reversed the arbitration decision based on the fact that the arbitrator had failed to consider whether the agent had received notice of the arbitration hearing.

7. On November 19, 2004, the NBA experienced a blight on the good name of the sport. With less than a minute left in a game between the Detroit Pistons and the Indiana Pacers, a fight broke out between players after Ron Artest committed a flagrant foul against Detroit Pistons player Ben Wallace. Players began to fight with one another, and the fight eventually moved into the stands as Artest began to fight Detroit Piston fans. NBA Commissioner David Stern subsequently levied fines against nine players and suspended them for a total of 140 games. Ron Artest was suspended by the NBA for the rest of the season. Two other Pacers players, Stephen Jackson and Jermaine O'Neal, were also suspended, Jackson for 30 games and O'Neal for 25. The NBA immediately took action and appealed the commissioner's ruling to a grievance arbitration, stating that the CBA did not allow such punishment by the commissioner. The league argued that any appeal must be made directly to the commissioner, not a grievance arbitrator. The opinion in *National Basketball Association v. National Basketball Players Association* (2005) was the result of the NBA filing a declaratory judgment action asserting that the arbitrator did not have jurisdiction to hear the appeal. Under what circumstances does the commissioner have the sole authority to render discipline for player misconduct and hear appeals of any decision that is rendered? When is a decision by the commissioner of a sports league arbitratable?

Unfair Labor Practices

1. Immediately after the NFL's first CBA was agreed to, NFL owners unilaterally instituted a rule that imposed a $200 fine on any player who left the bench during a fight. The NFLPA argued that the unilateral implementation of this rule was a "refusal to bargain" in violation of federal labor law. The owners argued that the commissioner had established the rule under his authority. The NLRB determined that the rule originated from the owners and that because the rule was a mandatory subject of bargaining, it was an unfair labor practice to unilaterally implement the rule (*NFLPA v. NLRB*, 1975).

2. Consider the case of Korey Stringer, the former Minnesota Vikings player who died after collapsing on the playing field. Stringer, an All-Pro lineman, died in a team practice that was being held in conditions of high heat and humidity. Stringer weighed 335 pounds and was in full pads at the time of his death. Stringer's death was the first recorded death from heatstroke in the NFL. Stringer's estate subsequently filed a wrongful death lawsuit against the Minnesota Vikings for $100 million.

KEY TERMS

Employee

Employer

Labor dispute

Unfair labor practice

REFERENCES

Allen v. McCall, 521 So.2d 182 (1988).

Allen, K., & Brehm M. (2005). Black ice. NHL season canceled. *USAToday.com*. Retrieved from http://usatoday30.usatoday.com/sports/hockey/nhl/2005-02-16-season-cancel_x.htm

Antitrust quotes. (2001). USAToday.com. Retrieved from http://usatoday30.usatoday.com/sports/baseball/stories/2001-12-05-antitrust-quotes.htm

Baumann, A. (2012). Play ball: What can be done to prevent strikes and lockouts in professional sports and keep the stadium lights on. *Journal of the National Association of Administrative Law Judiciary, 32,* 251–307.

Berry, R.C., Gould, W.B., & Staudohar, P.D. (1986). *Labor relations in professional sports.* Westport, CT: Greenwood Publishing.

Bloom, B.M. (2006). Bonds fined for apparel violation. MLB.com. Retrieved from http://m.mlb.com/news/article/1409123/

Brown University, 342 N.L.R.B. 483, 493 (2004).

Curt Flood Act of 1998, Pub. L. No. 105-297, 112 Stat. 2824 (1998).

Deubert, C., & Wong, G.M. (2009). Understanding the evolution of signing bonuses and guaranteed money in the National Football League: Preparing for the 2011 collective bargaining negotiations. *UCLA Entertainment Law Review, 16,* 179–236.

Eichelberger v. NLRB, 765 F.2d 851, 856 (9th Cir. 1985).

Federal Baseball Club of Baltimore, Inc. v. National League of Professional Baseball Clubs, 259 U.S. 200 (1992).

Feldman, G. (2012). Antitrust versus labor law in professional sports: Balancing the scales after *Brady v. NFL* and *Anthony v. NBA. University of California-Davis Law Review, 45,* 1221–1330.

Griffin v. International Union, United Automobile, Aerospace, and Agricultural Implement Workers of America, UAW, 469 F.2d 181, 182 (4th Cir. 1972).

Herring v. Delta Airlines. Inc., 894 F.2d 1020, 1023 (9th Cir. 1990).

Kansas City Royals v. Major League Baseball Players' Association, 532 F.2d 615 (8th Cir. 1976).

Kelci Stringer v. NFL, et al., Case No. 2:03-cv-665 (S.D. Ohio).

Krueger-Wyman, A.C. (2012). Collective bargaining and the best interests in basketball. *Virginia Sports and Entertainment Law Journal, 12,* 171–197.

Mackey v. National Football League, 543 F.2d 606 (8th Cir. 1976).

Major League Baseball Players Association v. Garvey, 532 U.S. 1015 (2001).

McNeil v. National Football League, 790 F. Supp. 871 (D. Minn. 1992).

MLB.com. (2014). MLB records seventh best attendance total ever in 2014. Retrieved from http://m.mlb.com/news/article/96990912/mlb-records-seventh-best-attendance-total-ever-in- 2014/

MLB, MLBPA reportedly reach tentative deal on five-year CBA. (2006). SportsBusiness Daily. Retrieved from http://www.sportsbusinessdaily.com/Daily/Issues/2006/10/Issue- 29/Leagues-Governing-Bodies/MLB-MLBPA-Reportedly-Reach-Tentative-Deal-On- Five-Year- CBA.aspx?hl=MLB%2C%20MLBPA%20reportedly%20reach%20tentative%20deal%20 on%20five-year%20CBA&sc=0

National Basketball Association v. National Basketball Players Association, Ron Artest, Stephen Jackson, Anthony Johnson, and Jermaine O'Neal, 2005 WL 22869 (S.D.N.Y. 2005).

National Basketball Players Ass'n Charge Against Employer, Nat'l Basketball Ass'n, Case No. 02-CA-040518 (N.L.R.B. May 24, 2011).

National Labor Relations Board v. Allis-Chalmers Mfg. Co., 388 US 175, 180 (1967).

National Labor Relations Board v. Coast Delivery Service, Inc., 437 F.2d 264 (Cal. 1971).

National Labor Relations Board v. Fotochrome, Inc., 343 F.2d 631 (1965), *cert. denied,* 382 U.S. 833.

National Labor Relations Board v. Miranda Fuel Company, 140 N.L.R.B. 181 (1962).

National Labor Relations Board v. Nordstrom d/b/a Seattle Seahawks, 292 NLRB 899 (1985).

National Labor Relations Board v. Stowe Spinning Co., 165 F.2d 609 (1947), *rev'd on other grounds*, 336 U.S. 226 (1949).

National Labor Relations Board v. Town & Country Elec., Inc., 516 U.S. 85, 86–87 (1995).

North American Soccer League v. N.L.R.B., 613 F.2d 1379 (5th Cir. 1980).

Northwestern University, 2014 NLRB LEXIS 298 (N.L.R.B., Apr. 24, 2014).

Office of Public Affairs. (2015). Board unanimously decides to decline jurisdiction in Northwestern case. National Labor Relations Board. Retrieved from https:www .nlrb.gov/news-outreach/news-story/board -unanimously-decides-decline- jurisdiction -northwestern.case

Peters v. Burlington Northern R. Co., 931 F.2d 534 C.A. 9 (Mont. 1990).

Powell v. National Football League, 690 F. Supp. 812, 1988 U.S. Dist. LEXIS 7859, 128 L.R.R.M. (BNA) 3119, 110 Lab. Cas. (CCH) P10758, 1988-2 Trade Cas. (CCH) P68156 (D. Minn. 1988).

Powell v. National Football League, 930 F.2d 1293, 1989 U.S. App. LEXIS 20824 (8th Cir. Minn. 1989).

Powell v. National Football League, 139 F.R.D. 381, 1991 U.S. Dist. LEXIS 16502 (D. Minn. 1991).

Radovich v. National Football League, 352 U.S. 445 (1957).

Shapiro, J.S. (1993). Warming the bench: The nonstatutory labor exemption in the National Football League. *Fordham Law Review*, *61*, 1203–1234.

Sharpe v. National Football League Players Ass'n, 941 F. Supp. 8 (D.D.C. 1996).

Shaw, B. (2014). The solution to the NHL collective bargaining disputes: Mandatory binding arbitration. *DePaul Journal of Sports Law & Contemporary Problems*, *10*, 53–81.

Snyder, B. (2007). *A well-paid slave: Curt Flood's fight for free agency in professional sports.* New York: Penguin.

Sprewell v. Golden State Warriors, 275 F.3d 1187, 2001 U.S. App. LEXIS 28424 (9th Cir. Cal. 2001).

St. Clair v. Local 515, Int'l Bhd. of Teamsters, etc., 422 F.2d 128, 130 (6th Cir. 1969).

Staudohar, P.D. (2005). The hockey lockout of 2004-05. Monthly Labor Review. Retrieved from http://www .bls.gov/opub/mlr/2005/12/art3full.pdf

Stevens, D. (1998). *Baseball's radical for all seasons: A biography of John Montgomery Ward.* Lanham, Md.: Scarecrow Press.

Steele v. Louisville & N.R. Co., 323 U.S. 192 (1944).

Strang, K. (2013). NHL, union have tentative agreement. ESPN.com. Retrieved from http://espn.go.com/nhl /story/_/id/8817955/nhl-nhlpa-reach-tentative -agreement

Thompson v. Brotherhood of Sleeping Car Porters, 316 F.2d 191 (4th Cir. 1963).

Toolson v. N.Y. Yankees, Inc., 346 U.S. 356 (1953).

Trotter v. Amalgamated Ass'n of Street Railway Employees, 309 F.2d 584 (6th Cir. 1962), *cert. denied*, 372 U.S. 943 (1963).

White v. National Football League, 822 F. Supp. 1389 (D. Minn. 1993).

Wiestart, J.C., & Lowell, C.H. (1979). The law of sport. Indianapolis: Bobbs-Merrill.

Wong, G.M. (2010). *Essentials of sports law.* Santa Barbara, Calif.: ABC-CLIO.

Yoffie, A.G. (2015). There's a new sheriff in town: Commissioner-elect Adam Silver & the pressing legal challenges facing the NBA through the prism of contractions. *Jeffrey S. Moorad Sports Law Journal*, *21*, 59–90.

Yoost, S.M. (2006). The National Hockey League and salary arbitration: Time for a line change. *Ohio State Journal on Dispute Resolution*, *21*, 485–537.

Walter A. Kelly, 139 N.L.R.B. 744 (1962).

AGENTS

LEARNING OBJECTIVES

By the end of the chapter, the reader will be able to:

1. Identify the duties and responsibilities of sport agents
2. Recognize key provisions of representation agreements between athletes and agents
3. Identify the primary responsibilities of a sports agent when negotiating a player contract
4. Describe the varying state and federal regulations that sport agents are subject to
5. Describe the sport agent regulations set forth by the NCAA, universities, and player's associations

RELATED CASE

Case 11.1   Champion Pro Consulting v. Impact Sports Football, 116 F. Supp. 3d 644 (2015)

INTRODUCTION

Sports agents generally did not exist prior to the era of free agency in sports. Now almost every professional athlete has an agent representing his or her interests. From NFL superstars to players in the Women's National Basketball Association, professional athletes have selected agents to handle issues such as contract negotiations, endorsements, business matters, legal issues, and financial planning (Mitten, Davis, Smith, & Berry, 2009).

The idea of sports agents can be traced as far back as the career of Harold "Red" Grange, better known as the "Galloping Ghost." Grange was the original star of professional football and is thought by some to have been the greatest professional football player ever and one of the main reasons the professional game gained such popularity. Upon his arrival in professional football, the Chicago Bears put together a barnstorming tour in which they displayed his talents, playing 19 games in 62 days. In the 1920s his agent, Charles "Cash and Carry" Pyle, represented Grange in a variety of deals, including his playing contract, endorsement deals, and movie rights. The day after Grange played his last game at the University of Illinois in 1925, Pyle negotiated a contract with George Halas of the Chicago Bears on behalf of his client for a purported $3000 per game and a percentage of gate receipts (Masteralexis, Masteralexis, & Snyder, 2013).

Hollywood movie producer and sports agent J. Williams Hayes represented All-Star pitchers Sandy Koufax and Don Drysdale in contract negotiations with the Los Angeles Dodgers in the mid-1960s. The era of free agency had not yet arrived in professional sports, so the use of an agent was unusual at that time. In the mid-1960s, Major League Baseball (MLB) players were still shackled by the dreaded reserve clause, which gave a player only two options: he could either retire or be traded to another team. Koufax and Drysdale threatened to hold out and not play for the 1965 season unless the Dodgers agreed to increase their salaries. In 1964 Koufax had earned $85,000 as one of the best pitchers in baseball, and Drysdale had earned $80,000. Their agent suggested they engage in a joint holdout and then promptly demanded $1 million over three years to be divided equally between the two or, alternatively, argued that each should receive $167,000 annually. The Dodgers rejected the offer but eventually increased their salaries to $125,000 for Koufax and $115,000 for Drysdale for the next season. Superstars such as Grange, Koufax, and Drysdale thus used the services of an agent, but they were certainly the exception during their era. The overwhelming majority of athletes went unrepresented.

The former Detroit Tigers great Earl Wilson was one of the first players to use the services of an agent when he called upon attorney Bob Woolf to negotiate his playing contract with the Boston Red Sox in 1964. During contract negotiations, however, Wilson was prevented from bringing not only his agent to the negotiations but also any family members. If Wilson needed counsel regarding his contract during the negotiation process, he was required to leave the meeting and telephone Woolf from a pay phone. This is quite a different environment from the high-powered negotiations that can occur today between a player and management. Woolf would later represent such notable athletes as Joe Montana, Larry Bird, and Carl Yastrzemski.

The use of agents has increased substantially in the past 25 years; in 2013, there were approximately 4300 athletes in the four major sports leagues in the United States and an estimated 1600–1800 certified player agents (Masteralexis, Barr, & Hums, 2012). This increase can be attributed to many factors, including the increase in popularity of sports, the broadcasting of sports on television, the rising salaries for professional players, the extensive and complex nature of collective bargaining agreements (CBAs) in professional sports, the rise of labor unions, and the increased ability of a player to generate income in addition to his or her playing contract.

Today, many large sports representation firms exist, such as the International Management Group (IMG), Assante Sports Management Group, and SFX Sports. They represent a myriad of different athletes for a variety of different matters. IMG was the first large sports management firm. It was founded by Mark McCormack, who met Arnold Palmer while playing golf for William & Mary College. After McCormack graduated from law school, Palmer asked him to review an endorsement contract. That was the start of a sports management firm that now has 70 offices in 30 countries and represents such notable athletes as Tiger Woods and Peyton Manning. Sports firms have become a "one-stop shop" for professional athletes, handling both the athletes' business and personal needs.

Sports agents can be lawyers, certified public accountants, financial planners, or business executives. An agent must possess a good working knowledge of the sport in which he or she practices, must understand the economic issues of the sport, and must have a working knowledge of labor relations, contracts, and business. These are all essential to any agent who represents professional athletes. For instance, an agent negotiating an NFL contract for a top draft pick must understand the ramifications of the salary cap, know the categories of free agency under the CBA, be able to negotiate a contract with an NFL team executive, and be able to interpret and analyze specialized legal clauses pertinent to his or her client's contract. Finally, the agent must have knowledge about the financial and tax ramifications of any deal that is entered into on behalf of the player.

An agent must also build a relationship of trust with his or her client. The agent is acting as a *fiduciary* on the part of a player, so it is essential that open communication and trust exist between the two parties so the agent may achieve the best results for the player. A network of contacts is important to an agent as well. The more individuals an agent knows, the better he or she is able to perform the duties of an agent. It is an advantage for agents and their client if the agent is able to establish professional working relationships with general managers, owners, and other executives of professional teams. If a player's agent is "connected" with the sports world, the agent will have a definite advantage over those agents who are not and may be able to achieve a better result for his or her client. This is one of the major reasons it is so difficult for new agents to break into the agent business: players tend to flock to the agents who are experienced and who already have clients and connections within the sports world.

As will be explored later in this chapter, many steps have been taken to regulate agent conduct and to ensure they are qualified to represent professional athletes. The popularity and intrigue of representing professional athletes has caused a glut of agents in the market. In actuality, the majority of registered sports agents with the four major professional leagues have no clients; a very small number of agents represent a large number of players, leaving the majority of agents with no clients (Mitten et al., 2009). Coaches have agents as well, but their numbers are even smaller. The majority of coaches needing agents are at the National Collegiate Athletic Association (NCAA) Division I college level in football and basketball. This scarcity has created fierce competition for clients among agents for players and coaches alike.

DUTIES AND RESPONSIBILITIES OF AGENTS

A sports agent may be called on to perform many functions for the client. These tasks can include tax preparation and advice, marketing of the athlete, legal advice, estate and financial planning, career counseling for the athlete's post career plans, and advice on media relations. Negotiating a contract for an athlete is just one of the many responsibilities an agent may have in the representation process (Mitten et al., 2009).

The law has defined *agency* as "the fiduciary relation [that] results from the manifestation of consent by one person to another that the other shall act in his behalf and subject to his control, and consent by the other to so act" (Restatement (Third) of Agency §1). The agency relationship involves a principal, who retains an agent to represent the principal's interests to a third party. In the sports context, the principal is the athlete, and the agent is the party the athlete retains to represent him or her. Both agency and contract law govern this relationship (see also Chapter 8).

Additionally, the law imposes a fiduciary duty on an agent. This duty involves a relationship of trust and confidence between the agent and the principal. In any agency relationship, one party agrees to act on behalf of the other and in the latter's best interest. One of the primary functions of the agent is to carry out the desires and wishes of the principal. The agent must be loyal to the principal and furthermore it is incumbent upon the agent to act solely and exclusively in the best interest of the principal and not in the interest of the agent or other parties (Mitten et al., 2009).

An agent has certain duties under the law that must be discharged to the principal. These include a duty to: (1) act in the best interest of the principal; (2) keep the principal informed of all significant matters concerning the agency relationship; (3) obey instructions given to the agent by the principal concerning the agency relationship; (4) account to the principal for all funds handled on the principal's behalf; and (5) exercise reasonable care in the performance of the agent's duties (Restatement (Third) of Agency §8).

One of the primary functions of an agent is to avoid all actual or potential *conflict of interest*. It is incumbent upon the agent to avoid a conflict of interest so that the agent can dedicate his or her efforts fully to the principal's concerns. Conflicts of interest raise concerns about an agent's fiduciary duty required under the law. For example, it would be a conflict of interest and a breach of an agent's duty of loyalty to the principal to represent two principals in the same transaction unless both principals were fully aware of the situation and consented to the representation. If an agent makes full disclosure of any conflict of interest and the athlete is fully aware of the existing conflict, the agent will not have breached any fiduciary duty owed to the principal (athlete). Other possible conflict situations could exist for an agent by representing players on the same team at the same position. They could also exist if an agent represented a coach and player on the same team. The standard representation agreement for NFL contract advisors specifically requests that the agent disclose whether he or she also represents anyone in a management capacity for an NFL club. Lastly, an agent also has a duty of confidentiality which requires the agent to keep all information received by the principal in confidence during the relationship. The agent's duty of confidentiality continues even after the agent–athlete relationship has been terminated.

REPRESENTATION AGREEMENTS

Terms and Conditions

What terms and conditions should govern the player/agent relationship outside the scope of the common law duties imposed on the parties? Prior to the union influence in sports, agents and players would negotiate individual contracts for representation. This resulted in many different versions of representation agreements, with different fee structures and different legal obligations placed on the parties. With the rise of the influence of unions in sports, major sports leagues began to require agents to use a "standard representation agreement" when signing a potential client to a contract. This has created uniformity of representation agreements and allows the parties to have a better understanding of their obligations.

The NFL Players Association (NFLPA) and the National Basketball Players Association (NBPA) have standard representation agreements that dictate the terms and conditions between an agent and a player. All agents desiring to represent players in the NFL and NBA must use the standard representation agreement or they cannot represent a player; these agreements do not have term limits and can designate a multi-year relationship. By contrast, the MLB Players Association (MLBPA) still allows agents to develop their own representation agreements with players, but agreement may only be executed for one year.

The NFLPA standard agreement contains clauses dealing with the fiduciary responsibility of the agent, arbitration provisions governing disputes between players and agents, and fee structures. The influence of the NFLPA has led to a concise agreement that the parties sign that allows the player to terminate the relationship between the parties upon five days' written notice. The following are selected excerpts from the NFLPA standard representation agreement.

This AGREEMENT made this _____ day of _____, 201_, by and between _____ hereinafter (Player), _____ and thereinafter (Contract Advisor)
WITNESSETH:

In consideration of the mutual promises hereinafter made by each to the other. Player and Contract Advisor agree as follows . . .

2. Representations
Contract Advisor represents that in advance of executing this Agreement, he/she has been duly certified as a Contract Advisor by the NFLPA. Player acknowledges that the NFLPA certification of the Contract Advisor is neither a recommendation of the Contract Advisor, nor a warranty by NFLPA

of the Contract Advisor's competence, honesty, skills or qualifications.

Contract Advisor hereby discloses that he/she (check one): [ ] represents or has represented; [ ] does not represent and has not represented NFL management personnel, any NFL coaches, other professional football league coaches, or college football coaches in matters pertaining to their employment by or association with any NFL club, other professional football league club or college. (If Contract Advisor responds in the affirmative, Contract Advisor must attach a properly completed and signed SRA Coaches and NFL Personnel Disclosure Form.)

3. Contract Services
Player hereby retains Contract Advisor to represent, advise, counsel, and assist Player in the negotiation, execution, and enforcement of his playing contract(s) in the National Football League. In performing these services, Contract Advisor acknowledges that he/she is acting in a fiduciary capacity on behalf of Player and agrees to act in such manner as to protect the best interests of Player and assure effective representation of Player in individual contract negotiations with NFL Clubs. Contract Advisor shall be the exclusive representative for the purpose of negotiating player contracts for Player. However, Contract Advisor shall not have the authority to bind or commit Player to enter into any contract without actual execution thereof by Player. Once Player agrees to and executes his player contract, Contract Advisor agrees to also sign the player contract and send a copy (by facsimile or overnight mail) to the NFLPA and the NFL Club within 48 hours of execution by Player. If Player and Contract Advisor have entered into any other agreements or contracts relating to services

other than the individual negotiating services described in this Section, describe the nature of the other services covered by the separate agreements:

4. Compensation for Services

A. If Contract Advisor succeeds in negotiating an NFL Player Contract acceptable to Player and signed by Player during the term hereof, Contract Advisor shall receive a fee as set forth below. CONTRACT ADVISOR AND PLAYER AGREE AND ACKNOWLEDGE THAT THE AMOUNT OF SUCH FEE IS FREELY NEGOTIABLE BETWEEN THEM, EXCEPT THAT NO AGREED UPON FEE MAYBE GREATER THAN:

(1) Three percent (3%) of the compensation received by Player for each playing season covered by a Player Contract which is the result of negotiations between Contract Advisor and an NFL Club; or

(2) The lesser percentage specified in Section 4(B) of the Regulations in a case where Player signs a one-year tender as a Franchise, Transition, or Restricted Free Agent player.

B. The fee for Contract Advisor's services shall be as follows (Both Contract Advisor and Player must initial the appropriate line below):

	Contract Advisor	Player
Three Percent (3%)	_____	_____
Two-and-one-half Percent (2 1/2%)	_____	_____
Two Percent (2%)	_____	_____
One-and-one-half Percent (1 1/2%)	_____	_____
One Percent (1%)	_____	_____
Other (specify)	_____	_____

In computing the allowable fee pursuant to this Section 4 the term "compensation" shall include only base salaries, signing bonuses, reporting bonuses, roster bonuses, Practice Squad salary in excess of the minimum Practice Squad salary specified in Article 33 of the Collective Bargaining Agreement, and any performance incentives actually received by Player. The term "compensation" shall not include any "honor" incentive bonuses (i.e., ALL PRO, PRO BOWL, Rookie of the Year), or any collectively bargained benefits.

…

5. Payment of Contract Advisor's Fee

Contract Advisor shall not be entitled to receive any fee for the performance of his/her services pursuant to this Agreement until Player receives the compensation upon which the fee is based. However, Player may enter into an agreement with Contract Advisor to pay any fee attributable to deferred compensation due and payable to Player in advance of when the deferred compensation is paid to Player, provided that Player has performed the services necessary under his contract to entitle him to the deferred compensation. Such fee shall be reduced to its present value as specified in the NFLPA Regulations (see Section 4(B)). Such an agreement must also be in writing, with a copy sent to the NFLPA.

8. Disputes

Any and all disputes between Player and Contract Advisor involving the meaning, interpretation, application, or enforcement of this Agreement or the obligations of the parties under this Agreement shall be resolved exclusively through the arbitration procedures set forth in Section 5 of the NFLPA Regulations Governing Contract Advisors.

…

12. Term

The term of this Agreement shall begin on the date hereof and shall continue for the term of any player contract executed pursuant to this Agreement; provided, however, that either party may terminate this Agreement effective five (5) days after written notice of termination is given to the other party. Notice shall be effective for purposes of this paragraph if sent by certified mail, postage prepaid, return receipt requested to the appropriate address contained in this Agreement. Notwithstanding the above, if this Standard Representation Agreement is being signed by a prospective rookie player (a "rookie" shall be defined as a person who has never signed an NFL Player Contract) prior to the date which is thirty (30) days before the NFL Draft, then this Agreement shall not be terminable by Player until at least 30 days after it has been signed by Player.

If termination pursuant to the above provision occurs prior to the completion of negotiations for an NFL player contract(s) acceptable to Player and signed by Player, Contract Advisor shall be entitled to compensation for the reasonable value of the services performed in the attempted negotiation of such contract(s) provided such services and time spent thereon are adequately documented by Contract Advisor.

If termination pursuant to the above provision occurs after Player has signed an NFL player contract negotiated by Contract Advisor, Contract Advisor shall be entitled to the fee prescribed in Section 4 above for negotiation of such contract(s).

In the event that Player is able to renegotiate any contract(s) previously negotiated by Contract Advisor prior to expiration thereof, Contract Advisor shall still be entitled to the fee he/she would have been paid pursuant to Section 4 above as if such original contract(s) had not been renegotiated. If Contract Advisor represents Player in renegotiation of the original contract(s), the fee for such renegotiation shall be based solely upon the amount by which the compensation in the renegotiated contract(s) exceeds the compensation in the original contract(s), whether or not Contract Advisor negotiated the original contract(s).

If the Contract Advisor's certification is suspended or revoked by the NFLPA or the Contract Advisor is otherwise prohibited by the NFLPA from performing the services he/she has agreed to perform herein, this Agreement shall automatically terminate, effective as of the date of such suspension or termination.

(NFLPA Regulations, 2012, Appendix D, 1-5).

AGENT FEES

Some professional sports leagues have set limits on the fees agents can charge for negotiating a player's contract. The MLBPA allows the market to govern the fees of player agents and has not set any limitations on agent fees. The agent fee is negotiated between the player and his agent. However, an MLB agent cannot charge a fee to a player unless the player's salary, after deducting the agent's fee, exceeds the minimum salary guaranteed by baseball's Basic Agreement. Prior to the 1987 CBA, the limit on fees for agents in the NFL was 5%. Since that time the fees for agents have slowly been reduced. The current maximum fee allowed by the NFLPA for an agent negotiating a player contract is 3%. However, as shown in the above sections of the NFLPA standard representation agreement, the fee is negotiable between players and agents.

Even if an agent is successful in negotiating a player contract, there is no guarantee the agent will receive a fee. A player could be drafted in the NFL draft or sign a rookie free agent contract and subsequently be cut from the team; in this case, the agent would receive no fee. The agent could negotiate an NFL player contract in April but the player can be cut from the team the week before the first game in September. The agent would receive no fee even though he or she had negotiated the player's contract and may have expended sums on recruiting, training, and other expenses on behalf of the player. Most leagues require the agent to provide an itemized list of expenses incurred by the agent and to seek approval by the player before incurring any expenses. If a dispute arises between a player and an agent over fees, the matter is required to be settled through binding arbitration.

The fee limitations set by the leagues only apply to player contracts and not endorsement contracts or other work performed by the agent. Agents can charge a higher fee for endorsement contracts or other legal or business-related work performed on behalf of the client. Large sports management firms charge as much as 20% for the negotiation of an endorsement contract on behalf of a client. However, some players have chosen to pay agents an hourly fee to negotiate a contract or perform business services (Berger, 2007). Some believe this results in a lower fee for the agent, depending on the amount of the contract being negotiated.

Competition Among Agents

The competition for top draft picks in professional sports is extreme and fierce and sometimes can lead to questionable behavior among agents vying for top athletes. There are many reasons for increased competition for clients, including the increase in the number of agents and the amount of money involved in the transactions. It is sometimes difficult to prove that another agent improperly solicited or stole a client. The testimony that is needed to establish such proof often must be extracted from the player who has just recently retained the very agent who is accused of the impropriety. The player is often not willing to testify against his or her new agent, which makes it difficult for the agent who is alleging the wrongdoing to prove misconduct.

Common law remedies are available to agents who believe that other agents have improperly solicited or taken clients from them. An agent will sometimes assert that the competing agent engaged in acts that constitute the tort of wrongful interference with contractual relations. As discussed in chapter 8, a tortious interference with contract claim requires a plaintiff to prove that a valid, enforceable contract exists between two parties; a third party must know that this contract exists; the third party must intentionally cause one of the two parties to the contract to breach the contract; the interference must be for the purpose of advancing the economic interest of the third party (*Kallok v. Medtronic, Inc.*, 1998).

Litigation between prominent agents Leigh Steinberg and David Dunn highlights the problem of competition for clients in the sports business. Dunn left the employment of Steinberg to begin his own sports agency and took with him several significant clients of the firm. Steinberg sued Dunn, alleging that Dunn breached a covenant not to compete that he had signed with the firm whereby Dunn was to not solicit clients or take clients with him when he left the firm. The case went to trial in Los Angeles, and a jury returned a verdict in favor of Steinberg in the amount of $44.66 million in 2002. While the verdict was subsequently overturned by the United States Ninth Circuit Court of Appeals, the initial verdict illustrates the potential breach of covenant not to compete and unfair competition in sport agency (Jury Awards Steinberg $44.6M, 2002).

Sports Contract Negotiation

An agent who negotiates a contract on behalf of a player must properly arm himself or herself with sufficient information to represent the client. This information might include the following: (1) the collective bargaining agreement; (2) the standard player contract; (3) the league bylaws and constitution; (4) relevant court cases or administrative proceedings dealing with issues relating to the negotiation; (5) contracts of similar players; and (6) information relating to player salaries and benefits (Mitten et al., 2009).

An agent must understand terms such as *free agency*, *salary cap*, and *rights of first refusal* and possess a general understanding of how the economics of sports leagues operate to get his or her client the best contract available. Professional unions can be very helpful to agents in the negotiation of contracts. They can provide information on contracts signed by players so the agent can compare a proposed contract to signed contracts already entered into. Information relating to player salaries, bonuses, and contractual terms is readily available to agents today. Salaries of players are printed in newspapers and posted on the Internet. This information was not always available to agents in the past, making it difficult to be able to negotiate a good contract on behalf of a client. For example, in the 1980s, none of the NBA players' salaries or contract terms were available to agents or players; the only people who had information on players' contracts were the few player agents who had actually negotiated those contracts (Simon, 1993).

Salary negotiations for many players can be relatively simple. Players drafted in the later rounds of the NFL draft will most likely earn the league minimum salary with a small bonus and will sign the standard player contract. The only negotiating left to the agent would be the amount of the bonus. Collective bargaining has set the minimum salaries of most professional leagues, thereby reducing some negotiations to a relatively simple process for later-round draft picks and undrafted free agents. However, star players' contracts will require a knowledgeable and skilled negotiator. An agent who is familiar with the economic structure of the league as well as the relevant contract provisions that might be included in such a contract

will have an advantage during negotiations. If an agent has negotiated previous contracts with an owner or a general manager of a particular team, the agent might have gained valuable knowledge for the next negotiation. Knowing the ropes gives the agent and player a negotiating advantage.

A player's representative must consider the following during negotiation of a player contract: (1) Potential contract guarantees; (2) Incentives or bonus provisions; (3) No-trade clauses; (4) No-cut clauses; (5) Signing bonuses; (6) Injury protection provision; (7) Disability insurance; and (8) Renewal contract provisions.

Having a database of salary information is essential to negotiation. Agents must be familiar with players who are similarly situated in relation to the agent's client. Understanding performance statistics is also essential for the negotiation of a good contract. If a team offers an offensive lineman a $1 million bonus for being named NFL most valuable player, the agent would be wise to spend negotiation capital elsewhere. Negotiating a bonus for an American player in the Canadian Football League (CFL) for Most Outstanding Canadian would obviously be fruitless. Knowing what bonuses are attainable for a player is essential for the negotiation of a good contract. Understanding how each club in a league operates is also valuable. If an agent represented an undrafted free agent in the NFL, the agent would want to perform due diligence to determine whether the team has a history of signing a large number of undrafted free agents or whether it is a team that signs a large number of veteran free agents. Other considerations might be a factor during negotiations as well. For instance, some states have a state income tax. That issue may be a deciding factor between two offers made to a player. A player's personal preference regarding a particular team or location may also dominate the negotiations.

Negotiating strategies will change for different player contracts in different situations. A sports agent must understand the particularities of the sport his or her client plays to get a good deal on the player's behalf. If an agent is representing a player labeled as a "franchise player" by the Denver Broncos under the NFL's CBA, negotiations would surely differ from those of an agent representing a punter drafted in the seventh round by the Detroit Lions. Each player representative brings to the table a set of negotiating skills and tactics. Negotiating a sports contract takes excellent negotiating skills combined with a special knowledge of the sporting world.

Agents and players have employed a variety of negotiation strategies over the years in the attempt to secure a better contract. Holding out for a better contract is a ploy that has been used by many players, but renegotiation of contracts has led to many players signing contracts in their last season of their current contract. Renegotiation of a contract by a player is also a tool that has been used many times for leverage to a better contract. Some players and agents will attempt to renegotiate a contract to which they had previously agreed, citing a change in circumstances since the original deal was structured.

Another way for an athlete to gain an advantage during negotiation is to receive competitive offers from other teams. This was more common when major sports leagues had competition that could match the salary offers of the major teams. For example, in the 1980s the United States Football League (USFL) was a start-up league that went head to head with the NFL in signing players. Many NFL stars actually signed large contracts with the USFL and later played in the NFL, including Jim Kelly, Steve Young, and Herschel Walker. Heisman Trophy winner Walker signed a three-year, $3.9 million contract with the New Jersey Generals of the USFL. The Generals sold 36,000 season tickets, almost half of them purchased between Walker's signing and the opening game. Rival leagues can assist a player during negotiations if the league can compete with an established sports league. The CFL cannot match the offers of the NFL; therefore, players do not

have the leverage to negotiate using offers from the CFL as a valid tool when negotiating with an NFL team. In today's sports market, there are no realistic rivals to the four major sports leagues in the United States that could provide negotiation leverage for a player.

Free agency has clearly had an effect on a player's ability to negotiate a better contract. Since the institution of free agency in sports, player salaries have risen dramatically. Negotiations with different teams can clearly lead to different results. A baseball agent knows what Major League teams are willing to offer a contract to a free agent player. The Yankees and Red Sox are traditionally active in the free agent market in baseball, whereas the Tampa Bay Rays and Kansas City Royals are not. An agent would do well to understand the economic structure of baseball and its impact on free agency to gain an advantage for his or her client during negotiations.

REGULATION OF SPORTS AGENTS

Necessity for Regulation

Many different entities have attempted to regulate sports agents. Sports agents are primarily regulated by NCAA regulations, the Uniform Athlete Agent Act (UAAA), which has been adopted by 40 states along with Washington, DC, and the U.S. Virgin Islands, the federal Sport Agent Responsibility and Trust Act (SPARTA) and the regulations of the professional athlete players associations in the professional leagues (Masteralexis et al., 2013). All these entities have a vested interest in protecting players from the unethical and illegal conduct of sports agents. Each has attempted, through its own respective processes, to ensure that the individuals representing a player are qualified and are engaging in ethical and legal conduct while performing the duties of a sports agent.

Regulation by the NCAA, Universities, and Colleges

The NCAA is the governing body for collegiate athletics in the United States. Its membership consists of over 1250 private and public colleges and universities. One of the primary missions of the NCAA is to maintain the concept of amateurism. The NCAA also has the difficult tasks of maintaining the integrity of athletics at the collegiate level and of monitoring the activities of student-athletes, agents, coaches, boosters, and others involved in athletic programs. The NCAA has the power to discipline agents, student-athletes, and universities if they are found to be in violation of NCAA rules or regulations.

The NCAA has promulgated numerous rules and regulations involving the conduct of agents. Specifically, an athlete will be declared ineligible to participate in intercollegiate sport "if he or she ever has agreed (orally or in writing) to be represented by an agent for the purpose of marketing his or her athletic ability or reputation in that sport. Further, an agency contract not specifically limited in writing to a sport or particular sports shall be deemed applicable to all sports, and the individual shall be ineligible to participate in any sport" (NCAA Division 1 Manual, 2014–2015). Further, student athletes will lose their eligibility if they receive any item of value from an agent. Receipt of benefits from a perspective agent is a clear violation of NCAA policy. While these policies are clear regarding prohibited conduct and penalties for athletes (and subsequently institutions), the regulations do not provide any recourse against the agent, since the agent is not a member of the NCAA (Materalexis et al., 2013).

There are many recent examples to demonstrate that NCAA policies have not deterred inappropriate agent behavior. In 2014, agent Noah Lookofsky reported paying former UCLA Bruin basketball player Tyler Honeycutt over $55,000 while he was enrolled at UCLA. Further, Lookofsky estimates that impermissible benefits are the norm, and that over 60% of Division 1 college basketball players receive money either before or during their time on campus (Hart, 2014). Given that many other high profile athletes, such as Cam Newton, O.J. Mayo, Maurkice Pouncey, A.J. Green, and Dez Bryant have all been accused within the past five years of receiving improper gifts or benefits while in college, the NCAA regulations do not seem a likely deterrent (Brautigan, 2010).

In addition to the NCAA regulations, colleges and universities have taken steps to ensure that student-athletes are protected from unscrupulous agents. Many athletic departments and professional sports counseling panels of universities have "agent days" on campus to allow agents to be interviewed by student-athletes. Universities believe they can better control the conduct of agents on campus by hosting such events. The University of Alabama and Ohio State University are two major universities that have held very successful agent days. At Alabama, agents who have at least five current clients are able to make a 20-minute presentation to rising senior football student-athletes and their parents. The university stresses this is the only chance that agents will have to meet with student-athletes prior to the end of the season. Agents are able to present materials to prospective clients as well as to make a short oral presentation. The purpose of agent day is to regulate contact between the university's student-athletes and agents and to give student-athletes a wide variety of agents from which to choose.

State Regulation

An agent will sometimes have clients in different states and will be faced with the dilemma of how to comply with each state's law regarding athlete agents. A California agent may be recruiting a student-athlete at Louisiana State University who is from Florida. Where would the agent register to be in compliance with state law? What law or regulations would apply to his or her actions?

In 2000, the National Conference of Commissioners on Uniform State Laws drafted the UAAA; at that time, 28 states had differing laws regulating agent conduct (Masteralexis et al., 2013). The UAAA is a uniform act regulating athlete agents who deal with student athletes. Specifically, the UAAA requires an agent to register in each state he/she conducts business, prohibits an agent from making false promises or furnishing anything of value to a student athlete, and requires written notifications to a university when a student athlete retains an agent (Masteralexis et al., 2013). The UAAA also addresses the contents of a representation agreement, sets forth a list of prohibited acts for agents, and provides a remedy for schools that are harmed by an agent's actions or conduct.

As of August 2015, the UAAA had been adopted by 40 states and two territories; three states have non-UAAA legislation (California, Michigan, and Ohio) and seven states have no regulatory legislation at all (Alaska, Maine, Massachusetts, Montana, New Jersey, Vermont, and Virginia) (UAAA Laws, 2015). One of the purposes of the passage of the UAAA was to create uniformity among the many states that had passed laws dealing with athlete agents; however, this uniformity has not been completely achieved. For example, in 2011, Arkansas passed the Athlete Agent Reform Act, which significantly broadens the definition of sport agent, and increases the penalties agents in Arkansas face for improper conduct with a student athlete. Specifically, the statute defines an athlete agent as a person authorized by a student athlete to enter into an agreement on his or her behalf, a person who works on behalf of another agent (runners, recruiters, service providers, etc.), and/or a person who represents to the public that he is an athlete agent (Arkansas Athlete Agent Reform Act, 2011). "Additionally, family members who offer or solicit, on their own behalf or the student-athlete's behalf, any sort of financial benefit or gift not allowed by the NCAA will be considered athlete agents under the Act" (Heitner, 2011, p. 1). Regarding penalties, improper conduct

is punishable by fines up to $250,000 and/or six years in jail.

The Arkansas law is harsher than many other state counterparts; however, regardless of penalties, recent examples demonstrate the potential impact of the UAAA laws. Although charges under state UAAA laws are rare, six individuals were indicted between 2013 and 2015 under the North Carolina Uniform Athlete Agent Act in connection with the football scandal at the University of North Carolina (UNC) at Chapel Hill. Former UNC tutor Jennifer Wiley Thompson was the first to be charged under the law; she was charged with four felonies for providing cash packages and airfare to a UNC football player in attempts to get the player to sign with Terry Watson. Sports agent Watson was himself charged with 14 felony counts for giving improper gifts of cash and travel expenses to three UNC football players over a 5 month period in 2010 (Sports agent, 2013). In addition to others, Chris Hawkins, a former UNC football player, was the most recent arrest; his indictment was for two counts of violating the law, also for giving impermissible gifts as well as failing to register in the state (Former UNC Football Player, 2015). Without question, the ongoing investigation in North Carolina is an example of the pervasive nature of improper agent conduct, as well as the potential impact of the UAAA laws as a form of agent regulation.

Federal Regulation: Sport Agent Responsibility and Trust Act

In 2006, Congress passed SPARTA, the first-ever federal law aimed at regulating sports agents. The law was an effort by the federal government to add uniformity to agent regulation. The act does not preempt any state laws relating to agents but instead was meant to supplement the already existing Uniform Athletes Agent Act.

The goal of SPARTA is to keep college athletes eligible and to protect them from unscrupulous agents. It sets forth guidelines for agents regarding the recruiting of student-athletes and delineates penalties for those agents who violate the act. The act also gives a state attorney general the right to bring a civil lawsuit against any agent who violates the act. Universities have also been given the right to bring a civil lawsuit against any agent who causes damage to the university for improper conduct under the law. (Sport Agent Responsibility and Trust Act, §§ 7801–7807, 2006).

Player's Association Regulations

Agent certification falls under the purview of player associations. All of the player's associations, except for the Major League Soccer Players Union, regulate agent certification and conduct (Masteralexis et al., 2013). Player associations (unions) clearly have an obligation to ensure that agents are qualified to represent union members; as such, initial agent certification, agent conduct, discipline, and re-certification all fall under the scope of what is regulated by player's associations.

Sports agent certification criteria are dictated by the player's associations, often including minimum benchmarks for education and experience. NFLPA regulations require that all new applicants not only have a four-year college degree from an accredited university but also possess a postgraduate degree from an accredited college or university. The applicant must also pass a written examination. The exam covers issues dealing with collective bargaining, player benefits, and other matters relating to the representation of NFLPA players.

Further, most player's associations set forth performance requirements and membership fees. The NFLPA requires that an agent must negotiate one NFL standard player contract every three years or be required to apply for recertification by the union. Also, the annual dues to be a certified agent have risen exponentially in the past several years. In 1985, the application fee to become an NFLPA contract advisor was a mere $35. In 2014, the dues owed for a season for an NFLPA contract

advisor were $1200 if the contract advisor represented less than 10 active players and were $1700 if the contract advisor represented 10 or more active players. Lastly, the applicant is also required to attend a seminar approved by the NFLPA to remain certified with the league.

One of the more powerful tools available to a player's association is the power to discipline an agent for improper conduct. Every professional sports union sets forth in its regulations the type of conduct that is prohibited by agents. When agents engage in prohibited conduct, the union can fine the agent or revoke the license granted to the agent. Punishment by the union can range from a reprimand to decertification. Agents are provided with an appeal process for any discipline they may receive.

In December 2003, arbitrator Roger Kaplan found that former NFL player and agent Sean Jones had violated NFLPA regulations in his financial dealings with former NFL player Chris Dishman but reduced the union's discipline from decertification to a two-year suspension. Dishman sued Jones in a civil lawsuit and received a judgment in the amount of $396,000 (Stienbaker, 2007).

In 2004, the NFLPA disciplinary committee filed a complaint against contract advisor Hadley Engelhard stating that he gave his NFLPA website password to a reporter and also changed his agent fee for a player without properly informing the player. The disciplinary committee of the NFLPA voted to issue a letter of reprimand and levied a fine of $10,000 for each offense.

NFL agent Jerome Stanley was suspended by the NFLPA's disciplinary committee for missing a deadline to file for free agency on behalf of his client, Dennis Northcutt of the Cleveland Browns. Northcutt had signed a seven-year contract with the Browns that required him to notify the team by November 19 if he was going to void the final three years of the contract. Northcutt indicated he was eager to test the free agent market and was anticipating receiving in the neighborhood of a five-year contract with a $5 million signing bonus. He was unable to void the contract because of the missed deadline by his agent.

The NFLPA also expressed concerns about whether contract advisors had insurance coverage available to them for any potential liability that might result from their negligent actions as contract advisors. The NFLPA Executive Committee subsequently required that all contract advisors obtain malpractice insurance to cover any potential liability they may face when performing their duties as a contract advisor.

While every major sports player's association has regulations dealing with agent misconduct, MLB updated its regulations in 2010 in an attempt to prevent improper agent conduct and client stealing, both of which were distracting players and having a negative impact on player salary negotiations. The updated regulations required an agent to inform the MLBPA if he or she had contact with a player that was not his or her client; further, agents are not allowed to promise anything of value to a player that he or she does not represent. Further, the regulations disallowed an agent change during the time period where a player was eligible for free agency or salary arbitration, unless the MLBPA was consulted first. The new regulations also impose mandatory arbitration for dispute resolution (Masteralexis, et al., 2013).

CONCLUSION

Sport agents play a significant role in the sport industry, impacting professional and collegiate sport alike. While sport agency can certainly be lucrative for those who successfully represent professional athlete clients, the industry is also wrought with a myriad of potential legal issues. Those involved in athletics administration must be aware of the legal landscape that impacts sport agency; those that aspire to work as sport agents must understand the duties, responsibilities, legal obligations, and broad scope of regulatory functions.

DISCUSSION QUESTIONS

Duties and Responsibilities of Agents

1. What are the basic qualifications a sports agent should possess? Should each agent be required to have a graduate degree or to have substantial business experience before being certified as a sports agent?
2. Art Shamsky is just starting out in the agent business. He has negotiated one contract for a player in the CFL but has not negotiated any NFL contracts. He is contacted by a cousin whose roommate is a potential high-round draft pick in the NFL. Shamsky is able to sign the player to a standard representation agreement. Shamsky begins to call various scouts of NFL teams to tell them about the player. All the scouts agree that the player will go no lower than the third round of the upcoming NFL draft. Based on this information and other research Shamsky has performed, he assures the player that he will be taken in the first three rounds of the NFL draft. Shamsky also tells the player he will be able to get him at least a $300,000 signing bonus based on the information he has received from the NFL scouts and general managers.

DISCUSSION QUESTIONS (CONTINUED)

The player is actually drafted in the sixth round of the NFL draft and only receives a signing bonus of $85,000. The player fires Shamsky and plans to file a civil lawsuit against him based on breach of contract and breach of fiduciary duty. Will the player win his lawsuit? Does the agent have any defenses to the lawsuit?

3. Under what circumstances could a player win a case against an agent for breach of fiduciary duty?

4. In *Bias v. Advantage International, Inc.* (1990), the estate of Len Bias sued his agent, alleging that the agent failed to perform his duties. Len Bias was the second round draft pick of the Boston Celtics in the 1986 NBA draft; however, he died of a cocaine overdose two days after being drafted. Specifically, Bias's estate alleged that the agent failed to obtain a life insurance policy for Bias, even though the agent claimed a policy had been secured. Further, the estate alleged that the agent failed to finalize an endorsement contract with Reebok on behalf of Bias, and was instead attempting to negotiate a contract for multiple clients, which resulted in Bias's endorsement contract being delayed. Do you believe the agent breached his fiduciary duty? Do you believe that the agent breached the fiduciary duty owned to Len Bias by negotiating endorsement contracts for several players at the same time? What is a reasonable time period for an agent to complete the negotiation of an endorsement contract on behalf of a player?

Representation Agreements

1. Review the provisions of the NFL Standard Representation Agreement found in this chapter. Is the standard representation agreement a good idea? What are the advantages and disadvantages of such an agreement? Why do some leagues require standard agreements and some do not?

Agent Fees

1. Should unions be able to set limits on fees for agents or should the market control agent fees? Should all unions have a set fee for agents?

2. In *Brown v. Woolf* (1983), the agent negotiated a five-year contract for an NHL player valued at $800,000; however, the team experienced financial difficulties shortly thereafter and the team defaulted on its obligation to pay. Ultimately, the player received only $185,000. Although the player received significantly less money than contracted for, the agent received and retained his full 5% ($40,000). Is it appropriate for the agent to take the entire fee he was owed under the contract even though the player received a reduced amount of what he was owed under the contract? Is an agent ever required to reduce his or her fees during negotiations? At what point during the negotiations is an agent allowed to take his or her fee?

(continues)

DISCUSSION QUESTIONS (CONTINUED)

Conflicts of Interest

1. Which of the following pose a conflict of interest for a sports agent?
   a. Representing two players on the same team at the same position.
   b. Representing a player and coach on the same team.
   c. Representing NFL management personnel and a player simultaneously.
   d. A sports management firm that continues to represent a player who retires and later becomes the general manager of a Major League team.
2. What are the potential problems that exist for an agent who represents a player for both contract negotiations and financial matters?
3. Assume that an agent represents two NFL players who play the same position and are both unrestricted free agents. During negotiations with an NFL club, the agent is told by the general manager that salary cap considerations only allow the signing of one star player. Does the agent have an irreconcilable conflict of interest in this scenario? What are the agent's duties in this case? Suppose a team tells an agent that his client, player A, needs to take a salary cut to make room on the squad for player B, who is also represented by the agent. What conflict of interest issues arise under the circumstances? Can the agent continue to represent both players?

The Regulation of Sports Agents

1. Who should have the primary responsibility for regulation of sports agents: the state, universities, leagues, unions, or the NCAA?
2. At what point should a players' union step in and regulate a dispute between agents over the signing of a player? Do you think this type of activity is unusual in the sports agent business?
3. Should there be a Uniform Code of Ethics for sports agents? If so, what should be contained in the code?
4. Paul Thomas is an attorney who is trying to break into the sports agent business. A friend of his knows a possible first-round NFL draft pick who is attending the University of Oklahoma. The friend introduces Thomas to Jamison, who is in his junior year at the university. Jamison tells Thomas he is "taking offers" from potential agents and that he needs about $2500 a month for the rest of his college career to maintain his "lifestyle." Thomas agrees to pay Jamison and continues to pay him $2500 through the player's senior year. After Jamison's senior year, Oklahoma is invited to play in the Alamo Bowl against Northwestern, with a payout to each university of $1.2 million. Three days before the bowl game, Jamison is declared ineligible and Oklahoma is banned from playing in the bowl game by the NCAA because of violations of NCAA rules. An investigation by the NCAA, based on a tip, revealed the payments by the agent to the player. The University of Oklahoma now seeks to recover $1.2 million because of the lost bowl game opportunity. It seeks damages to the reputation of the university as well. It

DISCUSSION QUESTIONS (CONTINUED)

names Thomas and Jamison as defendants in a civil lawsuit. Will the university prevail? What is the relevant law in this case? What damages has the University of Oklahoma sustained?

5. Do you agree with the NCAA rules regarding agents? Do you believe agents should be able to make contracts with student-athletes prior to the expiration of their eligibility? Is the regulation of agents a job more suited for the university where the student-athlete is matriculating? The NCAA's general rule relating to agents states that an individual will be deemed ineligible if he or she has agreed orally or in writing to be represented by an agent. How will the NCAA monitor oral promises between agents and student-athletes?

KEY TERMS

Agency
Conflict of interest
Fiduciary
Free agency

Rights of first refusal
Salary cap
Salary Negotiations

REFERENCES

15 USCA §§ 7801–7807 (2006).

Arkansas Athlete Agent Reform Act (2011). Arkansas Code § 17-16-102.

Berger, B. (2007). Making a case for doing away with full-time agents. Sports Business Radio, Retrieved from http://sportsbusinessradio.com/blogs/2007/11/making-case-doing-away-full-time-agents

Bias v. Advantage International, Inc., 905 F.2d 1558 (D.C. Cir.1990).

Brautigan, B. (2010). Cam Newton and 10 college athletes in scandal: Is it their fault or the system? Bleacher Report. Retrieved from http://bleacherreport.com/articles/514177-10-college-athletes-involved-in-scandals-is-it-their-fault-or-the-system

Brown v. Woolf, 554 F. Supp. 1206 (D.C. Ind. 1983).

Former UNC football player arrested in sports agent probe. (2015). Associated Press. Retrieved from http://www.foxsports.com/college-football/story/university-of-north-carolina-robert-quinn-sports-agent-probe-051215

Hart, D. (2014). UCLA Bruins basketball: Scandal brewing over agent paying Tyler Honeycutt? LA Sports Hub. Retrieved from http://lasportshub.com/2014/04/10/ucla-bruins-basketball-scandal-brewing-agent-paying-tyler-honeycutt/

Heitner, D. (2011). Arkansas' new athlete agent law may be used as national model. Sports Agents Blog. Retrieved from http://sportsagentblog.com/2011/11/22/arkansas-new-athlete-agent-law-may-be-used-as-national-model/

Jury awards Steinberg $44.6M in lawsuit with former partner. (2002). SportsBusiness Daily. Retrieved from http://www.sportsbusinessdaily.com/Daily/Issues/2002/11/Issue-47/Sports-Industrialists/Jury-Awards-Steinberg-$446M-In-Lawsuit-With-Former-Partner.aspx

Kallok v. Medtronic, Inc., 573 N.W.2d 356 (Minn. 1998).

Masteralexis, L.P., Barr, C.A., Hums, M. (2012). Principles and practice of sports management (4th ed.). Sudbury, MA: Jones and Bartlett.

Masteralexis, J., Masteralexis, L., and Snyder, K. (2013). Enough is enough: The case for federal regulation of sports agents. *Jeffrey S. Moorad Sports Law Journal, 20*(1), Article 3.

Mitten, M., Davis, T., Smith, R., & Berry, R. (2009) *Sports law and regulation: cases, materials, and problems* (2nd ed.). New York: Aspen.

National Collegiate Athletic Association, NCAA Division I Manual 1 (2015).

NFLPA Regulations Governing Contract Advisors. (2012). Retrieved from https://nflpaweb.blob.core.windows .net/media/Default/PDFs/Agents/2012_NFLPA _Regulations_Governing_Contract_Advisors.pdf

Restatement (Third) of Agency § 1(1) (2006).

Restatement (Third) of Agency § 8(1) (2006).

Simon, R. (1993). *The game behind the game: Negotiating in the big leagues.* Stillwater, Minn.: Voyageur.

Sport Agent Responsibility and Trust Act, 15 USCA §§ 7801-7807 (2006).

N.A. (2013). Sports agent Terry Watson faces 14 felony counts in UNC scandal. WRAL Sports Fan. Retrieved from http://www.wralsportsfan.com/sports-agent -connected-to-unc-scandal-charged/12976259/

Stienbaker, J. (2007). Ex-Oiler Jones indicted on fraud charges. Amarillo Globe News. Retrieved from http://amarillo.com/stories/061507/nfl_7782483 .shtml#.VeDhIpc0AqN

UAAA Laws in the 50 States. (2015). Retrieved from http:// fs.ncaa.org/Docs/ENF/UAAA/map/index.html

INTERCOLLEGIATE AND INTERSCHOLASTIC ATHLETIC ISSUES

LEARNING OBJECTIVES

By the end of the chapter, the reader will be able to:

1. Identify the governance structure of intercollegiate athletics
2. Identify the governance structure of interscholastic athletics
3. Identify the requirements for state action in a constitutional law analysis
4. Consider whether the NCAA and state athletic associations are classified as state actors
5. Identify the United States Constitution Amendments that are most often used by student-athletes filing constitutional law challenges
6. Consider the various standards used to determine whether student speech is protected under the First Amendment
7. Consider emerging free speech issues such as online virtual speech and social media restrictions for student-athletes
8. Identify the dichotomy present in the Establishment Clause and the Free Exercise clause
9. Recognize the key findings in cases that determine whether the Establishment clause or the Free Exercise clause have been violated
10. Consider how the Due Process Clause may impact student-athlete eligibility
11. Consider how the Equal Protection clause may impact student-athlete eligibility

RELATED CASES

Case 12.1   Hayden ex rel. AH v. Greensburg Community School, 743 F. 3d 569 (2014)

Case 12.2   KOUNTZE INDEPENDENT SCH. DIST. v. Matthews, 482 SW 3d 120 (2014)

INTRODUCTION

Intercollegiate and interscholastic sports are widely popular; millions of students participate annually in both levels. Student-athletes at both levels of play are *amateur athletes*; governing bodies at both levels create rules and regulations that govern play. These *governing bodies* may be formal, such as the National Collegiate Athletic Association (NCAA), the National Federation of State High School Associations (NFSHA), or a state athletic association; however, individual educational institutions and coaches also create institutional rules and/or policies that govern play. This chapter will first consider the governance structure of both intercollegiate and interscholastic athletics, and then detail the challenges faced by each. The NCAA, the NFSHA, state athletic associations and various educational institutions included therein have all faced constitutional challenges to various rules and policies, as well as legal issues regarding rule-making processes, enforcement procedures, and eligibility rules. This chapter will address each of these areas of concern.

NCAA

College sports in America are both popular and lucrative. Collegiate student-athletes compete in a variety of sports, including baseball, football, basketball, ice hockey, golf, rodeo, fencing, water polo, gymnastics, bowling, volleyball, track and field, wrestling, and lacrosse. Millions of fans attend college sporting events and watch them on television every year. Participation in and the viewing of college athletics is a national pastime and can also be extremely lucrative for some of those involved. Several associations govern intercollegiate athletics in the United States; however, this chapter focuses solely on the NCAA because it is the most powerful of the associations and is the primary rule-making body for collegiate athletics in the United States.

Structure and Organization

As briefly discussed in chapter 11, the NCAA is the primary organization governing collegiate athletics in the United States. It is a private organization that administers the athletic programs of many universities and colleges. The NCAA was founded in 1906 during the presidency of Theodore Roosevelt. The Intercollegiate Football Rules Committee, founded in 1894 by the then college football powerhouses of Harvard, Yale, the University of Pennsylvania, and Princeton, had been the regulating body for college football in 1905. That year, 62 colleges sent representatives to a meeting called by New York University Chancellor MacCraken because of his concern about injuries and deaths in college football; during the 1907 season there were 11 student-athlete deaths and 98 serious injuries of student-athletes (Football Deaths, 1907). The meeting culminated with the formation of the Intercollegiate Athletic Association of the United States, which would, several years later, become known as the NCAA. The NCAA now sponsors athletic championships in a wide variety of sports.

Headquartered in Indianapolis, Indiana, the NCAA has a large staff consisting of departments for championships, business, compliance, enforcement, publishing, and legislative services, to mention a few. Its membership comprises more than 1250 institutions, which are organized into separate divisions based on competitiveness: Divisions I, II, and III. Division I is divided further into I-A and I-AA. Division I offers full athletic scholarships and is the most competitive. Division II offers athletic scholarships as well, and the student-athletes compete at an intermediate level. Division III has no scholarships and is the least competitive of the divisions but may be the most collegial. Schools compete in different divisions based on student population and athletic participation. Both small private schools and large public universities play in NCAA Division I-A football, which has approximately 120 teams. For example,

Ohio State University in Division I-A has an undergraduate student population in excess of 50,000 while Wake Forest University has an undergraduate population of approximately 4800 undergraduate students. The Demon Deacons compete in Division I-A football in the Atlantic Coast Conference.

Athletic conferences are also members of the NCAA. Universities and colleges are divided into various conferences for athletic purposes. In the past five years there has been an extensive reorganization of collegiate athletic conferences. Member institutions have attempted to switch conferences to align themselves with powerhouse athletic programs; the primary motivating force behind the moves is college football. The Big Ten Conference now has 14 teams and the Big East Conference and the Atlantic Coast Conference have also had members leave and establish a new makeup for the conferences in the past few years. Much is at stake in college sports for student-athletes, coaches, administrators, and universities. The NCAA will continue to try to find the right combination of administration and enforcement to strike the ideal balance between academics and athletic success.

The NCAA has expressed its fundamental purpose in its constitution; specifically, the NCAA states that "competitive athletics programs of member institutions are designed to be a vital part of the educational system" (NCAA Manual, 2015). Further, the NCAA aims to "maintain intercollegiate athletics as an integral part of the educational program and the athlete as an integral part of the student body and, by so doing, retain a clear line of demarcation between intercollegiate athletics and professional sports" (NCAA Manual, 2015).

The NCAA is governed by a detailed set of manuals containing its bylaws for each division and is directed by an 18-member council, an executive committee, and paid staff members. Division I-A powerhouse conferences and universities constitute the majority of the membership appointments for the management council

and the board of directors. The NCAA sets forth the rules and regulations with which all member institutions, coaches, and student-athletes must abide. The bylaws published by the NCAA give guidance regarding a myriad of issues relating to collegiate sports, including eligibility, drug testing, use of agents, recruiting, the amateur status of student-athletes, and financial aid. As members of the association, all institutions are required to comply with all NCAA regulations. If an institution fails to follow NCAA bylaws, then the NCAA is empowered to act appropriately against the institution in an attempt to ensure its compliance and can penalize the member institution for any major or minor violation. The enforcement bylaws empower the NCAA Committee on Infractions (COI), set forth the policies and procedures of enforcement proceedings, delineate available penalties, and grant a right to appeal to member institutions.

All individuals employed by member institutions have a duty to cooperate with an NCAA investigation. The institution may begin its own investigation into any alleged violations as well and may do so in an attempt to fend off the NCAA's investigation and mitigate any penalty that may be assessed. Many institutions will immediately begin their own investigation once they have received notice from the NCAA that the athletic program is being investigated. The NCAA's enforcement powers are extensive and have been used in the past to penalize those universities that violate NCAA rules. Some have argued that the NCAA has been too harsh in enforcing its bylaws and needs to be reformed (Yeager, 1992).

NCAA Enforcement

The NCAA enforcement program aims to eliminate violations of NCAA rules and impose appropriate penalties should violations occur. Each NCAA member is responsible for conducting its athletic program in a manner consistent with NCAA rules and regulations. NCAA bylaws give the organization the necessary authority to investigate alleged violations of its rules. The NCAA's COI investigates and renders decisions regarding infractions by member institutions. The committee is able to conduct investigations into any conduct that it believes is in violation of NCAA rules and regulations. A member institution is able to conduct its own internal investigation as well, and the NCAA looks favorably upon any action taken by member institutions in good faith to remedy improper conduct. Any discipline rendered as a result of an investigation must be performed in a fair and legal manner.

The first step in the investigation process is evaluating the gathered information to determine whether it is credible. If it is not deemed credible, the case will be closed. If it is determined that the information is credible, then the NCAA will notify the member institution that an investigation will be initiated. The notice will generally provide the school with details concerning the investigation, including names of witnesses, when the violation or violations occurred, and the individuals involved.

After the investigation is complete, the COI conducts a hearing. The committee then prepares a public report that details the infractions, actions taken by the member institution in its attempts to remedy the infraction or infractions, and the discipline rendered by the committee. The member institution has the right to appeal the decision of the committee.

A wide range of penalties is available to the NCAA if violations are found, including loss of scholarships, forfeiture of tournament money, ineligibility for postseason play, limitations on television appearances and recruiting, public censure, financial penalties, and the expungement of team or individual records. The NCAA also has the power to give the "death penalty" to a sports program, a term that became more widely known after Southern Methodist University's football program was canceled for a period of time because of NCAA violations.

NATIONAL FEDERATION OF STATE HIGH SCHOOL ASSOCIATIONS/STATE ATHLETIC ASSOCIATIONS

Participation in *interscholastic athletics* is at an all-time high; millions of student-athletes participate in a variety of sports at the high school level every year (High School Athletics Participation Survey, 2013–2014). As a result of this increased participation, extensive regulation has occurred. The premier governing body for high school sports in the United States is the National Federation of State High School Associations (NFHS), founded in 1923. The NFHS comprises the high school athletic or activities associations of 50 states and currently governs more than seven million high school student-athletes. Its stated purpose is to "serve its members, related professional organizations, and students by providing leadership for the administration of education-based interscholastic activities, which support academic achievement, good citizenship, and equitable opportunities" (NFHS Handbook, 2013–2014). Further, the NFHS and its member state associations build awareness and support, improve the participation experience, establish consistent standards and rules for competition, and help those who oversee high school sports ("About Us," 2015).

The NFHS has multiple roles regarding interscholastic athletic governance. In addition to representing millions of athletes, the organization compiles national records, assesses participation rates, coordinates officials' certification, promulgates rules for 16 boys and 16 girls sports, organizes national conferences, and acts as an advocate for youth sports (Masteralexis, Barr, & Hums, 2012). The organizational structure for these functions has three primary components; a legislative body, made up of one representative from each state, an elected board of directors, responsible for the annual budget and establishing committees, and a paid professional and administrative staff of approximately 50 members.

As noted, the NFHS encompasses each of the 50 *state athletic associations*; these associations have structures similar to the national model. State associations are responsible for determining athlete eligibility policies (discussed later in this chapter), as well as overseeing state level championships. Each state association varies regarding size and scope of activities; however, the governance functions are similar across all associations (Masteralexis et al., 2012). Given the increasing number of interscholastic athletes, this level of sport is highly regulated, and the state associations are responsible for providing such. "State associations have had to develop increasingly sophisticated and elaborate regulations to govern interscholastic athletics" (Mitten, Davis, Smith, & Berry, 2009, p. 24). While the state level regulations are often elaborate, local school districts do have autonomy in creating policies for their respective athletic programs; however, school level policies must adhere to the general rules promulgated for all state association members (Mitten et al., 2009).

Constitutional Law Considerations

Amateur athletics have been a fertile ground for constitutional challenges in the past several decades. As the popularity and profitability of high school and college sports have increased, so to have the regulatory policies set forth by the governing bodies. As a result, both intercollegiate and interscholastic athletic governing bodies (national and state associations and local school districts) have faced a multitude of challenges under constitutional law. Specifically, student-athletes have argued that governing bodies have compromised their rights of free speech, freedom of religion, search and seizure, due process and equal protection under the United States Constitution. This section will first review the threshold requirement for a constitutional challenge, *state action*; then, the First, Fifth,

and Fourteenth Amendments will be specifically discussed (the Fourth Amendment search and seizure protections were addressed in chapter 7).

State Action

As mentioned in chapter 7, governmental action must comply with the constitutional rights of individuals; however, private actors do not have such concerns (*Burton v. Wilmington Parking Authority*, 1961). An individual who is alleging a denial of his or her constitutional rights must first establish that the action being taken is one by a governmental entity. If the plaintiff cannot establish "state action" on the part of the entity, then the constitutional claim will fail. In some cases, state action is easy to establish. If a plaintiff is challenging a policy implemented by a state university or public high school, the state action requirement is met; however, other cases are not quite as clear. Amateur athletic associations such as the NCAA and state high school athletic association are private associations but, under certain circumstances, may perform similar functions as a governmental entity.

Courts have applied certain tests to determine whether the defendant is a state actor. The *public function theory* substantiates state action when a private association is performing a service typically performed by the government. The *entanglement or nexus theory* considers whether there is a close nexus between the state and the challenged action; if so, the court may consider the defendant a state actor. Does the law recognize interscholastic and intercollegiate governing bodies as state actors, thereby invoking constitutional considerations? To answer this question, the NCAA and interscholastic governing bodies must be analyzed separately.

NCAA

There is a long history of cases where courts have considered whether the NCAA is a state actor. In the 1970s, many courts used both the public function and entanglement theories to determine that the NCAA was a state actor (Wong, 1988, citing *Howard University v. NCAA,* 1975; *Parish v. NCAA,* 1973; *Buckton v. NCAA,* 1973; and *Associated Students v. NCAA,* 1974). However, in 1988, the United States Supreme Court heard *National Collegiate Athletic Association v. Tarkanian* (1988), and determined that the NCAA did not meet the state action requirements. Specifically, Jerry Tarkanian, head basketball coach for the University of Nevada-Las Vegas (UNLV) brought suit in Nevada state court, alleging that he had been deprived of his Fourteenth Amendment due process rights in violation of 42 U.S.C. § 1983 after UNLV informed Tarkanian that it was going to suspend him. The suspension, which came in 1977, was predicated by a report by the NCAA detailing 38 violations of NCAA rules by UNLV personnel, including 10 involving Tarkanian. The NCAA placed the university's basketball team on probation for two years and ordered UNLV to sever all ties between its intercollegiate athletic program and Tarkanian, under threat of further discipline (p. 181).

The act challenged by Tarkanian (his suspension) was committed by UNLV, and a state university without question is a state actor. When a state actor decides to impose a serious disciplinary sanction upon one of its tenured employees, it must comply with the terms of the Due Process Clause of the Fourteenth Amendment to the Federal Constitution. Thus when UNLV notified Tarkanian that he was being separated from all relations with the university's basketball program, it acted under color of state law within the meaning of 42 U.S.C. § 1983. However, Tarkanian argued that the NCAA was a state actor as well because it misused power that it possessed by virtue of state law. He claimed that UNLV delegated its own functions to the NCAA, clothing the NCAA with authority both to adopt rules governing UNLV's athletic programs and to enforce those rules on behalf of UNLV. Further, Tarkanian argued that

UNLV had delegated its authority over personnel decisions to the NCAA; therefore, the two entities acted jointly to deprive Tarkanian of liberty and property interests, making the NCAA (as well as UNLV) a state actor (p. 182).

In the initial lawsuit, Tarkanian obtained injunctive relief and an award of attorney's fees against both UNLV and the NCAA; the injunctive relief prohibited UNLV from suspending Tarkanian (under directive of the NCAA). The initial court found that the events that led to Tarkanian's suspension constituted "state action" by both UNLV and the NCAA. Over the next several years, multiple appeals followed, with the Nevada Supreme Court upholding the finding that the NCAA is a state actor. Specifically, the Nevada Supreme Court held that the NCAA engaged in state action when it conducted its investigation and recommended that discipline for Tarkanian. However, the United States Supreme Court granted certiorari to review the case and reversed the ruling, finding that *the NCAA is not a state actor.* The court held that the NCAA neither exercised nor held governmental power when it threatened to expel a state university from membership if the university did not take specified action (p. 197). Instead, the court found that UNLV chose to conduct its athletic program in compliance with the NCAA's policies in order to maintain NCAA membership (p. 199).

Tarkanian argued that the power of the NCAA was so great that the UNLV had no practical alternative to compliance with its demands. The court recognized that UNLV's conduct was influenced by the rules and recommendations of the NCAA, but emphasized it was UNLV, the state entity, that actually suspended Tarkanian. When considering whether UNLV's actions in compliance with the NCAA rules and recommendations turned the NCAA's conduct into state action, the court found it did not. The court was not willing to assume that a private monopolist can impose its will on a state agency by a threatened refusal to deal with it, and even if it could, the court would not conclude that such a private party conduct constitutes state action.

SCHOOL AND STATE ATHLETIC ASSOCIATIONS

As noted earlier, state athletic/activity associations govern interscholastic athletics. Often, the state association is a private entity engaging in conduct that has the characteristics of a "state actor" or is actually a de facto state actor. Given that the state level associations often establish and enforce the rules regarding athletics participation, eligibility, and penalties, there is ample case law that considers whether a state high school athletic association is a state actor.

The most notable case is *Brentwood Academy v. Tennessee Secondary School Athletic Association* (2001). The Brentwood Academy (Brentwood) case addressed the issue of whether the Tennessee Secondary School Athletic Association (TSSAA), which was "incorporated to regulate interscholastic athletic competition among public and private secondary schools," engaged in state action when it enforced one of its rules against a member school (p. 290). Specifically, TSSAA sanctioned Brentwood after the TSSAA's Board of Control found that that Brentwood had committed a recruiting violation when it wrote to incoming students and their parents about attending spring football practice. TSSAA placed Brentwood on probation for four years, declared certain teams ineligible for post-season competition for two years, and imposed a $3000 fine. Brentwood filed a lawsuit alleging that TSSAA imposing the sanctions constituted state action, and that the action was a violation of the First and Fourteenth Amendments. The district court found in favor of Brentwood and enjoined (prevented) TSAA from imposing the sanctions; however, the United States Court of Appeals for the Sixth Circuit reversed finding

no symbiotic relationship or nexus between the TSSAA and the state, which would warrant a finding of state action. The United States Supreme Court granted certiorari to render a final decision.

The United States Supreme Court considered multiple factors in its analysis. First, the court considered TSSAA membership and recognized that public schools constituted 84% of TSSAA's members; further, public school faculty and administrators provided TSSAA's leadership. The court was also influenced by the fact that TSSAA's primary revenue source was gate receipts from tournaments between TSSAA-member schools, and TSSAA employees were treated like state employees by virtue of their eligibility for membership in the state retirement system.

Using these factors, the court stated that "there would be no recognizable Association, legal or tangible, without the public school officials, who do not merely control but overwhelmingly perform all but the purely ministerial acts by which the Association exists and functions in practical terms" (pp. 299–300). Given the above analysis, the United States Supreme Court held that because of "the pervasive entwinement of state school officials in the structure of the association," TSSAA's regulatory activity constituted state action (p. 291). The court also acknowledged that the analysis of whether state action existed was a "necessarily fact-bound inquiry" and noted that state action may be found only where there is "such a close nexus between the State and the challenged action that seemingly private behavior may be fairly treated as that of the State itself."

Although the court acknowledged that whether a state athletic association is a state actor is a case specific, fact bound inquiry, the overwhelming majority of cases that have considered this issue have reached the same conclusion. Several states have considered this issue and reached the same conclusion including Illinois, Arizona, Missouri, Ohio, Louisiana, Oklahoma, Mississippi, West Virginia, Massachusetts, and Pennsylvania

(Wolohan, 2013). Based on the significant case law precedent, state high school athletic associations are generally considered state actors when they pass regulations regarding a student-athlete's participation in sports.

With the exception of the NCAA (which is a significant exception), many governing bodies for intercollegiate and interscholastic athletics are considered state actors; as such, these entities must be aware of the protections afforded student-athletes by multiple Constitutional Amendments. The First Amendment (freedom of speech and freedom of religion) and the Fifth and Fourteenth Amendments (due process and equal protection) have been used by an overwhelming number of student-athletes at all levels to challenge perceived inequities in intercollegiate and interscholastic sport governance.

First Amendment

The First Amendment of the Constitution affords many protections. Specifically, the Amendment states "Congress shall make no law respecting an establishment of religion, or prohibiting the free exercise thereof; or abridging the freedom of speech, or of the press; or the people to peaceably assemble and to petition the Government for a redress of grievances" (United States Constitution, Amendment I). Of the freedoms afforded by the First Amendment, citizens most commonly challenge freedom of speech and freedom of religion; this is also true for student-athletes.

Free Speech

There are decades' worth of case law clarifying the freedom of speech afforded by the First Amendment in various settings. Although straightforward in concept, the judiciary has clarified and further defined this freedom over time. With regard to interscholastic students (including student-athletes), the law has evolved as well.

As noted in chapter 7, students do not "shed their constitutional rights to freedom of speech of expression at the schoolhouse gate" (*Tinker v. Des Moines Sch. Dist.*, 1969, p. 506). However, it is equally clear that school authorities have a strong and valid interest in maintaining school discipline and in carrying out their educational mission.

The *Tinker* case (1969), established the standard that prohibiting student speech or expression, without any evidence that the restraint is necessary to avoid substantial interference with school discipline or the rights of others, is not permissible under the First Amendment (p. 508). However, *Bethel Sch. Dist. v. Fraser* (1986), held that the First Amendment rights of public school students "are not automatically coextensive with the rights of adults in other settings" and that schools may prohibit on-campus student speech that is vulgar, lewd, or indecent because such discourse is inconsistent with the fundamental values of public school education (p. 683). The *Bethel* court determined that a school's interest in prohibiting vulgar and lewd speech outweighs whatever First Amendment interests a student might have, and that in the pursuit of pedagogical goals, school authorities are entitled to regulate speech in a way that would be impermissible outside the school context (pp. 683–685). Further, in *Hazelwood Sch. Dist. v. Kuhlmeier* (1988), the United States Supreme Court held that when a school sponsors an activity in such a way that students and others may reasonably perceive the activity as having the school's permission, the school has the right to restrict student speech (p. 273). Lastly, *Morse v. Frederick* (2007), extended the lewd speech standard from *Bethel* to speech that advocates for students to violate school policy, holding that the First Amendment did not protect such speech (Morse, p. 2622).

Each of the above cases involved speech that occurred on school property. In *Tinker* (1969), students wore armbands protesting the Vietnam War; in *Bethel* (1986), the lewd phrases were part of a student assembly speech; in *Hazelwood* (1988), student authored school newspaper articles were censored; and, in *Morse* (2007), students violated school policy with a banner advocating drug use. While varying in communication channels, all of these forms of speech occurred at school. What is the standard when "speech" is virtual, and only exists on the internet? Many recent cases have considered this emerging legal issue, with mixed results.

In *Doninger v. Niehoff* (2011), the plaintiff authored a blog post calling school administrators "douchebags" after they canceled a "battle of the bands" competition; as a result, she was told she could not run for student council secretary. The plaintiff filed a lawsuit alleging that the school violated her First Amendment rights when they disciplined her for an online blog post she made off school grounds on her personal time. In finding for the school, both the district court and the United States Court of Appeals for the Second Circuit applied the *Tinker* standard. The courts held that the school did not violate plaintiff's right to free speech because her conduct posed a reasonably foreseeable risk that it would come to the attention of school authorities and materially and substantially disrupt the work and discipline of the school. Although the speech in this case was online, the *Doniger* court did not consider that material.

However, in *J.S. v. Blue Mountain School District* (2011), the United States Court of Appeals for the Third Circuit reached a different result. The plaintiff, an eighth grade student, created a fake MySpace page for the school principal. The profile characterized the principal as a sex-obsessed pedophile, and it was laced with profanity and other negative comments about the principal and his family. The school suspended the two students for 10 days after determining that the students had violated the school discipline code, which prohibited making false accusations against school staff members. The plaintiff filed a

lawsuit alleging that the schools punishment for non-disruptive, out-of-school speech violated her First Amendment rights. The Third Circuit court applied both the *Tinker* and *Bethel* standards to the case, and held that the school violated plaintiffs' rights because the student's conduct did not cause a substantial disruption in school, and the standard for lewd speech does not apply to off-campus speech. Also of note is *Kowalski v. Berkley County Schools* (2011), in which the United States Court of Appeals for the Fourth Circuit held that off-campus speech consisting of bullying and harassment that was intended to impact the school environment is not protected by the First Amendment.

In a student-athlete specific case, *T.V. v. Smith Green Community School Corporation* (2011), the plaintiffs were members of the volleyball team who the school suspended from participating in any extra-curricular activities (athletic or otherwise) for a full academic year. The volleyball players took multiple sexually suggestive and graphic photos at a sleepover party, using a phallic lollipop as a prop. The students posted the photos on their MySpace and Facebook accounts, and shared the photos virtually through these mediums. After a parent of another volleyball player advised the school about the photos, the school principal disciplined the girls, claiming that the photographs constituted a violation of the student handbook and could result in school disruption. In applying the *Tinker* standard, the district court found that while showing an actual school disruption is not required to limit student speech, a specific and significant fear of disruption is; a remote apprehension of disturbance is not sufficient. Because the school officials in this case could not point to any students creating or experiencing actual disruption during a school activity, the court found that the punishment imposed on the plaintiffs violated their First Amendment rights.

Given the above case law, there are two primary issues to consider when evaluating whether student speech protected by the Constitution. First, how is the speech classified, and second did the speech occur virtually and off-campus, or more traditionally and on school grounds. Regarding speech classification, three distinct types of student speech have emerged: (1) obscene, vulgar, and plainly offensive speech; (2) speech that bears the permission of the school; and (3) speech that falls into neither of these two categories. Per *Bethel* (1986) and *Hazelwood* (1988), the First Amendment does likely not protect the first two categories. However, speech that falls into neither of the two categories is governed by the standards set forth in the *Tinker* case, and school officials must justify their decision to restrict speech by showing facts that might reasonably have led school authorities to forecast substantial disruption of or material interference with school activities (*Tinker*, 1969, p. 514). Regarding how and where the speech occurred, traditional, on-campus speech is easier to assess. However, virtual off-campus speech presents significant challenges. There is clear dissent in the courts, with the federal appellate courts reaching different conclusions when applying the same standards for analyzing student speech. Although the United States Supreme Court failed to grant certiorari on this issue three separate times in 2011, this is very much an emerging issue that the United States Supreme Court is likely to settle eventually (Lindsay, 2012).

Lastly, it is worth noting that when college students have filed lawsuits alleging imposition on their speech rights, the majority of courts have clearly found in favor of the students, refusing to place exceptions on free speech rights in a university setting. There are exceptions to this, most notably *Tatro v. University of Minnesota*, (2012), which applied the *Tinker* standard to a university student and found in favor of the University. However, most courts agree that "college-age students being exposed to a wide range of intellectual experience creates a relatively mature marketplace for the interchange of ideas so that the free speech

clause of the First Amendment with its underlying assumption that there is positive social value in an open forum seems particularly appropriate" (*Antonelli v. Hammond*, 1970).

Another emerging issue regarding free speech that does significantly affect college athletes relates to social media. With new technologies and social media platforms emerging almost daily, and millions of users globally across multiple platforms, the reach of social media is significant (Han, Dodds, Mahoney, Schoepfer, & Lovich, 2015). Social media use is also especially high among collegiate student-athletes. Specifically, a 2012 study indicated "93.5% of student-athletes had a Facebook account, 72.2% of student-athletes had Twitter accounts, and 64.8% had an Instagram account" (Han, et al., 2015 quoting DeShazo, 2013).

Given the pervasive use of social media by student-athletes, the regulation of its use is not surprising; in the past 10 years, many college athletic departments have disciplined student-athletes for alleged inappropriate social media use. The NCAA does not specifically require member schools to regulate social media; nor do college conferences. However, many college/universities have strict policies in place. For example, student-athletes have been suspended or otherwise disciplined for doing the following on Facebook: posting inappropriate photos on personal pages; using racial derogatory language; posting photos related to hazing incidents; and using expletives (Han et al., 2015). Additionally, inappropriate tweets have also resulted in sanctions against both student-athletes and universities. In 2014, a Kent State suspended a wrestler indefinitely after a series of tweets containing homophobic language and slurs. In 2012, Notre Dame, the University of Michigan and the University of Minnesota reported secondary recruiting violations based on tweets exchanged between athletes and recruits (Han et al., 2015).

In addition to disciplining student-athletes for social media use, college/university athletic departments are also monitoring or restricting student-athlete use of various social media platforms. Some monitoring is informal, such as coaches requiring athletes to allow coaching staff access to the accounts. For example, a team policy may be that all athletes must accept friend requests on Facebook, or a follower request on Twitter from a designated coach to allow the coach to monitor the social media activity. Other monitoring, however, is far more formal. Some teams choose to purchase "monitoring software systems such as Varsity Monitor, UDiligence, Centrix, and Fieldhouse Media that identify keywords on student-athlete social media accounts that may tarnish the reputation of the student-athlete, team, or university" (Han et al., 2015, p. 9). Specifically, athletic departments purchase the software and require student-athletes to install it on all computers, tablets, and cell phones (Han et al., 2015). Even stricter than monitoring, are coaches who ban use of social media entirely, either during the season, or for the entire year. Boise State's Chris Petersen, South Carolina's Steve Spurrier, and Florida's Jimbo Fisher are coaches who have banned Twitter in-season; Old Dominion's Bobby Wilder banned his football players from using Twitter year round (Steinbach, 2012).

Clearly, colleges and universities are concerned about the impact student-athlete social media use will have on the reputation and success of their athletic programs. However, does that concern warrant the potential violation of student-athlete free speech rights under the First Amendment? Legal scholars have varying opinions regarding the constitutionality of the restrictions, monitoring and sanctions; further, courts have yet to consider this issue. Some scholars advocate that these practices are constitutional, reasoning that free speech does not entitle a person to say whatever they want, for any reason, without having repercussions. Further, these scholars assert that as long as the school has a good reason, to maintain order and discipline, it can regulate speech (Steinbach,

2012). Alternatively, some legal experts argue that these practices present significant legal concern, and could potentially be actionable under the First Amendment.

Freedom of Religion

In addition to the language guaranteeing freedom of speech, the First Amendment also provides the freedom of religion, set forth in the *Establishment clause* and the *Free Exercise clause*. The Establishment clause to the First Amendment "protects every individual's right to freedom of belief while the Free Exercise Clause protects the individual's freedom to practice his [or her] religion" (*Malnak v. Yogi*, 1977). Specifically, state actors must not create a rule or policy respecting an establishment of religion, or prohibiting the free exercise thereof. Problematically, there is an inherent dichotomy in these two clauses. If an interscholastic or intercollegiate governing body (assuming they are a state actor) specifically allows or prohibits religious based expression, that action may violate freedom of religion protections. As with freedom of speech, courts have specifically addressed and clarified the religious freedoms of school students in the past several decades; Establishment clause cases analyze a student's right to be free from religion, and Free Exercise clause cases analyze a student's right to freely express his or her religion.

The Establishment clause, at its core, advances the common notion of "separation of church and state" (*Everson v. Board of Education*, 1947). As such, plaintiffs have called on the courts to determine what constitutes a state actor establishing religion, in violation of the First Amendment. Courts have considered this question in many contexts, not exclusively in the school setting; however, the legal standards that have emerged from the case law are applicable in the school setting.

Specifically, three standards have evolved from the case law; the "Lemon test" (*Lemon v. Kurtzman*, 1971), the "Coercion test" (*Lee v. Weisman*, 1992), and the "Endorsement test" (*Lynch v. Donnelly*, 1984). To determine if a challenged rule or practice establishes religion, the *Lemon test* uses a three-criteria analysis: (1) does the rule have a secular (non-religious) purpose; (2) does the rule advance (or inhibit) religion; and (3) does the rule foster an excessive entanglement between religion and the state actor (*Lemon v. Kurtzman*, 1971). By contrast, the *Coercion test* considers whether a challenged rule or practice "obliges the participation of objectors" (*Jones v. Clear Creek Independent School District*, 1992, p. 970). This test did evolve from a school setting case and found the school unreasonably coerced students to participate in a religious activity. Lastly, the *Endorsement test* evaluates whether a challenged rule or practice communicates a message that endorses a particular religion, thus establishing religion and violating the First Amendment (Brown-Foster, 2010). The state actor cannot endorse, promote, or favor any religious belief or practice (*County of Allegheny v. American Civil Liberties Union*, 1989).

Although all three tests are still valid legal precedent, courts considering Establishment clause cases where school students (or their parents) are the plaintiffs tend to rely on the Coercion or Endorsement tests to determine if schools are encroaching on religious freedoms. In addition, school setting cases have challenged establishment of religion in many contexts other than athletics. There is significant case law discussing whether prayer at graduation and other school ceremonies is constitutional. The majority of these cases hold that administrative control is likely to render a prayer or religious speech constitutionally impermissible; however, prayer that students independently initiate and lead is likely constitutional (Brown-Foster, 2010, citing *Alder v. Duvall County School Board*, 2001; *Jones v. Clear Creek Independent School District*, 1992; *Santa Fe High Independent School District v. Doe*, 2000).

Regarding athletic events, the case of note is *Santa Fe High Independent School District v. Doe* (2000), in which the United States Supreme Court decided that delivering a prayer over the public address system prior to a football game was an unconstitutional establishment of religion. Specifically, the high school in question had a policy that allowed a student elected student chaplain to deliver a prayer prior to the start of each home football game. Students at the school (and their mothers) filed a lawsuit alleging that this practice violated the Establishment clause. While the lawsuit was at the district court level, the school modified the policy to require a student vote to determine whether the pre-game activities would include an invocation (the term prayer was eliminated), and which student would lead the invocation. The district court further modified the policy to allow only a "nonsectarian, nonproselytizing" invocation (*Santa Fe v. Doe*, 2000, p. 291). Even after the school district modified the policy, the Court of Appeals and United States Supreme Court struck down the policy as unconstitutional establishment of religion. In doing so, the court relied on facts of the case that demonstrated the school was still distinctly involved in the religious activity, although it claimed otherwise. The prayer turned invocation had a long history in the school of delivering a religious message, the principal was heavily involved in the student election process, and a stated purpose of the invocation was to "solemnize the event" (*Santa Fe v. Doe*, 2000, p. 295). Using both the Coercion test and the Endorsement test in its analysis, the United States Supreme Court held that students who attended the football games were coerced to listen to the message, and that those listening to the Santa Fe invocation would unquestionably perceive it as endorsed by the school.

As noted, the Establishment clause is only one aspect of protected religious freedoms; many cases also consider the Free Exercise clause in the school setting. Specifically, many interscholastic athletes have tested their rights under the Free Exercise clause of the First Amendment. These cases have included issues such as the scheduling of practices and games, the conducting of prayer sessions before games, the wearing of religious headwear during competition, and grooming policies. For example, in *Keller v. Gardener Community Consolidated Grade School District* (1982), an elementary school student and his father challenged a rule that required attendance at practice in order to play in the game. Eleven-year-old Joseph Keller missed practice because he attended religion classes scheduled by his Catholic Church at the same time as basketball practice. The coach failed to make an exception for Joseph, and a lawsuit followed. In finding in favor of the defendant school district, the court considered whether the coach's rule violated the plaintiff's right to freely exercise religion. Given that the church offered the plaintiff's religion classes at times other than the scheduled practice time, the court found that the plaintiff did not establish interference with his free exercise of religion, but only with his selection of a church in which to pursue his religion. The court also considered the impact on the basketball program of an alternative to the current school policy and found that an alternative scheduling arrangement would not be appropriate because the school could not successfully pre-arrange a practice schedule that would accommodate the religious education class of each of the many participants in the athletic program.

By contrast, plaintiffs in *Menora v. Illinois High School Association* (1982) successfully challenged their religious free exercise rights. Specifically, student sought to wear a yarmulke during a high school basketball game and the school refused. A state association forbid basketball players to wear hats or other headwear, with the sole exception of a headband no wider than two inches, while playing. The primary concern behind this prohibition was that the headwear might fall off in the heat of play and one of the players might trip or slip on it, fall, and injure himself. The plaintiffs in the case were five members of interscholastic basketball

teams at two Orthodox Jewish high schools, the high schools themselves, and the players' parents. The plaintiffs challenged the rule as an infringement of the religious freedom of orthodox Jews who are required by their religion "to cover their heads at all times except when they are (a) unconscious, (b) immersed in water or (c) in imminent danger of loss of life" (p. 1032). The plaintiffs asserted that Orthodox Jews who play basketball comply, or at least try to comply, with this requirement by wearing yarmulkes (small skullcaps that cover the crown of the head) fastened to the hair with bobby pins. With yarmulkes forbidden, plaintiffs asserted that the rule forced them to choose between their religious observances and participating in interscholastic basketball, which was the only interscholastic sport in which the athletes at plaintiff schools participate (p. 1033). The district court ruled in favor of the plaintiffs, holding that the state did not assert a safety rule sufficient to overcome the plaintiffs' First Amendment right to exercise their religious beliefs. The United States Court of Appeals for the Seventh Circuit vacated that decision and remanded the case back to the district court, requiring the plaintiffs to suggest alternate headwear that would satisfy the state association's safety requirements, yet also comply with the tenants of Orthodox Judaism. On remand, the district court again found for the plaintiffs (they had successfully asserted an alternate solution).

More recently, the courts considered the Free Exercise clause in the coaching context, addressing whether a school can restrict a coach from participating in pre-game prayers with student-athletes. In *Borden v. School District and the Township of East Brunswick* (2008), the head football coach led his team in prayer prior to games, at pre-game dinners, and in the team locker room; the coach had a 23-year history of these religious observances. The school received a complaint about the activities, and the school district informed Borden he could no longer participate in the religious activity. Borden complied and no longer led the prayers; however, he was present in the room with a bowed head when his students led the prayers. The school district again instructed Borden that he was not to participate at all in the religious observances, and Borden filed a lawsuit alleging that the restrictions violated his protected free exercise rights. On appeal from a district court ruling in favor of the school district, the United States Court of Appeals for the Third Circuit upheld the school district policy. The court found that the school did not violate Borden's free exercise rights, and that Borden's participation in the religious activities was unconstitutional endorsement of religion, which the school had a right to prevent. The court reasoned that Borden's 23-year history of praying with the team in multiple venues could not be erased, and that such history would lead any observer to conclude that Borden, as a representative of the school, was endorsing religion. Borden appealed his case to the United States Supreme Court; however, they denied certiorari, leaving the Third Circuit ruling in effect.

Although *Borden v. Township of East Brunswick* (2008) is a free exercise case, it also serves as another example of a courts reluctance to hold constitutional prayer in a school setting that school administrators or employees direct or otherwise influence. This echoes previous cases that find religious activity that is voluntary and led by students permissible, while religious activity that schools influence is not.

Coach Borden is not the only coach to come under fire for praying with student-athletes. In September 2015, the Freedom from Religion Foundation (FFRF) produced a report titled *Pray to Play: Christian Coaches and Chaplains are Converting Football Fields into Mission Fields* (Seidel, 2015). The report contends that many public state universities allow coaches and Christian chaplains to lead teams in bible study, pre-game prayer, and chapel services (p. 3). Further, universities fund these chaplains, as well as provide meals, tickets, and travel to reimburse the services (p. 3). The report alleges that these practices are pervasive and an unconstitutional Establishment clause violation. Given the current climate in society regarding religious practice and religious freedom, these practices will likely continue until a court (the United States Supreme Court) eventually determines whether these challenged practices are permissible.

FIFTH AND FOURTEENTH AMENDMENTS: DUE PROCESS, EQUAL PROTECTION, AND STUDENT-ATHLETE ELIGIBILITY

The Fifth Amendment of the United States Constitution contains the *Due Process Clause*; this clause states that no person shall be deprived of life, liberty, or property without due process of law (United States Constitution, Amendment V). The Fourteenth Amendment of the United States Constitution provides that no state shall deny to any person equal protection of the laws; this is known as the *Equal Protection Clause* (United States Constitution, Amendment XIV). Thus, the Fourteenth Amendment applies the Due Process clause (and all other Amendments) to the states. Interscholastic and intercollegiate athletes have used both the Fifth and Fourteenth Amendments to challenge eligibility decisions related to rules such as transfer policies, conduct codes, personal appearance and grooming standards, and maximum age limits. These lawsuits often include a combination of federal constitutional issues and state law issues; also, many combine both due process and equal protection challenges.

There are two significant considerations in any Due Process Clause analysis. First, did the state actor deprive an individual of life, liberty, or property? Second, were an individual's substantive or procedural due process rights violated? In considering the first question in the athletic context, sport-governing bodies never deprive a person of life. However, courts have addressed whether a governing body has compromised a student-athletes liberty or property interests related to sport participation. Of these two considerations, the most common is the property right; student-athletes in both high school and college have alleged that governing bodies have violated their protected property rights.

Prior to the 1970s, courts defined property rights in a traditional sense; property was considered something of value that could be exchanged or possessed. However, courts began to broaden this definition in the early 1970s to include anything that an individual was entitled to (*Board of Regents v. Roth*, 1972). In *Goss v. Lopez* (1975), the United States Supreme Court stated that high school students have a constitutionally protected property right in education, and that a state actor cannot revoke that right without fair process. Classifying education as a protected property right gave rise to a litany of cases that asserted the education right included a right to participate in interscholastic athletics, as interscholastic sports are part of a student's overall education. While some courts agreed with this assertion (*Butler v. Oak Creek-Franklin School District*, 2000; *Duffley v. New Hampshire Interscholastic Athletic Association*, 1982), the majority of jurisdictions have found that there is no protected property right in interscholastic athletics participation (Wolohan, 2013, citing *Bruce v. S.C. High School League*, 1972; *Albach v. Odle*, 1976; *Hamilton v. Tennessee Secondary School Association*, 1976; *Menke v. Ohio High School Athletic Association*, 1981; *Simkins v. S.D. High School Activities Association*, 1989). College athletes playing on scholarship have fared better when asserting a protected property right; such right is typically found in their scholarship. Additionally, there is limited case law assigning

a property right to a future professional career (Wolohan, 2013).

Returning to the second question above, assuming a student-athlete has established a liberty or property right in their athletics participation, courts must next consider whether a student's rights to substantive or procedural due process have been violated. Substantive due process "guarantees basic rights that cannot be denied by governmental action" (Wong, 1988). Substantive due process considers whether state actors apply rules in a fair and consistent manner. In the absence of fraud, mistake, collusion, or arbitrariness, the courts generally will not interfere with the internal affairs of state actors and voluntary associations, and will not question the substantive fairness of a rule. Next, procedural due process guarantees the process used to deprive an individual of a right is fair. Per *Goss v. Lopez* (1975) and other similar cases, procedural due process requires published standards, notice of the charge against the student, advance notice regarding the time and location of a hearing, an impartial decision maker, writing findings, and an appeals procedure (Wolohan, 2013).

State actors must adhere to due process protections when student-athletes meet the necessary criteria; so to, they must provide equal protection under the law. The Equal Protection Clause is found in the Fourteenth Amendment and guarantees that no person is discriminated against under the law or "singled out from similarly situated people" unless there is a constitutionally permissible reason for doing so (Wong, 1988). The Equal Protection Clause provides individuals with a means of challenging the constitutionality of a rule or law that has deprived them of a fundamental right or has singled them out for different treatment based on their membership in a prescribed category of people. In addition, the Equal Protect Clause only provides protection against intentional discrimination.

Specifically, courts use three separate standards to determine whether a state actor has violated a person's equal protection rights. The first standard is *strict scrutiny*; this says that a state actor's rule or law must be necessary to achieve a compelling state interest. This standard is used if the challenged rule or action discriminates against individuals based on their race, ethnicity, or national origin. Next, is *intermediate scrutiny*, which requires a state actor's rule or law to be substantially related to an important state interest; this standard is used if the challenged rule or action discriminates against individuals based on gender. The third standard is the *rational basis* test, which is used by all plaintiffs who are members of all other groups. Rational basis requires that the state actor's rule or law be reasonably related to a legitimate state interest.

As noted, interscholastic and intercollegiate student-athletes have used both the Due Process Clause and the Equal Protection clause to challenge various rules and policies of schools and state associations related to eligibility. Athletic eligibility is the key to participation in amateur sports, and sports' governing bodies must deem student-athletes eligible. Athletic associations providing eligibility rules dictate who can participate as well as how student-athletes can participate. High school and collegiate competition is considered "restricted" competition. A local school district, the state high school athletic association, or both may regulate an interscholastic athlete. At the intercollegiate level, athletic conferences and the national governing entity govern the eligibility and rules of participation of the student-athlete.

Governing bodies at both levels base eligibility on many requirements; student-athletes have challenged most of them. For example, student-athletes often challenge transfer regulations. In *Indiana High School Athletic Association v. Carlberg*, 1997, plaintiff Jason Carlberg was a student at Brebeuf Prepatory Academy as a freshman and a member of the swim team. Prior to his sophomore year, Carlberg transferred to Carmel High School for academic reasons, and did not

change his permanent address. The Indiana High School Athletic Association (IHSAA) applied its transfer rule and determined that for his first year at Carmel High, Carlberg was not eligible to be on the swim team (he was eligible for all other sports). After Carlberg exhausted all appeal mechanisms afforded by IHSAA, he filed a lawsuit claiming that application of the transfer rule violated his due process (procedural) and equal protection rights under the United States Constitution. The trial court agreed with Carlberg and enjoined IHSAA from enforcing the transfer rule; the appellate court upheld this decision. However, the Indiana Supreme Court reversed, finding that Carlberg had no constitutional right to participate in interscholastic athletics (property right), thus the IHSAA did not owe Carlberg procedural due process. Regarding the equal protection claim, the court found that Carlberg was not a member of a suspect class or quasi-suspect class, thus the rational basis test was appropriate. Under this standard, the IHSAA needed to prove the rule was reasonably related to a legitimate state interest. The court held that preserving the integrity of interscholastic athletics and preventing recruiting at the high school level provided a rational basis for the rule.

Other eligibility rules often challenged relate to student conduct. In *Brands v. Sheldon Community School* (1987), the high school declared a state champion wrestler ineligible after allegations surfaced that he and three other students had multiple acts of sexual intercourse with a 16-year-old student at his home. These acts violated the school discipline policy, which allowed for punishment if a student's conduct was detrimental to the best interests of the school district. After a series appeals at the school level, and a successful grant of *injunctive relief*, which allowed Brands to participate in sectional qualifying competition, the district court reviewed the claim. Brands claimed that his suspension violated his rights to equal protection, substantive due process, and procedural due process, among other constitution law claims. The court found that no equal protection claim existed because the plaintiff was not a member of a suspect or quasi-suspect class, and the *rational basis test*, when applied to the facts, showed that the school's discipline code was reasonably related to a legitimate school interest.

Regarding due process, the court considered whether Brands had a property right to participate on the wrestling team. Specifically, the court considered whether a future potential college scholarship established a property right, or whether the school disciplinary policy itself, which required mandatory procedural measures when a student was suspended, established a property right. When considering the potential scholarship, the court distinguished this case from others that have found a property right in the initial grant of a college scholarship. Because Brands had not yet received one, the court found no property right. When considering whether the disciplinary policy itself created a property right, the court did not specifically answer the question. Rather, the court found that even if a property right existed, the school satisfied the procedural due process requirement by providing Brands notice of the charges, a hearing, and an opportunity to appeal. As for substantive due process, the court found that the school did not deny Brands his basic rights, and that his discipline was consistent with other students who violated the disciplinary policy.

A more recent example of a student conduct challenge is *Sacramento State University Men's Rowing Club v. California State Univ.* (2014). The plaintiff student organization was a Tier One Rowing Club, open to students only as a club sport. In December 2012, a rowing alumni and assistant coach for the program competed with the team in a Holiday Row competition. The plaintiff argued that such alumni participation was customary when current team members did not fill a boat; however, the assistant director for Club Sports suspended the team for 10 weeks.

The plaintiff filed a lawsuit alleging that when the University suspended the organization, they did so without affording the plaintiff procedural due process. The plaintiff argued that the University created a property right to participate in extra-curricular activities when it adopted mandatory policies governing club sports. The University disagreed, maintaining that the plaintiff did not have a property right, because the policies did not contain mandatory procedures, rather the procedures were permissive. As such, the University maintained that it did not owe the club due process. In finding for the University, the district court found that the plaintiff failed to demonstrate a protectable property interest necessary for the claim to proceed. The district court stated "a clear majority of courts addressing this question in the context of interscholastic or intercollegiate athletics has found that athletes have no legitimate entitlement to participate" (*Brands v. Sheldon Community School*, 1987). The district court also found governing policies permitted the University to discipline the club, but did not establish entitlement to participate or due process. Previous cases have found that documents such as student conduct codes are sufficient to create a property right (*Butler v. Oak Creek-Franklin School District,* 2000), but the *Sacramento* district court was unwilling to do so.

Personal grooming and appearance cases are also common. In *Hayden ex rel A.H. v. Greensburg Community School Corp* (2014), an eighth grade male student tried out for the boys basketball team, and was given a roster spot. However, the school athletic code had a "Dress and Grooming" policy that prohibited boys from having long hair; specifically, the rule required that boys wear their hair above the ears and collar. When the student showed up for practice without having cut his hair, the coach dismissed from the team. The boy's mother discussed the policy with the coach, the school principal, and the superintendent, but the school provided no recourse. As such, the mother filed a lawsuit on her son's behalf, claiming that the school's policy and his dismissal from the team violated substantive and procedural due process rights, and that the policy constituted sex discrimination in violation of the Equal Protection clause because no female trying out for any sport was subject to a like grooming policy. After careful analysis, the district court found in favor of the school district on all claims.

First, the district court considered whether the student had a protected liberty or property interest in participating in interscholastic athletics. Following the majority of cases that find no property right in extracurricular activities, the court rejected the property right. However, the court did find that a person's liberty interest in wearing their hair in a style of their choosing is a protected right. Even with this finding though, the district court held that school students are not entitled to the same level of protection as regular citizens, and that schools may enforce dress and grooming codes without compromising a students protected liberty interests. Regarding the due process claims, the court held that even in the case a liberty interest did exist, the school afforded the student procedural due process when the mother met with the coach, principal and superintendent. Regarding substantive due process, the court rejected the plaintiff's claim that the school applied the rule against her son in an arbitrary manner. Regarding the equal protection claim, the district court based its finding for the school district on the fact that plaintiffs could not prove the gender-based discrimination was intentional, and intentional discrimination is requisite for an equal protection claim to succeed.

On appeal, the United States Court of Appeals for the Seventh Circuit reversed, in part, the district court's ruling. The appellate court agreed that no due process violations (substantive or procedural) existed; however, the appeals court did substantiate an equal protection claim, arguing that the plaintiffs established a case of discrimination and that the school intentionally imposed a gender-based standard when regulating the hair length of male students. This decision was narrow, and based on procedural issues within the case; however, the case does serve as precedent that grooming policies that differ based on gender may violate student rights to equal protection.

CONCLUSION

Interscholastic and intercollegiate governance are elaborate functions; both levels of sport have a myriad of rules and policies that dictate student-athlete rights and responsibilities. While the governance structures at both levels are well defined, issues still arise related to creating and enforcing rules. In addition, student-athlete constitutional rights (assuming the governing body is a state actor) further compound the challenges in interscholastic and intercollegiate sport governance. Administrators at both levels of sport must be aware of the legal issues surrounding sport participation and rules enforcement, and the potential legal challenges student-athletes may bring. Further, administrators must recognize that many of the legal issues are currently unsettled, and student-athletes may continue to test the availability of legal remedy.

DISCUSSION QUESTIONS

State Action

1. In *Howard University v. NCAA* (1975), a case prior to *Tarkanian*, the NCAA was held to be a
    state actor. *Howard* dealt with a soccer player who the NCAA declared ineligible. The asso-
    ciation sanctioned Howard University as a result of the violation. The court, in finding state
    action on the part of the NCAA, stated:

    > Approximately half of the NCAA's 655 institutional members are state or federally sup-
    > ported. Since financial contribution to the NCAA is based upon institutional size, and
    > since public universities generally have the largest student bodies, the public institu-
    > tions provide the vast majority of the NCAA's capital (the NCAA's annual administrative
    > budget at the time of the suit being $1.3 million). Principal power in the Association
    > lies with the Convention, which is made up of representatives of the member institu-
    > tions. The Convention elects the governing Council and the NCAA's principal officers,
    > adopts and amends the constitution and Bylaws, and reviews all Council and committee
    > actions. As can be seen from this description, the state instrumentalities are a dominant
    > force in determining NCAA policy and in dictating NCAA actions. That conclusion is
    > buttressed by reference to the record before us which documents that both the President
    > and Secretary-Treasurer were representatives of public instrumentalities and that state
    > instrumentalities traditionally provided the majority of the members of the governing
    > Council and the various committees. Thus, governmental involvement, while not exclu-
    > sive, is 'significant,' and all NCAA actions appear 'impregnated with a governmental
    > character.'
    >
    > The NCAA's regulation and supervision over intercollegiate athletics is extensive and
    > represents an immeasurably valuable service for its member institutions. The NCAA
    > conducts championship events in most sports for the benefit of its member institu-
    > tions. The Association regulates the amateur status of student-athletes, sets financial aid
    > policies, prescribes playing and practice seasons, fixes minimum academic standards,
    > establishes standards for approved extra events and determines eligibility for intercol-
    > legiate competition and NCAA championships. The NCAA also negotiates television
    > contracts, the proceeds of which, $13,000,000 annually, flow directly to the partici-
    > pating schools, primarily the public universities. The foregoing analysis indicates that
    > the NCAA and its member public instrumentalities are joined in a mutually beneficial
    > relationship, and in fact may be fairly said to form the type of symbiotic relationship
    > between public and private entities which triggers constitutional scrutiny. (pp. 219–220)

    Do you agree with the court's analysis in *Howard*? What was different about the NCAA's
    makeup at the time the court decided the *Howard* case as opposed to today? One of the
    arguments made by the court in *Howard* in support of state action by the NCAA was the

(continues)

DISCUSSION QUESTIONS (CONTINUED)

$13 million it received in television contracts annually. The association clearly receives in excess of that today. Does that affect your decision concerning the NCAA and state action?

2. What is the basis for courts determining that the NCAA is not a state actor? Under what circumstances could the NCAA become a state actor?

First Amendment: Freedom of Speech

1. Reconsider the case law that analyzes whether schools can discipline students for speech that occurs off school property, on a student's own time. If you were an Athletic Director at a public high school, would you specifically create a policy regulating this speech? Why or why not? What does the case law tell you regarding what type of discipline might be appropriate?

2. If you were an Athletic Director at a state college or university, would you monitor or restrict student-athlete social media use? Why or why not?

First Amendment: Freedom of Religion

1. Kathy Mitchell is a devout Christian. She attends church regularly and is active in her youth group at church. She is an honor student and an All-District basketball player at Lamar High School. As part of her way to show her faith, she wears a cross around her neck on a chain. She wears the cross during games as well. During a game with their archrival, the opposing coach requests that the referee require Mitchell to remove her cross, citing a rule of the local High School Athletic Association that states: "During practice or competitive events student-athletes are prohibited from wearing any form of jewelry." Mitchell refuses to take off the cross, and the referee forfeits the match against Lamar High School. Mitchell files a lawsuit against the Association alleging religious discrimination. Will she win? What defenses are available?

2. The *Borden* case provides a clear standard for what coaching behaviors are constitutionally permissible regarding team prayer. Given these standards, why do so many coaches continue to lead team prayers (as evidenced in the FFRF report). Is there an inherent relationship between religion or prayer and sports that makes these actions seem permissible? If you were an athletic director at a public high school, college or university, would you allow your head coaches to lead their teams in prayer or otherwise pray with the team? Would it matter which area of the country you were in?

Due Process, Equal Protection, and Student-athlete Eligibility

1. As the majority of cases in this chapter make clear, high school students do not have a protected property interest in participating in sports. Usually, the courts will not find a right to participate in interscholastic athletics, but rather find that participation is a privilege, and therefore not entitled to Due Process claims. This is rooted in an even stronger debate:

DISCUSSION QUESTIONS (CONTINUED)

whether there is a constitutional right to an education, and further, whether athletic participation is a component of education. What do you think?

2. A minority of student-athletes succeed on due process and equal protection claims. When taken into consideration along with other constitutional protections and majority outcomes, one could argue that student constitutional protections have greatly diminished in the past 50 years. Do you agree? Is this worrisome?

KEY TERMS

Amateur athletes

Coercion test

Due process clause

Endorsement test

Entanglement or nexus theory

Equal protection clause

Establishment clause

Free Exercise clause

Governing bodies

Injunctive relief

Intermediate scrutiny

Interscholastic athletics

Lemon test

Public function theory

Rational basis test

State athletic associations

State action

Strict scrutiny

REFERENCES

About Us. National Federation of State High School Associations. (2015). Retrieved from http://www.nfhs.org/who-we-are/aboutus

Associated Students v. NCAA, 493 F.2d 1251 (9th Cir. 1974).

Bethel Sch. Dist. v. Fraser, 478 U.S. 675 (1986).

Borden v. School District and the Township of East Brunswick, 523 F.3d 153 (3rd. Cir. 2008).

Brands v. Sheldon Community School, 671 F.Supp. 627 (N.D. Iowa 1987).

Brentwood Academy v. Tennessee Secondary School Athletic Association, 531 U.S. 288 (2001).

Brown-Foster, S. (2010). Religious Issues. In *Law for Recreation and Sport Managers 3rd ed.* (p. 524-534). Dubuque, IA: Kendall Hunt.

Buckton v. NCAA, 366 F. Supp. 1152 (D. Mass. 1973).

Burton v. Wilmington Parking Authority, 365 U.S. 715 (1961).

Butler v. Oak Creek-Franklin School District, 116 F.Supp.2d 1038 (2000).

Chandler v. McMinnville Sch. Dist., 978 F.2d 524, 529 (9th Cir. 1992).

County of Allegheny v. American Civil Liberties Union, 492 U.S. 573 (1989).

Football's death record of 1907. (1907). *New York Times,* November 24.

Goss v. Lopez, 419 U.S. 565 (1975).

Griffin v. Illinois High School Association, 822 F.2d 671 (1987).

Hayden ex rel A.H. v. Greensburg Community School Corp, 743 F.3d 569 (7th Cir. 2014).

Hazelwood Sch. Dist. v. Kuhlmeier, 484 U.S. 260 (1988).

High school athletics participation survey. (2014). Retrieved from http://www.nfhs.org/ParticipationStatics /PDF/2013-14_Participation_Survey_PDF.pdf

Howard University v. NCAA, 510 F.2d 213 (D.C. Cir. 1975).

Indiana High School Athletic Association v. Carlberg, 694 N.E.2d 222 (1997).

Jones v. Clear Creek Independent School District, 977 F.2d 963 (1992).

Keller v. Gardener Community Consolidated Grade School District, 552 F. Supp. 512 (D.C. Ill., 1982)

Lee v. Weisman, 505 U.S. 577 (1992).

Lemon v. Kurtzman, 403 U.S. 602 (1971).

Lindsay, M. (2012). Tinker goes to college: Why high-school free speech standards should not apply to post-secondary students—Tatro v. University of Minnesota. *William Mitchell Law Review, 38*(4), Article 5.

Lynch v. Donnelly, 465 U.S. 668 (1984).

Malnak v. Yogi, 440 F.Supp. 1284 (D.C. N.J. 1977).

Masteralexis, L. P., Barr, C. A., Hums, M. (2012). *Principles and practice of sports management* (4th ed.). Sudbury, MA: Jones and Bartlett.

Menora v. Illinois High School Ass'n, 683 F.2d 1030 (7th Cir. 1982).

Mitten, M., Davis, T., Smith, R., & Berry, R. (2009). *Sports law and regulation: Cases, materials, and problems* (2nd ed.). New York: Aspen.

Morse v. Frederick, 127 S.Ct. 2618 (2007).

NCAA v. Tarkanian, 488 U.S. 179 (1988).

NFHS Handbook. (2013–2014). Retrieved from https://www .nfhs.org/media/885654/2013-14-nfhs-handbook.pdf

Parish v. NCAA, 361 F. Supp. 1220 (W.D. La. 1973).

Sacramento State University Men's Rowing Club v. California State Univ., 2014 WL 546694 (E.D. Cal. Feb. 11, 2014).

Santa Fe High Independent School District v. Doe, 530 U.S. 290 (2000).

Seidel, A. (2015). Pray to play: Christian coaches and chaplains are converting football fields into mission fields. Freedom from Religion Foundation Report. Retrieved from https://ffrf.org/images /PraytoPlayReport.pdf

Steinbach, P. (2012). Schools attempting to control athletes' use of social media. Athletic Business. Retrieved from http://www.athleticbusiness.com/articles/article .aspx?articleid=3927&zoneid=8

T.V. v. Smith Green Community School Corporation, 807 F.Supp. 2d 767 (2011).

Tinker v. Des Moines Sch. Dist., 393 U.S. 503 (1969).

United States Constitution, Amendment I.

United States Constitution, Amendment V.

United States Constitution, Amendment XIV.

Wong, G.M. (2010). *Essentials of sports law* (4th ed.). Santa Barbara, Calif.: ABC-CLIO, LLC.

Yeager, D. (1991). *Undue process: The NCAA's injustice for all.* Champaign, Ill.: Sagamore (1991).

INTERNATIONAL SPORTS

John J. Miller
John T. Wendt

LEARNING OBJECTIVES

By the end of the chapter, the reader will be able to:

1. Appreciate globalization, represented by Olympic competition, as it applies to the legal aspects of sport
2. Understand the importance of the Ted Stevens Olympic and Amateur Sports Act
3. Comprehend the status of the Court of Arbitration for Sport
4. Understand the responsibilities of the World Anti-Doping Agency
5. Analyze the rulings of both the Court of Arbitration for Sport and the World Anti-Doping Agency
6. Understand the issue of ambush marketing as it applies to the Olympic concerns
7. Analyze how different countries provide protection against ambush marketers

RELATED CASES

INTRODUCTION

The international environment of sport is one that is consistently and constantly evolving. As such, terms such as globalization (and the associated concept of Americanization) and international expansion are common themes in various areas of sport management. *Globalization* can be viewed as a process, rather than a product, as it effects a variety of items such as economical, political, social, and cultural implications (Eitzen, 2006). Eitzen further viewed the interconnectedness of the world's people by stating that globalization is a "process whereby goods, information, people, money communication, sport, fashion, and other forms of culture move across national boundaries" (p. 210). It is widely viewed as being culturally universal and as a global phenomenon (Li, Hofacre, & Mahony, 2001). Eitzen (2006) stated "sport transcends national boundaries. It is both a product and a source of globalization. There are migration flows of athletes between and among nations. Some athletes are global icons" (p. 240).

This book has mainly focused on U.S. sports law. However, many of the same issues exist on the international level as well. Noted international sports law expert James A.R. Nafziger (2006) has stated succinctly about the role and future of international sports law:

> The globalization of sports competition is a sign of our times. Inspired by the modern Olympic Games, nurtured by communications technology, and fueled by high-profile professional athletes and commercial interests, the process of globalization continues apace. In this process international sports law is gradually assuming a prominent role. (p. 861)

It is obvious that sports have exploded on the international level. It is common to view athletes across the globe compete in a myriad of international events, including the FIFA World Cup, World Cup of Cricket, the Olympics, the British

Open, the Ryder Cup, the World Baseball Classic, Wimbledon, and the Tour de France, just to mention a few. However, when international sports events are mentioned, the Olympics are the first to come to mind. While numerous legal aspects may be addressed regarding the Olympics, to do so adequately, would leave out a number of issues. As such, two relevant legal concerns from the viewpoints of the athletes and organizations, drug testing and ambush marketing, are discussed in this chapter. For example, many legal issues present themselves for athletes who participate on an Olympic level. Determining the rights of athletes who are participating at the Olympic level involves a web of institutions, organizations, governing bodies, and decision makers. How can athletes challenge a decision by an international body dealing with his or her eligibility or drug testing? What laws apply under such circumstances? Can a decision of an international tribunal be binding on a nonresident athlete? Could an athlete appeal such a ruling? If so, where is the appeal heard, and what law should be applied? How do U.S. courts view a decision from an international body? Additionally, with the amount of money major companies supply to become corporate sponsors, what protections are they afforded? Are there effective means to combat against ambush marketing? If so, how do different countries address the concept of ambush marketing? These and many more issues and questions concerning drug testing and ambush marketing are present for athletes and sponsoring companied that can be both complicated and confusing.

THE OLYMPIC GAMES

The Olympic movement consists of multiple governing bodies in a complicated structure that is both international and domestic. The *International Olympic Committee* (IOC) has the responsibility of overseeing and monitoring Olympic activities throughout the world. The IOC recognizes international sports federations (IFs) and *national Olympic committees* (NOCs). *International sports federations* define eligibility for international competition and administer Olympic programs for a particular sport. An NOC is the sole authority for representing a particular country at the Olympic Games. NOCs in turn recognize *national governing bodies* (NGBs), which administer each Olympic sport and selection of athletes for that sport. The U.S. Olympic Committee (USOC) is the U.S. representative to the IOC. Olympic athletes are under the authority of the IOC, IF, NOC, and NGB and are therefore subject to their rules and regulations, and their discipline, if necessary.

The 1980 Summer Games were held in Moscow, Russia—the first Olympic Games to be held in a communist country. However, because of the 1979 Soviet invasion of Afghanistan, the United States along with 65 other countries elected to boycott the 1980 Games. Due to the boycott by the United States, 25 athletes and 1 member of the Executive Board of the defendant USOC, moved for an injunction to bar the USOC from carrying out a resolution, adopted by the USOC House of Delegates on April 12, 1980, not to send an American team to participate in the 1980 Olympic Games held in Moscow (*DeFrantz v. U.S. Olympic Committee,* 1980). The plaintiffs alleged that in preventing American athletes from competing in the Summer Olympics, defendant has exceeded its statutory powers and has abridged plaintiffs' constitutional rights. Ultimately, the court held that the plaintiffs had failed to state a viable claim under the Ted Stevens Olympic and Amateur Sports Act (formerly known as the Amateur Sports Act of 1978) or for alleged constitutional violations.

THE TED STEVENS OLYMPIC AND AMATEUR SPORTS ACT

Most courts agreed with the *DeFrantz* ruling finding that no private cause of action exists under the Amateur Sports Act, now referred to as the Ted Stevens Olympic and Amateur Sports Act. For nearly a century (1888 to 1978) amateur sport in the United States was under the auspices the Amateur Athletic Union (AAU) often in conflict with the National Collegiate Athletic Association (NCAA) especially over Olympic participation and athletes rights in participation (Nafziger, 1983). In response to that conflict in 1975, the President's Commission on Olympic Sports was established to decide on the most feasible way to correct any disputes or the best means of correcting the disputes and inefficiencies that existed (H.R. Rep. No. 95-1627, 1978). The Commission preferred a vertical sports structure under which the USOC would function as the primary coordinating body for a variety amateur sports organizations in the United States. While the Commission wanted a way to resolve any issues or conflicts between athletes, NGBs, and other amateur sports organizations, the federal government was not to be the administrator of amateur sports in the United States. As a result, the United States Congress was asked to authorize its recommendation by amending the USOC charter.

The recommendations resulted in the establishment of the Ted Stevens Olympic and Amateur Sports Act (Sports Act) (36 U.S.C. § 220501(a) (2006)). The Sports Act gives the USOC the authority to serve as the U.S. coordinating body for international amateur athletic competitions. The purpose of the Act is to coordinate amateur athletic activity, give amateur athletes certain rights, and provide a mechanism for national governing bodies. The Act amends statutory provisions that relate to the USOC and states that the USOC can recognize any amateur sport group or NGB that files an application and is eligible. The Sports Act provides the USOC with complete jurisdiction over "all matters pertaining to Unites States participation in the Olympic Games" (36 U.S.C. § 220503(3)(A). Only one NGB can be recognized for each sport. An NGB must be incorporated as a domestic, nonprofit corporation with the purpose of advancing "amateur" athletic competitions. The act also gives detailed information about an NGB's duties and provides guidance on Olympic competitions.

For an amateur sport organization to be recognized as a *national governing body* of a sport it must meet certain statutory eligibility requirements (36 U.S.C. § 220522(a)). For example, the requirements mandate that the organization must be independent in governing the sport. Secondly, the organization cannot be a member of more than one international sports federation for its sport. Third, the organization must open its membership to anyone. Fourth, any resolution of grievances from its membership must be dealt with swiftly and in an equitable manner (36 U.S.C. §§ 220522(a)(5)–(7), (13)). To provide the effectively prompt resolution of disputes, the statute mandates that an organization agrees to a binding arbitration in any debate concerning the opportunity of an athlete to compete (36 U.S.C. § 220522(a)(4)(B)). As a result, this statute provides the national governing body of a sport the ability to institute "procedures for determining eligibility standards for participation in competition" (36 U.S.C. § 220523(a)(5)). Thus, the organization in charge of a particular sport has the authority to decide if an athlete can compete as long as it follows the binding arbitration clause of the Sports Act.

Numerous problems can arise concerning jurisdiction and choice of law. However, national courts are not the most convenient places to resolve the kinds of disputes that might occur on an international level in the sporting world. With the sporting world becoming more international, a body was necessary to handle disputes arising from international sports events on a worldwide basis. Therefore, the IOC established the *Court of Arbitration for Sport* (CAS) in 1984, discussed in the next section.

THE COURT OF ARBITRATION FOR SPORT

The CAS was created in 1981 when the IOC, headed by then-President Juan Antonio Samaranch, wanted a sports-specific authority to resolve sports-related disputes quickly and cost effectively. In 1983, the IOC ratified statutes to establish the CAS with the tribunal starting to operation in 1984 (History of CAS, 2015). The CAS provides the means to facilitate the settlement of sport-related disputes by means of procedural rules adapted to the specific needs of the sport world providing expedited, yet thorough relief. In fact, the essential feature of the CAS is the ability to render swift and substantial justice with all (Benz & Sternheimer, 2015).

Many commentators have noted that the CAS is developing its own rule of law—"lex sportiva" (Vaitiekunas, 2014). The law that the CAS applies to the merits of the case include Procedural Rule R45 that states, "The Panel shall decide the dispute according to the rules of law chosen by the parties or, in the absence of such a choice, according to Swiss law. The parties may authorize the Panel to decide ex aequo et bono" (Tribunal Arbitral du Sport/Court of Arbitration for Sport, 2015b). Under the principle of "ex aequo et bono" a court is allowed to look beyond the strict construction of the law and decide a case on the principles of what is "fair and just" under the circumstances. Procedural Rule R58 provides:

> The Panel shall decide the dispute according to the applicable regulations and the rules of law chosen by the parties or, in the absence of such a choice, according to the law of the country in which the federation, association or sports-related body which has issued the challenged decision is domiciled or according to the rules of law, the application of which the Panel deems appropriate. In the latter case, the Panel shall give reasons for its decision. (Tribunal Arbitral du Sport/ Court of Arbitration for Sport, 2015b.)

If the parties fails to agree on the applicable law, Swiss law will apply.

The CAS consists of 300 arbitrators from 87 countries chosen for their specialist knowledge of arbitration and sports law (Tribunal Arbitral du

Sport/Court of Arbitration for Sport, 2015c). The International Council of Arbitration for Sports (ICAS) oversees and administers the CAS. The Olympic Charter provides CAS with exclusive jurisdiction for all disputes related to the Olympic Games as "Any dispute arising on the occasion of, or in connection with, the Olympic Games shall be submitted exclusively to the Court of Arbitration for Sport, in accordance with the Code of Sports-Related Arbitration" (Olympic Charter, Rule 61, 2). In addition, signatories accepting the Code include the World Anti-Doping Agency (WADA), the IOC, all IFs, the International Paralympic Committee, all national Olympic Committees and Paralympic Committees, national major event organizations, and national anti-doping organizations (NADOs) (CAS Code, Article 23.1).

The CAS addresses issues dealing with eligibility, suspension of athletes, athlete drug testing, television rights, licensing, sponsorship, and the nationality of athletes for purposes of competition. CAS Procedural Rule R47 states that an "appeal of a decision of federation…may be filed with CAS if the statutes or regulations of the said body so provide" (Special provisions applicable to the appeal arbitration procedure, 2015, para. 1). Typically, when athletes become members of their International Federation, they are bound by the IF's rules and regulations, which call for decisions and appeals to be heard by the CAS (Connolly, 2006).

Participants may also choose mediation as a method to attempt to resolve the dispute. Of the cases heard by CAS, approximately 45% relate to appeals by the Federation Internationale de Football Association (FIFA); 30% of cases address doping violations; 15% are categorized as appeal cases; and 10% are considered international commercial cases (Reilly, 2012). CAS awards are usually enforceable through the 1958 Convention on the Recognition and Enforcement of Foreign Arbitral Awards (The New York Convention) which allows for enforcement of arbitral awards across international boundaries (Connolly, 2006; Cox, 2014).

Finally, as noted CAS arbitrator Dr. Dirk Reiner Martens has stated, "A CAS award upholding a federation's decision to suspend an athlete from competition for a doping violation is 'enforced' by the sports community by simply not allowing this athlete to compete during the applicable period" (Martens, 2014). Under The Ted Stevens Olympic and Amateur Sports Act, a U.S. athlete has the right to a hearing to determine whether they have committed a doping offense before the America Arbitration Association/North American Court of Arbitration for Sport (Tygart, 2003).

WORLD ANTI-DOPING AGENCY

Cyclists and other endurance athletes in the nineteenth century often used combinations of strychnine, caffeine, cocaine, and alcohol to boost their performances. At the 1904 Summer Olympic Games in St. Louis, Thomas Hicks, the winner of the marathon was visibly under the influence of the strychnine and brandy that was administered to him during the course of the race. The use of amphetamines to combat fatigue, heighten endurance, and elevate mood was discovered during World War II and their use was adapted by some athletes to improve their athletic performances. However, the side effects of amphetamines became apparent at the 1952 Winter Olympics when several speed skaters became ill and needed medical attention after taking amphetamines and at the 1960 Games in Rome Danish cyclist Kurt Jensen collapsed and died from an amphetamine overdose (Wendt, 2004).

In 1966 UCI (cycling) and FIFA (football) were among the first IFs to introduce doping tests in their respective World Championships. In 1967 the IOC instituted its Medical Commission and set up its first list of prohibited substances. The first drug testing procedures at Olympic Games themselves were in 1968 with the Winter Games in Grenoble and the Summer Games in Mexico City (Wendt,

2004). The majority of international federations introduced drug testing by the 1970s. However, the use of steroids, as previously mentioned, was prevalent particularly in strength-related contests (Miller, 2009). This was due to the lack of adequate testing measures. A consistent way to analyze the presence of steroids was instituted in 1974, which was the same year the International Olympic Committee added steroids to its prohibited substance list. The implementation to determine steroid use as well as its presence on the banned list resulted in a large number of athletes being barred from strength-related events (Miller, 2009).

Arguably, the most defining moment in doping in the modern Games occurred at the 1988 Summer Olympics in Seoul, Korea. Shattering the world record Canadian sprinter Ben Johnson won the 100-meter dash so easily that he raised his hand in victory the last ten meters. However his gold medal and record were stripped away when he tested positive for anabolic steroids. Given the incredible television and media visibility, there were calls for anti-doping regulation (Wendt, 2004).

After the events of the 1998 Tour de France, sometimes referred to as the "Tour of Doping," the IOC organized a world conference to consider options in the fight against doping in sports. This World Conference on Doping in Sport produced the Lausanne Declaration on Doping in Sport, which fashioned an independent international anti-doping agency, with the aim to have it completely ready for implementation by the 2000 Sydney Olympics (Miller, 2009). This independent organization, known as the *World Anti-Doping Agency* became the first and only international scientific research program that synchronized advanced detection methods of prohibited drugs in sports in 2001 (Miller, 2009).

In 2003, the Copenhagen Resolution was adopted by all the attending members at the World Conference on Doping. The members included the IOC, the International Paralympic Committee, all Olympic sports, national Olympic and Paralympic committees, athletes, NADOs, and international agencies to fight against doping in sport. The Copenhagen Resolution provided for the acceptance of the World Anti-Doping Code (hereafter referred to as the Code; Miller, 2009). The acceptance of the Code created the first formalized recognition of rules and responsibilities to counteract doping practices in sports where none may have previously existed. As a result, anti-doping endeavors have continued to reach an exceptional level of coordination and uniformity as the same fundamental procedures are typically employed when testing across sports, and the same substances are banned in the majority of international competitions under the Code (Miller, 2009). The Code has been accepted by the entire Olympic movement, NADOs, and recognized by more than 170 governments through the UNESCO Convention Against Doping.

The WADA also maintains a *Prohibited List*, which is a cornerstone of the World Anti-Doping Code and a key component of harmonization of the anti-doping movement. A substance shall be considered for inclusion on the Prohibited List if the substance is a masking agent or meets two of the following three criteria:

1. it has the potential to enhance or enhances sport performance;
2. it represents a potential or actual health risk; or
3. it is contrary to the spirit of sport.

The list is updated annually and is readily available online or as an "app" to all athletes and athlete support personnel. The Prohibited List is the International Standard for identifying substances and methods that are prohibited both in and out of competition (World Anti-Doping Agency, 2015b). Athletes are held to be strictly liable for what they take and what is in their body and athletes can commit an anti-doping rule violation occurs whenever a prohibited substance (or its metabolites or markers) is found in bodily specimen (World Anti-Doping Agency, 2015d). This included whether or not the athlete intentionally or unintentionally used a prohibited substance or was negligent or otherwise at fault. However, the athlete may attempt to reduce a penalty be showing that they bore no fault or no significant fault.

Adams v. Canadian Centre for Ethics in Sport (2008)

If exceptional circumstances exist, the athlete is categorized under *No Fault or Negligence* by which the athlete is considered blameless and is not penalized any period of ineligibility. The definition of No Fault or Negligence is predicated on the athlete's knowledge of the conditions that caused the violation. To do so the athletes are required to prove that had no knowledge or suspicion that they had been administered a prohibited substance. Thus, to be considered blameless, athletes must prove that the prohibited substance entered into their system without any knowledge of the contamination. If it can proven that an opponent sabotaged an approved nutritional supplement, the athlete may be considered blameless.

An unusual case involving the No Fault or Negligence category occurred in *Adams v. Canadian Centre for Ethics in Sport* (2008). Jeffery Adams was a Canadian, elite-level, track-and-field wheelchair athlete. Because of his paraplegia Adams was required to self-catheterize to urinate. Additionally, because he was funded by the Canadian government, he was required to submit to doping procedures. After he participated in an athletic event he used a catheter to provide his urine sample to the Canadian Centre for Ethics in Sport (CCES). The sample tested positive to a cocaine, which is a banned substance.

While at a Toronto bar, named the Vatikan, Adams claimed that an unknown woman forced him ingest cocaine without his consent six days before he was to compete. Adams stated that he passed urine using a catheter, also referred to as the "Vatikan catheter," shortly after he ingested the cocaine. When he provided the urine sample to the CCES, he used the Vatikan catheter that contained traces of cocaine. The CCES concluded that Adams committed an anti-doping violation because his urine sample tested positive to a banned substance. While the CAS found that Adams committed the strict liability violation of a presence of a prohibited substance, it also reported that Adams could not be held negligent or at fault. The Court concluded that he was the victim of an assault (the Vatikan incident) and that he could not have reasonably known about the contamination risks regarding the Vatikan catheter. As a result, CAS removed the two-year ban he received from CCES and reinstated his eligibility to receive financial aid from the Canadian government. It should be noted that Adams is a very rare case where it was recognized as an "exceptional circumstance" and the CAS removed all penalties (White, 2008).

World Anti-Doping Agency v. Hardy (2010)

Jessica Hardy has been a U.S. national swimming champion and world record holder. Hardy qualified for the Beijing 2008 Olympic Games in four events (50 meters freestyle, 100 meters breaststroke, 4 × 100 meters freestyle relay, 4 × 100 meters medley relay). At the urging of her coach she took supplements to improve her performances. Despite assurances from the company, the product contained clenbuterol, a banned substance and she tested positive. Hardy voluntarily withdrew from the United States Olympic Team and at her hearing before the American Arbitration Association (AAA) Panel she argued that exceptional circumstances that might reduce or eliminate the presumptive two year period of ineligibility.

The AAA Panel found that under the totality of the circumstances her case was "truly exceptional" however, they did find that she took supplements in spite of warnings from the U.S. Anti-Doping Agency (USADA) and her own hesitation due to risk of contamination. As such the Panel found that she acted with "fault of negligence" in committing an anti-doping regulation. The Panel provisionally reduced the period to one year pending the IOC's grant of a waiver of IOC Rule 45, or "The Osaka Rule" (*USADA and Jessica Hardy, Interim Arbitral Award*, 2009).

The *Osaka Rule* was an IOC Executive Board Unpublished Memorandum regarding participation in the Olympic Games. Under the Osaka Rule if an athlete receives a ban of more than six months they cannot compete in the following Olympic Games. It should be noted that the Osaka Rule came into effect only three days prior to Hardy testing positive. Because Hardy's ban was longer than six months, she would be ineligible to compete at the following Games, the 2012 Olympic Games in London. Hence, that "penalty is shockingly disproportionate to her degree of fault" as she would be punished twice (in 2008 and 2012) for the same offense (*USADA and Jessica Hardy, Interim Arbitral Award*, 2009).

Both the Fédération Internationale de Natation (FINA, the IF for swimming) and WADA appealed the Interim Award to the CAS who agreed with the AAA Panel that the circumstances of Hardy's case were "truly exceptional" but decided not to issue a decision of Rule 45 because they lacked jurisdiction and dismissed her appeal. The IOC determined later that it would not apply rule 45 to Hardy because of the timing of the enactment of Rule 45 (*WADA v. Jessica Hardy and USADA*, 2010) And in 2012 she went on to win an Olympic Gold Medal on the 4 × 100 Meter Medley Relay and Bronze Medal on the 4 × 100 Meter Freestyle Relay.

LaShawn Merritt and the United States Anti-Doping Agency (2011)

In a similar Rule 45 (Osaka Rule) case LaShawn Merritt, Olympic and World Track and Field Champion in the 400 meters, tested positive for dehydroepiandrosterone—a banned steroid that he said he consumed unknowingly in an over-the-counter male enhancement product (Extenze) (*USADA v. LaShawn Merritt*, 2010). The AAA/CAS Panel found that Merritt had proved that he tested positive as a result of taking ExtenZe and that he did not do so to enhance his sports performance. Merritt asked for the elimination or reduction of the period of eligibility based on the exceptional circumstances that they bore "no fault" or "no significant fault" for the violation. The Panel found that the Merritt was not significantly at fault in that when he bought the ExtenZe "enhancing his sports performance was the last thing on Mr. Merritt's mind." Hence, in Merritt's case "there was a complete 'absence of intention to gain [an] advantage [over] competitors." But, the Panel did note that Merritt's "negligence necessitates a serious consequence" and imposed an ineligibility period of 21 months (*USADA v. LaShawn Merritt*, 2010).

Similar to Jessica Hardy's case, Merritt also asked the Panel to look at Rule 45 because he, too, would be prohibited from competing in the 2012 Olympic Games in London. The CAS Panel also found that Rule 45 was, in effect a second disciplinary sanction over and above the consequences for a doping violation already provided in the Code, and as such was not in compliance with the Code itself and that Rule 45 was invalid and unenforceable (*United States Olympic Committee v. International Olympic Committee*, 2011).

British Olympic Association v. World Anti-Doping Association (2011)

Finally, the CAS reconciled these cases in a dispute involving British track star, Dwain Chambers. Chambers was an Olympic sprinter and was the fastest European at the 2000 Olympic Games in Sydney, Australia. However, Chambers had taken the banned drug, THG, was caught in the BALCO doping scandal and served a two-year ban. After the ban he returned to the track and wanted to compete for the British Olympic Team especially at the 2012 Games which were held in London, England. The problem was that the British Olympic Association (BOA) had a policy, Bye-Law 25, which prohibited anyone who has been found guilty of a doping offence from representing Great Britain for life in any future Olympic Games. The BOA argued that Bye-Law 25 was supported by 90% of Britain's athlete and allowing "dopers" on the team would "damage the credibility and reputation of the team in the eyes of the athletes and the public" (Wendt, 2012).

Based on the *U.S. Olympic Committee v. International Olympic Committee* (2011) award, WADA challenged the BOA bye-law because it, too, changed the substance of the sanctions imposed in the WADA Code. The CAS Panel noted that in while the BOA and WADA and BOA were both pursuing the fight against doping, they were using different means. Importantly, the main issue was whether the British Olympic Association could pursued on its own or would it be best to address the policy through the WADA code (*British Olympic Association (BOA) v. World Anti-Doping Agency*, 2012). Similar to *USOC*, the CAS Panel ultimately concluded that because the BOA bye-law was a second doping sanction, the bye-law was not in compliance with the Code and the appeal of the BOA was rejected. Eventually, Chambers went on to represent Team GB and was a semi-finalist in the 100 meters.

2015 World Anti-Doping Code

The 2012 BOA case against the WADA represented the culmination of the quest for harmonization between parties in the fight against doping. This concerted fight then moved to the third review of the World Anti-Doping Code and has resulted in the 2015 Code. There have been significant changes between the 2009 and 2015 World Anti-Doping Code. The new version of the Code

focuses on "fairness and firmness" providing for longer periods of ineligibility for real cheats, yet allowing for more flexibility in sanctioning. For example, under the 2009 Code for a first offense, the sanction was two years while a second violation resulted in a lifetime violation to the offending party. But starting January 1, 2015, athletes may receive a four-year ban from competition for a first offense. In addition, any athlete who refuses to participate in, evades, or tampers with the sample collection process, may also face a sanction of up to four years (USADA, 2015). Under the older rules the penalty could be reduced if the athlete could prove to the comfortable satisfaction of the Panel that the athlete bore "no fault" or "no significant" fault. Under the new rules, where the athlete can establish no significant fault the penalty may range from at a minimum a reprimand and at a maximum two years (USADA, 2015).

The 2015 Code amendments also emphasize the increasing importance of investigations and use of intelligence in the anti-doping fight. Hence, with the focus on those who intentionally cheat, versus accidental doping, the new version of the Code allows for a reduction in sanctions for athletes who give substantial assistance to WADA. For example, Russian star Liliya Shobukhova, who won both the London and Chicago marathons had her ban reduced by accepting responsibility for an anti-doping rule violation and providing information to WADA that was "of substantial value in uncovering and investigating anti-doping rule violations committed by other individuals, including athlete support personnel" (World Anti-Doping Agency, 2015f, para. 4).

The new Code also reaches beyond athletes who intentionally cheat to include athlete support personnel. Coaches, trainers, or other athlete support personnel were originally outside the jurisdiction of anti-doping authorities. However, under the new Code athletes are prohibited from associating with coaches, trainers, physicians, or other athlete support personnel who are sanctioned and/or criminally convicted of doping. The athlete must receive notice of the violation and be given an opportunity to explain the situation.

Under both the old and new Code athletes have to make their whereabouts known to USADA and make themselves available for out-of-competition drug testing. Under the 2009 Code an athlete who had three missed tests (referred to as "whereabouts violations") in an 18-month period would have been deemed to have committed an anti-doping violation. Under the 2015 Code that time period has been changed to a rolling 12-month period and may lead to a loss of funding, medals, prizes, and other money (USADA, 2014).

AMBUSH MARKETING

Another area that has recently gained legal prominence internationally is *ambush market-ing*. According to Grady and McKelvey (2008) ambush marketing can be defined as "a company's intentional efforts to weaken its competitor's offi-cial association with a sport organization, which has been acquired through the payment of spon-sorship fees" (p. 8). Grady and McKelvey (2008) further described the goal of ambush marketing as being "designed to intentionally confuse the buying public as to which company is in fact the official sponsor of the particular sports property or event" (p. 9). Some major companies—such as McDonald's, Samsung, Nike, and Coca-Cola—spend tremendous amounts of money to attain sport sponsorships, especially at competitions with international appeal such as the Olympics and the World Cup. Because of the amounts of money involved in sport sponsorships, there is an emphasis in determining the best return of investment. However, since ambush marketing promotes potential confusion in the minds of the consumer, these companies could lose millions of sponsorship fee dollars.

Ambush marketing first came to the light during the Olympics of the 1980s and 1990s. For example, ambush marketing occurred in the 1984 Los Angeles Olympic Summer Games when Fuji bought exclusive sponsorship rights, only to see rival Kodak imply its association with the event by sponsoring the U.S. Olympic track team and tele-vision broadcasts of the Summer Games. In the 1988 Olympics a reversal occurred as Kodak was the official sponsor but Fujifilm sponsored the highly successful United States swimming team. This strategy enabled Fuji to be connected with the Olympics at a decreased cost (Meenaghan, 1996).

The trend continued at the 1992 Barcelona Olympics when Visa paid $20 million to be the official credit card sponsor (Elliott, 1992). How-ever, right before the beginning of the games, credit card competitor, American Express, tele-vised commercials stating "And remember, to visit Spain, you don't need a Visa" as well as "Obviously, we're here for more than just the fun and games" (Elliott, 1992). Famously, at the 1996 Atlanta Olympic Games, Nike purchased billboards that were highly visible around the Atlanta metropol-itan area and supplied U.S. Olympic Sprinter and two-time gold medalist Michael Johnson with gold shoes. However, Nike was not an official sponsor of the 1996 Olympics, the official sponsor was Reebok.

At the 2000 Sydney Olympic Games, the Aus-tralian airline, Quantas, used the promotion "the spirit of Australia," which in many ways mimicked the Sydney Olympic slogan "share the Spirit." As a result, many consumers were under the impression that Quantas was the official sponsor of the Olym-pics when it actually was Ansett Air. McDonald's is part of the IOC's "The Olympic Partner" or "TOP" Program, which is "is the highest level of Olympic sponsorship and provides sponsors with exclusive worldwide marketing rights to the Sum-mer, Winter and Youth Olympic Games" (Inter-national Olympic Committee, 2015). Yet in 2010 Subway used a creative ad of Olympian Michael Phelps swimming to the Vancouver Games to give the appearance that they were an official sponsor (Boudway, 2014).

Types of Ambush Marketing

According to Berger-Walliser, Stallings-Williams, Walliser, and Bender (2012) ambush marketing can take several forms: 1) predatory, 2) coattail, 3) self-ambushing, 4) controversy, 5) associative, 6) distractive and insurgent, 7) unintentional, and 8) saturation. *Predatory ambushing* strikes at an event sponsor, leaving the consumers confused as to which organization is the official sponsor. An example, of predatory ambushing would be from the 1992 Barcelona Olympic Games in which American Express (a non-sponsor) advertised "And remember to visit Spain, you don't need a Visa" even though the credit card company Visa was the official sponsor of the 1992 Games. *Coattail ambushing* occurs when a company gains publicity through sponsoring a sports event without being a sponsor of the overall event. Coattail ambushing occurred in the 1984 Olympics at which Kodak, which sponsored the event participants ambushed Fuji which sponsored the event, not just the participants. *Self-ambushing* involves a practice that breaches the limits of a company's sponsoring agreement in a way that oversteps the sponsorship of the event by another sponsoring organization. For example, an official sponsor of the Union of European Football Associations (UEFA) European Championships, Carlsberg, distributed headbands and t-shirts at the tournament with the company's logo. However, this violated a sponsorship agreement of another company that was permitted to hand out these items. *Controversy ambushing* occurs when an organization produces an advertising scheme to sponsor an event with knowledge that it will not be accepted. The organization banks on the hope that through the controversy associated with the event, they will gain attention without having to pay a sponsorship fee. *Associative ambushing*

employs imagery to generate "an illusion that an organization has links to a sporting event or property" (Chadwick & Burton, 2010, p. 8). An example of this type of ambush marketing occurred at the 2008 Beijing Olympic Games where Nike, as a non-sponsor, made liberal use of the number 8, which symbolizes good luck in the Chinese culture. *Distractive and insurgent ambushing* uses distractions surrounding the event to draw attention to a product without making specific mention of the event (Chadwick & Burton, 2010). *Unintentional ambushing* occurs when a company's product is prominently, but inadvertently, mentioned by the media but the company is not a sponsor of the event (Chadwick & Burton, 2010). *Saturation ambushing* occurs when advertising for an event is significantly increased but there is no reference to the contest (Chadwick & Burton, 2010).

Although sponsors will often refrain from paying huge amounts of money if the ambushers obtain similar benefits at little or no cost, Sandler and Shani (1989) indicated that in many cases the consumers actually remember the ambushing company better than the sponsoring agency. Additionally, it is problematic for a plaintiff to demonstrate that consumer confusion is created due to ambush marketing. For example, several studies have revealed that sponsorship targets lack knowledge regarding the levels of sponsorship and the rights associated with assorted sponsors (Grady & McKelvey, 2008; McKelvey & Grady, 2004; Shani & Sandler, 1998).

International Application of Law to Protect Against Ambush Marketing

What was once thought to be an important extra enticement to Olympic selection committees, anti-ambush marketing has become a fundamental item for a site to be even considered. According to McKelvey and Grady (2004), many countries have enacted legislation to better protect sponsors from potential ambush marketing. However, the ability of ambush marketing to flourish depends on the law in the specific nation as what is allowed in some jurisdictions can be unlawful elsewhere. In the past 25 years, there have been efforts by a number of countries that have introduced significant legal protection of Olympic symbols against ambush marketing. According to Scassa (2011), "The insufficiency of existing legal recourses to address ambush marketing is one of the justifications for enacting specific legislation to target this activity" (p. 356). Specific legal protections have been addressed in Australia, Canada, Germany, United Kingdom, and the United States.

AUSTRALIA

Australia offers protections against ambush marketing through two primary acts of legislation: the *Olympic Insignia Protection Act 1987 and the Sydney 2000 Games (Indicia and Images) Protection Act 1996.* Specifically, the Olympic Insignia Protection Act 1987 by:

1. making the Australian Olympic Commission (AOC) the owner of copyright in the Olympic symbol;
2. making the AOC the owner of certain Olympic designs (for the purposes of the Designs Act);
3. providing that the Olympic motto, the Olympic symbol, and certain other Olympic images (including the Olympic torch and flame) must not be registered as trademarks; and
4. prohibiting the commercial use of certain Olympic expressions unless the user holds a license granted by the AOC (Olympic Insignia Protection Act 1987 (Cth) ss. 5–6, 8, 18–19 (Austl.)).

Additionally, when Australia was awarded the Olympic Games for 2000, the Australian Senate Legal and Constitutional References Committee instituted protection of Olympic insignia and sponsorship for the Sydney Olympics through the Sydney 2000 Games (Indicia and Images) Protection Act 1996 (Cth) (Cashing in on the Sydney Olympics: Protecting the Sydney Olympic Games from ambush marketing: Report, 1995). The Sydney 2000 Games (Indicia and Images) Protection Act 1996, also referred to as the Sydney 2000 Games Act, protected the Sydney Olympic and Paralympic Games official sponsors from ambush or parasitic marketing practices by commercial rivals.

The Sydney 2000 Act offered a licensing scheme that constricted the use, for commercial purposes, of a range of words, phrases, and images. The scheme prevented an unlicensed company from using words, phrases, or images to suggest a sponsorship arrangement with the games or other support for them. The list included: "games city," "millennium games," "Sydney games," "Sydney 2000," any combination of the words "games" and "2000" (or "two thousand"), "Olympiad," "Olympic," "share the spirit," "summer games," "team millennium"; the use of the word "Olympian" or "Olympic" with "gold," "silver," or "bronze"; the use of any visual or aural representation representing a connection with the Olympic or Paralympic Games) (Intellectual Property Laws Amendment (Border Interception) Bill, 1999, para. 1).

Specifically, Section 3 of the Sydney 2000 Games Act identified the following protections against ambush marketers:

(1)(a) to protect, and to further, the position of Australia as a participant in, and a supporter of, the world Olympic and Paralympic movements; and

(1)(b) to the extent that it is within the power of the Parliament, to assist in protecting the relations, and ensuring the performance of the obligations, of the Sydney 2000 Games bodies with and to the world Olympic and Paralympic movements; in relation to the holding of the Sydney 2000 Games.

(2) These objects are to be achieved by facilitating the raising of licensing revenue in relation to the Sydney 2000 Games through the regulation of the use for commercial purposes of the indicia and images associated with the Games.

CANADA

While no laws openly bar ambush marketing in Canada, the most applicable ones address laws relating to *passing off* as well as those associated to interference with contractual relations. The tort of passing-off mandates that the plaintiffs needs to exhibit that they have 1) goodwill in the trademark at issue, 2) been a misrepresented which likely to lead to confusion, and 3) have suffered or is likely to suffer some damage as a result (Gervais & Judge, 2005; Morcom, Roughton, Graham, & Malynicz, 2005). Under Canadian laws that prohibit passing off, a company could claim that another organization wrongly advertised thereby suggesting that deliberately causing confusion in the mind of the consumer. *The Competition Act of 1985* can also assist in preventing advertising false or misleading statements as it states:

No person shall, for the purpose of promoting, directly or indirectly, the supply or use of a product or for the purpose of promoting, directly or indirectly, any business interest, by any means whatever, knowingly or recklessly make a representation to the public that is false or misleading in a material respect (Section 1).

It is noteworthy that false advertising is not a tortious action under the Competition Act of 1985 meaning that the negatively affected party (i.e., organization) is not responsible for deciding the resources to be allocated for prosecution, only the pertinent authorities. Additionally, the sponsorship misrepresentation may be difficult in a misleading or material respect as it does apply to the safety or quality of the product.

Olympic and Paralympic Marks Act of 2007

The *Olympic and Paralympic Marks Act of 2007* (OPMA) is event-specific anti-ambush marketing legislation that was ratified in time for the 2010 Vancouver Olympic Winter Games.

OPMA Section 3(1) states that: "No person shall adopt or use in connection with a business, as a trade-mark or otherwise, an Olympic or Paralympic mark or a mark that so nearly resembles an Olympic or Paralympic mark as to be likely to be mistaken for it."

The statute refers to ambush marketing by association as it applies to a period of time imposed by regulations leading up to as well as after the Games. In this period, individuals may not "promote or otherwise direct public attention to their business, wares or services in a manner that misleads or is likely to mislead the public" (Olympic and Paralympic Marks Act of 2007, s. 4) Specifically, OPMA prohibits an organization from advertising that:

(*a*) the person's business, wares or services are approved, authorized or endorsed by an organizing committee, the COC or the CPC; or (*b*) a business association exists between the person's business and the Olympic Games, the Paralympic Games, an organizing committee, the COC or the CPC (Olympic and Paralympic Marks Act of 2007, s. 4).

The rights outlined in OPMA (2007) rests with the event organizers. Under OPMA (2007), the Canadian public is not required to be confused regarding the origin of the defendant's wares or services. Rather, it must be proven that the public was either misled or likely to be misled to believe that either official endorsement of the product or a type of association existed with the Games or its organizers. Moreover, OPMA is more straightforward in obtaining an injunction against any alleged ambush marketers by eliminating the necessity for a plaintiff to exhibit permanent damage during the specific period of protection. Finally, OPMA (2007) offers additional remedies including "damages, accounting of profits, and destruction or delivery up of offending wares" (Olympic and Paralympic Marks Act of 2007, s. 5(1)).

GERMANY

The primary legal source in Germany, as a civil law country, is codified law. One strategy to legally fight ambush marketing in Germany is through the use of trademark law. According to article 5(1) of the *European Trade Marks Directive* a registered trade mark shall confer on the proprietor exclusive rights therein. The proprietor shall be entitled to prevent all third parties not having his consent from using in the course of trade:

(a) any sign which is identical with the trade mark in relation to goods or services which are identical with those for which the trade mark is registered;

(b) any sign where, because of its identity with, or similarity to, the trade mark and the identity or similarity of the goods or services covered by the trade mark and the sign, there exists a likelihood of confusion on the part of the public which includes the likelihood of association between the sign and the trade mark (Council Directive 2008/95, 2008 O.J. (L 299) 25, art. 5(1)).

The following, therefore, may be prohibited under OPMA:

(a) affixing the sign to the goods or to the packaging thereof;

(b) offering the goods, or putting them on the market or stocking them for these purposes under that sign, or offering or supplying services thereunder;

(c) importing or exporting the goods under the sign;

(d) using the sign on business papers and in advertising. (Council Directive 2008/95, 2008 O.J. (L 299) 25, art. 5(3))

Olympia Schutz Gesetz (OlympSchG)

To entice the IOC to consider Germany for the 2012 Olympic Games, specific Olympic trademark protection statute was introduced and passed in 2004. The so-called *Olympia Schutz Gesetz (OlympSchG)* protects specific words and symbols associated with the Olympics as the sole property of the German National Olympic Committee and the IOC, independent of the product or event category with which Olympic signs or words are associated (Ericsson, 2014). While the Olympia Schutz Gesetz is much more extensive that the normal German trademark protection laws, the OlympSchG is not based on harmonized European Union law (Berger-Walliser et al., 2012).

UNITED KINGDOM

Laws had been passed in the United Kingdom to provide additional safeguards to some of the Olympic trademarks (Ericsson, 2014). In particular, the *London Olympic Games and Paralympic Games Act of 2006* offered increased sponsorship protection to the 2012 London Olympic Games sponsors against ambush marketing. For example, in the London Olympic Games and Paralympic Games Act 2006, event zones around the Olympic venues and routes were established. Should a party desire to advertise in these zones, the party would have to receive authorization from the London Organising Committee of the Olympic and Paralympic Games (London Olympic Games and Paralympic Games Act, 2006). The parties effected by this piece of legislation includes "anyone directly or indirectly responsible for the advertising activity, including those who arrange for advertising, any businesses whose products or services are advertised, and owners, occupiers, or managers of land on which the advertising takes place" (London Olympic Games and Paralympic

Games (Advertising and Trading) (England) Regulations, 2011, § 6).

Individuals whose were wear clothes, exhibit tattoos, or carry items exhibiting specific brands are do not apply to this regulation "unless the individual knows or has reasonable cause to believe that he or she is participating in an ambush marketing campaign" (London Olympic Games and Paralympic Games (Advertising and Trading) (England) Regulations, 2011, § 8(1)). Thus, any individual who is not authorized to represent an organization that may create an association between that person and the 2012 London Olympic Games would be held in breach of the Act resulting in a fine (Collett & Johnson, 2006).

It should be noted that ambush marketing campaigns often leave event organizers with inadequate time to determine if there is any evidence of confusion or harm (Johnson, 2011). Without evidence of confusion or harm the plaintiff cannot prove that there is a likelihood of damage arising from the ambush activity. For example, while the Canadian Olympic and Paralympic Marks Act eliminates the requirement for irreparable harm during the designated protection period, the London Olympic Games and Paralympic Games Act 2006 does not provide comparable stipulations.

UNITED STATES

The problem with ambush marketing in the United States is that the law is on the side of the ambushers as it does not include counterfeiting or unlawful use of trademarks, tradenames, or symbols (Berger-Walliser et al., 2012). For example, in *San Francisco Arts and Athletics, Inc. v. U.S. Olympic Committee* (1987), the United States Supreme Court held that permitting the USOC absolute right to use the word "Olympic" did not breach the United States Constitution's First Amendment. However, fourteen years later, the Federal court in *U.S. Olympic Committee v. American Media, Inc.* (2001), ruled that the *Ted Stevens Olympic and Amateur Sports Act* (OASA) did not prohibit ambush marketing.

Traditionally, in the United States, actions related with ambush marketing are normally not at the level of fraud, misrepresentation, or otherwise misleading practices that are required for a successful cause of action for unfair business practices (Berger-Walliser et al., 2012). In the United States, there are two legal methods to protect against ambush marketing tactics: the Lanham Act (2006) and the Ted Stevens OASA. The *Lanham Act*, a federal statute, offers protection against advertisements that may be construed as being misleading. In particular, two sections of the Lanham Act (Section 32 and Section 43(a)) that do not allow any registered mark that is likely to cause confusion, mistake, or deception to be used in state commerce. For example, Section 32 of the Lanham Act § 1114 states that:

(1) Any person who shall, without the consent of the registrant –
(a) use in commerce any reproduction, counterfeit, copy, or colorable imitation of a registered mark in connection with the sale, offering for sale, distribution, or advertising of any goods or services on or in connection with which such use is likely to cause confusion, or to cause mistake, or to deceive; or
(b) reproduce, counterfeit, copy, or colorably imitate a registered mark and apply such reproduction, counterfeit, copy, or colorable imitation to labels, signs, prints, packages, wrappers, receptacles or advertisements intended to be used in commerce upon or in connection with the sale, offering for sale, distribution, or advertising of goods or services on or in connection with which such use is likely to cause confusion, or to cause mistake, or to deceive, shall be liable in a civil action by the registrant for the remedies hereinafter provided.
Under subsection (b) hereof, the registrant shall not be entitled to recover profits or damages unless the acts have been

committed with knowledge that such imitation is intended to be used to cause confusion, or to cause mistake, or to deceive.

Additionally, Section 43(a) of the Lanham Act states that:

(1) Any person who, on or in connection with any goods or services, or any container for goods, uses in commerce any word, term, name, symbol, or device, or any combination thereof, or any false designation of origin, false or misleading description of fact, or false or misleading representation of fact, which –
(A) is likely to cause confusion, or to cause mistake, or to deceive as to the affiliation, connection, or association of such person with another person, or as to the origin, sponsorship, or approval of his or her goods, services, or commercial activities by another person, or
(B) in commercial advertising or promotion, misrepresents the nature, characteristics, qualities, or geographic origin of his or her or another person's goods, services, or commercial activities, shall be liable in a civil action.

Examples could include an organization depicting five interlocking circles, each a different color but are the same as the colors of the five Olympic rings. The OASA designates certain Olympic related words and symbols as being the exclusive property of the U.S. Olympic Committee (USOC) and "prohibits their unauthorized use, and subjects the unauthorized user to civil actions and remedies" (36 U.S.C § 2205 (2006)).

However, the Lanham Act is somewhat limited because ambush marketers can circumvent it by not using the trademark and the Act does not prohibit the activities most often related to ambush marketing. According to Davis (1996),

> The difficulty with ambush marketing is that the law is on the side of the ambushers. Purely defined, ambush marketing does not involve counterfeiting or the illegal use of trademarks, tradenames or symbols. Companies simply develop a creative advertising campaign around the event, never use the event logo, trademark or tradename and capitalize by association with the event without paying for official sponsor status. (p. 430)

Thus, while the Lanham Act does not provide ironclad protections from particularly creative marketers, it is considered the preeminent federal law for asserting claim of unfair competition (*Majorica v. Majorica International Ltd.*, 1988).

CONCLUSION

While there is little doubt that globalization of sports is occurring, each country still maintains its own federal laws that athletes will be held accountable. However, there are sports organizations such as the CAS that are tasked to settle sports-related disputes through arbitration. As such, this chapter was written to describe issues that are most common when applied to athletes and organizations that participate in international sporting competitions. Examples presented in this chapter include the different national statutes that impact ambush marketing within certain countries. Conversely, the CAS facilitates or arbitrates the settlement of any private disputes that develop in activities related to sports. The selection of arbitration for the settlement of a dispute creates a legal relationship external to federal laws of specific countries.

DISCUSSION NOTES

1. What sport do you think has the most international appeal? What are the major sports leagues doing on an international level to increase their appeal? Would an NBA division in Europe be feasible? What other major sports could function on a full-scale international level? What legal issues would a professional league have to concern itself with if it were to expand its regular-season schedule to Europe or other overseas venues?
2. Track and field star Butch Reynolds was required to exhaust all of his administrative remedies before the district court could accept the case. The *Reynolds* case displays the procedural quagmire that some athletes are placed in by a decision of an international or national sporting body. How would you propose to resolve such a case?
3. In *Slaney v. IAAF* (2001), a female track participant was disciplined for a positive drug test that indicated the possibility of blood doping violations. When she sued the IAAF and the USOC on state and civil Racketeer Influenced and Corrupt Organizations Act claims, the courts granted the defendants' motion to dismiss.

The Olympic Games

1. The USOC is considered a private entity and not a state actor. In *San Francisco Arts and Athletics, Inc. v. U.S. Olympic Committee* (1987), the USOC and IOC sued under the Amateur Sports Act to prevent the defendants from using the word "Olympics." San Francisco Arts and Athletics was promoting the "Gay Olympic Games" and was using those words on its letterhead, mailings, and other materials. The United States Supreme Court ruled in favor of the USOC. The USOC has had a trademark in the word "Olympic" since 1986, and the Amateur Sports Act gave statutory protection to the USOC for use of the word. Furthermore, the court found that "the USOC is a 'private' corporatio[n] established under Federal law." (36 U.S.C. § 1101(46)). The court found that the USOC was not a governmental actor. National governing bodies are also not state actors. What are state and governmental actors? Why is it important to know the difference between state and governmental actors?
2. *Martinez v. U.S. Olympic Committee* (1986), involved a 21-year-old boxer, Benjamin Davis, who died from severe brain stem injuries. He had participated in a Golden Gloves tournament and collapsed during his second fight. The court noted that the lawsuit was the first brought under the Amateur Sports Act for injuries in an event sponsored by the USOC. The court, in finding in favor of the defendant (the USOC), stated:

    > The Act states that purposes of the USOC include promotion and support for amateur athletic activities, promotion of public participation in amateur athletic activities, and assistance to organizations in the development of amateur athletic programs. 36 U.S.C. § 374(5), (6) and (7). We find no indication in the Act that Congress intended the USOC to be liable to athletes injured while competing in events that were not fully controlled by the USOC. Therefore, we uphold the district court's dismissal of

(continues)

DISCUSSION NOTES (CONTINUED)

Martinez's suit because she failed to state a federal cause of action on which the court could grant relief (p. 18).

What does the Amateur Sports Act cover in regards to athlete incurring an injury?

3. The first games for disabled athletes were held in 1948 in England. In the 1960 Olympics in Rome, an Olympic-style competition was held for disabled athletes. Since that time, games have been held every four years. The Paralympian movement has grown extensively since its inception. In *Shepherd v. U.S. Olympic Committee* (2006), the plaintiff alleged discrimination against the USOC based on Title III of the Americans with Disabilities Act (ADA) and Section 504 of the Rehabilitation Act. In *Shepherd*, the plaintiff alleged that the USOC operated "places of public accommodation," thereby making it a covered entity under Title III of the ADA. The plaintiff stated that Section (L), "a gymnasium, health spa, bowling alley, golf course, or other place of exercise or recreation," was applicable. What rights are owed to disabled athletes by the USOC?

4. In *Stop the Olympic Prison v. U.S. Olympic Committee* (1980), the plaintiffs printed a "Stop the Olympic Prison" poster in protest against the use of the Lake Placid Olympic Village as a prison after the Olympics were over. The court held that the use of the village was not in violation of trademark law because the posters were not sold commercially and there was no likelihood of confusion.

The Court of Arbitration for Sport

1. What are your impressions of the CAS? What disadvantages are there to this type of dispute resolution system? How would you limit its jurisdiction? What types of disputes should it handle? Should all Olympic athletes be required to use the CAS as the exclusive method for resolving Olympic disputes?

KEY TERMS

Ambush marketing

Associative ambushing

Coattail ambushing

Competition Act of 1985

Controversy ambushing

Court of Arbitration for Sport

Distractive and insurgent ambushing

European Trade Marks Directive

Globalization

International Olympic Committee

International Sports Federations

Lanham Act

London Olympic Games and Paralympic Games Act 2006

National Governing Body

National Olympic Committee

No Fault or Negligence

Olympia Schutz Gesetz (OlympSchG)

REFERENCES

Adams v. Canadian Centre for Ethics in Sport (2008) CAS2007/A/1312 (16 May 2008).

Amateur Athletic Union. (2015). AAU: About the Sullivan Award. Retrieved from http://aausports.org/Sullivan

Associated Press. (2011). IOC declares Jessica Hardy eligible. ESPN.com. Retrieved from http://sports.espn.go.com/oly/news/story?id=6444781

Australia. Parliament. Senate. Legal and Constitutional References Committee. (1995). Cashing in on the Sydney Olympics: Protecting the Sydney Olympic Games from Ambush Marketing: Report. Parliament of the Commonwealth of Australia.

Benz, J., & Sternheimer, W. (2015). Expedited procedures before the Court of Arbitration for Sport. Retrieved from http://www.tas-cas.org/fileadmin/user_upload/Bulletin_2015_1_internet3.pdf

Berger-Walliser, G., Stallings-Williams, M., Walliser, B., & Bender, M. (2012). Bavarian blondes don't need a Visa: A comparative law analysis of ambush marketing. *Tulane Journal of International and Comparative Law*, 21, 1–35.

Boudway, I. (2014, February 3). *Does a $5 footlong make you think of the Olympics?* Retrieved from http://www.bloomberg.com/bw/articles/2014-02-03/subway-olympics-ambush-marketing-master

British Olympic Association (BOA) v. World Anti-Doping Agency, CAS 2011/A/2658 (2012).

Chadwick, S. & Burton, N. (2010). Ambushed! *Wall Street Journal*, R4.

Chambers v. British Olympic Association, [2008] EWHC 2028 (QB) (Eng.).

Collett, P., & Johnson, N. (2006). Don't be ambushed in 2012. *Brand Strategy*, 199, 34–35.

Connolly, R. (2006). Balancing the justices in anti-doping law: The need to ensure fair athletic competition through effective anti-doping programs vs. the protection of rights of accused athletes. *Virginia Sports and Entertainment Law Journal*, 5, 161–199.

Cox, T.W. (2014). The international war against doping: Limiting the collateral damage from strict liability. *Vanderbilt Journal of Transnational Law*, 47, 295–329.

De Frantz v. United States Olympic Committee, 492 F. Supp. 1181, 1980 U.S. Dist. LEXIS 14024 (D.D.C. 1980).

Eitzen, D.S. (2006). *Fair and foul: Beyond the myths and paradoxes of sport* (3rd ed.). Lanham, Md.: Rowman & Littlefield.

Elliott, S. (July 15, 1992). Jousting by mass marketers is the newest Olympic sport. *New York Times*, D1.

Ericsson, S. (2014). Ambush marketing: Examining the development of an event organizer right of association. *Intellectual Property, Unfair Competition and Publicity—Convergences and Development (EIPIN Series)*. Cheltenham, UK: Edward Elgar.

Gandert, D. (2012). The Battle before the games: The British Olympic Association attempts to keep its lifetime ban for athletes with doping offenses. *Northwestern Journal of International Law and Business Ambassador*, 32, 53–80.

Gervais, D., & Judge, E.F. (2005). *Intellectual property: The law in Canada*. Toronto, ON: Carswell.

Grady, J., & McKelvey, S. (2008). Trademark protection of school colors: Smack apparel and sinks decisions trigger color-ful legal debate for the collegiate licensing industry. *Journal of Legal Aspect of Sport*, 18(107), 207–242.

International Olympic Committee. (2015b). *Sponsorship*. Retrieved from http://www.olympic.org/sponsorship?tab=the-olympic-partner-top-programme

Johnson, P. (2011). *Ambush marketing and brand protection* (2nd ed.). Oxford: Oxford University Press.

Lanham Act, 15 U.S.C §§ 1051-1141 (2006).

Li, M., Hofacre, L.M., & Mahony, D.F. (2001). *Economics of sport*. Morgantown, W.Va.: Fitness Information Technology.

London Olympic Games and Paralympic Games Act, 2006, c. 12, § 21(2) (U.K.).

London Olympic Games and Paralympic Games (Advertising and Trading) (England) Regulations, 2011, S.I. 2011/2898, (U.K.).

Majorica, S.A. v. Majorica Int'l, Ltd., 687 F. Supp. 92, 96 (S.D.N.Y. 1988).

Martens, D.R. (2014). The role of the arbitrator in CAS proceedings. Retrieved from http://www.tas-cas.org /fileadmin/user_upload/Bulletin_2014_2.pdf

McKelvey, S. & Grady, J. (2004). An analysis of the ongoing global efforts to combat ambush marketing: Will corporate marketers "take" the gold in Greece? *Journal of Legal Aspects of Sport*, 14, 24–34

Miller, J. (2009). Drug issues in sport: Steroids illegal-performance enhancement. In J. Lee & J. Lee (Eds.), (pp. 19–41) *Criminal and sport behavior*. Durham, N.C.: Carolina Academic Press.

Morcom, C., Roughton, A., Graham, J., & Malynicz, S. (2005). *The modern law of trademarks* (2nd ed.). London: Lexis Nexis Butterworths.

Nafziger, J. (1983). The Amateur Sport Act of 1978. *BYU Law Review*, 1983(1), 47–99.

Nafziger, J.A. (2006). The future of international sports law. *Willamette Law Review*, 42, 861–876.

Olympic and Paralympic Marks Act. (2007). Retrieved from http://www2.parl.gc.ca/HousePublications/Publication .aspx?Docid=3044596&file=4

Reilly, L. (2012). An introduction to the Court of Arbitration for Sport (CAS) & the role of national courts in international sports disputes. *Journal of Dispute Resolution*, 2012, 63–81.

San Francisco Arts & Athletics, Inc., 483 U.S. 522, 107 S. Ct. 2971, 97 L. Ed. 2d 427, 1987 U.S. LEXIS 2895, 55 U.S.L.W. 5061, 3 U.S.P.Q.2d (BNA) 1145 (1987).

Sandler, D.M., & Shani, D. (1989). Olympic sponsorship vs. "Ambush" marketing: Who gets the gold? *Journal of Advertising Research*, 29(4), 3–14.

Scassa, T. (2011). Ambush marketing and the right of association: Clamping down on references to that big event with all the athletes in a couple of years. *Journal of Sport Management*, 25, 354–370.

Shani, D., & Sandler, D.M. (1998). Ambush marketing: Is confusion to blame for the flickering of the flame? *Psychology & Marketing*, 15(4), 367–383.

Slaney v. International Amateur Athletic Federation, 244 F.3d 580 (7th Cir. 2001).

Tribunal Arbitral du Sport/Court of Arbitration for Sport. (2015a). Frequently asked questions. Retrieved from http://www.tas-cas.org/en/general-information /frequently-asked-questions.html

Tribunal Arbitral du Sport/Court of Arbitration for Sport. (2015b). History of the CAS. Retrieved from http:// www.tas-cas.org/en/general-information/history-of -the-cas.html

Tribunal Arbitral du Sport/Court of Arbitration for Sport. (2015c). Procedural rules. Retrieved from http:// www.tas-cas.org/en/arbitration/code-procedural -rules.html

Tribunal Arbitral du Sport/Court of Arbitration for Sport. (2015d). Statutes of ICAS and CAS. Retrieved from http://www.tas-cas.org/en/icas/code-statutes-of-icas -and-cas.html

Tygart, T. (2003). Winners never dope and finally, dopers never win: USADA takes over drug testing of United States Olympic athletes. *DePaul Journal of Sports Law & Contemporary Problems*, 1, 124–138.

United States Anti-Doping Agency. (2014). 2015 WADA Code Changes. Retrieved from http://www.usada.org /resources/2015code/

United States Olympic Committee v. American Media, Inc., 156 F. Supp. 2d 1200 2001 U.S. Dist. LEXIS 11523 (D. Colo. 2001).

United States Olympic Committee v. International Olympic Committee, CAS 2011/O/2422 (2011).

USADA and Jessica Hardy, Interim Arbitral Award, AAA No. 77 190 00288 08 2009 (2009). Retrieved from http:// www.usada.org/wp-content/uploads/AAA_CAS -Decision-Hardy-May-2009.pdf

USADA v. LaShawn Merritt, AAA No. 77 190 00293 10 2010 (2010).

Vaitiekunas, A. (2014). *The court of arbitration for sport: Law-making and the question of independence*. Bern, Switzerland: Stämpfli Verlag.

WADA v. Jessica Hardy and USADA, CAS 2009/A/1870 (2010).

Wendt, J. (2004). The new World Anti-Doping Agency and World Anti-Doping Code. *Midwest Law Review*, 19, 29–45.

Wendt, J. (2012). Toward harmonization: British Olympic Association v. The World Anti-Doping Association. *Marquette Sports Law Review*, 23(1), 154–169.

Wetten, R., & Willis, J. (1976). The effect of New York's elite athletic clubs on amateur athletic governance. *Research Quarterly*, 47(3), 499–505.

White, P. (2008). Malicious drugging and the contaminated catheter: Adams v Canadian Centre for Ethics in Sport. *Sports Law Ejournal*. Retrieved from http:// epublications.bond.edu.au/cgi/viewcontent .cgi?article=1007&context=slej

World Anti-Doping Agency. (2015a). 2015 World Anti-Doping Code. Retrieved from https://www.wada-ama .org/en/questions-answers/2015-world-anti-doping-code

World Anti-Doping Agency. (2015b). A brief history of anti-doping. Retrieved from https://www.wada-ama.org /en/who-we-are/a-brief-history-of-anti-doping

World Anti-Doping Agency. (2015c). Significant changes between the 2009 Code and the 2015 Code. Retrieved September from https://www.wada-ama.org/en /resources/the-code/significant-changes-between-the -2009-code-and-the-2015-code

World Anti-Doping Agency. (2015d). Strict liability in anti-doping. Retrieved from https://www.wada-ama.org /en/questions-answers/strict-liability-in-anti-doping

World Anti-Doping Agency. (2015e). WADA Prohibited List. Retrieved from http://list.wada-ama.org/

World Anti-Doping Agency. (2015f). WADA statement regarding Liliya Shobukhova's sanction. Retrieved from https://www.wada-ama.org/en/media/news /2015-08/wada-statement-regarding-liliya -shobukhovas-sanction

GLOSSARY

49% modified assumption of risk the plaintiff recovers only if his or her percentage of fault is less than the defendant's

50% modified assumption of risk prevents a plaintiff who is found to be more than 50% negligent from any recovery whatsoever

Acceptance willingness to be bound by the terms of the offer

Agency a fiduciary relationship between individuals that results in one party having the ability to act on behalf of the other, based on consent

Aggravated assault type of assault which includes the use of a weapon, the status of the victim, the intent of the perpetrator, and the degree of injury caused

Amateur athletes individuals who participate in sport without receiving financial compensation

Ambush marketing a company's intentional efforts to weaken its competitor's official association with a sport organization, which has been acquired through the payment of sponsorship fees

Anabolic steroids more appropriately termed anabolic-androgenic steroids are synthetic variations of the male sex hormone testosterone

Arbitration a form of alternative dispute resolution in which a neutral third party (the arbitrator) settles a dispute with a legally binding decision

Assault refers to the attempt or threat of violence

Associative ambushing employs imagery to generate a deception that an organization has links to a sporting event or property

Assumption of risk a plaintiff voluntarily enters a risky activity and understands that risk

Bona fide occupational qualification a job requirement that is reasonably necessary to the operation of a business. While the requirement many discriminate against a protected class, it is not considered illegal

Bonus clause contractual provision that stipulates performance bonuses based on statistics or achievements

Breach of duty determines whether a reasonable person in the position of the defendant acted negligently

Buyout clause contractual provision that releases one party from the obligations of a contract for a predetermined amount of money

Capacity legal ability to enter into a contract

Catastrophic potential immeasurable loss of life and economic consideration

Civil battery use of actual force or touching against another, resulting in a harmful or offensive conduct

Clause sub-section of a contract

Coattail ambushing involves gaining publicity through sponsoring a sports event without being an official sponsor of the overall event

Coercion test used to determine constitutionality of state action under the Establishment clause; considers whether individuals were coerced into religious practice

Collective bargaining the process in which a group of employees organize to negotiate with the employer regarding working conditions such as hours, wages, and so on

Commercialization the process of introducing a product into commerce thereby making it available on the market

Comparative negligence compares the defendant's negligence with the plaintiff's own negligence, and to quantify the comparison by estimating a percentage of fault to each party

Compensation financial obligations contained in a contract

Compensatory damages damages available to the non-breaching party to recover direct losses and costs

Competition Act of 1985 Canadian legislation that assists in preventing advertising false or misleading statements

Conflict of interest when a person or entity has a legal responsibility to more than party, and upholding one could potentially cause harm to the other

Consequential damages losses caused directly by a breach of contract

Consideration item or object of value given in exchange for a promise

Contributory Negligence occurs when the plaintiff contributes to the injury suffered

Controversy ambushing occurs when an organization produces an advertising scheme to sponsor an event with knowledge that it will not be accepted

Court of Arbitration for Sport facilitates the settlement of sport-related disputes by means of procedural rules adapted to the specific needs of the sport world

Criminal battery criminal intent to do wrong, i.e., to cause a harmful or offensive contact

Criticality assessment recognizes and examines organizationally significant assets, infrastructure, and critical functions

Curt Flood Act of 1998 limits professional baseball's antitrust immunity

Damages occurs when the plaintiff suffers a significant injury, either physically or emotionally as determined by the court

Defamation act of harming the reputation of another by making a written or oral false statement to a third person

Disparate compensation occurs when individuals are compensated differently based on status or membership in a protected class

Disparate impact discrimination occurs when a policy that appears to be neutral has a disproportionate impact on one group

Disparate treatment discrimination occurs when individuals receive different treatment based on status or membership in a protected class

Distractive and insurgent ambushing uses distractions surrounding the event to draw attention to a product without making specific mention of the event

Due process clause requires that state actors provide fair and proper rules and rules enforcement before denying someone life, liberty or property

Duties and responsibilities clause specifies of the job responsibilities in a contract agreement

Duty to mitigate reasonable steps to lessen or mitigate the damage incurred in a breach of contract. Steps must be taken by the injured party

Duty a special relationship between two or more parties that may be created by statute, contract, or common law

Effective accommodation method of demonstrating Title IX compliance that requires an educational institution to demonstrate all interests and abilities of the underrepresented sex are being met

Eleventh Amendment prevents federal law-based suits against any of the U.S. states

Employee any individual who has agreed by contract to perform specified services for an employer in exchange for money

Employer an individual or organization who hires another person to perform a service under an express or implied agreement and has the right to control the manner and means of performing the services

Endorsement contract an agreement under which an individual receives consideration for use of that individual's person, name, image, or likeness in the promotion of any product, service, or event

Endorsement test used to determine constitutionality of state action under the Establishment clause; considers whether the government inappropriately endorsed one religion over others

Entanglement or nexus theory considers whether government involvement or entanglement with a private actor conduct is sufficient to transform the private actor into a state actor

Enterprise Risk Management the process of planning, organizing, leading, and controlling the activities of an organization to reduce potential risks to the organization

Equal Employment Opportunity Commission federal agency that enforces the federal laws prohibiting discrimination

Equal protection clause found in the Fourteenth Amendment of the United States Constitution; requires that states apply the laws equally to all citizens, and not arbitrarily discriminate

Establishment clause found in the First Amendment of the United States Constitution; prevents a state actor from establishing religion

Ethical dilemma a complex situation that often involves a psychological conflict between moral imperatives in which neither resolves the situation in an ethically acceptable fashion

Ethical risks involve actual or potential harm to the reputation or beliefs of an organization

European Trade Marks Directive used in Germany to confer on the proprietor exclusive rights

Exclusivity form of sponsorship where the sponsor is the only business in the product or service category with the ability to sponsor the event

Expressed assumption of risk participants are required to sign an assumption of risk form before being allowed to compete

Falsifiying information involves altering, changing, or modifying a document for the purpose of deceiving another person or organization. It can also involve the passing along of copies of documents that are known to be false

Federal Baseball v. National League of Professional Baseball Clubs (1922) declared that professional baseball was not a business that was involved in interstate commerce

Fiduciary a relationship involving trust between individuals

Financial risks involve the assets of the organization and include theft, fraud, loans, license fees, attendances, membership fees, insurance costs, lease payments, pay-out of damages claims or penalties and fines by the government

Football Bowl Subdivision (FBS) top level of intercollegiate football competition in the United States

Foreseeability the degree to which an organization knew, or should have known, that a participant/spectator/employee may be exposed to harm

Free agency freedom to negotiate; in the sport context, the ability to negotiate a contract with any team without restrictions

Free Exercise clause found in the First Amendment of the United States Constitution; prevents a state actor from impeding the free exercise of a person's religion

Globalization a process whereby goods, information, people, money communication, sport, fashion, and other forms of culture move across national boundaries

Governing bodies an organization that has regulatory and/or sanctioning power over a specific sport entity

Grievance something believed to be unfair or wrong that gives rise to a complaint

Gross negligence when there is a conscious and voluntary indifference of reasonable care resulting in a foreseeable and significant injury

Hazing any activity expected of someone joining a group that humiliates, degrades, abuses, or endangers, regardless of the person's willingness to participate

History and continuing practice method of demonstrating Title IX compliance that requires an educational institution to demonstrate a history or program expansion for the underrepresented sex, or specific plans to do so in the future

Hostile environment unwelcome sexual conduct unreasonably interferes with an individual's job performance or creates a hostile, intimidating, or offensive work environment

Hostile work environment negative working conditions created by pervasive or overt discriminatory conduct, in many cases conduct of a sexual nature

Imminent apprehension element of assault in which the victim must be aware of the threat at the time it is made

Implied assumption of the risk defendant does not owe a plaintiff a duty of care for an injury that occurred from an inherent risk of a sport

Incentive clause provision of the contract that monetize achievements related to responsibilities and duties

Injunctive relief a non-monetary legal remedy in which a court orders a defendant to cease a certain action

Intent to cause apprehension an element of assault in which the act must be intended to be harmful or offensive contact

Intentional tort a civil wrong not arising from a breach of contract in which harm to another person was intentionally committed

Intermediate scrutiny a legal test used to determine the constitutionality of a challenged action. Specifically, this level of scrutiny assesses whether the challenged action furthers an important government interest using substantially related means

International Olympic Committee responsible for overseeing and monitoring Olympic activities throughout the world

International Sports Federations define eligibility for international competition and administer Olympic programs for a particular sport

Interscholastic athletics athletic competition between secondary schools

Interscholastic occurring between schools; in athletics, this refers to secondary schools

Jesse Owens an American track and field athlete and four-time Olympic gold medalist at the 1936 Berlin Olympics

Labor dispute includes any controversy concerning terms, tenure or conditions of employment, or concerning the association or representation of persons in negotiating, fixing, maintaining, changing, or seeking to arrange terms or conditions of employment, regardless of whether the disputants stand in the proximate relation of employer and employee

Lack of consent victim clearly expressed that he or she did not consent to the action

Lanham Act a federal statute in the United States that offers protection against advertisements that may be construed as being misleading

Lemon test a three-part analysis used to determine whether a state actor's conduct violates the Establishment clause

Libel written word is used to damage a person's reputation

Licenses provisions written into the contract that define allowable use of a logo, slogan, or official mark

Liquidated damages clause provision that stipulates the money to be received if either party breaches the contract

London Olympic Games and Paralympic Games Act 2006 British legislation that protects against ambush marketing in event zones around the Olympic venues and routes

Mackey v. NFL found that the Rozelle Rule violated antitrust laws

Mascot any person, animal, or object used to represent a group with a common public identity, such as a school, professional sports team, society, military unit, or brand name

Medical malpractice any act or omission by a physician during treatment of a patient that deviates from accepted norms of medical practice

Misrepresentation false assertion of fact related to contract terms

Mixed contributory & comparative negligence occurs when the plaintiff is determined to be more than 50% responsible of the injury

Monopoly the power to control prices or exclude competition

Morals clause contract provision that states a company can terminate the agreement if a player places the company in a bad light or brings harm to the company's reputation

Mutual mistake occurs when both parties share a misconception about a basic assumption of vital fact upon which they base their bargain

National Collegiate Athletic Association (NCAA) a voluntary organization through which the nation's colleges and universities govern their athletics

National Governing Body administer each Olympic sport and selection of athletes for that sport

National Labor Relations Act federal legislation enacted to "protect the rights of employees and employers, to encourage collective bargaining, and to curtail certain private sector labor and management practices, which can harm the general welfare of workers, businesses and the U.S. economy" (NLRB, 2016)

National Olympic Committee sole authority for representing a particular country at the Olympic Games

Negligence an unintentional tort in which the alleged wrongdoer does not intend the consequences of his or her actions to another a person, property, or reputation

No Fault or Negligence athletes are considered blameless and is not penalized any period of ineligibility by proving that they had no knowledge or suspicion that they had been administered a prohibited substance

No-trade clause provision that states a player cannot be traded without the player's consent

Nominal damages damages awarded when the law recognizes a technical invasion of the plaintiff's rights, but no economic harm has been done to the plaintiff

Nonstatutory labor exemption permits labor unions to negotiate and to create agreements with their employers regarding terms and conditions of employment, without fear of antitrust scrutiny applying to the agreements

Offer conditional promise made by an offeror to an offeree

Olympia Schutz Gesetz (OlympSchG) protects specific words and symbols associated with the Olympics as the sole property of the German National Olympic Committee and the IOC

Olympic and Paralympic Marks Act of 2007 Canadian event-specific anti-ambush marketing legislation that was ratified in time for the 2010 Vancouver Olympic Winter Games

Olympic Insignia Protection Act 1987 and the Sydney 2000 Games (Indicia and Images) Protection Act 1996 provide legal protection against ambush marketing in Australia

Osaka Rule if an athlete receives a ban of more than six months they cannot compete in the following Olympic Games

Parol evidence rule states that a valid contract is the final statement of agreement between the parties and that no prior or subsequent statements can be considered in the event of a contract dispute

Passing off a company alleges that another organization wrongly advertised to deliberately cause confusion in the mind of the consumer

Per se test under the Sherman Antitrust Act an activity that is anticompetitive on its face

Performance-enhancing drugs (PEDs) substances that are used to improve any form of activity performance in humans

Physical risks involving personal injuries, environmental and weather conditions and the physical assets of the organization such as property, buildings, equipment, vehicles, stock, and grounds

Places of public accommodation areas listed in Title III of the Americans with Disabilities Act that must specifically allow disabled individuals to participate equally in the goods, services, and accommodations provided by the establishment

Players unions labor organization that represents the respective interest of a group of like professional athletes. For example, the National Football League Players Association is the players union for NFL football players

Predatory ambushing leaves the consumers confused as to which organization is the official sponsor

Primary assumption of risk no duty of care is owed as to risks inherent in a given sport or activity

Private entity any entity that is not connected to the government

Probable cause a legal proof standard that requires sufficient suspicion, based upon known facts, that a crime has been committed

Prohibited List identifies substances and methods that are prohibited both in and out of competition

Protected classes the five categories of people covered by Title VII; race, color, national origin, religion, and sex

Proximate cause occurs when the breach by the defendant actually and proximately causes the plaintiff's injury

Public function theory considers whether a private entity is undertaking functions or assuming powers ordinarily performed by the government, and whether such conduct is sufficient to transform the private entity into a state actor

Punitive damages designed to punish a defendant for improper conduct

Pure comparative negligence a plaintiff may be awarded a proportionate allocation of damages unless the negligence was determined to be 100%

Qualified individual with a disability an individual with a disability who, with or without reasonable accommodations, can perform the essential functions of the employment

Quick look test practice has obvious anticompetitive effects, such as price fixing

Quid pro quo "this for that"; when sexual behaviors are directly linked to employment conditions

Race each of the major divisions of humankind, having distinct physical characteristics

Rational basis test a legal test used to determine the constitutionality of a challenged action. Specifically, this level of scrutiny assesses whether the challenged action furthers a legitimate government interest using rationally related means

Reasonable accommodation when an employer modifies an individual's work environment or job responsibilities that allow a qualified worker to perform the job

Reasonable cause a legal standard of proof that is a lesser standard than probable cause, but still must be based in fact

Reserve clause bound a player to a single team, essentially in perpetuity, so that a player had no freedom to change teams unless he was given his unconditional release

Respondeat superior doctrine type of vicarious liability, which makes an employer liable for the actions of an employee when the actions take place within the scope of employment

Respondeat superior when an employer or corporate entity is subject to liability for the actions (or inactions) or employees

Restraint of trade unreasonable if, under the totality of the circumstances, its anticompetitive effects outweigh its procompetitive effects

Reverse sex discrimination when a member of the traditionally majority group is discriminated against based on gender. For example, in athletics, a male coach alleging gender discrimination

Right of publicity grants a person the exclusive right to control the commercial value and exploitation of his or her name, likeness, or personality

Rights of first refusal in contract law, the right of one person or entity (the offeree) to agree to contract terms with the other party (the offeror) before an offer can be made to a third party

Risk avoidance occurs when the risk is too great and should be eliminated

Risk communication concentrates on an intentional transfer of information designed to respond to public concerns or public needs related to real or perceived hazards

Risk management process by which identifying, measuring, controlling and minimizing foreseeable risks is conducted to protect organizational assets

Risk reduction occurs when a risk cannot be avoided and efforts are made to decrease the damage or loss

Risk retention the organization assumes responsibility for foreseeable risks that might occur in the event

Risk transfer responsibility of a certain risk is shifted to another person or organization

Risks perception that human actions or events lead to consequences that harm others

Rollover provision a statement in a contract that specifies the agreement will be automatically extended for a new term if certain conditions are met

Rozelle Rule restricted the ability of a player to sign with a different team when the player's contract expired

Rule of reason plaintiff must show significant anticompetitive effects within a relevant market

Salary cap a rule limiting the amount of money a team can spend on player salaries

Salary Negotiations the process in which an employer and employer (team and player) negotiate wages

Saturation ambushing occurs when advertising for an event is significantly increased but there is no reference to the contest

Search and seizure the lawful examination of a person (or their property or effects) looking for evidence of wrongdoing or criminal activity

Secondary assumption of risk defendant owes the plaintiff a duty, but the plaintiff knowingly continues the activity despite verbal and written warnings regarding the risk and potential outcomes

Section 1 of the Sherman Antitrust Act prevents attempts by a company or individual to constrain the free market by means of price-fixing, refusals to deal, etc.

Section 2 of the Sherman Antitrust Act prohibits the use of monopolies, whether intended or unintended, and either by an individual company or companies, to restrain interstate commerce

Self-ambushing practice of breaching the limits of a company's sponsorship agreements in a way that oversteps another sponsor's marketing or advertising

Sexual harassment unwelcome sexual advances, requests for sexual favors, and other verbal or physical conduct of a sexual nature

Sherman Antitrust Act exists to promote customer welfare, protect individuals against the corruptive practices of big business, and offer individuals protection from monopolistic and anticompetitive behavior

Signing bonus a one-time bonus for signing a contract

Slander orally damaging a person's reputation

Sovereign immunity shields the state, its agencies, and its officials from lawsuits for damages, absent legislative consent to sue

Specific performance an equitable remedy available to the non-breaching party that calls upon the opposing party to perform the contract

Sponsorship contract binding agreement between an athlete or a sporting event that details obligations as agreed to in the sponsorship negotiations

Sports broadcasting exemption permits the sale of a television package to a network or networks in which the league members share equally, includes blackout rules

Sports ethics an individual or group activity pursued for exercise or pleasure, often involving the testing of physical capabilities and taking the form of a competitive game

State action a person or entity acting on behalf of the government

State actor a person or entity acting on behalf of the government

State athletic associations athletic governing bodies that regulate athletic eligibility, competitions and sanctions at the state level

Statute of frauds states that some certain contracts must be in writing to enforceable

Steroids era period of time in professional sports, particularly Major League Baseball, when a number of players were believed to have used performance-enhancing drugs, resulting in increased offensive output throughout the game

Strict scrutiny a legal test used to determine the constitutionality of a challenged action.

Specifically, this level of scrutiny assesses whether the challenged action furthers a compelling government interest using narrow and specific means

Substantial proportionality method of demonstrating Title IX compliance that requires an educational institution to demonstrate the number or participation opportunities for men and women and proportionate the enrollment rates of each gender

Ted Stevens Olympic and Amateur Sports Act gives the USOC the authority to serve as the U.S. coordinating body for international amateur athletic competition

Term the length of a contract

Termination clause states the conditions in which a party can be terminated

Termination without cause a premature termination of a contract prior to the end term date, normally involves payment of compensation to the coach who was prematurely terminated

Theory of the Threshold of Effective Zerohood likelihood of an incident occurring gets to be small enough, the probability of the incident occurring may be seen as no longer possible

Threat assessment prepares the organization to provide a better assurance of alertness in case of an incident

Tort an act of ommission or omission that wrongly leads to injury or harm to another individual to which the courts may impose liability

Tortfeasor a person who commits a tort

Tortious behavior an action or conduct that constitutes a tort

Trademark Trial and Appeal Board a neutral body that functions like a court for trademark matters at the USPTO. The Board's administrative trademark judges are authorized to determine a party's right to register a trademark with the federal government

Unfair labor practice Section 158 of the NRLA states that the term "unfair labor practice" means any unfair labor practice to include: (1) to interfere with, restrain, or coerce employees in the exercise of the rights guaranteed in Section 157 of this title; (2) to dominate or interfere with the formation or administration of any labor organization or contribute financial or other support to it: *Provided*, That subject to rules and regulations made and published by the Board pursuant to section 156 of this title, an employer shall not be prohibited from permitting employees to confer with him during working hours without loss of time or pay

Unilateral mistake occurs when one of the parties to the contract makes a mistake as to some material fact contained in the contract that has some adverse effect on the performance of the contract

Unintentional ambushing occurs when a company's product is prominently mentioned by the media but the company is not a sponsor of the event

United States Patent and Trademark Office (USPTO) an agency in the U.S. Department of Commerce that issues patents to inventors and businesses for their inventions, and trademark registration for product and intellectual property identification

Violence behavior involving physical force intended to hurt, damage, or kill someone or something

Vulnerability assessment estimates the susceptibility of potential damages by those desiring to create physical or psychological harm to an organization's infrastructure, including employees or patrons

Waiver or releases written articles in which a party releases or exculpates a second party from possible tort liability

Willful or wanton misconduct when an injury is intentional or act that caused the injury must have been performed under circumstances that exhibited a reckless disregard for the safety of others

With cause termination occurs when the employer terminates the contract prior to its expiration for reasons such as breach of contract, criminal conduct, improper behavior, or violation of team rules

Workers' compensation laws that establish an administrative process for compensating workers who were injured while on the job

World Anti-Doping Agency international scientific research program that synchronizes advanced detection methods of prohibited drugs in international sports

INDEX

D

concept of, 72–73
defined, 73
ethical, 72–73
as feelings, 72
financial, 72
legal, 73
physical, 72
unreasonably increased, 61
risk transfer, 84
Robertson v. National Basketball Association, 163
Robinson, David, 40
Robinson, Jackie, 8, 94
rodeo, 216
Rodgers, Aaron, 141
rollover provision, 138
Romanowski, Bill, 32
Roosevelt, Theodore, 216
Roseboro, John, 7
Roseboro, Johnny, 40
Roventini v. Pasadena School District, 25
Roy, Alvin, 6
Rozelle, Pete, 142, 179
Rozelle Rule, 156, 157–158, 179–180, 186
Rudolph, Wilma, 9
Rule 45 (Osaka Rule), 244
rule of reason analysis, antitrust law, 154–155
Russell, Bill, 8–9
Ryder Cup, 238

S

Saban, Nick, 4, 137
Sacramento State University Men's Rowing Club v. California State Univ., 231
Saelua, Jaiyah, 103
safe transportation, duty to provide, 27–29
safety
defined, 72
need for, 72
safety feature costs, 74–75
salary caps, 156, 159, 186, 205
in CBA, 178
salary(ies)
arbitration, 187–189

of coaches, 4
discrepancies in, 185
negotiations, 205
of players, 185–186
CBAs and, 178
Samaranch, Juan Antonio, 240
same-sex harassment, 52–53
Samsung, 246
Sanders, Anucha Browne, 50
Sandusky, Jerry, 26
San Francisco Arts and Athletics, Inc. v. U.S. Olympic Committee, 251
Santa Fe High Independent School District v. Doe, 226
saturation ambushing, 247
Schmidt v. Midwest Sports Events, Inc., 77, 84
School Success and Opportunity Act, 103
Schott, Marge, 9
Schultz, Gary, 27
search and seizure, unreasonable, protections against, 119
seat belts, 27
secondary assumption of risk, 61, 62
Second Mile, 26
Section 1, Sherman Antitrust Act, 152, 153–154, 167, 175, 180
Section 2 (monoplization), Sherman Antitrust Act, 154
security risk, 79
Seles, Monica, 7
self-ambushing, 247
Selig, Bud, 115
September 11, 2001 attacks, 76
sex discrimination, 93, 97. *See also* gender equality; Title IX
in athletics, 98
reverse, 96
Title VII on, 95–96
sexual harassment, 50–53
cases overview, 50
defined, 50–51
hostile environment, 51–52, 96–97
of opposite and same-sex members, 52–53
quid pro quo, 6, 51
race and, 52
religion and, 52